BLOOD
AND
IRON

Nothing will ever be the same again in Papua. Anyone who toiled over the Owen Stanley Ranges in wartime knows it will never be the same silent, sweet-smelling jungle track where man and his indecencies were almost unknown. It is a trail of blood and iron now, and in the memory of this generation will remain so.

– Dr Geoffrey Vernon

By the same author

When the Buffalo Fight
Into the Dragon's Jaws
The Battle of Long Tan
Against All Odds
Contact
The Fighting First
The Battle of the Bismarck Sea

BLOOD AND IRON

The Battle for KOKODA 1942

LEX McAULAY

ARROW

An Arrow Book
Published by
Random House Australia Pty Ltd
20 Alfred Street, Milsons Point, NSW 2061
http://www.randomhouse.com.au

Sydney   New York   Toronto
London   Auckland   Johannesburg

First published in hardback 1991 by Hutchinson Australia
This Arrow edition first published in 1992

National Library of Australia
Cataloguing-in-Publication Entry

McAulay, Lex, 1939-
Blood and iron.

Bibliography
Includes index.
ISBN 0 09182 628 4

1. World War, 1939-1945—Campaigns-Papua New Guinea.
2. Kokoda Trail (Papua New Guinea). I. Title.

940.5426

Cover photograph C/- Australian War Memorial (AWM No. 14028)
Cover design by Reno Visual Communications 11896
Printed and bound by Griffin Press, Netley, South Australia

10 9 8 7 6 5 4 3 2 1

Contents

CHAPTER 1
DISTANT THUNDER   1
JUNE 1942

CHAPTER 2
SOWING THE EAST WIND   22
JULY 1942

CHAPTER 3
STRENGTHENING GALE   63
AUGUST 1942

CHAPTER 4
TEMPEST   164
SEPTEMBER 1942

CHAPTER 5
TORNADO   278
OCTOBER 1942

CHAPTER 6
REAPING THE WEST WHIRLWIND   367
NOVEMBER 1942

APPENDICES   414
ACKNOWLEDGEMENTS AND SOURCES   417
FOOTNOTES   419
BIBLIOGRAPHY   423
INDEX   424

Dedication

This book is dedicated, firstly, to all those members of the Australian armed services who fought on or above the Kokoda Trail, and to those who supported them. Secondly, it is dedicated to the Australian women whose menfolk were in that and other campaigns, and especially to my mother, who had a husband and two brothers in the army and air force, and at the age of 23, with two young children and a newborn baby, was evacuated from Innisfail, North Queensland, to make a 1600-kilometre journey in wartime blackout and security conditions to Brisbane.

Measurements and distances

Measurements contained in material derived from Allied records are given in Imperial scale. Some metric equivalents are given in parentheses where applicable. Altitudes are in feet only, as is the convention in aviation. Short distances, usually expressed in yards, are not given metric equivalents but it is fair to assume that yards and metres are virtually interchangeable.

The measurements contained in material derived from Japanese records are given in metric with the Imperial equivalent in parentheses where necessary.

Chapter 1
DISTANT THUNDER
June 1942

The Kokoda campaign of 1942 has taken its place in Australian history alongside the landing at Gallipoli, the charge at Beersheba and the defence of Tobruk. The Gallipoli landings were pivotal in Australian self-perceptions and relationship with the Mother Country, Britain. The Kokoda campaign also marked a pivotal point in Australian awareness. It was that occasion when, for the first time, Australians were fighting for their own homeland without the protection of large and powerful friends.

The Royal Navy had long been put forward as defender of that part of the British Empire in the South Pacific. By early 1942, superior Japanese forces had forced the Royal Navy back to Ceylon (Sri Lanka) and the British Fleet did not return to the Pacific for more than 30 months. The United States Navy had been badly battered at Pearl Harbour, but in the Battle of the Coral Sea, in May 1942, repulsed a Japanese invasion aimed at Port Moresby, and managed to win a crucial victory at Midway in June 1942.

However, the US Navy was preparing to fight in the central Pacific and the Solomon Islands; there was little to spare for New Guinea and Australian waters. US and RAAF air forces were weak in striking power, and still had no fighter able to cope with the Mitsubishi A6M Zero, which had cleared the skies over China, Pearl Harbour, the Philippines, Malaya, the Netherlands East Indies (Indonesia), Rabaul and Darwin.

Northern Australia and New Guinea were undeveloped, in few ways able to support modern military operations on and over them. What forces Australia and the US were able to transport to New Guinea would be compelled to exist and fight at the end of a newly-established, inefficient and tenuous logistic system. One factor was to Allied advantage: in late 1941, a network of airfields was constructed in northern Queensland to facilitate US air movements to the Philippines. These airfields, often nothing more than dirt runways among unbroken expanses of Australian bush, were built by the Queensland Department of Main Roads. When the times, the environment and machinery available are considered, the construction work was a credit to that much-maligned organisation.

Without that network of airfields, which provided a string of havens for the small US air striking force from which they could fly to operate from Port Moresby, the campaigns in New Guinea may have been successful for the Japanese. Using the landing strips at Longreach, Cloncurry, Mareeba, the Townsville area, Cairns, Cooktown, Coen and Horn Island, the available squadrons could be dispersed relatively safely out of range of the Japanese. From the bases, they could fly up to Port Moresby for operations and then return to Australia for rest and maintenance. Port Moresby itself was the scene of more airfield construction work, but the complex of fields so well known later did not exist in June 1942. While the arrangement of having the squadrons based in Australia but flying operations from Port Moresby was inefficient, it did have the advantage of safety for the squadrons out of combat, and for the staffs and ground crews.

After the series of smashing Japanese victories across the Pacific and Indian Oceans, there was widespread concern in Australia that it was soon to be invaded. Only with postwar investigation was it found that while the Japanese Navy urged such a move, the Japanese Army did not agree. It was decided by Japanese Imperial General Headquarters not to invade in 1942, but to neutralise Australia by isolating it from its friends and Allies by occupying New Guinea, particularly its ports and airfield sites on the south coast. From there, air and sea power could cut Australia's lines of communication. Quite probably, in due course, Australia would have been occupied rather than invaded, and a system of administrators installed.

Australia had contributed greatly to the British war effort

against Nazi Germany, with raw materials, men, and units of the three Armed Services. The prewar British policy of requiring only materials from the colonies and dominions, while at the same time using every means possible to refuse or hinder development of any manufacturing capability, resulted in the desperate situation of 1942. Australia found itself with few tradesmen, few factories and lacking the national infrastructure necessary to support modern warfare. Quite apart from increased food production for export and increased quantities of all raw materials she had previously provided, Australia had to develop the capability to make aircraft, vehicles including armoured fighting vehicles, weapons of various types, ammunition, and naval and merchant ships.

While Germany was seen as the main enemy, and volunteer forces enlisted to fight her were raised, trained and sent overseas for service in the United Kingdom and North Africa, there was a perceived threat from Japan. Military officers who had persisted in warning about Japan in the 1930s had been disciplined for political reasons. However, as the international situation worsened, military formations for service in Australia and her territories were raised.

There was immediate dislike between those units raised for overseas service in the Second Australian Imperial Force (2nd AIF), proud inheritors of the First World War AIF traditions and honours, and the home service units, the Militia. Many uncomplimentary titles were bandied about, probably the most common in use being 'Choco', for chocolate soldier. AIF volunteers had an 'X' inserted after the letter identifying their state of enlistment, that is, 'N' for New South Wales, 'Q' for Queensland; so 'VX' identified a Victorian member of the AIF. Units raised for the 2nd AIF were prefixed by a '2/', as in 2/1st Battalion. Also, AIF members wore a grey border to their unit colour-patches worn on the uniform shoulder and hat-band (puggaree).

The drain on Militia units by soldiers and officers resigning to become AIF volunteers was so great that many were refused discharge or permission to do so. Some promptly went absent without leave and joined the AIF under a false name. But some AIF members were sent to Militia units, to their dismay. However, the Militia's 39th Battalion was destined to be the first Australian unit to inflict a setback to the advancing Japanese on Australian territory. The battalion was formed in September 1941, from personnel of 3 Division, 4 Division and 2 Cavalry Regiment. When units were informed that personnel were needed for 39th Battalion, 3 Division did the right thing and sent a good selection, but 4 Division off-loaded those who were not wanted, for one reason or another. 24/39th Battalion, an amalgamated unit, was subordinate to 3 Division, and this may have influenced the selection of better men for the new unit.

Commanding Officer of the 39th, Lieutenant Colonel Conran, personally accepted or rejected those officers presented to him on arrival. He insisted that all company commanders and all except two seconds-in-command be men with service in the First World War. The battalion formed at an AIF reinforcement camp, Darley. After checking those who were sent to him, Conran sent many of all ranks back to where they came from, but eventually had a battalion. He trained it in open warfare, suitable for the campaigns in the Middle East.

There was hard training in the months to December, with 13 days' leave in November. The battalion was to go to Port Moresby, to replace 49th Battalion. At the time, recruiting for the AIF had ceased, but a petition organised by the NCOs (non-commissioned officers) went round the battalion, asking that it be included in the AIF; more than 90 per cent of the battalion signed. The Militia classification remained.

On 29 December 1941 the ship *Aquitania* steamed from Sydney, in company with *Folke* and *Sarpedon*, for New Guinea and New Britain. As well as 39th Battalion, there were 53rd Battalion, 13 Field Regiment, 23 AA Regiment, 3 Field Ambulance, and the cadre of 30 Brigade HQ, under Brigadier Hatton. Some soldiers, particularly 53rd Battalion, were so recently in service that they were taught basic matters on the ships. On arrival at Port Moresby, 39th Battalion marched to 7-Mile Airfield; no one knew they were coming; the battalion was tasked to defend the airfield. Commercial enterprises in the town, such as BP and BNG, immediately had three prices: one each for soldiers, civilians and for natives.

After settling in, 39th Battalion deployed a rifle company, a machinegun platoon and a section of Bren gun carriers to Bootless Inlet, as that was thought to be the most likely place for a Japanese landing. Company positions were dug on top of the hills along 7-Mile Valley.

The commander in New Guinea, Major General Basil Morris, was well aware of the serious military situation, but was also appalled at the quality of the Militia infantry. The way in which some units had been recruited and brought up to strength for their deployment to New Guinea was and remains a low point in the history of the Australian Army, and is worthy of a book in itself. Generally speaking, parent units sent their worst men, or those threatened with punishment, to the battalions going north. Some were literally sent onto the transport ship with no warning, no chance to farewell family and friends, and in some cases without being told their destination. Yet later, with good leadership, many of these men performed to the highest standards in battle.

Australian forces allocated to New Guinea consisted of small base units and a headquarters at Port Moresby, and the main force for military operations consisted of the 39th, 49th and 53rd Militia Battalions with 13 Field Regiment of artillery, all commanded by Brigadier N. G. Hatton, as 30 Brigade. Air elements were equally weak, comprising Catalina flying boats, Hudson reconnaissance bombers and Wirraways, the latter being nothing more than armed training planes. The Navy had no ships available to send against the Japanese, but in the prewar years had organised a network of observers who would report by radio on enemy air and ship movements – the Coastwatchers.

In January, Rabaul had been easily captured by the Japanese 144 Infantry Regiment, who brushed aside the defending 2/22nd Battalion, losing a mere 16 killed and 39 wounded to gain the strategic harbour and airfields. Token forces of Independent Company platoons were positioned throughout the Solomons, but had no effect on the invading force. In March, Lae and Salamaua were captured without opposition by Japanese marines and II Battalion 144 Regiment (II/144).

Towards the end of January, after the first Japanese air attacks on the north coast, refugees began to arrive in a variety of aircraft. One party from the goldfields was said to have left at Salamaua some 50,000 ounces (1417 kg) of gold. They had only the clothes they wore.

On 27 January, Major General Morris had called to military service all white, fit males who were British subjects. However, this effectively removed from their necessary tasks the administrators and business people of the territory.

Port Moresby was attacked by Japanese aircraft on 3 February, and further raids followed. By 28 February, only two Catalinas and a Hudson remained serviceable for operations around New Guinea. The first fighter defence arrived on 21 March, when the RAAF's 75 Squadron flew in with their new Curtiss P40 Kittyhawks, which they had received just 10 days earlier. The story of 75 Squadron's epic and lone defence of Port Moresby for 44 days has been told in David Wilson's *The Decisive Factor – RAAF Fighter Squadrons at Port Moresby and Milne Bay*.

The Japanese bombings resulted in an exodus of natives from the danger area, but traditional hazards were greater. Tribal enemies were waiting, and killed many people trying to make their way home, though the greater number did not go far. David Marsh was a young Australian who had been working for the Kienzle family at Kokoda, and was recruited into the Australian New Guinea Administration Unit (ANGAU). He arrested 12 such local killers, but could do little other than 'sentence' them to work as carriers for his patrol force, releasing them after one patrol.

Once ANGAU was established, it proceeded to grow until it exceeded the prewar civil administration. However, at time of its inception, ANGAU officers often continued with their duties in much the same way as they had done as civilians, and the Assistant Resident Magistrates in the Kokoda and north coast areas were commissioned as lieutenants, with Thomas Grahamslaw at Awala as a captain, and Officer Commanding Northern District.

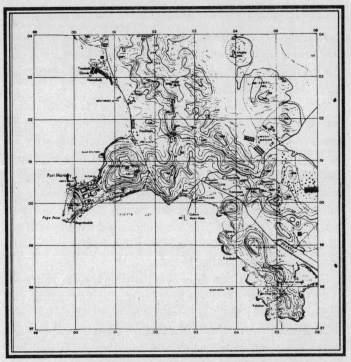

Port Moresby town area, April 1942.

The air raids became something of a break in the monotony for 39th Battalion. No battalion member was killed by the attacks, but some were injured. Because of the great amount of flying done by the RAAF Catalina flying boats and Hudson reconnaissance bombers, the Japanese thought there were more aircraft available than they could see from the air, and made the deduction that underground hangars were hiding the rest. Two US airmen taken prisoner at Rabaul on 18 April, after their 22nd Bomb Group B26 was shot down by a Zero, told the Japanese that they came from a base on a small island near Australia, where there were 400 aircraft in underground hangars.[1] This may have led to the Japanese deciding to make air attacks on the slopes of the hills around 7-Mile, but there were no such hangars.

At first, a total blackout of Port Moresby was enforced, but it was realised this only hindered the defenders. Approaching Japanese crews could position themselves by looking at the coastline, and so the lights were turned off only when the approaching bombers were close. Later, when outdoor films were shown, it was said that the Japanese used the illuminated screen as a reference point from which to make their bombing runs.

Radio Tokyo propaganda broadcasts referred to the defenders, and rather than lowering their morale, served to improve it. If the Japanese included them in their broadcasts, then they were assumed to be important. Throughout the war, and after, right up to and including Vietnam, propaganda and so-called psychological warfare activities had remarkably little affect, regardless of the nationality of the enemy concerned, be they Australian, American, Japanese, Korean, Chinese or Vietnamese. Exponents of this effort usually justify its use by asserting that the effect is cumulative and cannot be quantified.

However, general morale in 39th Battalion and the other units in the Port Moresby area was low, due to activities by their own higher echelons. Food was described as 'vile'. Much had been stacked in the open and had spoiled in the blazing heat. For the first three weeks, 39th Battalion had only their rifles and 20 rounds of ammunition. There were no cooking utensils, and the battalion had to make its own from tin cans. There were no mosquito nets and no repellant, no long trousers or long-sleeved shirts. A single, two-inch (50 mm) tap on the road supplied water for the entire battalion. There was no mail for the first month.

All of these things, plus the sense of isolation and of being sent away from Australia to defend the Godforsaken locale of Port Moresby, combined to reduce the typical high spirits of the average Australian. All the above aspects of physical comfort and well-being were easily solved, but the fact that they existed for a relatively small force deployed so close to Australia indicates the state of defence preparedness and Australia's ability to support a force sent on garrison duties.

Brigadier Selwyn H. W. C. Porter, whose AIF number was VX133, had commanded three 2nd AIF battalions, including the 2/31st on operations in Syria. Under his command, the battalion captured Jezzine from Vichy French. He arrived in Port Moresby on 17 April to take command of 30 Brigade. He was not pleased with the condition of his formation, but realised that it had been badly treated by higher headquarters, and that some of the older officers could not cope with the climate. He set about sending back unsuitable officers and bringing in AIF replacements. Some replacements were resentful at being allocated to a Militia unit. By June, Brigadier Porter had sent back all over-age officers in 39th Battalion, except for Captain Sam Templeton, OC B Company.

Porter found much that needed attention at Port Moresby, but understood the problems that had plagued Brigadier Hatton: the climate, the lack of supplies, lack of air defence, the constant requirement from New Guinea Force HQ for working parties to unload ships, build positions and work on the airfields, which left no time for training and resulted in lower morale in units that had not been keen to begin with. The supply staff, with few troops, faced an ever-increasing burden as what supplies did arrive had to be unloaded and dispersed according to sensible wartime requirements, to avoid clustering where they could be easily destroyed.

These matters have been described well in the official histories and other books and it is not intended to detail them here again.

The Papua New Guinea of the time was to be swept away forever by the war. The white administrators, police, planters, miners and others lived in a colonial fashion that was soon to disappear. The local population had no concept of 'nation' as understood by the Europeans. The local people were tribally oriented, and horizons extended to the district, such as Gulf District, West or Eastern District. Loyalty was to a bloodline, and even in the district there were deadly enemies. The local people went to work to gain material objects that would allow them, for example, to choose independently for a wife, rather than obey the tribal elders, who possessed the wealth of the tribe in the form of cowrie shells and similar items. Work was not seen as a career, but as a way to acquire things from the European shops. These Western items completely destroyed the old system of wealth. The steel implements, hurricane lanterns, torches, mirrors and so on brought instant standing to the young man who returned to the tribe with them.

David Marsh, the man who went to the territory in 1939, from school, with an agricultural background, and, as mentioned earlier, worked at Kokoda for the Kienzle family, was to spend the remainder of his life there, until retirement, and gain a deep insight into the region, the peoples, and their problems. During the coming campaign, he was to be employed in ANGAU, and after the war as a patrol officer. He was proud to be part of the process whereby Stone Age tribesmen who had not seen a white man until they were adults had grandsons who were helicopter pilots. But that was far in the future in 1942.

Marsh worked seven days a week for £20 a calendar month, which, of course, meant each year he worked a week for nothing. The Kienzles paid the native workers 10 shillings a month, and also sold them the desired items from their own store, at their set prices. Like many other plantation owners, they stood to gain nothing from idle labourers, so set high quotas of work, lifting the standard when the lesser amount was achieved. As the local people did not consider work a full-time career, employer and employee were at opposite ends of the spectrum.

However, it was realised that happy workers produced more, so the Kienzles allowed wives and families to accompany the workers at Kokoda. The women and children were responsible for growing the food consumed by the workforce, and as part of this policy, David Marsh had cleared a series of 50-acre (20-ha) vegetable garden plots. A grown man actively working requires eight pounds (3.6 kg) of sweet potatoes a day. These plots of vegetables were a windfall for the Japanese, and the quantity of food available from them assisted the Japanese forward to Port Moresby. Given the ineptness of the Japanese planners and logisticians, they may have believed that similar large areas of food existed further into the mountains, and, as will be shown, persisted in sending forward more ammunition than was needed, in place of food.

In the course of his work in the northern area, Marsh met and came to know the missionaries and plantation owners. Except for Father Benson, the rest were described as 'lovable, well-meaning but impractical, hopeless in looking after themselves'. Father

Holland was paid £32 a year, and lived at or lower than the standard of the local people, but was devoted to the natives. Like the others, he worked hard, going without to bring the word of God to the people. It seemed that many missionaries lacked a basic understanding of the native people. Two female teachers told Marsh, at Kokoda, that if the government and its power ever left the Buna–Gona area, the natives would kill them. Marsh found that these ladies had been forcing the teenage native girls in their class to strip naked before thrashing them for some misdemeanour. Such acts were bound to build up a reservoir of ill-will.

At the other end of the scale from a member of ANGAU was the flamboyant Supreme Commander South West Pacific Area (SWPA), US General Douglas MacArthur. MacArthur was son of a well-known US military hero, Arthur MacArthur, and had enjoyed a well-publicised career in the US Army before and during the First World War. After becoming US Army Chief of Staff, he had retired and gone to the Philippines as 'military adviser' to the Philippines Government. The US had captured the Philippines from Spain and promised independence to the islands in 1946.

When the Second World War spread to the Pacific with the Japanese attack on the US naval base at Pearl Harbour, Hawaii, on 7 December 1941, similar simultaneous attacks followed on the Philippines and Malaya. However, fog on Formosa (Taiwan) delayed the take-off of the Japanese air units tasked to strike the US bases in the Philippines, and the attacking force expected a sturdy defence from the alerted fighter squadrons. To their amazement, the US Air Force was on the ground. The Japanese made good use of this opportunity and eliminated the only real offensive force available to the Allies. MacArthur, for some reason which has not fully been explained, refused permission for his air units to attack, and though they had been airborne, had just landed again. Further Japanese air attacks followed and pounded the US naval and air bases. The Japanese Army did not land in force until 22 December, and advanced so rapidly that next day MacArthur withdrew to the Bataan Peninsula. There followed the creation of the myth of the great fighting defence of the Philippines by Mac-

Arthur's forces. Because the final surrenders of US forces in the Philippines did not take place until May 1942, whereas the British surrendered Singapore in February, it has been claimed that the British performed far less well than the defenders of the Philippines. In fact, as shown by detailed postwar investigation, there was far more actual fighting in Malaya than in the Philippines.

The Japanese had landed only about one-fifth the forces commanded by MacArthur, and bundled him back to Bataan with great ease. After some unsuccessful attempts to break through the defences on Bataan, the Japanese waited until April, then attacked and took the peninsula. The island fortress of Corregidor remained in Manila Harbour. A Japanese assault force landed on one of the few small beaches, broke out onto the island and captured it in less than 12 hours: 1000 Japanese against 12,000 Americans. Accounts of the action by US writers usually are careful not to mention the size of the Japanese assault force on Corregidor, nor of the force that defeated MacArthur.

MacArthur spent three months on Corregidor, during which 140 press releases were issued, mostly referring to only one person: MacArthur. Nearly all were written by him. The legend was boosted by the almost daily media reports in the United States extolling the heroic defence of the Philippines, and of the achievements of this one American commander who seemed to be giving the Japanese their only real problems and defeats.

However, in February, the governments of Australia and New Zealand, well aware that the US was the only possible source of assistance against the oncoming Japanese, informed Washington that a US theatre commander was acceptable to both countries. US President Franklin Roosevelt ordered MacArthur out of the Philippines, to Australia, as that commander. After a dangerous journey by navy PT boat and worn out B17 bomber to Darwin, DC3 to Alice Springs, and then by train, MacArthur arrived in Melbourne on 21 March. He was accompanied by his wife and son, and a selection of staff officers. This 'Bataan clique' remained with MacArthur and formed the cadre around which his General Headquarters (GHQ) South West Pacific Area (SWPA) was built.

They received all senior positions, and, in MacArthur's opinion, could do no wrong.

It was not widely known until postwar research discovered the documentation, but MacArthur and several of his senior officers received substantial payments, in addition to their military salaries, from the Philippines Government to look after the interests of the Philippines. The only officer who was offered and refused one of these payments was the then-Colonel Dwight Eisenhower, who had left the court intrigues and ineffective advisory role to the Philippines administration to return home. Eisenhower said that a letter of appreciation would be reward enough. MacArthur accepted US$500,000, and his senior officers lesser amounts.

In Melbourne, MacArthur was appalled to find that there was no congregation of large air, land and sea forces for him to take back to the Philippines. He apparently expected to find such a force ready for a counter-offensive, but does not appear to have given any thought as to where President Roosevelt might have acquired it. All that existed was a motley collection of some 20,000 troops of air and land units that had been en route to the Philippines when the Japanese attacked, and so had diverted to Australia.

MacArthur had long believed, with some justification, that he had many enemies in Washington, and that these people now were plotting to leave him with no forces to wage effective campaigns, let alone 'return to the Philippines'. The one bright spot was the euphoria with which he was received in Australia, and the almost complete submission with which Prime Minister Curtin complied with MacArthur's wishes.

Given the factors of the dangerous world and regional situation, MacArthur's immense ego, his considerable personal charisma and experience in politics, added to his status as representative of US military power, it is not surprising that Curtin allowed MacArthur to become virtual dictator of Australia. Curtin had earned his place in Australian history by his leadership during the war, and by standing up to British Prime Minister Winston Churchill and demanding, then continuing to demand, the return to Australia of the battle-experienced AIF formations from North Africa after

Churchill arrogantly and without consultation sent them to Ceylon (Sri Lanka) and en route to Burma. But Curtin was putty in Mac-Arthur's hands.

General Thomas Blamey, Commander-in-Chief of Australian Military Forces, had successfully resisted the attempts by the British Generals to have Australian formations broken up and fed piecemeal into their own organisation. This would have limited, in effect, Australian command to battalion level. However, Blamey too was outmanoeuvred by MacArthur, and ended up with the nominal title of Commander Allied Land Forces.

Of the greatest importance to maintenance of the MacArthur image and personal legend was Curtin giving control of the media to MacArthur. Nothing could be printed or broadcast without clearance from GHQ SWPA, or complying with its guidelines. Consequently, one man was seen to be fighting the Japanese. Blatant untruths, known as such to those in the military and to the journalists, were released as fact, but the only way to counter this arrangement was to go out of the SWPA.

In the Kokoda and following campaigns, MacArthur was to denigrate the Australians actually doing the fighting, so that Washington perhaps would accede to his demands for more US forces of all services.

After the Japanese landings at Lae and Salamaua in March, and their naval reverse in the Battle of the Coral Sea, in May it was realised that Allied positions would have to be held on the north coast of New Guinea. On 14 May, General MacArthur informed General Blamey that airfields were to be established for use against the Japanese at Lae and Salamaua, and that suitable sites seemed to exist between Abau and Samarai. On 14 May also, the ships bringing the US 32nd and final elements of the US 41st Divisions arrived in Melbourne. The Australian 14 Brigade – 3rd, 36th and 55th Militia Battalions – already had been ordered to Port Moresby, on Blamey's authority, and on 16 May Blamey replied to MacArthur that troops were available for the proposed airfields. On 20 May, MacArthur ordered that an airfield be built in the Abau –Mullins Harbour area, that air force squadrons at Port Moresby be brought up to full strength, and US anti-aircraft units move to Townsville, Mareeba, Cooktown, Coen and Horn Island. However, a reconnaissance of the Abau–Mullins Harbour area showed no suitable airfield sites existed, so it was recommended, and approved, that the better sites in Milne Bay be developed.

MacArthur told Blamey on 9 June that it was believed the Japanese intended going overland from Buna through Kokoda and on to Port Moresby. Three days earlier, 6 June, Major General Morris had tasked the Papuan Infantry Battalion (PIB) of 310 all ranks to reconnoitre the Awala–Tufi–Ioma area on the north coast. Two weeks later, Blamey ordered Morris to prepare to oppose Japanese forces on possible lines of advance from the north coast, and to secure Kokoda. On 24 June, Morris ordered 39th Battalion, less one company, with the PIB and small medical and supply elements to delay any Japanese advance on Kokoda, prevent Japanese movement through the Kokoda Gap, and meet any airborne landings in the area, with the first company of the 39th to depart on 26 June. This force for the protection of Kokoda would be 'Maroubra Force'.

This fear of airborne landings was common to both sides in the coming campaign, and is little considered in other studies of the events. However, it was a serious factor in those to be considered by commanders planning defensive measures in 1942. The Germans had made good use of airborne and air-landed troops in Europe and the Mediterranean, and the Japanese also had used them in their advance through the Netherlands East Indies.

The Europeans in Papua-New Guinea before the war were, perhaps, the most air-minded community in the world. Air travel was common between the mining settlements and the coast, and feats of air delivery of heavy mining machinery by local airlines had led the world in such matters in the 1930s. It was understood by many in the territory that air movement was essential, but the number of aircraft necessary for military operations simply was not available. Unfortunately for future Australian intentions, MacArthur did not like flying, and disliked his air commander and air staff.

All in New Guinea were aware of the formidable nature of the defensive task, and the unsolved problems of resupply. No military force had ever been deployed into the region, and all communications, supply and support arrangements would be developed from a completely bare beginning – nothing existed outside of Port Moresby.

MacArthur later claimed that immediately on arrival in Australia he reviewed the strategic situation and plans for the defence of Australia, discarded the so-called 'Brisbane Line' and decided to fight in New Guinea. His absolute control of the Australian media allowed this falsehood to be recorded as 'fact', and it has been repeated in subsequent writings. In May and June, as clearly shown by Dudley McCarthy in the Australian official history, available in Australia were most of the battle-experienced AIF Corps from North Africa, the two US Divisions, plus 10 other Australian divisions. The decision to fight in New Guinea, if taken so early, would have resulted in some movement north of combat units and logistics arrangements. Prime Minister Curtin and General Blamey were not informed of this radical and historic decision by MacArthur. In fact, MacArthur had issued a directive on 25 April, which described the defensive role for Allied Land Forces in preventing Japanese landings on the north-eastern Australian coast, and made no alteration to existing dispositions. In addition, until 20 July, MacArthur's headquarters remained in Melbourne – 2000 miles (3220 km) from Port Moresby.

For the first 15 days of June, Allied air operations consisted of fending off Japanese attacks on Port Moresby. Feelings were not improved by the news of the Japanese submarine attack on Sydney Harbour. The Japanese force that withdrew to Rabaul after the Coral Sea battle had intended to capture Port Moresby by amphibious assault, and they still intended to capture the town, its harbour and airfield sites. The Japanese were about to commit a force to take Port Moresby from the direction that many people believed impassable to any large body of men – from the north, over the Owen Stanley Ranges.

However, after the Japanese invasion of March, civilian refugees had successfully walked from the settlements on the north coast and inland all the way to Port Moresby, and if these people could do so, so could Japanese soldiers.

On 14 June, Lieutenant General Harukichi Hyakutake, commanding the Japanese 17th Army, was ordered by Imperial General Headquarters to prepare an overland invasion of Port Moresby, if a reconnaissance of the overland routes showed this to be feasible. Hyakutake selected Major General Tomitaro Horii to command the formation assigned to this task, to be called 'The South Seas Detachment'. Logically, an engineer unit would be best to carry out such a reconnaissance, and Colonel Yokoyama's 15th Independent Engineer Regiment was picked. The regiment had distinguished itself in the Malayan campaign. On 29 June, Horii's force was ordered to Rabaul.

The force consisted of:

144 Infantry Regiment – Colonel Kusunose (three battalions plus regimental troops).

55 Mountain Artillery Battalion – Lieutenant Colonel Hozumi.

15 Independent Engineer Regiment – Colonel Yokoyama.

1 Company 55 Engineer Regiment – Captain Takamori.

In addition there were anti-aircraft, supply, signals, medical, hygiene, cargo-handling and other relevant units.

On 30 June, Horii went to Davao (Philippines) and was given his orders on 1 July. The first landing force and advance element for the crossing of the mountains was the Yokoyama Advance Unit, comprised of the following units:

15 Independent Engineer Regiment – Colonel Yokoyama.

1st Battalion 144 Infantry Regiment (I/144) – Lieutenant Colonel Tsukamoto.

No. 1 Company 55 Mountain Artillery – Lieutenant Hamada.

Sasebo 5 Special Naval Landing Party (less two companies) – Commander Tsukioka.

15 Naval Pioneer Unit – Major Kukuchi.

In addition, there were signals and transport units, a hospital, a port-handling unit, medical and army service corps units detailed for the operation. In effect, the Yokoyama unit was an infantry-engineer group suitable for a landing and advance, able to be supported by its own elements from the beach after supplies were delivered. The Yokoyama force was to land near Buna and press on into the mountains to reconnoitre the route for the following main body for the occupation of Port Moresby. They were to quickly occupy a strategic line south of Kokoda on the western side of the ranges while examining the possibility of the Horii formation capturing Moresby by the land route, and build roads as well as moving forward supplies. As soon as I/144 was ashore, it was to move by motor transport and bicycle to the mountains, covering for the main party. All following units were to move inland as soon as possible by truck or on foot.

Engineer reconnaissance troops would be active with the advance troops. A platoon from No. 1 Company 15 Independent Engineer Regiment was to accompany the forward element of the infantry and reconnoitre the route. At the mountains, a platoon of infantry was to come under command of this Engineer platoon. The Engineers were to constantly report on the terrain and factors affecting the construction of roads for packhorses, light and heavy trucks. Behind them, the main body of the Engineers would be advancing while constructing roads, with the assistance of the Takasago (Formosan/Taiwanese) Volunteer unit and 400 coolies.

After landing operations were completed, part of 10 Independent Engineers were to reconnoitre the Kumusi River, to see if the Horii formation could advance along that, at least part way, to Papaki. At the same time, 10 Independent Engineers was similarly to reconnoitre the Mambare River and the road alongside it, reporting as soon as possible.

Duties for the transport, signals and medical units were those relevant to supporting the advance units. Colonel Yokoyama would be aboard the ship *Ayatosan Maru*, and intended landing with the second wave, then to accompany the infantry in their advance. The AA Company was to have half its force ashore by dawn, to cover the landing, and when all the unit was ashore, half was to move as quickly as possible to the newly established dump location and guard that. The power of air attack was well recognised.[2]

While the landing force would be of army troops, the navy also intended putting ashore a force to occupy and make usable an area near Buna selected as an airfield. However, a US–Australian team had closely checked the Buna area for possible airfield sites, and agreed that the location was not suitable. Instead, the Allies intended building airfields a little way inland. The Japanese went ahead, and put several thousand men to work – at the wrong place.

The Japanese military already had a vile reputation for their attitude to civilians, non-combatants and prisoners. Their behaviour in China had been reported in the Western press, and survivors of massacres and attacks on ships packed with refugees had spread their stories. In January, the survivors of 2/22nd Battalion at Rabaul had been murdered in and around the Tol Plantation on New Britain, and some of those lucky enough to live through this, or witness it, had made their way to New Guinea.

A document captured later at Milne Bay gave insight into the official policy of Japanese units. 'Notes for Unit Commanders' was published by the Imperial Japanese Navy's Kure 3rd Special Landing Party (3SLP) in February 1942, and was intended to inform and instruct unit leaders with a combination of 'lessons learned' from combat and instructions. Paragraph 45 stated that:

'To eradicate the sense of fear in raw soldiers carnivals of bloodshed (or) human sacrifices to the war god are most effective. Killings with the bayonet should be carried out whenever an opportunity occurs. Raw troops, being unused to fighting, suffer relatively heavy casualties, and attention should be paid to this point.'[3]

Bluntly, troops were to be taught to kill by bayoneting available prisoners or captives. Many photographs exist of this activity, most showing Chinese as the victims. The Japanese had studied their enemies, and produced writings for study by unit commanders. Points describing the Australians were: 'The enemy is a slow firer, but is skilful in covering jungle roads and precipices. He fires and throws grenades at close range. He is fond of using hand grenades. His fighting spirit is unexpectedly intense; he does not retreat in single combat; on being charged he will flee. One kilo [metre] to their front are scouts who usually flee immediately. Foot patrols usually operate 200-300 metres from the left and right, forward and rear of their positions.'[4]

Other comments on the qualities of the Australians were found in Japanese documents: 'The enemy confronting us in combat hereafter will be Australian and American Troops. As we experienced at the battle near Buitenzorg (Netherlands East Indies), the resistance put up by Australian troops is strong and their distinguishing feature is that they particularly excel in sniping. Their units assigned to defend areas near their homeland [sic] were especially excellent, and it was recognised by [Japanese] combat units in that area that they were putting up a stubborn resistance to our attacks.'[5]

The document went on to say that the future combat zones would be the Solomons and Papua. 'The said area is absolutely uncivilised and is infested with tropical diseases. The land is very mountainous, with dense jungles; along the shores are barrier reefs of coral. Villages are not much more than boat anchorages along the coast and are barely recognisable. As far as roads are concerned, there are only footpaths and horse-paths and it is not difficult to imagine they will be bad.'

There had been a great amount of concern in Australia for many years over alleged Japanese spying activities. This concern was well-founded, but the results gained by the Japanese perhaps were overestimated. The Japanese knew a great deal about the coastal settlements, even to the contents of individual buildings, but little or nothing of inland areas. Despite the reference to roads and footpaths above, it was believed that a good road linked Port Moresby and Kokoda, when in fact only a track existed. However, the road leading out of Port Moresby went in that direction, and ended abruptly at Ower's Corner. Japanese observers must have assumed the road continued, and this idea was to influence Japanese operations in the mountains.

However, if the Japanese had little idea of the inland, so did the Australian civil and military authorities. A completely false idea existed of a narrow Kokoda Gap, which could be defended by very few men, sometimes stated to be only two (one to fire and one to load), who easily could hold the arms-width defile and kill their attackers. Troops actually in combat, and their commanders, were plagued by headquarters referring to this non-existent pass. The most ludicrous suggestion came from General MacArthur's GHQ: that the pass be blown up. There was an even more misinformed suggestion – that the mountain ranges themselves be blown up!

The combatants on each side were to be poorly served by their respective theatre headquarters. Neither sent enough senior officers to assess the situation, at any time, and report. But all this was in the future.

In late June, the Japanese had allocated troops for the expedition through the New Guinea mountains, and MacArthur's GHQ had decided to establish an airfield with protecting infantry on the north coast. If MacArthur really had decided to hold the Japanese in New Guinea, it would be reasonable to expect a high priority given to such a move, and that units, equipment and materials would have been allocated. There was no such urgency evident, and the Japanese were to arrive first.

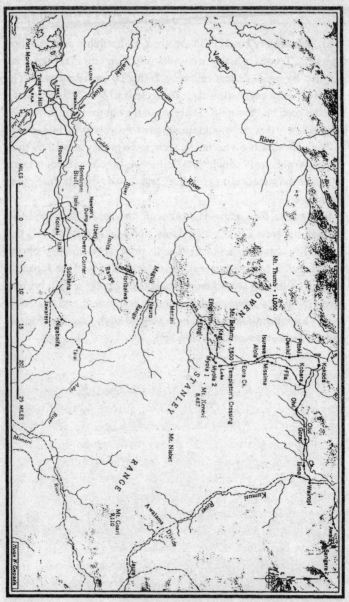

The Kokoda 'Track'.

Chapter 2
SOWING THE EAST WIND
July 1942

In Washington, the Joint Chiefs of Staff met and on 2 July decided on three tasks for the commanders in the South Pacific region. The first was to seize and occupy the islands of Santa Cruz, Tulagi and others in the Solomons by 1 August; the second was to seize and occupy the remainder of the Solomons, Lae, Salamaua and the north-east coast on New Guinea; task three was to seize and occupy Rabaul and nearby positions in the New Guinea–New Britain area. The first was the responsibility of Admiral Ghormley, Commander of the South Pacific Area, and the other two were allocated to MacArthur's South West Pacific Area. By any reckoning, these tasks were beyond the capabilities of the local Allied forces in mid-1942.

The world situation was not bright. In North Africa, Field Marshal Rommel had taken Tobruk and was advancing on Egypt; the besieged island of Malta in the Mediterranean was hanging on under intense German aerial attack; the Germans had begun a large and successful offensive in Russia; U-boats were wreaking havoc on the Atlantic convoys; the Japanese dominated Asia from Burma to Singapore, to Rabaul and north to Wake Island. The strategic defeats suffered by Japan in the Battles of the Coral Sea and Midway, in May and June, had no immediate effect on Allied defensive operations in New Guinea.

Lieutenant H. T. 'Bert' Kienzle, a plantation manager from Yodda, north of Kokoda, was the only European known to have walked the Kokoda Trail in recent times. He was commissioned into the Australian New Guinea Administration Unit, then told to organise and take charge of all native labour, and construct a road from Ilolo to Kokoda. On 3 July he was told that B Company 39th

Battalion was waiting for a guide to Kokoda. He found that 600 native carriers assembled for the porterage over the trail were very sullen and unhappy, as no proper thought had been given to their living conditions and general treatment. Instantly grasping the situation, Kienzle gathered the natives for a talk, in terms which they could readily grasp, and had work started on construction of clean, dry shelters for the men. Very quickly, this consideration resulted in an improvement in the situation.[1]

This incident, in fact, gives a more accurate picture of the 'fuzzy wuzzy angels' aspect of the Kokoda Trail than the wartime propaganda of faithful, stalwart peoples flocking to serve the white man against the Japanese. Without the expertise and local knowledge of the ANGAU members, who controlled the local people working as carriers, there would have been no fuzzy wuzzy angels.

However, two lieutenants of the 3rd Battalion, 14 Brigade, had walked the trail to Kokoda and back, from 13 June to 3 July, but as they had not returned by the time Kienzle was told to take the infantry company to Kokoda, and when they did arrive back had to complete their report on the 'military' aspects of the trail, there was no up-to-date information available. It seems the report the two men did compile was little used; perhaps the opinions of two recently arrived Militia subalterns did not carry sufficient weight.

B Company 39th Battalion prepared to move over the trail to Kokoda, and then to Buna. They were to be the unwitting pioneers in an epic of courage and physical exertion that was to affect the entire Australian Army and channel that army's efforts into mastering jungle warfare. There were no maps, no terrain studies, and very little information was available. It was accepted that Europeans could not travel through the mountains when carrying more than a very light load of personal belongings. Military operations had not really been considered, as the mountains were believed to be impassable to bodies of men.

For the first two weeks of July, the major military activity was by the air forces, particularly reconnaissance flights to the Solomons, puny raids on Rabaul, and fighter defence by US P39 squadrons over Port Moresby. On 4 July, four B25s were damaged in

combats; on 7 July, Allied Air Force (AAF) HQ authorised commanders of P39 squadrons to remove the outer wing .30-calibre
machineguns, ammo boxes and solenoids, in an attempt to improve its performance against the Mitsubishi Zero. Over the next
four days, B17s and a B24 reconnoitred Buka, Rabaul, Tulagi, Kavieng and Kokoda–Mambare. On 11 July, seven B17s attacked
Rabaul and two were attacked by fighters; one was damaged. P39s
intercepted a raid on Port Moresby, losing two and one damaged.
On 12 and 13 July, B17s reconnoitred Kavieng, Buka, Faisi, Tulagi and Kokoda, but another sent to Madang–Kavieng–Rabaul was
attacked for 40 minutes by three Zeros, sustaining damage to both
wings, the cockpit and to No. 4 engine, but no crew casualties. The
B17 returned with photographs of its targets. On 14 July, five B17s
set off from Cloncurry, via Horn Island, to attack Salamaua. On
take-off from Horn Island, two crashed, killing three crew members, then two became lost in clouds and went back to Cloncurry,
while only one went on to the target. The never-ending B17 reconnaissance missions were flown to Tulagi and Kavieng. On 15 July,
B17s went to Buna–Kokoda, Tulagi, and Nissan Island.

At higher levels, Ultra signals intelligence had warned that the
Japanese intended to land again on the north coast of New Guinea
and push overland to Port Moresby, but there was little detail
available. The Japanese Army code was not broken until 1943, and
the Japanese Navy changed its code. All that remained to the
Allied staff was analysis of the volume of Japanese radio traffic,
air reconnaissance, coast watchers and captured documents or prisoners. However, no Japanese had been taken prisoner and documents were few and far between. The initiative remained with the
Japanese.

Meanwhile, on 8 July, Lieutenant Bert Kienzle and B Company
39th Battalion began the march to Kokoda. With them were native
carriers, and Kienzle realised that he would have to deal with the
problems of establishing facilities and improving the track as they
went on. Nothing existed ahead of them in the form of rest camps,
supply dumps, medical facilities, or communications installations
such as telephone lines back to Moresby.[2]

The supply and transport organisation at Port Moresby had been warned that 39th Battalion would be moving to Kokoda, and that rations were to be delivered there by air. Nine flights, each of 4200 pounds (1905 kg) were to be available, but the rations had to be prepared in 40-pound (18 kg) packs. The soldiers worked around the clock in shifts to meet this requirement, and then were informed that the aircraft would not be available and the rations had to be repacked for delivery by carriers.

9 Company Australian Army Service Corps (AASC) had arrived for service in New Guinea after an uncomfortable voyage on an old, flat-bottomed Dutch ship. Ray Royal was a 20-year-old soldier who wanted to transfer from the Militia to the AIF, but his parents would not sign the papers; 21 was the age of maturity then. On the voyage, Ray had been among a number of Diggers detailed to make sure the officers were awake and out of their cabins if the ship was torpedoed. As it was obvious the officers were living in greater comfort, and there was much laughter and noise from their quarters, Ray decided that if the ship was hit, the officers could look after themselves. When the unit arrived at Port Moresby, all were amazed at the total lack of light discipline – Australia was firmly under blackout at night.

Later, 9 Company came to realise the importance of the single wharf at which they disembarked. Along it went all the cargoes destined for the support and fighting forces on the island, and all knew that if a ship were sunk alongside, or the wharf destroyed, the supply situation would soon be desperate.

Tales of the all-conquering Japanese were rife. Aboard ship, the Diggers were told that the Zeros strafed each arriving ship as a welcome. Sure enough, as the ship came into harbour, a flight of fighters dived towards it. The alert machinegun crews swung their weapons towards the planes and one nervous Australian gun crew fired, but were stopped after a few rounds by the American sergeant in charge of the guns – the fighters were US P39 Airacobras!

9 Company moved out to a camp at 'the 20-mile' distance from Moresby, and were regaled with tales of the Japanese supposedly creeping around at night. They soon experienced their first air raid,

a single flying boat that did little damage. Everyone had scattered to trenches or distant parts of the area. One of the Diggers had scaled a hill. When the 'all-clear' sounded, he decided he might as well sit there for a while and enjoy a contemplative pipe and the view. However, to the nervous people below, the flare of the match and repetitive glows as he got the pipe drawing well were signals from a spy to the dreaded Japanese aviators in the distance, and soon a hail of bullets was cracking around the lone smoker, who was yelling, 'Don't shoot! It's me, Harry!' Luckily, there were no accurate gunmen below.

An American fighter unit fought a 45-minute battle among themselves at one of the airfields, when glowing embers from a bushfire were taken for cigarettes. When calls to put out the cigarettes were ignored, it was immediately deduced that the smokers must be Japanese. The volley of gunfire went past the embers and into another group of tents, whose occupants returned fire, believing themselves to be under attack. Such was the degree of uncertainty in some areas of Port Moresby.

Until their vehicles and equipment arrived, 9 Company AASC was employed as labourers unloading ships. When the ship with their unit materials arrived, it was found that Sydney waterside workers had looted the batteries, tools and other items necessary for the company to function. It mattered not to the thieves that the items stolen were from a unit defending Australia against an enemy whose fleet had been in battle off the east coast of Australia. Replacement items had to be given high priority and flown from Australia before 9 Company could function. The company then began an 18- to 24-hour day, with the vehicles used almost nonstop. They could not be spared for maintenance, and eventually the unit created a section of mobile vans that patrolled the roads, working on the trucks as required and as the chance arose. In Ray Royal's opinion, the mechanics 'did a terrific job' keeping the vehicles on the roads. The intense pressure was kept up until the Buna campaign was well advanced and supply bases were established on the north coast of New Guinea.

MacArthur's GHQ ordered a reconnaissance of the Buna area

for airfield sites on 9 July, and this was done on the next two days, resulting in an unfavourable assessment of Buna, but a positive report was submitted on the neighbouring Dobodura area. GHQ SWPA decided to go ahead, and on 15 July ordered the occupation of the Buna area, by a force of infantry, engineers, anti-aircraft and radar units, which was to depart Port Moresby on 31 July.

At the same time, Japanese 17th Army was given approval by Imperial GHQ to go ahead with the reconnaissance of the mountain crossing to Port Moresby.

B/39 was recuperating at Kokoda after their march from Moresby. It was obvious to experienced men such as Kienzle that human carriers simply were not practical for such operations as might develop in the mountains. A native carrier consumed the equivalent of his own load in food in 13 days, and if there was one soldier to each carrier, then the rations were consumed in half the time. This was for only food, and took no account of any other item necessary for operations. As the walk to Kokoda took eight days, supply by humans was impossible. The only answer was large-scale air dropping or air landing. It was out of the question to consider road construction. Kienzle had supplies from his own home in Yodda brought to B Company, then set off again for Moresby.

Near Moresby, the remainder of 39th Battalion was training, and in the afternoon of 18 July, Lieutenant Colonel Owen was conducting a meeting of unit umpires when a message was delivered to him. He read it, then told the umpires to go back to their own companies. The battalion had been ordered across the Owen Stanleys. Warrant Officer George Mowat, CSM A Company, began a diary in a pocket notebook. Mowat was a First World War veteran and had won the Military Medal in France. He noted, 'Great excitement. Four hours movement order'.

George Mowat was born at Cressy, Victoria, in 1895, fourth son in the family, descendants of Scottish settlers who arrived in 1852. The family had a small farm, but was mainly occupied with providing Clydesdale workhorses for local activities such as carting, sinking dams and road-making. All farm produce was taken to Geelong by cart or wagon, until the railway was built. After passing his 8th grade, at the age of 12, young Mowat went to work for the local grocer for several years, then joined the family business. In 1914, at 19, George Mowat enlisted in the AIF and was on Gallipoli with the 24th Battalion. In France, where he was in the 58th Battalion, Mowat was wounded in action at Fromelles. He was hit in the thigh, but also temporarily deafened by the shell explosion, so while unfit to return to the 58th, he did a Lewis gun instructor's course. He won the Military Medal at Polygon Wood, and after the end of the war, married Norma Chapman, a nurse he had met when in hospital. They returned to Cressy, but the small farm and carrying business were not enough to support three families, so Mowat moved to Geelong.

He loved sport, but had to give up football, as he could not see well enough when his glasses were knocked off. He was a member of the RSL, and attended Anzac Day in Melbourne. When war was declared in 1939, Mowat was persuaded to give a demonstration of stripping and assembling the Lewis gun, while blindfolded, at the local RSL branch. Along with other ex-soldiers, he volunteered for the second great war. He was 44 years old. Mowat and other veterans were assigned to the 39th at Darley Camp, near Bacchus Marsh. When the battalion was warned for service in New Guinea, Christmas Day 1941 was the final occasion on which family and friends were able to visit members of the unit. The trains from Melbourne and nearby areas were crowded as relatives and friends went to spend what Elva Mowat recalled as 'an unforgettable Christmas Day with the men of the 39th'. Next day, the 39th departed for active service. Now they were preparing to cross the Owen Stanley Ranges.

On a higher level, a US officer was worried about the developing situation. Lieutenant Colonel David Larr, of MacArthur's G-3 (Operations) Branch, was disturbed by reports of Japanese shipping gathered at Rabaul, and by sightings of smaller ships probably practising amphibious landings near Talasea (New Britain). He thought these indicated a move on Buna, and urged that the Allied forces occupy the area at once. However, he was overruled; Guadalcanal had priority.

At Davao, in the Philippines, Japanese 17th Army Headquarters issued Operation Order A-10, concerning the invasion of eastern New Guinea. Order A-10 allocated the following tasks to army units, which were to cooperate with the navy:

• Nankai Detachment was to land quickly at Buna, advance along the Buna–Kokoda road and capture Port Moresby and the nearby airfields.

• 35 Infantry Brigade was to remain at Palau, prepared to make a landing east of Port Moresby to assist the advancing Nankai Detachment, as well as prepare to capture Samarai and islands to the east of Samarai.

• Ryuto Force was to land near Buna and establish a supply base for Nankai Detachment.

• 47 Field Anti-Aircraft Battalion was to land at Buna and provide AA defence for the area and the mouth of the Kumusi River.

• Units remaining under command of 17 Army were to advance to Rabaul, prepared for future allocation as deemed necessary, while 1st Debarkation Group would be responsible for transporting the units and allocation of boats for ship-to-shore operations.

• Reserves would be Yazawa Force and Aoba Force, at Davao in the Philippines.

Japanese optimism about their speed of advance from Buna to Port Moresby is shown by their allocation of supplies for the various formations. Major General Horii's Nankai Detachment was to take only two weeks' supplies from Rabaul; the others were to take one month's supplies.[3]

Meanwhile, the Australian C Company 39th Battalion moved to Ilolo, and B/39's stores arrived at Buna. At Kokoda, after recovering from the march up, B Company was training and familiarising itself with the local terrain and such features as rubber tapping. Warrant Officer Mowat, in A Company, wrote, 'All ready. Move held up for a few days. Route marches'.

The heavy weapons and supplies for B Company 39th Battalion arrived at Buna, and Captain Sam Templeton set off from Kokoda, with a carrying party, to collect them. Templeton, a mature man with wide military experience, believed to include submarine service in the First World War, and battle in the Spanish Civil War, must have been well aware of the immense problems facing his partly-trained company, more or less isolated on the northern face of the Owen Stanleys.

On 20 July, at 5.15 am, the Japanese convoy began to move out of Rabaul harbour and turn towards New Guinea. On *Ayatosan Maru* was the diarist of Sakigawa Transport Unit. He recorded that unit members were deeply moved at their departure from what had been an important outpost of Australian defence, but now was an advanced base of Japanese forces. He added that after six months in occupation, the unit had grown attached to Rabaul, and 'our emotion is profound'. The army passengers did exercises on deck, then practised assembly for the event of air attack, and had instruction in anti-aircraft firing. The sea was rough, and around them they could see the other ships. Later, the new operation was explained to the gathered troops, and the importance of the transport unit as a whole and of individuals was emphasised to the Sakigawa Tai (unit) soldiers.[4]

Meanwhile, Allied aerial operations continued, with reconnaissance flights, small attacks on Rabaul, and fighter defence of Port Moresby by US P39 Airacobras. On 16 July, a B17 went to Buna–Salamaua, and 11 others from Longreach flew to Port Moresby, to attack Rabaul next day, but one crashed at Horn Island, overshot the flarepath, burst into flames and all the crew were killed. On 17 July, a B17 reconnoitred Guadalcanal–Tulagi, and was attacked by three float-planes, one of which was seen going down in flames. Ten B17s set off from Moresby for Rabaul, but two landed back at Horn Island with oxygen problems, one returned due to the weather, and one returned with electrical failure. Lack of maps, navigation aids and adequate pilot training meant that single-engine fighters had to be accompanied north of Townsville by twin-engine aircraft as guides. On 18 July, a B24 flew to Kieta, Bougainville; an Australian 33 Squadron DH89 Rapide carrying Generals Scanlon, Vasey and some staff set off from Moresby to fly over the Kokoda area, and allow the generals to see for themselves the terrain, but the aircraft was forced back by weather. On

19 July, Lieutenant Don Tower, of US 435th Squadron, located a convoy in the vicinity of Rabaul, later assumed to be the Buna convoy, but there was nothing to indicate this at the time. Next day, 26 Japanese bombers escorted by 15 fighters bombed Port Moresby, and although US P39s took off, there was no interception and two US fighters crashed, while a B17 searched sea areas.

Below the fighters and bombers, A Company 39th Battalion began its route marches, which were to be up to 20 miles (32 kilometres) a day, and George Mowat noted, 'Very solid. Very hot'.

On 21 July, aboard Japanese ships heading for Buna, reveille was held, followed by physical exercises on deck. The Sakigawa Transport Unit had no cases of seasickness, and all were reported to be in good spirits. Then at 7.30 am, two enemy planes at 24,000 feet were seen, and all passengers went to action stations, but the planes went past to the south of the ships with no reaction. At 2.30 pm, passengers aboard the ships saw the coast of New Guinea. At the same time, Allied aircraft were seen, but again no attacks were made, and the diarist of Sakigawa Transport Unit put this down to lack of courage on the part of the Allied crews.[5]

However, the aircraft did report the convoy, but the bad weather precluded any accurate report, and all GHQ knew was that ships had been sighted on a course for the north coast of New Guinea.

The preliminary bombardment of the Gona–Sanananda area started at 4 pm as landing parties prepared to go ashore. At Buna Government Station, ANGAU Sergeant Barry Harper radioed Port Moresby before the enemy arrival and action, then asked for a reply. There was none, and though Harper kept on transmitting, Moresby did not acknowledge. Finally, the message was relayed by a three-man team of spotters at Ambasi, some 37 miles (60 kilometres) north of Buna. The three men, Hannah, Holyoake and Palmer, were later betrayed to the Japanese by local natives, and were killed. Private Gaina was one of 21 Papuan Infantry Battalion (PIB) soldiers under command of Lieutenant A. A. Smith and Sergeant Hill. Gaina remained loyal, and returned to tell how two men from Senani village led Japanese after the party.[6]

Major W. T. Watson, commanding the PIB, had his force spread

along parts of the coast or waiting at Kokoda. Because reports of
the landings were imprecise, Watson went forward to see for himself what was happening, as did Captain Grahamslaw, ANGAU,
with a small party. Watson was described as 'bluff, outspoken,
quick in the uptake and quick in speech. A man with the highest
standard of personal courage, and utterly intolerant of those who
lack resolution and coolness in danger. As a subaltern in the 1st
AIF, he probably won more decorations than any other artillery
officer of his rank. His officers say that he made the PIB'.[7]

At 4.30 pm, the ships began unloading off Basabua. Sakigawa
unit were grateful that their AA training had not been used. All
were in high spirits and aware of the important nature of their duties once ashore. Sergeant-Major Tanaka and two men went with
the second landing wave at 5.50 pm, to select the vehicle landing
point and assembly area, while the rest of the unit checked and
adjusted the unit vehicles and prepared them for unloading. The
need for speed was realised and understood. Food for the evening
meal and breakfast was issued, and as high waves made landing
operations extremely difficult, operations were suspended until
conditions calmed. People tried to sleep.[8]

At 5 pm, Lieutenant Tower flew a B17 to Buna and attacked the
invasion fleet with four 1000-pound bombs, but missed, and the
bomber was hit by intensely accurate fire from ships and shore. At
the same time, another B17 reconnoitred Kavieng–Rabaul. However, a strike force from Moresby soon arrived and from 6300 feet,
five US B26s attacked two transports and four destroyers off
Salamaua at 6.02 pm. Despite intense and accurate anti-aircraft
fire, one direct hit was scored on the stern of a transport, as well as
a cluster of near misses. A Japanese diarist recorded that *Ayatosan
Maru* was hit by three bombs, and 'the stern sank'. Toshiaki Sugimoto, 2 Platoon of Takasago Volunteer unit, noted that he was
ashore by 05.00 (5 pm), but the ship blew up at 06.00 [sic]. He may
mean at 6 pm, which would be the time of the B26 raid. He also
noted that three enemy aircraft were believed shot down.[9]

Seaman 1st Class Shunji Shin, 2 Company Sasebo 5 Special
Landing Party (2/Sasebo 5SLP), saw three enemy planes drop

bombs close enough to rock *Kinryu Maru*, but he was safely ashore by 6 pm and bivouacked about two and a half miles (four kilometres) from Buna. Toshio Watanabe noted in his diary that he had landed at Buna, and begun the advance to Port Moresby as the first battalion of the force. Takiwo Igaue, in Lieutenant Mayazaki's 2 Platoon, Lieutenant Ogawa's 1 Company of Tsukamoto's 1/144, was one of 170 men in the company. Lieutenant Nose's 3 Company also landed, and each of Nose's men was equipped with a bicycle. They began moving inland as fast as possible.[10]

At 9.30 that night, US time, Major General George C. Kenney, with his aide, Captain Bill Benn, took off from Hamilton Field, north of San Francisco. Kenney was to replace General Brett as air commander in Australia, was to shape the Allied Air Forces in the SWPA into the most innovative air formation in the Second World War and to see it advance from Melbourne to Japan over the wreckage of the Japanese Army and Navy air forces opposing him. It was certain that Brett was to be replaced, but the Japanese landing at Buna, despite the best his squadrons could do, was the final excuse needed by the Bataan clique that surrounded MacArthur.

At 6.25 am on 22 July, the first attack on the Japanese landing force was made by an RAAF Hudson, from 12,000 feet. The bombs fell 75 feet (23 metres) short of the target ship. The Hudson sent a sighting report, which was acknowledged in the usual way by Moresby, but, as they left the area, a message was received asking for their route, then another came in telling them to go to a rendezvous. The suspicions of the radio operator, Sergeant Juett, were aroused, and the message was not acknowledged. At Moresby, the crew found that base had not contacted them, or received the sighting report. The Japanese had been trying a little deception. Juett said that the radio procedure was perfect each time.

Next to bomb was a B17 flown by Lieutenant Robert M. Debord, who came in low, and bombardier Sergeant Richard Olson dropped more than a dozen 300-pounders. On the first run, five aimed at a destroyer missed, but the second attack was made on a transport, the bombs scoring hits amidships and on the starboard side. Two and a half hours later, the ship was seen still on fire, listing to port. This was almost certainly *Ayatosan Maru*, already hit by one bomb. In addition, Japanese sources stated that the destroyer *Uzuki* suffered 16 casualties and damage from near misses in this operation.

Aboard the ship, the Sakigawa unit had seen the Hudson, and recognised it as a reconnaissance flight. Then the diarist described an attack by five B17s in formation, which came through the fire from the ships' guns, 'impudently evaded the fire and calmly soared over the *Ayatosan Maru*, dropping countless bombs. The heavy bombs screeched as they fell, dropping all around the ship, almost lifting it from the sea. One bomb struck No. 4 hold, which was loaded with crude oil'. Fire broke out and the fire fighting unit worked hard; AA ammunition on the bridge was thrown overboard because of danger from the flames. The ship's papers, baggage and other items were put into a small boat and sent ashore, and later it was decided to abandon ship. Wounded were carried up on deck before being loaded into barges. Also going ashore was the Sasebo 5 Special Landing Party (5SLP), a marine unit that was to acquire an evil reputation for murdering civilian and military prisoners.

At 8.55 am, six US B25s bombed the smaller transport from 8000 feet, but claimed no hits. The Sakigawa diarist recorded the attack, noting that the bombs fell between *Ayatosan Maru* and *Ryoyo Maru* . Then, as the diarist described it, 'like a typhoon came the low-flying Spitfires! They strafed from about 50 metres the personnel making for shore in motor boats. The ship AA fired bravely, and those who crossed the line of death are truly flowers of the soldier's spirit'.

The attackers were a mixed formation of eight P400s from three squadrons at Moresby, and Captain Bob Faurot, with Lieutenant Charlie King, led a section down onto the barges. They attacked from only 30 feet, returning with two aircraft damaged. The Japanese had mistakenly identified them as Spitfires, but were sharp-eyed enough to see the damaged fighters, and believed they had been shot down. The Airacobras swept up and down the coast over Buna until the B25s arrived, the fighter pilots watched the bombers make four passes and noted one ship burning, then the formations went back to Moresby. Six B26s set off to attack the ships, but one returned to base. At 9 am the other five attacked, dropped 34 bombs from 7000 feet, and claimed a hit on a burning transport, but it was not proven by photographs. Crews saw a fighter pilot bale out. Eight P400s strafed barges at Buna–Gona at the same time, but Lieutenant David Hunter of the 80th Squadron was hit by ground fire when low over the sea. He parachuted onto Gona Beach. After the war, Hunter's personal ring was recovered at Rabaul, and it seemed he had been taken to New Britain before being killed by the Japanese. In this attack, one barge was sunk, and pilots reported seeing one transport burning, plus three destroyers offshore. Next to attack were 10 B17s, but one went back with engine trouble. At 10.35 am, the other nine dropped 72 500-pound bombs in a pattern on the transports, but there were no hits. The daily reconnaissance commitment was maintained, and B17s set off to reconnoitre Rabaul shipping, Tulagi and ships at Buna respectively. Eight A24 divebombers of the US 8th Attack Squadron were warned to move from Charters Towers to Moresby, in preparation for attacking the ships at Buna.

By 11.20 am, all personnel from *Ayatosan Maru* were ashore and moved to separate unit assembly places. All vehicles of the transport units still on the ship were lost, as it was impossible to unload them. Sakigawa Transport Unit had only seven vehicles ashore, including a side-car and a light armoured car. The others were three captured vehicles, a truck and a command car. The unit was going to find it difficult to fulfil its role in supporting the advancing infantry, engineers and artillery. *Ryoyo Maru* had weighed anchor and left, to avoid bombing, after landing only two captured trucks. About 1800 men of Yokoyama Force had landed, with 52 horses and several hundred Rabaul natives to assist as carriers. As well as the bad news of this landing, commanders in Australia were also presented with reports of four ships torpedoed and sunk off the east coast on this day.

Departing Port Moresby at 11.30 am, Pilot Officer Warren Cowan, of 32 Squadron RAAF, took his Hudson to the Buna landing

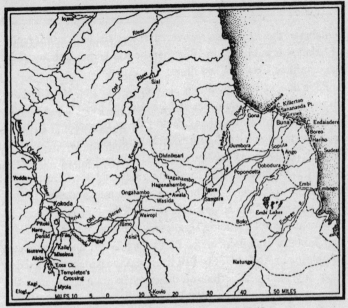

The Kokoda–Buna area, July 1942.

area, radioed his sighting report and that he had found two cruisers
heading for Rabaul, then attacked at low level. Overhead were
nine Zeros of the Tainan Kokkutai, from Lae. The Zeros dived
after the fleeing Hudson, and first to reach firing range was Japanese air ace Saburo Sakai. Then the Japanese were amazed to see
the Hudson turn on them and attack. By brilliant flying, Cowan
survived the one-sided contest for some time, as the Zeros crowded
each other away when clustering for the kill. Eventually, Sakai
closed in and put the rear turret gunner out of action. Cowan could
no longer be given warning of attack from that direction, and the
Japanese went in to 100 feet range, fired and ignited the petrol
spraying from the Hudson's tanks. The Zeros, according to Sakai's account, swung away and watched as Cowan tried to put the
burning Hudson down, but as it touched the trees the wings were
ripped off and the fuel exploded. According to Sakai, all the Japanese were impressed with the bravery and ability of Cowan's
crew, and Sakai himself has a special regard for Cowan as the best
opponent he met over New Guinea. After the war, the wreckage
of Hudson A16-201 was found near Popoga village, Buna, and the

remains of the crew were recovered. It was not until a biography of Sakai was published in 1986 that the RAAF became aware of the details of Cowan's last flight.

P39s attacked AA positions at Gona at 1.15 pm, and pilots reported seeing large numbers of Japanese and piled boxes of supplies as they roared overhead. Below them, the Sakigawa diarist recorded them again as Spitfires, and also that two trucks had their engines riddled and were unusable, so the vehicles were towed off and left at the headquarters location on the beachhead. Despite the losses, the unit received an order to prepare transportation for the main strength of the advance elements of the Japanese force.

Watching the advancing Japanese was a detachment of the Papuan Infantry Battalion under Lieutenant Wort, and Lieutenant Champion of ANGAU. The PIB itself was too widely dispersed to have any immediate effect on the invaders, but in any case the commander, Major W. T. Watson, had little information available to allow him to plan anything useful. At Moresby, Lieutenant Colonel Owen was ordered to concentrate 39th Battalion at Kokoda. There was one transport aircraft available in New Guinea.

The air attacks on Buna continued, and at 1.35 pm, strafing from 50 feet, P39s fired cannon and machineguns into the trees, saw nothing to report below them, but out to sea saw a burning ship: *Ayatosan Maru*. At 1.40 pm, six B26s attacked a destroyer off Buna, dropped 34 bombs, claimed one hit on the stern of the ship, but on return one aircraft belly-landed at 7-Mile Strip. At 14.50, eight RAAF P40s attacked with 500-pound bombs. At 5000 feet, they engaged eight Japanese fighters, hit one, but lost a P40, though the pilot was safe. Two hours later, nine P39s attacked a float-plane, and left it diving, smoking. At 5.45 pm, five US B25s dropped their bombs from between 3000 and 5000 feet on the beach at Buna. No ships were seen, but 20 barges were counted on the beach. Ten minutes later, a B17 arrived with 14 bombs, but as no ships were seen, dropped them on 22 motorised landing craft (MLC) counted on the beach, but no bombing results were claimed. Four other B17s could find no ships, so dropped 28 bombs on the burning ship. No hits were claimed.

The Japanese were moving inland to their assigned areas, and the engineers already had begun work on roads. Assisting them were the transport unit members, carrying logs, chaining them together to form a more solid surface through the muddy areas. 'Thus the fruits of our training were realised,' wrote the Sakigawa diarist. Working through the night, improving on the route behind the engineers, the transport soldiers caught up with the leading road-builders, and were allowed to sleep.

By the end of the day on 22 July, I/144 and the attached engineers had 900 men at Soputa, well away from the beachhead and bombing attacks. A patrol led by Lieutenant Chalk of ANGAU went into Sangara, and found the Japanese had been there. He took his men back to Awala, and waited for the Japanese to arrive.

After four hours of sleep, the Sakigawa unit was woken and work began immediately at 7.30 am on 23 July. The jungle was thick enough to cover their work from the air, but constant attention was paid to camouflage. In the distance, they could hear Allied aircraft arriving over Buna. First Allied aircraft over the beaches again this day was a Hudson of 32 Squadron RAAF at 6.30 am. This was Sergeant Airey, who dropped four bombs, and counted 25 barges on the beach. Next at 6.45 were four US P400s but they reported nothing from their mission.

C/39 began moving from Ilolo to Uberi, with the other companies following. Warrant Officer George Mowat noted that the company commander was 'called at a moment's notice. Platoon commanders, Company Quartermaster Sergeant and self stand by in readiness for instructions. Orders are to proceed by plane to Kokoda and then march to Buna. Spent considerable time allocating men and material to planes. To bed at 02.00 [2 am]'.

At Kokoda, Lieutenant Seekamp's 11 Platoon was moving forward to Awala, Mortimore's 12 Platoon had taken up position at Gorari, and Garland's 10 Platoon stayed to defend Kokoda airfield.

Seven B26s from Townsville set off for the target area, but only four bombed, at 11.15 am, dropping 19 500-pounders on the beach from 6000 feet. The other three were unable to descend through the clouds and returned with their bombs. At 12.45 pm, four P39s appeared over the invasion area, and two dived to attack the two three-inch AA guns emplaced at Gona Mission compound, with unknown results. A single B26 came in at 1.10 pm, and from 3900 feet through intense accurate AA dropped two bombs on a 5000-ton ship, 15 miles (24 km) south of Buna, claiming one hit amidships. A large orange flame flared, then fire could be seen on the surface of the sea, as if fuel had spilled and was burning. These piecemeal attacks have been related in some detail to indicate the weak force available. They achieved little and dissipated Allied air strength, but were to continue in this manner until March 1943, when at last the squadrons were concentrated to deliver a smashing blow to a Japanese convoy.

On land, the advancing Japanese were about to engage the force sent to delay them. At about 4 pm, some 1000 yards east of Awala, Chalk's patrol was waiting. Coming from the east were Japanese, while approaching from the west was Seekamp's platoon of B Company 39th Battalion. The Japanese arrived first, but with natives ahead of them as a screen. With small arms, Chalk's men fired, forcing the Japanese to deploy. Very quickly, the Japanese began to return fire with machineguns, mortars and a mountain gun. It was obvious Chalk really could do little to hold them, and he withdrew.

Captain Sam Templeton had ordered Seekamp to Awala, then returned to Kokoda to meet Lieutenant Colonel Owen. Major Watson ordered Seekamp to hold the Japanese for 30 minutes while the PIB established themselves some two or three miles (five kilometres) back at Ongahambo. But for some reason, Seekamp withdrew to Wairopi, on the far side of Ongahambo. Watson was forced to destroy the stores and buildings at Ongahambo, then go back to Wairopi with the few men left to him: his European officers and NCOs and a small number of staunch native soldiers – the majority had deserted.

At 4 pm, three B26s released 60 bombs along the shore northwest of Buna, reporting much smoke rising after the attack, and 30 minutes later, two more B26s attacked from 6000 feet, released 54 bombs into what was believed to be a stores area inland. No results were seen, but there was heavy machinegun fire and light inaccurate AA. Over the jungles, four P40s tasked to strafe the Mubo–Komiatum road also attacked a corvette and Zero-type float-plane at Salamaua, but one was lost. B17s had gone to reconnoitre Buka and Buna, and five B25s and five B26s returned from Moresby to their bases at Charters Towers and Reid River (Townsville) after their missions on 22 July. Six B17s set off from Mareeba, for recce and attack sorties on Lae and Buna, but two returned for mechanical reasons.

Throughout the day, the Sakigawa Transport Unit had slaved to improve the road leading inland from Buna. They completed six miles (10 kilometres) of rough track, including laying logs over mud, and the unit diarist noted that the difficulties were beyond description, adding, 'All officers and men realised their duty and proudly carried on'. One vehicle had to be abandoned due to lack of parts to repair a damaged gearshift, and work continued under the moon. Lack of sleep was beginning to be a problem.

After a short sleep, the Sakigawa transport soldiers were roused after midnight, early on 24 July, and went on with their road-building, pushing on to Soputa. Clouds came up, and it began to rain, adding to their difficulties in the darkness, but 'our duty to reach the front line would not let us rest for one moment'. At 5.30 am, they were allowed to rest, but only because the engineers were busy with a bridge ahead.

Again the early morning Hudson from 32 Squadron was first on the Buna scene, Sergeant Cowan dropping four 250-pounders at 6.30 am. Japanese documents reported that there were no casualties, but 100 rounds of cannon ammunition were blown up, the navy wireless station was destroyed and much equipment burned. At 8.50 am, eight P39s and P400s arrived over Buna as escort to eight A24s led by Major Rogers. Charlie King led the second section of the Airacobras, and admired the beautiful formation flying of the divebomber pilots. The A24s slid into echelon, peeled off and dived into the haze below, passing through AA bursting at 3000 feet, with gun-flashes from the ground clearly visible to the aircraft. Five divebombers, with four escorts, attacked from 2500 feet, dropping four 500-pounders among the barges and buildings. Another report claimed eight direct hits in the AA position. The only sign of Japanese activity was AA fire. Faurot went down in the dive with the A24s, to strafe, but the others remained with the A24s. Thirteen other P39s strafed Gona at 9 am, but no results were seen, and 10 minutes later, six B26s attacked the barges with 196 100-pound bombs, but again no results were seen.

Meanwhile, inland, Major Watson with Lieutenant Seekamp's platoon was in position on the western side of the Kumusi River, having destroyed the bridge at Wairopi. At 9 am, they received a radio message from Captain Templeton informing them that 1500-2000 Japanese were believed to have landed, so it was recommended they engage only in rearguard actions and fall back on Kokoda.

Later Captain Stevenson, Templeton's second-in-command, arrived with orders for Seekamp: he was to leave a lookout on the west bank, and fight a rearguard action back to Mortimore's platoon at Gorari. About midday, Lieutenant Jesser of PIB arrived, having swum the river. He had been reconnoitring the Japanese at Awala, and reported that they had not moved forward by 7 am. However, the Japanese I/144 and engineers were only about two hours behind Jesser, and soon appeared on the far bank of the river. After shots were fired by both sides, the Australians moved back to Gorari and took up position behind Mortimore's platoon.

Meanwhile, closer to the coast, Captain Grahamslaw, of the ANGAU, with native soldiers, was on a reconnaissance patrol to locate the Japanese. He noted much Japanese air activity, and when he reached the Popondetta Road he put scouting parties out to the flanks and went to a place where he could observe the track at a creek crossing. He settled down and watched the passing Japanese, but then a shot from one of the scouts was answered by Japanese gunfire and he had to leave, as he could hear the Japanese coming. By 3 pm, he was again squatting in the bush watching large numbers of Japanese passing along the track. Later that night he was only a few yards from the track, still observing, and waited for dawn.[11]

Moresby was attacked by 18 Japanese bombers, with 16 fighters as escort, and their bombs destroyed petrol supplies. Eight P39s were scrambled from Moresby, but because of misunderstanding the ground controller, no interception was made and the Airacobras returned to base. At 2 pm, seven B26s dropped 191 100-pounders on the Gona Mission area, and barges were seen burning as the bombers departed. Japanese documents recorded a direct hit on a Company headquarters, ammunition exploded, and one man was killed, another wounded. Three B25s also attacked the Buna–Gona area, but four more B26s tasked to attack a warship reported at Salamaua did not take off on the mission. Nine B25s flew from Charters Towers to Moresby, and two B17s set off to reconnoitre Tulagi–Guadalcanal and Huon Gulf–Buka.[12]

By the end of the day, the Sakigawa Transport Unit had reached its allocated area in the jungle 1000 metres south of Soputa, prepared a vehicle park and carefully camouflaged the entire area against air attacks. Sentries were posted at night, and the first transportation task was done: a radio unit was driven in three trucks from Buna to Popondetta.

Lieutenant General Hyakutake arrived in Rabaul, and found that Yokoyama Force had been sending reports of good progress in New Guinea, so Hyakutake recommended to Imperial GHQ that the assault on Port Moresby go ahead. However, Yokoyama's reports only described the successful landing and the advance to date. There was nothing Yokoyama could have written about the mountainous terrain yet to be encountered, the availability of food, engineering problems or any other matter from further inland. Hyakutake may have been keen to get on with the capture of Moresby, but neither he nor any member of his staff seems to have considered tasking any of the aviation units available to do a reconnaissance of the route through the mountains. There were no army aircraft in the region, though there was the Navy 11th Air Fleet, but there may have been inter-service problems involved.

In Port Moresby, Lieutenant Kienzle, of ANGAU, reported to Major General Morris on the situation regarding carrier use and supplies along the Kokoda Trail. A Company 39th Battalion waited all day for its flight to Kokoda. At 4 pm, trucks picked up the gear and men, and took the soldiers to Koitaki. No one knew where the gear went. 'Japs reported to have landed. Plane trip cancelled,' wrote George Mowat.

Just after midnight, on 25 July, a RAAF Catalina dropped bombs in the area between the Kumusi River and Mangrove Island, disturbing the rest and night activities below them. A RAAF 32 Squadron Hudson flown by Sergeant N. B. Clarke left Moresby with a mixture of bombs and flares to harass Gona. One bomb hit an ammunition dump, but the crew saw an unidentified aircraft near them, assumed it was Japanese, and decided to leave. They still had two bombs and three flares, so dropped them all at once. The flares ignited, illuminating an area of some 80 square miles (200 sq km), and the crew felt very much exposed, but slipped into a cloud.

Lieutenant Colonel Owen and Captain Templeton had moved forward from Kokoda during the night, and arrived at the Gorari location about 2 am. Owen decided to fight at a place 800 yards east of Gorari, and supervised the positioning of his platoons there, with the PIB soldiers on the flanks. He then set off back to Kokoda, to meet elements of the battalion coming by air.

At 6.35 am, three US B25s dropped eight bombs onto Gona Mission, with unobserved results, then there was a break for almost four hours, until 10.20 am, when eight B25s escorted by six P400s were attacked by eight Zeros. The Japanese exploited the speed and agility of the Zero, and would fly below the bombers, then chandelle up into their formation, rolling across and down on the other side, firing as they did so. Six B25s were hit by cannon and machineguns, all 64 bombs were jettisoned, but crews claimed three Zeros destroyed. The six P400s also carried a 300-pounder each, to release on Gona and the Kokoda road, but results were unobserved. No Zeros were claimed, but one US fighter was missing, and another pilot wounded, his plane damaged and unserviceable. More B25s returned at 5.20 pm, aiming 45 bombs from 10,000 feet at barges and targets inland; no results were observed. At 1.30 pm, a B17 en route to Rabaul–Kavieng, was 60 miles (100 km) north-east of Buna when it was attacked by fifteen Zeros at 4000 feet. The B17 escaped into cloud, but had been well hit: cannon and machinegun strikes were made on the wings, fuselage, tail, fin and rudder, nose and ball turret; No. 2 engine cut out, No. 3 engine was damaged; two gunners were wounded and required hospital treatment when the B17 returned. However, days of intense Japanese fighter combat such as this were rare. Despite having the advantage of bases on the north coast, and a superior fighter, the Japanese failed to secure air superiority over the Buna landing area, or over the invasion path inland, or even over the sea routes. For their part, Allied air force commanders continued to send their aircraft to attack in penny-packets.

Sakigawa Transport Unit was settling in, with kitchen and latrines, canteen purchases, and truck supply tasks done as ordered. The Japanese diarist noted that natives informed them of the presence in a village only about one mile (1.5 km) away of three armed enemy. All the unit except a dozen left as guards went to capture these men, but could not find them, despite searching the area with assistance from the natives. The diarist also wrote of the continuous passage overhead of Allied aircraft, and of the camouflage precautions for all vehicles and especially for drying of laundry, to avoid giving telltale signs of occupation to the planes. Another order had been received: personnel were not to be carried in the few trucks, only supplies.

The armed enemy may have been Captains Grahamslaw and Austin, of ANGAU, and their party. Grahamslaw had been evading the Japanese since watching them pass along the Popondetta track, and now he decided to go to Wairopi. However, Captain Austin had supplies hidden in the hills and intended going there, as he had trouble walking far and was not able to make the journey to friendly territory. In the morning, Grahamslaw would find the PIB and natives with them had gone in the night. He went on, arriving back at Port Moresby on 9 August.

Things were not going so well for the Japanese advance elements, who were ambushed by Mortimore's platoon of 39th Battalion. All was quiet, then Japanese with bicycles appeared on the track, just as the Lewis light machinegun team was changing. The gun teams changed every hour so the men stayed alert. However, the Japanese saw the shrubbery move, and at once abandoned their bikes and disappeared into the bush. No Australian fired, which was a credit to their personal and unit discipline. This was their first engagement with the enemy, moreover an enemy about whom many tales had been told emphasising his military qualities.

Eventually, when nothing further happened, the Japanese scouts came back onto the track. Nothing happened, so more Japanese appeared behind them, and the advance continued to Gorari. Mortimore had placed the single available Bren left of the track, with the Lewis slightly forward on the right. The leading Japanese was almost on the Lewis gun, and Private Arthur Swords was looking down the enemy rifle barrel when Mortimore gave the fire order. A hail of bullets went down the track, hitting about 15 Japanese, but the remainder began manoeuvring against the ambush party. Mortimore held as long as possible, then brought his platoon out and back to Oivi, where a two platoon position was established, with the third on the way from Kokoda to join them.

Lieutenant Colonel Owen informed New Guinea Force HQ at Port Moresby of events, asked urgently for at least two fresh companies to hold the flanks at Oivi, told HQ the airfield at Kokoda would be open, and asked to be informed by 3 am if the troops would not be coming by air. Just beginning the journey over the trail was A Company. They had been taken by truck to the end of the road, their packs and heavy equipment loaded onto carriers, and began the march. The sheer lack of knowledge of the trail and the conditions in the mountains can be gauged by the comments made in his diary by Warrant Officer George Mowat. As the company set off, he noted, 'Very picturesque scene. First stage to Uberi; 2 1/2 hours travel. Everyone looking forward to trip'. Later, he added, 'Trail rough, steep and slippery; arrived 18.00 [6 pm]. Native village. Good meal'.

Travelling with them was Lieutenant Bert Kienzle, of ANGAU, continuing his work of organising the native carriers and the flow of supplies to Kokoda. Ahead of them on the trail was the redoubtable Dr Geoffrey F. Vernon, a First World War veteran who had served as a medical officer in the Light Horse. Partly deaf, independent and capable, he used his deafness selectively to ignore orders he did not like. With Bert Kienzle, he was one of two great characters of the prewar white men on the Kokoda Trail. Vernon knew that the 39th had no medical officer, and calmly set off up the trail to do his best to look after the young men of the battalion.

During the afternoon, near Nandi, Fiji, Major General Kenney and Captain Benn had experimented with low-level skip-bombing attacks from a borrowed B26. Though RAF squadrons in the United Kingdom had been successful, despite heavy losses, against German shipping with such tactics, Kenney was first to encourage it in the Pacific war. To do so, he had to overcome the emphasis on high-level precision bombing as taught and practised by the bombardment schools and staffs in the US. Actually, RAAF Hudsons had some success with such attacks on Japanese ships off New Britain early in 1942, but only one of the three aircraft survived Japanese AA and fighters in the first strike.

Two RAAF Catalinas harassed the Buna–Gona area during the night, dropping 16 bombs across suspected dump areas. Below them, crews could see the ship still burning. In what was becoming a regular arrival time, at 6.30 am, on 26 July, a Hudson of 32 Squadron RAAF dropped four bombs into an area five miles (eight kilometres) south-east of Gona, and one caused four secondary explosions. The Zeros were up again this day, and disaster struck a formation of US B25s at 8.15 am. Crossing out of New Guinea to attack Japanese flying boats expected at Gasmata, the B25s were intercepted by 15 Zeros. Two B25s went down in flames, and the other three were damaged. One, rear fuselage blazing, broke in half; another was burning fiercely, and the co-pilot could be seen half out of his hatch, while two parachutes were seen after men baled out of the bottom hatch. One Zero was claimed destroyed. Above was the fighter escort, six US P39s, but they were two minutes behind the B25s, and failed to intercept. The Japanese were the elite Tainan Kokkutai from Lae, and claimed three B25s destroyed, among 10 pilots.

At Kokoda Airfield, Lieutenant Colonel Owen was to be disappointed at the amount of airlifted reinforcements delivered to him. Instead of two companies, only one platoon arrived, in two widely-separated flights. All D Company was driven in trucks to 7-Mile aerodrome, and the Diggers looked around at the activity, noticing US Negroes working on the airstrip. 16 Platoon, commanded by Lieutenant Doug McClean, was divided into two plane loads, and McClean climbed aboard the single available DC3 (C47 in the USAAC) with 14 men. Remaining were Sergeant Ted Morrison, 15 men and the platoon's two Bren guns, still in their boxes. McClean left and after a short flight the plane arrived over Kokoda, but on the ground the watchers were deficient in aircraft recognition, and did not identify the distinctive shape of the DC3/ C47 until the plane had circled many times, then began removing the runway obstructions placed there to prevent Japanese air assaults. Paratroopers, gliders and air-landings were in the minds of many Allied defenders coming to grips with the age of air mobility; the Germans in Holland and Crete, and the Japanese in the Dutch East Indies, had aroused fear and anxiety in the minds of many Allied commanders. Later, at Buna, the Japanese themselves were to spend many sleepless hours worrying about an airborne invasion there. While the transport plane circled Kokoda, seven Zeros flew over, but the slow C47 was hidden in cloud. The Japanese were the Tainan Kokkutai formation chasing the surviving B25s to Moresby. Eventually, McClean's men were landed and sent at once to Oivi, some four hours' march away.

Back at 7-Mile, Sergeant Morrison's half-platoon was boarding when the pilot asked if the weight had been checked, adding that landing at Kokoda had been difficult due to the weight of McClean's group. In the best tradition of Australian sergeants, Morrison assured the American that weight was correct, knowing well that with an extra man and the two Brens in boxes his party was heavier than the first. They took off and arrived at Kokoda with no problem noticed by passengers, probably another testimony to the strength and durability of the Douglas DC3 design. Lieutenant Colonel Owen greeted Morrison, having known him in his prewar Militia days, then told him to go at once to join McClean at Oivi. Morrison had no idea where Oivi was, so asked, and was told to follow 'that track and you'll get there'!

Captain Sam Templeton had gone to Oivi, and when McClean's party arrived, placed them in position with Mortimore's and Seekamp's platoons. At about 3 pm, the first Japanese attack came in, and was held, but eventually the defence was compressed into a perimeter about 50 yards across. Firing continued as the Japanese probed the position, and it became obvious that the Australians were surrounded. Templeton knew Morrison was moving towards the location, and became concerned that he might be ambushed. At about 5 pm, Templeton decided to go back along the track to meet and warn Morrison. He left the Australian position, and disappeared into the gloom under the trees. There were a few shots, then silence. Templeton did not return, nor did he meet Morrison. Japanese documents indicate that he was taken prisoner, and information from him was passed to higher Japanese headquarters. He is not known to have been sent to the Buna area, so it is reasonable to assume that after interrogating him, the Japanese killed Captain Sam Templeton somewhere in the Oivi area.

Morrison's party had already met some B Company people going back along the track, and was told that Oivi was surrounded, so he decided to return to Kokoda and report this to Lieutenant Colonel Owen. After they had started again for Oivi, Owen called Morrison's group back to Kokoda. He had decided to go back to Deniki, after destroying all stores at Kokoda. Meanwhile, advancing along the track towards Kokoda, Dr Vernon arrived at Eora Creek camp, and recorded his disapproval of its location. It was on a small knoll, high above the rushing water, but the banks were so steep that at night one had to take precautions to avoid sliding into the creek. He was to pass through the camp often, and always thought it 'a dreary windswept sunless perch with great mountain walls towering on each side. The approaches were very bad'.

A Company 39th Battalion had been marching since 6 am, on their second stage, to Ioribaiwa. CSM George Mowat, still ignorant of what was before the company, noted, '9 hours. Magnificent scenery. Hills awfully steep, crossed lots of rivers. Everyone very tired. Reckoned succeeding stages could not be harder'.

In their vehicle park area near Soputa, the Japanese Sakigawa unit had been allowed to rest and sleep all morning, then after lunch began digging trenches and carrying out vehicle maintenance. As they had not been discovered by Allied aircraft, morale was high that afternoon and evening.

Not far away, in the darkness at Oivi, Major Watson estimated that some 20 light machineguns were firing on his position, but luckily most rounds were going high. It seemed that most of the Japanese were to his rear, that is, between Oivi and the next village, Pirivi. Lieutenant McClean and Corporal Pyke crawled forward at about 8 pm and launched a grenade attack, resulting in loud cries and groans from their victims. The Japanese tried calling out in English to trick the Australians, to no avail. Guided by a large, brave Papuan, Lance Corporal Sanopa, Watson's command moved first to the south, where there seemed to be fewest Japanese, and then circled back to Kokoda. However, in the pitch black, heavy rain and trackless jungle, progress was very slow and by dawn the group was only some two miles (3.2 kilometres) from Oivi.

Oivi was still defended by Private Swords, the Lewis gunner, Private Taylor and four other men of 16 Platoon, who had been told that the move back was to take place, but not actually informed when it did occur. In the silence after the others had gone, one of the other men realised no one else was left with them, and told Swords of this development, which surprised and dismayed them. Keeping their heads, the six decided to detour around the obvious place where Japanese might be expected on the Kokoda track, and then press on to rejoin the rest of the Watson force. This worked to a certain extent, and the rain must have helped their escape, but without a compass progress was difficult, so the six decided to halt for the night.

At 5.45 pm, two B26s took 50 100-pound bombs to attack the Awata–Wairopi Road, but thick clouds foiled the attempt, so they attacked a destroyer, which outmanoeuvred their bombs as the B26s tried to cope with heavy overcast and a 2800-foot cloud base, then during the night, two Catalinas dropped high-explosive and incendiary bombs across the Gona area. A B24 and B17s reconnoitred Kieta, Kavieng and Tulagi.

On 27 July, Shunji Shin, of 2 Company Sasebo 5SLP, was relieved of duty at 9 am, and went to look at a 23-year-old US 2nd Lieutenant pilot who had been taken prisoner. Very few Japanese had ever seen a foreigner. Shin had noted in his diary some detail of the numerous attacks on the beachhead area in previous days, and the tasks carried out by 5SLP, including carrying rice from the beach to warehouses.[13]

Elsewhere in the beachhead area, the Japanese located one of the parties of Europeans and loyal PIB trying to escape. Corporal Tapora was looking for food, but was seen by Japanese on horses and mules, and a chase developed. Seventeen PIB deserted, leaving only Sergeant Aria, Corporal Detapora, Private Wamu and Private Gaina. Private Gaina was acting as forward scout, and found that the Senani village men had lead the Japanese in behind him, to surround the party of Europeans. Sergeant Aria and Private Wamu were captured with them – Lieutenant Smith, Sergeant Hewitt, Miss Hayman, Miss Parkinson, five US airmen and the three Army signallers. All were later killed by Japanese or natives.[14]

Other loyal PIB soldiers were continuing to fight. Sergeant Katue and 15 men were near Ongahambo, and shot three Japanese on bicycles, then shot another five at Sangara Mission.[15]

Meanwhile, in the Kokoda area, Lieutenant Colonel Owen had reached Deniki, and was surprised to find Major Watson and most of his party had already arrived there, led by Sanopa along a track from Oivi to Deniki. Still out in the jungle was Private Swords and his party of five other men, who eventually found a track going towards Kokoda and followed it, using correct tactical procedures for spacing, changes of forward scout and such. They arrived at Kokoda late in the day.

Moving up to Deniki from the south was Dr Vernon. His personal carrier was so nervous that he was left at Eora camp to look after some gear. Vernon acquired a police constable as guide, and a couple of Kokoda natives as carriers, but as they met more and more people going the other way, they too became so scared that finally he sent them back. Vernon walked on alone, carrying what he could manage. Further back, George Mowat was on the six-hour stage to Nauro. Rain during the night made the track slippery, so that in places the troops had to crawl upwards on hands and knees. 'Hills and yet more hills. Native villages very attractive', he wrote, adding, 'Clean, nicely laid out, and beautifully made'.

Aerial activity for the day began at 9.20 am, when three US B26s released 76 bombs over the Gona area, watched the explosions among the trees, but could not report any results. Five A24s, with 12 P39s as escort, brought their 500-pound bombs to the Buna area to attack shipping, but none were seen, so they bombed the road at Serananoi, causing a small ammunition dump to explode. The sky was overcast at 15,000 feet, and very cloudy over the mountains. Below the P39s, 10 Japanese transport unit trucks had been on a task in the area when the aircraft arrived, quickly drove under the shelter of trees, and none were damaged. Nine B17s went to attack ships at Buna, but did not find any, and other B17s were sent to reconnoitre Kavieng, Buna–Gona, Malaita in the Solomons, and Goodenough Island–Gasmata–Lae–Salamaua.

As dawn on 28 July seeped under the rubber trees at Kokoda, Private Swords and his five companions woke, having spent the night in the tents erected for accommodation when B Company arrived there. No Japanese were near. After searching among the damaged and destroyed materials left by Owen, they collected what food was possible and set off in the rain for Deniki.

Outside Deniki, Lieutenant Colonel Owen was surprised by the arrival of Swords and the five others. When told that the Japanese had not occupied Kokoda, Owen decided at once to go back and hold it. He had 77 men, all tired, feeling the effects of three sleepless nights, the strain of battle, and cross country movement in rain and cold. With them now was the redoubtable Dr Vernon. Owen told Vernon to remain at Deniki, where casualties would be sent.

Owen's force reached Kokoda at 11 am, to find that no Japanese had arrived. At once, he positioned his platoons on the eastern tip of the ridge on which the Kokoda buildings stood, and where the

Oivi track came in. Garland's 10 Platoon was on the right, then the remaining Papuans, Seekamp's 11 Platoon was on the tip of the plateau, with 16 Platoon on the left, the RAP behind 16, and Mortimore's 12 Platoon in the rubber trees astride the Deniki track.

Gradually the Japanese closed on Kokoda, made their reconnaissance, and began firing ranging rounds from mortars, then firing machineguns to test the defences. No one was in doubt an attack would come. An attempt to fly another platoon to Kokoda failed because when the planes arrived the defenders took so long to run out to the airfield and remove the obstructions that the US pilots became concerned at spending so much time in a place where they could be attacked, and flew back to Port Moresby. The pilots also were angered because a Bren gunner had smashed a window in a new C47, and was ready to fire on any Zeros that approached.

Here was another lost opportunity. General Kenney, always ready to demonstrate the advantages of air power, would have been keen to develop such an air-landing, if he had known of the possibility. However, he had not yet taken command. During the afternoon, Kenney arrived in Brisbane and reported to MacArthur's headquarters. He was subjected to a discourse from the Chief of Staff, Major General Richard K. Sutherland, who denigrated the incumbent air forces commander, General Brett, and all aspects of the air forces, and also described the Australians as being 'undisciplined, untrained, over-advertised and useless'. No fool, Kenney realised that his survival as a US officer required careful handling of the situation.

In Rabaul, on this day, 28 July, General Hyakutake was given permission by Imperial GHQ to go ahead with the attack on Port Moresby using forces allocated to the expedition: Horii's South Seas Detachment, Yazawa and Aoba units. In the Soputa area, 2nd Lieutenant Ito and 36 men of the transport unit, guided by natives, left to capture two 'English soldiers', returning to the Sakigawa truck park at 7.30 pm. The diarist made no reference to prisoners.

CSM George Mowat, with A Company 39th Battalion, was on the fourth day's march, eight hours to Efogi, described as, 'Slip, slide, slither, climbing almost perpendicular; descent likewise. Beautiful ferns; trees with moss to the top. Lost a few men on this stage; extra hard'.

The rain falling on the northern slopes of the Owen Stanleys at dawn that day was coming from clouds with a base at 4000 feet, and these conditions interfered with a sortie to Lae and Salamaua by a single B26, so at 6.55 am, the crew dropped 72 bombs on Gona Mission instead. Conversely, three more B26s tasked to attack Lae–Salamaua turned back at 1 pm, because the weather was too good: ceiling at 10,000 feet and visibility 10-15 miles (17-24 km); too clear to risk approach to either target. Zeros had hammered the B25s in recent days, and in this case, discretion was to be observed. In an attempt to relieve supply problems caused by reliance on native carriers, air drops were made at Efogi and Kagi, but only 540 pounds (245 kg) were recovered at Efogi, and 2500 pounds (1134 kg) at Kagi. During the day, a B17 reconnoitred Kavieng–Rabaul, while a P38 flew from Townsville to Iron Range on Cape York Peninsula, tasked to photograph the coast to Port Moresby, then Buna–Gona–Sogeri. At night over the Gona area, two RAAF Catalinas cruised back and forth, dropping 152 bombs. They were replaced by two more in the early morning, which dropped 128 bombs at barges. Japanese documents stated one large and one small MLC were sunk, and one large and two small ones were 'made useless' by bombs from this attack. The Japanese were sending their own harassing flights, and Port Moresby experienced Raid 74, when a four-engined flying boat scattered 16 bombs across the area, but did no damage.

On 29 July, the Japanese began their attack on Kokoda at about 2 am, closing on the ridge tip positions under cover of heavy fire and the darkness, but aided by moonlight in the open areas. They came, in what seemed little regard for tactical dexterity, right up the tip against Seekamp's platoon position. Fierce firing and grenading held them for the moment.

Lieutenant Colonel Owen was at the edge of the steep slope, and was throwing a grenade when a Japanese bullet hit him over the right eye. Lieutenant Peter Brewer, of ANGAU, told Sergeant

Wilkinson, adding that Owen was still clutching a grenade, and to be careful. Wilkinson took a stretcher down to the trenches, but could not find Owen, so Major Watson went with him to the pit. Then Wilkinson realised Dr Vernon was with them, instead of being back at Deniki. Because of the Japanese close by, only whispers could be used, but Vernon was too deaf to hear. The stretcher was left on top of the embankment and Owen hauled up to it. Watson and Wilkinson took his shoulders and Vernon the legs. Owen's weight drove Wilkinson's fingernails into the flesh, and his fingers were sore for days afterwards. While the other two carried the stretcher to the house, Wilkinson ran ahead and lit the lantern. The Japanese had not fired while they were rescuing Owen, but began shooting at the light. Wilkinson later said that 'nervous' was an understatement, as he was 'downright scared'.

It was a mortal wound and despite the brave action by Major Watson, Dr Vernon and Sergeant Wilkinson in dragging him back, then giving what treatment possible in the circumstances, it was obvious Owen was dying. For his part, Dr Vernon 'was very glad to have Jack Wilkinson with me'. They had known each other prewar at Misima, and Vernon appreciated Wilkinson's capabilities, courage and military experience in Greece and Crete. 'I felt every confidence in him,' added Vernon.

Mist had formed under the moonlight, and parties of Japanese were creeping around in the long grass. Heavy fire, coming up the slope, shot the grass roof to pieces and shot away a verandah post, causing one end of the floor to collapse. Every time Wilkinson raised the lantern to assist Vernon with treatment for Owen and several other casualties who had arrived, more shots cracked into the building. The situation became difficult for Major Watson to control, as Japanese were infiltrating the positions and becoming mixed with Australians. Walking wounded were sent on back, Vernon and Wilkinson gathered what medical equipment they could, other cases were evacuated, and the position was given up to the Japanese. The mist aided the Japanese, but also allowed the Australians to break contact and set off back to Deniki.

Wilkinson went to catch up with the wounded, but at the edge of the rubber plantation Vernon turned back. As a young medical officer in the Sinai in 1915-18, he had it 'dinned into me that the place of the MO was at the tail of a retreating column, with the second-in-command'. He'd found such escapes from the Turks exhilarating, and decided to wait and leave with the last person in authority. However, the passing 39th men did not seem to know or to care much where the officers were. Vernon went on back to Kokoda, noting the smaller parties passing, thickening mist and moonlight shadows under the trees, and was about to leave again when he met Major Watson, Lieutenant Brewer and a few others.

Watson told him they were the last. Brewer was sent on ahead and Watson walked slowly along. Dr Vernon thought Watson was tired, but he was going slowly to ensure all the soldiers had gone first. He was in good spirits and Vernon realised that Watson 'had not turned a hair over the night's events'. Meanwhile, Wilkinson had not gone far. He had stopped also, until he found out what had happened to Vernon, and when he was recognised coming along with the last of the soldiers, Wilkinson set off again for Deniki.

Probably the last 39th Battalion men to go were Privates Parr and Hollow, a Bren gun team. Parr waited until a bunch of about 20 Japanese was almost on him, then fired a full magazine of 28 rounds into them, estimating that he hit about 15, before moving away into the rubber trees, into the welcome shadow and avenues of clear movement through the plantation, to the edge of the jungle and the Deniki track.

The Japanese Sakigawa unit spent the morning of 29 July on vehicle maintenance, and the afternoon divided between road repair and attending the unloading of cargo from *Ryoyo Maru*; more ships had arrived. Orders were that food and ammunition were to be unloaded first, and only one more truck had been landed when the ship had to depart the danger zone near the beach. Another 24 men of the unit came ashore, but others remained aboard *Kotoku Maru* when it also left the landing area.

The US 3rd Attack Group was to suffer another heavy loss this day, when several experienced and dedicated crews were lost in a dive-bomber attack on the ships. Seven A24s, led by Major Floyd

Rogers, took off with P39 escort, but over the mountains, due to heavy cloud, the fighters lost contact. Knowing how important it was to attack the newly arrived ships, Major Rogers continued with the mission. As the A24s began their approach down the northern slopes of the Owen Stanleys, they were intercepted by Zeros. Rogers went on. The P39s briefly saw Zeros and A24s in the area, and one Zero was reported hit, but heavy cloud rendered the fighter escort ineffectual. One A24 dropped its bomb over the mountains, but the others tried to score hits on the ships. From analysis of Japanese documents, Rogers is believed by the author to have been the successful pilot who hit *Kotoku Maru* at No. 5 hatch, but, under fighter attack and in the AA barrage, all the other bombs were misses. Japanese AA gunners claimed two A24s shot down.[16]

Rogers was seen on fire, crashing into the sea, and the A24s flown by Captain Schwab, Lieutenants Casseks, Dean and Purker failed to return. Purker and his gunner, Sergeant Hoppe, were reported to be 'safe' on the beach at Ambasi, but were not seen again. Lieutenant Hill flew his damaged plane to Fall River, where his gunner, Sergeant Sam, died of wounds. The only untouched A24 to return to Moresby was flown by Lieutenant Ray Wilkins, who then believed that he was sure to survive the war. He remained in the SWPA when he could have returned to the US, and eventually returned to the 8th Squadron as commander in mid-1943. His only breaks from the war were leaves in Australia, and he became engaged to an Australian woman, with a marriage date set. On his 82nd mission, 2 November 1943, he was shot down into Simpson Harbour at Rabaul while leading the squadron in the famous mast-height attack against Japanese merchant and naval ships concentrated there. He was awarded the Congressional Medal of Honor.

Floyd Rogers had led the first unit of US tactical bombers from Australia to Port Moresby, on 31 March 1942. Thirteen A24s had set off from Charters Towers that day, but due to mechanical problems, only six arrived at Port Moresby. The situation there was such that only two 500-pound bombs were available, and the A24s had to bring their own from Horn Island. Rogers, Schwab, and the others, including the gunners, had flown their A24s while waiting for better aircraft, and went into this attack knowing the chances of survival were slim. In the long term, Rogers and the other men were not lost in vain. The ships were forced to stop unloading, and the cargoes did not reach shore. The Japanese were operating with such a narrow margin of supply that this setback to the logistics program had a significant effect on the Japanese ability to advance. Elsewhere, US B17s tasked for various targets and missions were forced to turn back because of bad weather over New Guinea or over their targets. However, a B17 reconnoitred Kavieng–Rabaul–Gasmata, and a P38 photographed Buna–Kokoda.

At Deniki, Major Watson's tired force from Kokoda had reoccupied water-logged huts and water-filled pits, and waited for reinforcements to arrive. Since first engaging the Japanese, Lieutenant Colonel Owen and 10 others had been killed and more were missing. They had certainly inflicted several times that number of casualties on the advancing Japanese, and delayed their forward movement. As well as Captain Templeton, the Japanese may have captured six other Australians. Yokoyama's advance unit reported capturing Templeton and one other, then, 'five more prisoners' were mentioned in Intelligence Report No. 4 from 18th Army Headquarters. None were referred to by Japanese at Buna, nor are they known to have reached Rabaul. Yokoyama's Engineers or Tsukamoto's I/144 presumably killed them after interrogation.[17]

Struggling along to join the force at Deniki were the platoons of A Company. George Mowat recorded the two and a half-hour stage to the camp as 'extra hard climb, 1 1/2 hours to the top, 1 hour descent. Native carriers marvellous. Received instructions to push on with all speed. Things serious at front. Left packs here, carried own equipment. Blankets put in bags, sent ahead by carrier'. Also coming up were Captain Merritt's E Company (retitled from Machine Gun Company), Captain Bidstrup's D Company of two platoons but reinforced with AA Platoon, and Headquarters Company. Instruction on the Bren gun was given on the way, with AA Platoon receiving a very basic introduction to the weapon on a rest day at Kagi. One aspect that was not explained was the gas valve, which could halt firing as carbon built up. Subsequently, when the gun stopped after a certain amount of firing, no one knew how to fix them, and some guns were thrown away. But the defenders at Deniki were to be allowed a few days respite, as the Japanese themselves were to consolidate and reorganise around Kokoda.

In Brisbane, General Kenney had paid a call on General Brett, and been told briefly of the relationship between the air forces and the rest of the US force. Then Kenney went in to meet Douglas MacArthur, aware that the first thing he had to do was assure that supreme egotist that he had Kenney's absolute loyalty. At an appropriate time in the conversation, Kenney did so. The situation as described by MacArthur was bleak: only Australian Militia forces were fighting the Japanese in New Guinea, though the Australian 7th Division was soon to become available; the US 32nd and 41st Divisions were partly trained and could not be sent into action; the naval elements were small and there were no amphibious forces for the necessary landings to retake territory held by the Japanese; the air forces also were small and their performance so far had failed to impress MacArthur. In fact, as he described it, everybody from Washington to Australia had failed to provide him with the forces he demanded, and with which he was to return to the Philippines. Presumably, little was said about the destruction of the US air formation in the Philippines as a result of MacArthur's orders.

Far to the north, at Buna, after the slaughter of the A24s, unloading resumed of the undamaged cargo in *Kotoku Maru*. Despite rough seas, work went on through the night, and next day Shunji Shin and other men of Sasebo 5SLP were allowed to rest.

Early on 30 July, a Catalina dropped the usual harassing bombs over the Buna–Gona area. Many sorties this day were flown by B17s on long-range reconnaissances, but at 6 pm, eight B17s from Mareeba attacked a convoy at sea. Five hits were claimed on a transport ship, and flames were visible 30 miles (48 km) from the burning *Yokohama Maru*. Cloud base was down to 1500-2000 feet, and B17s that had not bombed attacked a destroyer and 'the Gona wreck', *Ayatosan Maru*. Another six also tried to attack the ships, could not find them, so returned to base. Four RAAF Hudson sorties were flown over the Buna area, from 9 pm through to midnight, with nothing to report from the crews for damage inflicted. Three Japanese bombers attacked Port Moresby, but inflicted only slight damage to a transport aircraft.

General Kenney was looking over the air formations he was to command, and flew to Port Moresby on his first tour of inspection. There he found things not to his liking. First was the integrated RAAF–US organisation at all levels of command, extending into the crews of aircraft. He knew that MacArthur did not approve, and also had been told by General George C. Marshall in the US that Marshall did not approve of such arrangements. He also found that the US bomber crews jettisoned all bombs and extra fuel tanks when attacked by fighters, afraid that a single machinegun bullet would explode the lot. Kenney saw there was so little warning time, the Moresby fighters had no hope of climbing to height and intercepting. In addition, everyone was short of parts, and valuable aircraft were caught on the ground during raids for want of minor items such as tail-wheels. He rapidly came to understand that almost anything he did would constitute an improvement, and determined to remove anyone of senior rank unable to conform to his ideas of operating a wartime air force, to improve the parts situation, and to reward achievement, no matter how small.

Still struggling forward to the battle were the soldiers of A Company 39th Battalion. 'Sixth stage, Eora Creek, 10 hours 30', wrote George Mowat. Perhaps somewhat sarcastically, he added, 'Today we rose to great heights. Crossed the OS Range at 7500 feet [2285 metres]. Phew, what a climb. Had a lot of rain. Each day has been a bit stiffer'.

On the northern side of the mountains, loyal Sergeant Katue, of PIB, continued his patrolling and showing loyalty to the Australian flag. He and his men shot six Japanese and two Orokaiva natives in the Beama village area while going to Tufi. He acquired more ammunition and continued patrolling, dispensing summary justice by shooting two chiefs who urged the people to support the Japanese. Later he shot two more Japanese and took a wounded third man prisoner near Pongani.[18]

Early on 31 July, the nightly harassment by Catalinas resulted in 128 bombs falling on dumps and the general Buna–Gona area. The Sakigawa diarist recorded a two-hour harassment by an enemy bomber that dropped bombs near them, but did no damage. Three B17 reconnaissance sorties were flown, searching for shipping, to Buna–Gona–Gasmata and to the Lae area for ships, while a B24 went to Buka. At noon, four B17s tried to find ships off Buna, could not, so bombed Gona.

General George Kenney flew from Moresby to Townsville, determined to begin shaping his new command. He told General Royce that he would be returning to the US to a training formation, then placed Ken Walker in command of the bomber force, with authority to ignore the intricate Australian–US command structure, issue orders, and shape the bombing squadrons into an effective part of the Allied effort. While at the headquarters, he met an RAAF officer who impressed him. Group Captain Bill ('Bull') Garing, with operational experience in Europe, had extensive pre-war knowledge of New Guinea, and was able to answer Kenney's questions while demonstrating mental agility and eagerness to get on with the war. They were to develop a close working relationship, with mutual respect. In the afternoon, Kenney visited his 19th Bomb Group, at Mareeba. He found that of the 32 B17s on strength, 18 were unserviceable for want of parts. He was informed that the system required a correctly filled-in form to go from Mareeba to Charters Towers, to Melbourne, to the huge base at Tocumwal in Victoria before any action could be taken. Often four weeks would go by, and then sometimes the request would be returned as not correctly written. Kenney told the Group Commander, Colonel Carmichael, to halt operational flying and get as many aircraft as possible ready for operations in about a week, when the squadrons would support the coming Guadalcanal landing. He also told Carmichael to submit recommendations for medals for deserving personnel.

Meanwhile, climbing the Kokoda Trail with A Company 39th Battalion, CSM George Mowat recorded the day as, 'Stage 7. Isurava, 7 hours. Hills not so steep, lots of rivers. Tree roots are a trap. Wend way around mountain side, 100-foot [30-metre] fall if you slip. Crawled across 80-foot river on narrow tree trunk. Received Bren guns here'. Kienzle, who had accompanied A Company with 122 carriers, was told to remain in the rear and organise supplies of ammunition and food to be sent on to the battalion up the track.

In Rabaul, Lieutenant General Hyakutake had concluded talks with his Japanese air and naval counterparts. It was agreed that Vice-Admiral Gunichi Mikawa's 8th Fleet would cooperate with the plan to move more army units to northern New Guinea and also to provide the shipping necessary for the seaborne landing at Port Moresby as Horii's forces came over the mountains from the north, as well as prepare the airfields at Buna and Gona for use by the main force. The Kawaguchi Detachment (brigade force) would be delivered to Samarai, at the eastern extremity of New Guinea. Vice-Admiral Nichizo Tsukahara would provide air support with his 11th Air Fleet. X-Day was at first to be 7 August, but later was changed to 16 August.

July ended with little good news for the Allies. The Japanese now had a formidable force in New Guinea despite the best efforts of the Allied air forces, and were advancing in strength against a weak Australian unit, so far unable to concentrate more than a company equivalent against them. The Japanese were trained and experienced, while the young Australians of 39th Battalion were learning about jungle warfare in the hardest way possible.

Two factors were some cause for comfort: New Guinea was neutral, and the climate, terrain and weather were as hard on the Japanese as on the Allies. The Japanese air forces had been involved to a remarkably minor extent. Raids on Moresby were one thing, but there was relatively little fighter presence over the Buna beachhead, and nothing over the Kokoda force. Japan had won too many victories too easily. This lack of thorough understanding at high levels of the principles of war was to become increasingly evident to perceptive Allied observers, of which General George Kenney was one. But at the end of July 1942, to the disquiet of many in the Port Moresby area, not to mention Townsville, Brisbane and Melbourne, the seemingly unstoppable Japanese army was advancing again.

Chapter 3
STRENGTHENING GALE
August 1942

At Giruwa on 1 August, Sergeant Ikeshima and 18 men of the Sakigawa Transport Unit spent all day near the food dump making a concealed truck parking area. Twenty-nine survivors of the unit who had been aboard *Kotoku Maru* when it was bombed finally arrived, after walking for two days from a point 18 miles (30 km) north of the Mambare River. Eleven vehicles and much personal equipment had been lost with the ship – the sacrifice of Major Rogers and the A24 crews had not been in vain. As the new arrivals had no vehicles, they were put to work on road maintenance. They had no tools, and a request to another unit resulted in five picks being delivered, so all tools from the trucks were collected and brought to the bivouac area for use on the roads.

Meanwhile, General George Kenney returned to Brisbane from his visit to Port Moresby, Townsville and Mareeba. He telephoned (US) Air Force Headquarters in Melbourne and gave an order that all relevant items of supply for the bombers in North Queensland were to be sent at once, regardless of whether the paperwork was completed correctly or not. Kenney then went to see MacArthur and told him of his orders to prepare the B17s for use against Rabaul in support of the Guadalcanal operation, to which MacArthur agreed. Kenney then outlined his plans: use the B17s against Rabaul, and the B25s and B26s against the airfields at Buna, Salamaua and Lae until the Japanese did not bother to fill in the bomb craters, while using everything else to support the troops on the Kokoda Trail.

Kenney also decided to send back to the US all personnel who had been in the Philippines and Java campaigns, on the grounds that they were operationally tired. He privately thought that these men had been beaten mentally by the Japanese, by the long period of retreat and of operating for seven months with minimal support in a hostile environment.

At sea from Rabaul were more members of the Takasago (Formosa/Taiwan volunteers) Unit, who had seen a reconnaissance aircraft detect them, and survived an attack by bombers at 1.15 pm, with all bombs missing. 'Uchida', a diarist in 15 Pioneers, aboard *Nankai Maru*, watched the B17s coming in at low level, and drop eight bombs that exploded very close to the ship's hull, the shock temporarily halting the vessel.[1]

Marching away from Buna towards the mountains were troops who had landed. Akira Teruoka and the Tanaka unit, 55 Division Medical unit, began walking at 3 pm, and kept going for six hours before they made camp. Everything was carried on their backs — no trucks were available. In the mountains, 2nd Lieutenant Onogawa, 2 Platoon, 3 Company, I/144 Regiment, had looked around at the fog in the Kokoda basin, and wondered if that was why the enemy had not counter-attacked. He could hear light machinegun fire, but no rifles or grenades, and was pleased that the Japanese Army had taken the location. At 10 am, he took 90 men — two-thirds of the company — back to collect rations, and also bring back bicycles. His group returned with 70 bicycles and food for 135 men, but the journey would take three days in all.

Onogawa may not have been so pleased if he knew that the force opposing the Japanese had been only one company of semi-trained troops, who had caused such a delay to the advance. Marching to Deniki on the last stage of their march to battle was A Company 39 Battalion. They had a six-hour journey, 'easy compared with previous days', wrote CSM George Mowat. 'Traversed through lovely gullies. A rock gardener's dream: ferns, moss, tiny rivulets, etc. One lovely big waterfall. Weather very much cooler the last four days; pullovers necessary at night. Reached Deniki, took up position. Everything quiet.'

Air activity on 1 August was relatively slight after that of preceding days. B17s went off on the usual reconnaissance missions to Gasmata, Rabaul and Guadalcanal. Six from Mareeba set off to attack an aircraft carrier at Rabaul, but only one located the target and the others bombed in the Gona area. Three P400s also bombed the area during the day. At 8.15 am on 2 August, five B17s searched the Buna–Gona area for ships, none were located, so they dropped 14 bombs along the beach. Nine Zeros attacked head-on from below; one B17 was lost and two damaged. At 8.20 am, four P400s dropped bombs on Kokoda, then strafed. No enemy were seen. Five B26s and 11 P400s were to attack ships in the Buna–Gona areas, but could not locate any. Eight Japanese fighters attacked, and in the combats three Zeros were claimed destroyed and one probably destroyed, but two P400s were missing. Tainan Kokkutai recorded one loss, but claimed two B17s and four fighters.[2]

Because of the difficulties of night marching, Akira Teruoka's unit decided to march from early morning to midday, and set off before dawn along the road to the mountains. Also working in the early hours were the trucks of the Sakigawa Transport Unit. Beginning at 2 am, 10 vehicles carried rice from the landing area to the intermediate dump. All transport unit members were waiting for the arrival of the new commander on the next ship.[3]

Long carrier lines were coming forward from Eora. Bert Kienzle had left Eora Creek at 8 am and heard the aircraft pass overhead, then the explosions. He was going to the vicinity of where, on pre-war flights to Kokoda, he had seen what appeared to be open areas. Kienzle and his group marched on through the rain. The cold, wet night was spent huddled together for warmth around fires on the mountain ridge. He knew that somewhere close by were the lakes he had seen from the air.

Early on 3 August, two RAAF Catalinas harassed Lae and Salamaua. Later, two formations of P400s reconnoitred Buna–Gona and Lae–Salamaua, with little to report, and six B26s took off to attack ships in Collingwood Bay, but could not locate the target.

Below the searching aircraft, the Sakigawa Transport Unit was tasked to move a dump, to bring supplies from Giruwa, and to provide vehicles and men to work with the field hospital close to the front line. The unit diary noted that soldiers from the front had gone to the intermediate dump and simply taken their unit requirements instead of liaising with the Sakigawa unit. It seems some aspects of soldiering are international.

On the mountain ridges, as dawn came, Lieutenant Bert Kienzle set off at 7 am, looking for his remembered open areas. The natives with him said that the area was forbidden by tribal legend, and no one went there. Kienzle overrode this with an order from the government and they went on. At 7.25 am, he came out of the trees to see a dry lake-bed spread before him, large enough for air drops. As it had no native name, he called it Myola, from the name of the wife of Major Elliott-Smith, OC ANGAU. Myola was an Australian Aboriginal term meaning 'break of day'.

From Port Moresby, as yet unaware of the discovery of the lake-bed, Major General Morris informed Australian Army Headquarters that the supply situation for the forces at Kokoda and Wau were 'most serious'. He added that transport planes, with parachutes, were immediately required to be permanently stationed at Moresby, or operations would be in jeopardy and forward troops would starve.

In Brisbane, in the morning, Major General Brett spoke briefly to Major General Kenney, and went to say farewell to his commander, MacArthur. Brett told Kenney that this would be only the eighth time he had seen MacArthur since MacArthur arrived in Melbourne in March. Kenney took the point: he could not allow Richard Sutherland to dominate the air commander, or restrict his access to the Supreme Commander SWPA. Later, Kenney spoke to MacArthur about the Kokoda Pass defences, and allegedly said that he thought the Japanese would break through there. How he came to have such a grasp of the land campaign after a single brief visit during which he was occupied with all aspects of air matters is unknown. Everyone at GHQ apparently believed in the mythical 'Kokoda Pass' – the very narrow defile that easily could be defended in the extreme case of the Japanese ever progressing that far, but Kenney after one quick visit was fully informed. It is noticeable that in his memoirs Kenney never admits being surprised by anything done by the enemy, and always was able to predict the outcome of events.

At 3 pm, nine Japanese aircraft arrived at Buna airfield. The Sasebo 5SLP had been working all day on the airfield to prepare it for the arrival of the Japanese planes. After they landed, the work was inspected and recommendations for improvements given. The men would work on the airfield for the next two days.[4]

The presence of these Japanese planes was not known to the US fighter pilots who flew to attack Japanese ground targets in the afternoon. Four P400s strafed the rest house at Oivi at 3.55 pm, and saw six people, possibly in uniforms, running. Eight other fighters provided escort. Visibility was maximum, with the clouds only on the peaks.

The Japanese Yazawa Butai (41 Regiment) was preparing to go to New Guinea and issued 'Intelligence Report No. 1'. In the 'General Situation' paragraph, readers were informed that the US was making Alaska and Australia secure, strengthening her own internal military preparations and 'preparing frantically' to counterattack the Japanese forces. The air arms of Japan had achieved an advantageous situation in eastern New Guinea, and were facilitating the invasion of Port Moresby, and of the enemy advance base (Kokoda), plus having 'firm control of the Coral Sea, vital for operations against Australia'.

The 'Enemy Terrain Situation' included information from an unnamed Australian captain taken prisoner in the Kokoda area, which was that a battalion of about 1000 men, commanded by a colonel, had arrived in that area some 10 days before. (This must have been Captain Templeton.) In addition, there were believed to be 500 to 600 Papua-New Guinea troops with European officers along the Mambare River, but Allied submarine and air strength in eastern New Guinea did not seem to be adequate. New Guinea was described as mountainous, with heights up to 4000 metres [13,000 feet], with heat, cold and rain, with only poor roads, pack trails and paths.[5]

It may be that Templeton, after capture, and knowing well the need for time, exaggerated the force supposedly confronting the Japanese (1000 Australians and 500 native troops) in a last effort to influence them to proceed cautiously.

On the morning of 4 August, General Brett left for the United States, and Kenney became Allied Air Force commander. Almost immediately, Kenney confronted Sutherland and it was decided once and for all who was really commanding the air forces. Kenney then worked out a reorganisation of the air forces into separate RAAF and US commands.

In the Japanese rear areas at Soputa–Buna, the Sakigawa Transport Unit checked the condition of the roads, and found that while they were hard and dry at the moment, rain would make them difficult to use. It was estimated that man-packing could deliver three tons a day, regardless of weather, to the dump area. Still making his way to the front was Akira Teruoka, Tanaka Unit, 55 Division Medical Unit. After 5 am reveille, they marched from 8 am till 5 pm, crossing many suspension bridges, and bivouacked near a fallen Allied aircraft close to a large river. The daily marches would continue for the next few days.

At Deniki, Major Alan Cameron arrived to take command of Maroubra Force. Like Lieutenant Colonel Owen, Cameron had been with 2/22nd Battalion on New Britain, and had escaped in an open boat with 12 other men. He had been promoted to major and posted as Brigade Major 30 Brigade, but now had been sent forward to the battle area. A few members of 39th Battalion had arrived in the rear areas, having more or less left the unit on their own initiative, and Cameron was scathing in his comments on those men.

However, on the positive side, hard working Army signallers completed a telephone line from Port Moresby to Deniki, having laid some 66 miles (106 km) of wire through inhospitable country. This was a great addition to the force, ensuring that communications could be maintained day and night. The radios in use at the time were often ineffective because of distance, weather, climate and terrain. Meanwhile, Lieutenant Kienzle had begun work on cutting a new track to link the newly-named Myola Lake with Eora, and the Kagi–Eora–Templeton's Crossing track. The lake area was east of Kagi, and even if supplies were air-dropped there, the items would still be some two or three days walk from the front line. However, it was an improvement over carrying every item from the beginning of the Kokoda track. Aerial activity was confined to reconnaissance flights in the region by US Airacobras.

A convoy was forming at Rabaul, to reinforce the Buna–Gona operation. On 5 August, Toshio Sato, a linguist, counted 600 men of a naval airfield unit boarding *Kinai Maru*, part of 3000 men in 14 and 15 Naval Pioneer units. 'Uchida' saw 900 Koreans of 15 Pioneer Unit come aboard *Nankai Maru*, but later he transferred to *Kenyo Maru* with more Koreans.[6]

Twenty tons of local rice was taken from Giruwa to the Sambo dump by Sakigawa Transport Unit during the day, and two platoons patrolled for six miles (10 km) around the unit camp. 2nd Lieutenant Onogawa noted the first enemy air attack for some days, which destroyed some equipment where he had camped about eight kilometres (five miles) from the Kumusi River on his way back to Kokoda. He had started his resupply party marching at 3.30 am, after finding that his company had already moved on.

The only two aircraft available at Moresby for supply drops returned to Australia, but Major General Morris was told that one would be stationed permanently at Moresby. He signalled that a minimum of two transport planes was necessary, but none were available at that time, that resupply by native carriers was impossible, and they were expected to desert if the trail came under air attack, and that Kokoda had been lost because of the cumbersome procedure for ordering planes.

Again there was little air activity. B17s and an LB30 flew to Madang, Rabaul and on sea searches, with nothing to report. From Australia, seven B26s and eight B25s flew to Port Moresby to prepare to attack Lae and Salamaua next day. Using the new telephone line, Lieutenant Kienzle arranged for air drops from Moresby to be made at Myola Lake.

In Australia, General Kenney had gone to Mareeba to see B17s set off for Rabaul, then to Charters Towers, to visit the 3rd Group and the air depot there. He was not pleased with the emphasis on paperwork at the depot, and the days of some senior people there were numbered, while juniors who showed signs of understanding what Kenney wanted were soon to be promoted and given command.

On 6 August, from Rabaul, Japanese ships *Kinai Maru*, *Kenyo Maru*, *Nankai Maru* and cruiser *Tatsuta*, with two destroyers and two sub-chasers, left for Buna. Once at sea, the units were told their destination: Gona, New Guinea, to establish an airfield for the invasion of Port Moresby.[7]

2nd Lieutenant Onogawa, hurrying to catch his unit, left his previous night's camp at 4 am, reaching Oivi three hours later. He pushed on to Kokoda, noting that air attacks became more severe. In the evening, he would rejoin his company, which had suffered heavy losses in action against the Australians.

Air attacks on 6 August were directed at Japanese airfields, and at 7.28 am, seven B25s attacked Salamaua airfield from 5000 feet. Large fires were started and fuel and ammunition dumps were hit. Six B17s had gone from Mareeba to Lae, but clouds covered the airfield and no bombs were dropped, though when six B26s attacked Lae at 10.26 am, visibility was 15 miles (24 km), under a solid overcast. At 5.20 pm, six B26s returned to Lae, placing their bombs on the runway and nearby; visibility then was unlimited. From 10.25 pm, three RAAF Catalinas dropped bombs on the runway area at Lae; crews saw many fires in the Buna–Gona area. Three B17s attacked Guadalcanal targets.

At Buna, the Japanese Sasebo 5SLP was removed from airfield construction work, with platoons sent to assist AA guns at Buna. The Sakigawa Transport Unit had been busy since 6 am, 10 trucks carrying 19 tons of rice, canned fish and rye. There was the first sign of concern over the constant demands for foodstuffs from frontline units, compared with amounts delivered to the dumps.

The Australian D Company 39th Battalion reached Deniki during the day. This meant that the battalion was complete, as a unit, for the first time in seven months. The force available to Major Cameron now was 464 members of 39th Battalion, about 43 PIB officers, NCOs and soldiers, and a few ANGAU officers and NCOs with 14 native police. Cameron knew that recent patrol actions had favoured the Australians, and he was well-briefed by the

39th Battalion Intelligence Officer, Lieutenant McNamara.

Cameron decided to attack and dislodge the Japanese from Kokoda. He intended to send A Company to attack from the north-east, C Company from the south-east, and use D Company to ambush the Oivi track, to prevent Japanese reinforcements arriving to assist in the battle. Deniki and surrounds would be held by the other companies.

At 11.40 am on 7 August, 13 B17s attacked Vunakanau airfield, Rabaul. Crews claimed the high number of 75 Japanese aircraft destroyed on the ground. Zeros intercepted, but gunners claimed seven destroyed. One B17 was destroyed and five others damaged. With support from Kenney and MacArthur, a recommendation for the US Congressional Medal of Honor was forwarded and the medal awarded posthumously to the pilot of the lost B17, Captain Harl Pease. According to Kenney, Japanese messages intercepted reported that only 30 planes remained usable at Rabaul, but no captured document, diary or other Japanese message found by the author mentions a major loss of aircraft in this raid.

Apart from the Rabaul raid, six B26s bombed Lae at 2.46 pm, and claimed their bombs hit the centre of the runway, but Australian Army observers in the hills reported that the bombs fell on the west side of the airfield; visibility was unlimited. One B26 was damaged by anti-aircraft fire, and one made a forced landing 100 miles (160 km) north of Moresby. Eight B25s were turned back by weather.

On this day, Kenney was presented with the figures of his air strength: US fighters 245, but 170 unserviceable; heavy bombers 62, 19 unserviceable; transports 36, of 19 different types, half usable. RAAF fighters 40, at Darwin, Moresby and Mareeba; bombers 30 reconnaissance type (Hudsons). Kenney informed Washington of the details, and of the fact that the Japanese could have replacements and reinforcements in the region in two days; he desperately needed more and better aircraft. He also asked for his air force to be allocated a number, to give it much-needed identity.

2nd Lieutenant Onogawa noted information from battalion headquarters (I/144, Tsukamoto battalion) on the recent battle east of Oivi: the enemy were identified as 39th Battalion, and of the 120 Australians engaged, 55 were claimed killed and two captured, including Captain Templeton; two automatic rifles, three machineguns and 32 rifles, 175 grenades, plus two radios were captured during six night attacks by the Japanese. At Kokoda, 150 members of 39th Battalion were attacked, losing 20 dead and some prisoners, plus two machineguns, five automatic rifles, 20 rifles and 180 grenades. The number of dead Australians was greatly exaggerated, as Lieutenant Colonel Owen, Major Watson and Captain Templeton had nowhere near the 200-plus men necessary to meet the Japanese figures. As shown, only B Company was involved in the actions at Oivi and Kokoda. The number of weapons and grenades claimed captured also was grossly exaggerated. Perhaps 'creative accounting' was necessary to give a good impression at Japanese HQ in Rabaul. The identity of the other 39th Battalion man claimed to have been captured was not included in any Japanese document later taken by Allied forces.

Signs of rising problems in the Japanese logistics area near Buna were becoming evident. Commanders were making more reconnaissances of the roads, dumps and arrangements for delivering food. Labour units would not be available to units for internal tasks, but from now on would be used for road maintenance. Transport units also would be required to do road works as well as vehicle maintenance. The cumulative effect of attacks on shipping at sea and at the beachhead resulted in less than the estimated amount of vehicles and men getting ashore, plus the unforeseen fighting by the Australian Militia in the depths of the distant ranges combined to expose weaknesses in Japanese logistic planning.

US Marines and Army units had landed on Guadalcanal, Tulagi and nearby islands. About 18,500 Americans went ashore, and what supplies could be unloaded were dumped on the shorelines, but in a confused mass. The ships were loaded in New Zealand by the units themselves, as the local waterside workers refused to do so in the rain. Union principles were stronger than patriotism, even when other men were going to do the fighting for the wharfies. The Japanese defenders numbered only about 700, but the inexperienced US staffs had estimated them at between 3100 and 8000. The US carrier force, under Vice Admiral Jack Fletcher, withdrew for tactical reasons, but the amphibious force, under Rear Admiral R. K. Turner, was not about to remain without air cover, so it also withdrew, as did the warship screen commanded by Rear Admiral Sir Victor Crutchley. Major General Vandergrift's marines were alone on the island.

However, unknown to them at the time, the US landings had one important effect in Rabaul: the Japanese command, so busy with its own offensive intentions, did not know what to do about the Guadalcanal situation. Horii's force was destined for Kokoda and the advance to Port Moresby; Yazawa and Aoba forces were still at Palau; Kawaguchi force would have to go to Guadalcanal instead of to Samarai. However, Ichiki force, originally intended to land on Midway, was available, and so was sent to counter-attack the Americans. At the same time, the Japanese detected the Australian–US airfield-building at Milne Bay, so decided to attack this also. In 15 Pioneers, Japanese scribe 'Uchida' glumly wrote that the expected ships had been bombed while at sea, and because of the Guadalcanal actions, had returned to Rabaul. 'The enemy has control of the air around Buna and Lae.'

Playing their small but constant part in the campaign, five RAAF Catalinas during the late night and early morning of 8 August had harassed Buna, Lae and Vunakanau.

Early on the morning of 8 August, 39th Battalion began moving out of Deniki for the attack on Kokoda. D Company began the march, with Warrant Officer Wilkinson, Sergeant Evensen and 16 Papuans. A Company started off at 7 am, guided along a little-used track by Lieutenant Peter Brewer and the respected Lance Corporal Sanopa, of the Papuan Constabulary. Captain Dean's C Company, with four Australians and 17 members of the PIB, left their area at 8 am, tasked with attacking up the Kokoda–Deniki track.

D Company began engaging Japanese at Pirivi, south of the Kokoda–Oivi track, as foraging parties were encountered. The fighting was often at close range and hand-to-hand, with the bayonet used, as well as clubbed rifles. This combat delayed the company, but Lieutenant McClean's 16 Platoon reached the Oivi track in time to get into position and ambush a large party of Japanese hurrying to Kokoda. But Crawford's 17 Platoon was just getting into position when Japanese coming from Kokoda arrived and there was no chance for an ambush. Firing began and the Japanese inflicted casualties, one being Crawford, wounded when a bullet hit his helmet, driving jagged edges of metal into his head and making it difficult for Jack Wilkinson to remove it without inflicting further injury. Another man was killed outright while kneeling in a fire position on the track, and in one of the strange aspects of violent death, the man's body was instantly held rigid.

Crawford was sent back with an escort of two men, but when they reached the rear guard for D Company, supplied by 10 men of the battalion AA platoon under Sergeant 'Bunny' Pulfer, Crawford evidently decided that he could make the rest of the journey to Deniki safely alone, and ordered the other two men to remain. Corporal Wyld, senior man of the escort, insisted that they should take Crawford to Deniki, but Crawford pulled his pistol to reinforce his orders, went off down the track and was never seen again. It is believed he fell from a log over one of the wild creeks, and was swept away.

Meanwhile, his platoon had been taken over by Sergeant Marsh, who found that the Japanese had surrounded them, penetrating the 60 yards of jungle between the platoon and Captain Bidstrup's company headquarters; two runners simply disappeared in that short distance. Bidstrup ordered 16 and 18 Platoons to withdraw, but did not know what had happened in 17 Platoon. The company had suffered at least 11 killed, wounded or missing.

Major Elliott-Smith, of ANGAU, accompanied Captain Dean's C Company in the attack on Kokoda. Elliott-Smith and Major Watson moved with the company headquarters. On the right of the track, movement was noticed in the shrubbery, and at once the area was lashed with fire from Bren and Thompson guns, killing seven Japanese, but two others escaped.

Unknown to Major Cameron, the Japanese had placed machineguns with a good field of fire covering the creek crossing and climb up from the water. The company was held by machinegun fire, coming across the steep gorge, and two Australians were wounded. Cameron, Elliott-Smith and a patrol went down to the right, intending to cross the river and attack the Japanese positions. They got into the riverbed without much difficulty, but were confronted on the far bank by a sheer cliff, and could not climb out, so had to work their way along to the main crossing. By this time, Dean and the company were on the lower side of the road at the crossing.

At the crossing place, on the 'Japanese side', was a clearing some 150 yards across, and from cover on the far side, the Japanese were firing at any sign of movement. Dean, Cameron and Elliott-Smith moved together, and Dean began to climb over a log to join some of his company when a single shot rang out. Dean said, 'Through the stomach, too', and fell dead. C Company placed heavy small arms fire onto the Japanese position, and advanced, to find seven dead Japanese around a light machinegun. One more nearby tried to run but was killed; he was an officer. There were many bloodstains and blood-trails showing more casualties had been inflicted. Elliott-Smith was impressed by the conduct of the Papuan Infantry Battalion men throughout the action, and more so when they buried Dean under heavy fire, 'with not the slightest sign of panic'.[8]

It was evident that with one rifle company, Cameron could not shift the Japanese in this sector, and he ordered a withdrawal. Some 11 wounded were being cared for by Chaplain Earl. The aggressive Japanese followed the company back to Deniki, and harassed the positions there into the evening.

Meanwhile, A Company arrived at Kokoda itself with no enemy contact. Part of the way, the platoons had waded along the river, and arrived after an air strike on Kokoda. At 10.20 am, 16 P400s dropped 500-pound bombs on Kokoda and Yodda, then strafed, silencing a machinegun post. No enemy were seen by the pilots at Yodda, but six were noticed at Kokoda. Visibility was 10 miles (16 km), cloud base at 6000 to 7000 feet.

A Company went into the attack in three waves, passing

through the rubber plantation, and arrived at about 1.30 pm. It may be that there were no Japanese encountered as they had been drawn off to deal with C and D Companies. For whatever reason, the Australians found themselves in undisputed possession again of Kokoda, and a platoon went to the airfield. There was no word from the other companies in the attack, and no sign of them.

The rifle platoons were positioned once more to defend the tip of the ridge. 8 Platoon, under Sergeant Guest, held the eastern side, overlooking the Oivi track; Lieutenant Trotter's 7 Platoon was on the west, overlooking the airfield; and 9 Platoon under Lieutenant Neal some 100 yards to the south, in the tall rubber trees. There were distant sounds of battle, but no Japanese presence close by.

Following their own planned activities for the day, after a very early reveille, 2nd Lieutenant Onogawa's unit of I/144 departed camp at 3.30 am, moved through the area and took up position on top of a hill. A three-man reconnaissance patrol was sent out and returned with information on the terrain and signs of enemy. It was not realised that the Australians had moved around to the flank and were pushing to Kokoda.

Meanwhile, Brigadier Arnold Potts, commander 21 Brigade, with his Brigade Major, H. B. Challen, had arrived at Port Moresby. His 2/14th and 2/16th Battalions had sailed from Australia on 6 August. However, on his arrival, Potts was met by Major General Morris, who did not know Potts and his men were coming.

At Kokoda, at dusk, Staff Sergeant Jim Cowey fired a Verey flare from the airfield, a pre-arranged signal to Major Cameron that A Company was in possession. However, it seems no one was watching for the flare, or it was not seen. Then it began to rain heavily. However, there were no Japanese about, and A Company spent a peaceful night. CSM George Mowat noted that there was no sign of the other rifle companies, and 'Skipper worried. Settled down for the night. Everything quiet. Cooked and ate Jap rice'.

Meanwhile, having held position near Pirivi throughout the afternoon, just before dusk Captain Bidstrup began to move D Company back, coping with flank and frontal attacks by the surrounding Japanese. The Australian wounded were carried on stretchers fashioned from copra bags. Again, Sergeant Pulfer's AA Platoon men were the rear guard. In addition, they were to make contact with the separated 17 Platoon, under Sergeant Marsh. Pulfer's two scouts had barely passed out of sight around the first bend in the track when they came running back with news of a large force of Japanese approaching. Rapidly going back to a suitable section of track, the 10 men set up an ambush with the Bren covering the killing ground. Jack Boland signalled for the spare Bren magazines to be passed up, and the Japanese came into view on the wide well-made track, bunched up and about eight abreast. Then Pulfer decided not to fire, as his task was to defend the rear of the company, and the party moved away past Pirivi and after D Company. Those who were present believed that a large number of Japanese could have been mowed down, perhaps some of those who engaged them and D Company next day. After creeping along in the pitch black night, reduced to following the lead man who crawled along feeling for the track with his hands, the group stopped for the night to rest and sleep.

The AA Platoon soldiers were not far from D Company. During the night, two more men from D Company were lost. From the separate 17 Platoon perimeter, Private Joe Dwyer went to find water for the wounded and did not return. Private Robinson went to find Dwyer and did not return either. Jack Wilkinson sat up all night tending one of the wounded, Private Hanlon, who had a sucking back wound. There were no rations in the company.

A Company 39th Battalion was holding Kokoda; C Company had returned to Deniki, which was being harassed by Japanese; D Company was waiting out the night in the jungle at the village of Komondo, some two miles (3.2 km) from Pirivi.

During the day, a DC3 dropped supplies at Wau, but at Myola Bert Kienzle waited for air drops. Eleven B26s attacked Lae and Salamaua airfields and anti-aircraft positions; weather was clear, visibility unlimited. Six B25s bombed through intense, heavy but inaccurate anti-aircraft fire onto Salamaua airfield, and 10 B26s attacked a ship near O'Dea's house at Salamaua, scoring one direct hit and leaving the ship burning. Again, the workhorse B17s flew reconnaissance flights to Kavieng and Rabaul. Six more B17s from Mareeba searched the Vitiaz Straits for shipping, but found none, so two bombed Lae from 26,500 feet, placing 14 bombs onto the airfield. During the night, six RAAF Catalinas went to Vunaka-nau, Buka and Lae.

Members of Japanese Sasebo 5SLP were told that because of the interruptions to the shipping schedule, food for August would be reduced. Advancing into the mountains, Akira Teruoka and the rest of 55 Division Medical unit camped by the 'suspension bridge of a large river', in heavy rain. They were at Wairopi, and the bridge was to be heavily bombed during the next two months.

Again on 9 August, the Japanese ships from Rabaul turned back to harbour there, rather than go on to Buna. The command staff could not make up their minds what to do or where to send troops. Two reconnaissance planes were seen, but the ships were not attacked. The Japanese soldiers were told that in a battle off Guadalcanal–Tulagi, 12 Japanese planes had been lost, but 37 US aircraft had been destroyed, two cruisers sunk and two more on fire, two destroyers and 10 transports sunk, with another transport on fire. For once, the claims were reasonably correct, as the Allied warships had been soundly defeated, but the transport ships had not been attacked. During the night, in the Battle of Savo Island, Allied cruisers USS *Quincey*, *Vincennes* and *Astoria*, and HMAS *Canberra* were sunk, cruiser USS *Chicago* badly damaged and destroyer *Ralph Talbot* damaged, but no Japanese ships were lost and only cruisers *Chokai* and *Aoba* were damaged. Eight Japanese ships defeated 12 Allied vessels by superior use of torpedoes and gunfire in relatively narrow waters.

On 9 August, as dawn crept under the jungle and bush around Kokoda, a patrol from D Company found the 10 men of Sergeant Pulfer's AA Platoon section, and they went back to Captain Bid-strup's location. Bidstrup knew nothing of the outcome of the previous day's fighting, even whether 39th Battalion still held Deniki. He decided to send Pulfer and a small group to see what the situation was there. A native policeman led the patrol across country, right out of the jungle to Deniki, and word went back to

Bidstrup that C Company under Captain Jacob held the position. Bidstrup's men began moving to Deniki, which took most of the day. It was particularly exhausting for those carrying Private Bernie Hanlon, with a lung wound. Hanlon's greatest worry was the problem he was causing the rest of them, fully aware of his size and weight. They arrived at about 5 pm, hungry and tired. Meanwhile, actions had been fought elsewhere.

At Deniki, Sergeant Pulfer's men had been absorbed into Jacob's C Company, and together with other Diggers had been sent forward of the main position there, to cover a long, sloping ridge. All was quiet, then suddenly a number of Japanese appeared crossing the ridge, fire was opened, and Pulfer was shot dead in the exchange of shooting.

At Kokoda, the Japanese were reacting and more lessons in jungle warfare were being learned the hard way by A Company. Lieutenant Colonel Owen's body, apparently ignored by the Japanese, was found and buried, and a patrol led by Lieutenant Sorenson, second-in-command of A Company, went out through the rubber trees, along the Deniki track direction, met no enemy, and returned by 10 am. No sooner had the patrol settled back when soldiers were seen coming through the rubber trees and it was thought they were C Company, advancing along the track to Kokoda as part of Cameron's attack.

A Company soldiers stood in plain view, peering in the gloom along the rows of rubber trees, but the distant men had no questions to settle about identities, and opened fire. Larry Downes was acting as 9 Platoon sergeant, and saw the first shot kill Private Williams, who'd run up from 8 Platoon area. The second cracked past Downes's ear. Private McLeod called he could see the firer, and aimed a round from his .303 at the enemy, worked the bolt for another shot, but the third bullet from the Japanese hit and killed him on the spot. Whoever the enemy was, he fired accurately in the dimness under the trees. Alex Lochhead noticed that the oncoming men were not dressed like 39th Battalion, and also had palm fronds in their helmet netting, and then the fight was on. George Mowat noted 'Our line held fire, and appeared to inflict heavy casualties'.[9]

A section from 7 Platoon had been positioned past the airfield on the Yodda side, under command of Sergeant Win Murray. Also with them was Sergeant Les Simmons, the Band Sergeant, accompanying A Company as Regimental Aid Post (RAP) Sergeant. The section was Corporal J. D. McKay's 1 Section, and with Simmons, McKay led the small force back when the firing began. They left the track to avoid ambush, climbed the escarpment and arrived at the rear of Kokoda village. Lieutenant Frank Trotter sent McKay and the section to the assistance of 9 Platoon, and they covered the last 30 yards on their stomachs, under the hail of Japanese fire from rifles, machineguns and mortars.

The Japanese then began their usual tactics of probing the flanks to determine the size and strength of the opposition, to locate automatic weapons and headquarters positions, and put in several attacks, which were all thrown back. The Australians gradually realised that certain of the Japanese moves were simply intended to draw fire, and often A Company obliged. Privates Smythe and Dridan, a Bren crew, were located and engaged by a Japanese machinegun and a sniper, wounding both Australians. Alex Lochhead noticed that a fern seemed to have sprouted suddenly at the base of a tree only 50 yards away. It was a Japanese with camouflaged helmet peering around; Lochhead shot him. So the fighting went on through the day. It became obvious that no other Australians were going to arrive at Kokoda – A Company was on its own.

2nd Lieutenant Onogawa was told that the Australians had recaptured Kokoda, inflicting more than 20 casualties on Takamori (engineer) unit, and No. 1 Company (of I/144) had returned to the battle, with fighting going on through the day.

On 9 August, one B17 attacked Gasmata, and a Catalina harassed Lae at night; areas through which shipping for New Guinea would pass were searched by B17s. A DC2 delivered supplies to Wau once more, but at Myola, Kienzle and his group still waited for aircraft to appear and begin drops to them. As far as he could see, this was good flying weather, but no aircraft arrived. Dr Vernon did come to the position, to inspect medical conditions for the carrier force. At 3.45 pm, seven B26s attacked Salamaua from just under the cloud base, and hits were claimed on a ship and other targets on shore. Five B17s attacked Simpson Harbour at Rabaul at 5.50 pm, through intense AA fire from the ships below. B17 gunners claimed seven of 15 intercepting Zeros, but one B17 was shot down, another ditched off New Guinea, while another on two engines made it to Port Moresby for a crash-landing, and was later used as spare parts. In the previous three days, 55 sorties had been flown against the airfields, Lae and Salamaua.

Watching the air battles were more men of Takasago Volunteers, who were told four bombers were brought down by AA fire. Aboard *Kinai Maru*, translator Toshio Sato was told that in this attack nine enemy were shot down, but later noted a single night bomber dropped five bombs on the airfield, destroying two planes and 'causing great damage to petrol and other supplies'.[10]

An RAAF Catalina had gone through intense heavy anti-aircraft fire to bomb Lakunai and Vunakanau, starting fires that were visible 50 miles (80 km) away. Japanese documents other than Sato's diary stated that in this attack two navy fighters, two navy carrier-borne bombers and eight army light bombers were destroyed, and three carrier-borne bombers were badly damaged, for a total of 12 destroyed and three damaged. It was one of the most successful single-aircraft raids of the campaign. The Catalina, flown by Flight Lieutenant Wearne and Pilot Officer Priest, of 11 Squadron, had dropped 500- and 250-pound bombs on the target, reporting that 'two bombs started very large fires, destroying one bomber; one bomb among buildings caused large red fires and explosions, increasing after each bomb dropped'.

General Kenney was informed that his air force would be numbered '5', and so was titled one of the greatest tactical air forces of the Second World War. He claimed that his fighters had been busy along the Kokoda Trail since 4 August, but apart from the references above, there is no reflection of this in Japanese documents, the operations room logbooks at Townsville or Port Moresby, or in his formation's reports to GHQ SWPA.

As night fell at Kokoda, the Japanese quietly advanced, using the information they had gathered during the day about the Australian positions. Under the rubber trees there was no glimmer of light, and it was a matter of waiting patiently for the unseen foe to come within bayonet or rifle butt range. This is easier said than done, and the A Company success that night again indicated the high standard achieved by this battalion, first to fight the well-trained and experienced Japanese in New Guinea.

2nd Lieutenant Hirano, 3 Platoon, No. 1 Company I/144, related how the attack began at 10.20 pm. Because of the dark and heavy rain, the platoon could not be assembled properly, but the attack went in. The Japanese advanced stealthily on hands and knees until they met the Australian sentries under the rubber trees. A Corporal Hamada killed one with a bayonet, but the platoon was scattered and forced to withdraw by return fire, being unable to reorganise and attack again that night. Private Hirose was killed, and in the confusion, the Australian grabbed by Hirano was wounded by a grenade thrown by Hamada. Control and assembly of the platoon was impossible in the night conditions, and Hirano became disoriented. He thought he was reorganising the platoon, but found he was in grenade range of the Australians, instead of at the rear of his own men. It was a failure. Hirano noted that 1 Platoon attacked unsuccessfully at 3 am, and regretfully recorded his 'tears of bitterness' over the daily loss of men. Cold and hungry, he waited for the new day.

Another grey dawn slipped gradually under the rubber plantation at Kokoda, and the tired A Company men looked around. Alex Lochhead, who had seven men in his section the previous dusk, now had four. He could see two dead Australians in his area, but could not recognise them, and called to Roy Baxter, who had two killed and one wounded, and who thought Les Skinner also was dead. The Japanese were not too far away, and every time Lochhead tried to go to the dead Australians, a light machinegun fired at him. He could see that they had been killed by stab wounds.

More probes followed, with sniping and machinegun harassment throughout the day. Six mortar bombs fell, but were duds, and to add to the uncertainty, a voice from the side of the plateau kept calling in English for help, but no one knew if it was a Japanese trick, and accurate gunfire was aimed at everyone who tried to see over the edge for the caller. One of Lochhead's men was missing, but it was thought the caller might have been one of Templeton's from B Company. The matter was never resolved.

Yet another lesson was learned. J. D. McKay's section had taken position in a convenient stormwater drain in the rubber plantation near 9 Platoon, but were pinned there by fire, losing one man. Eventually they realised the Japanese were up in the rubber trees, firing down, with a good view along the drain.

A Company held for another day. It was men such as these who were denigrated by the far away Generals MacArthur, Sutherland and, on occasions, Kenney, who had no idea of the conditions under which the enemy was engaged on the Kokoda Trail.

Under a cloudy sky, Akira Teruoka's unit was up at 5.30 am and moved to a field hospital located near Kokoda airfield. At dusk, rifle fire could be heard only about 1000 yards away, but no fighting developed around his unit. He was told that an estimated platoon of enemy had engaged the engineers, killing 10 and wounding 11 on 8 August.

No attack missions were recorded as flown from Port Moresby on 10 August. A Company soldiers at Kokoda recall that a single P39 circled, waggled its wings to the waving Aussies, and flew away. The daily long-range flights to Rabaul and sea searches were flown, with no sightings. General Kenney had gone to Port Moresby, to talk General Ken Walker and Colonel Carmichael into skip-bombing, but found them both very reluctant to depart from the tenets of high-level precision bombardment. He also found that he had another bombardment unit, the 43rd Group, but it had no aircraft and its personnel were scattered all over eastern Australia in a variety of jobs.

39th Battalion's 17 Platoon, cut off in the fighting on the Oivi track on 8 August, had quietly left their position at dawn on 9 August and moved through the bush, carrying two wounded, to Deniki. They arrived during the afternoon, but brought no word of A Company. Nothing was known of Symington's force since Lance Corporal Sanopa had come back with some Japanese documents taken by A Company when it retook Kokoda in the afternoon of 8 August.

A Company had held without word from its parent battalion, and it was obvious it could not remain. The only food was captured Japanese rice, cooked by the company clerk and brought forward under fire, and the last ammunition reserve had been issued to the platoons. Some B Company Lewis gun drum magazines had been found with ammunition in them. Captain Symington decided that if there was no contact with higher headquarters before dusk, he would begin to withdraw, but first go north towards Yodda, where there seemed to be fewest Japanese. The Japanese force was estimated to be about 300, with heavy machineguns and mortars. By mid-afternoon, it was obvious the Japanese were preparing for a greater effort, and much shouting of orders could be heard. One man with a bull-like voice was presumed to be the commander.

2nd Lieutenant Onogawa had been told that 50 or 60 Australians were fighting on at Kokoda, 'resisting desperately from AA trenches we built there. Though they are our enemy, their bravery must be admired. Compared to those we met at New Britain, these soldiers seem to be an entirely different people. A general attack will be carried out this evening'.

Lieutenant Hirano had gathered his platoon to await orders to attack. While there, Private Miyabe was killed by a hit in the head from a sniper. He briefed his section commanders at 2.30 pm (4.30 pm local time), and the attack went in at 5.40 pm local time, with machinegun support from 2nd Lieutenant Shimomura's 1 Platoon, 1 MG Company. The assault got to within 70 yards of the Australian positions, and held. It rained again. The Japanese then used smoke to mask movement and attacked again, but water had affected the smoke candles and they were not as effective. Hirano's platoon charged an empty position, but when they crept up onto another, were held back by the Australian fire. Then 2 Platoon went in and the Australians moved back. At 7 pm (9 pm local time) Hirano's men occupied a house at Kokoda; he had four wounded.

By now, A Company was about to run out of ammunition, and survivors of the action believe that they could have held longer if more ammunition had been available. Still Japanese were being felled, and the platoons gradually thinned out and went back in the dusk. Wounded men and empty Bren guns were taken to company headquarters, and at 7 pm, in darkness, assisted by rain, the withdrawal began. It was presumed, perhaps hopefully, that in the darkness the Japanese may have fought each other. This attack was heard by Akira Teruoka at the hospital.

The Japanese assault had not covered the western side of Kokoda, which allowed A Company to leave successfully and loop back to Deniki. Company HQ went off down the side of the ridge moving towards Yodda, followed by 7 Platoon, then 8 Platoon with the wounded Les Skinner. 9 Platoon was to bring up the rear, with J. D. McKay's section, but not all of them received the actual word to go and in any case were trying to hold off the attacking Japanese. The main body of the company successfully crossed Madi Creek, which ran between Kokoda itself and the airfield, but in the dark and rain some elements became separated. Skinner died when being taken across the creek, presumably from the shock of the sudden immersion in cold water adding to the ill-effects of his massive thigh wound.

J. D. McKay's position had two Bren guns firing, the Japanese paused, then surged on again and ran past. It was decided to go back, as the position had been overrun, but one of the Bren gunners, Scattergood, stood firing from the hip, was hit, and not seen again as the section went back to the company position. McKay's section found one of their own section casualties, Private Stormont, in the HQ dugout, but his wound was too big and it was evident he was dying. He had been hit in the back by a sniper in a tree when the section was pinned in the stormwater drain earlier. They had to leave him and move on into the darkness.

The rest of the company had gone, but Staff Sergeant Jim Cowey had remained to assist McKay's section, which had been isolated for much of the day, and now were separated from the company. Cowey had already met and kept with him a few of the last to leave, and was determined to make sure every man possible was informed of the evacuation and given assistance if necessary.

Cowey was a remarkable man, having served in the First World War in the 46th Battalion, been commissioned and awarded the Military Cross, then at the age of nearly 52 years, he volunteered for service in the Second World War, in 39 Battalion. Setting an example of calmness, Cowey gradually brought together the last living Aussies at Kokoda, and told them that they would quietly walk out of the area. All around were Japanese searching buildings and grenading weapon pits, but Cowey realised that running or moving quickly would attract attention, so led his small party through the rubber trees, off the ridge, over the bridge spanning Madi Creek between the town and airfield, over the airstrip and into scrub, where he told the group to rest and wait until daylight.

In the rain, cold and darkness, scattered parties of Australians tried to rest, and Japanese searched the position they had taken after so much trouble.

During the day, Lieutenant General Rowell had left Brisbane en route to Port Moresby, to assume command there. He had rather expected to be allocated a military aircraft, but instead flew as far as Townsville in a civilian airliner. Next day was to provide another insight into the transport aircraft situation. Also wondering about the transport aircraft was Lieutenant Kienzle. He set off from Myola to Eora, where he was needed to oversee solution to problems arising from the continuous use of the native carriers, without allowing them rest.

One Catalina harassed Lakunai in the early hours of 11 August; only four reconnaissance missions were flown from Port Moresby.[11]

At daybreak on 11 August, west of Kokoda, Staff Sergeant Jim Cowey roused his small party of A Company men and began to take them back to Deniki. He took the lead, and organised the group into an infantry section arrangement, with Alex Lochhead bringing up the rear. At every halt, he would point out to the group the tactical lessons encountered or observed. It was thought a unit of Japanese was trying to catch them, so he took his party along creeks, but moving gradually back to Deniki.

Also at daybreak, 21 men of 8 Platoon, commanded by Sergeant Bill Guest, separated from the main body of the company, began their own journey back. After some wandering, Private Bluey Murray said he believed that he could lead the way back to the airstrip and was told to do so. Sure enough, at about 8 am he brought the group to the edge of the jungle at the airfield. All was quiet. Corporal Allen Smith courageously volunteered to check the small hut where air passengers had waited in peaceful times, and returned with the news that no Japanese had been there. Once again, light fog assisted the Aussies, and they were able to cross the airfield unseen, get into the kunai grass and find a track that eventually led them to a deserted village. There they took stock – there was one stretcher case, with multiple groin wounds, and several walking wounded. They had two Bren guns without ammunition, so these were hidden after the breech-blocks were thrown away; one Tommy gun with one magazine; rifles with little ammunition; one haversack of Japanese rice.

From Rabaul, the convoy again set off for New Guinea. Aboard were the Tomita Butai, under Colonel Yoshinobu Tomita, and a company of the Takasago Volunteer Unit.[12]

Lieutenant General Rowell, on the final leg of his journey to take command in New Guinea, found himself aboard a US military DC3/C47, flown by a civilian pilot under contract, in which the passengers sat on narrow seats or on mail bags. For some reason, about halfway to Port Moresby, the pilot began circling as close to sea-level as he could. Rowell had no time for this nonsense and sent his Operations Officer, Brigadier Henry Rourke, to tell the pilot to stop circling and get on to Moresby, but the co-pilot had already protested and the DC3 continued to 7-Mile. It was necessary for arriving aircraft to follow a designated route to allow identification and avoid being attacked by fighters or anti-aircraft guns. The pilot, whether to show who was boss or because of some other reason, made a pretence of following regulations, but landed safely. Rowell climbed down and was met by Major General Morris and other officers.

With Rowell in command on arrival, Morris became commander of ANGAU, responsible for government of the native civil population. Rowell found the situation was:

• Milne Bay, held by 7 Infantry Brigade (Militia), with 75 and 76 Squadrons RAAF; 18 Brigade (AIF) of 7 Australian Division was due there on 21 August.

• Port Moresby, held by 30 Infantry Brigade (Militia), with 39 Battalion opposing the Japanese on the Kokoda Trail, and 14 Brigade; HQ 7 Division and 21 Brigade (AIF) were en route and due on 17 August.

• Kokoda, 39 Battalion of 30 Brigade, in action against the Japanese.

• Wau area, an independent company and elements of NGVR operating against Japanese airfields at Salamaua and Lae, with another independent company at Moresby waiting to be flown to Wau.

• Australia, 25 Brigade of 7 Division available but dependent on shipping and the operational requirements in New Guinea.

Rowell was aware at once that the most pressing problem was at Kokoda, which had to be recaptured as soon as possible, and operations prepared against Buna from Kokoda and Milne Bay. The commando operations from Wau would receive such support as available. He also was aware that the size of any force deployed onto the Kokoda Trail depended on the amount of supplies that could be delivered to it.

Rowell had been told that neither MacArthur's GHQ nor Blamey's Allied Land Forces HQ believed the Japanese posed a direct threat to Port Moresby, as both HQs were comfortable in the belief that the mountains were impassable to a large force necessary for modern war. MacArthur's Intelligence Officer, Willoughby, had convinced himself that the enemy only wanted airfield sites on the north coast. Both headquarters also still believed in the 'Kokoda Gap', supposedly the only pass through the ranges, so narrow that a man could touch each wall with outstretched arms, and that could be held by a couple of determined men, rather like Horatius at the Tiber Bridge and Leonidas at Thermopylae.

Again, the lack of combat units available to Rowell in early August, three months after General Blamey sent 14 Brigade to Port Moresby, shows how little MacArthur really had done to 'fight the Japanese in New Guinea'.

Meanwhile, near Kokoda, Staff Sergeant Cowey's party found the main Kokoda–Deniki track and began following it. They came to the Japanese base area, with supplies piled at the base of trees, Japanese writing on pieces of material, hitching ropes for the packhorses and such, and realised just what size force had been met by C Company when it tried to advance along the track to Kokoda on 8 August. Cowey continued along the track, to the dismay of some of the others. Suddenly they met Privates Drummond and Spriggs, also alone, with their Bren. The gun had seized, but they had only one magazine with three rounds left. Cowey called a halt. There were 10 in the group, with Tommy guns, rifles and a few grenades, but little ammunition. Cowey led them on, but a Japanese machinegun opened fire, narrowly missing his head with the first burst. Cowey then demonstrated coolness under fire to the other Aussies. He leaned against the tree nearby, brought up his .303 rifle, aimed and shot dead the Japanese gunner, who was pushed aside by his partner, so Cowey reloaded at the shoulder and shot dead this man also, then continued to kill every Japanese who climbed behind the gun. Of course, a hornet's nest had been aroused, and the Japanese were swarming.

It seems the Japanese overestimated the protective qualities of the trees and large slab-like roots that project from certain tree trunks in the region. Cowey directed the others to fire through the wood, and the .303 bullet, travelling at 2440 feet per second (744 metres), punched through and into the sheltering Japanese. At the right moment, Cowey calmly told the others to withdraw, and they moved off the track, into the bush, and around the Japanese position. Soon after, the Australians came on a Japanese outpost, which was destroyed with a grenade, killing two soldiers sitting there. The small group moved off, intending to circle from the west back to Deniki. Alex Lochhead had noticed one thing that impressed him. Some of the Japanese were six feet (183 cm) tall, not at all the little fellows so beloved of the propaganda machinery.

At 9 am, Akira Teruoka's unit set off for Kokoda airfield, listening to the sound of battle, probably Cowey's small engagement. When they arrived, he saw his first Australian casualties, estimated them to be in total about 20, and helped carry a dozen Japanese wounded to the field hospital. Lieutenant Onogawa wrote, 'Though the Australians are our enemies, they must be admired'.

Through the day, the separated elements of A Company made their way back, avoiding contact with the Japanese. Captain Symington and the main body arrived at the village of Naro, between Kokoda and Deniki, waited a while and then patrolled the area. At dusk, Cowey's party arrived at the village, went into it, and were met by Symington's group, just returning there. Symington already had sent a message by runner to Major Cameron telling him of the arrival at Naro, and asking for assistance with the wounded.

For his part, Cameron had arranged for food and ammunition to be dropped at Kokoda early in the morning, but of course this all fell into the hands of the Japanese. When the message arrived, he sent a party of PIB natives and Warrant Officer Jack Wilkinson to Naro. It was expected that Deniki would be attacked soon, and after Wilkinson left at 5.15 pm, his party saw Japanese on the track, but dodged into the long grass and played possum. The Japanese were only feet away, but did not detect the group. Travelling became very difficult in the pitch black, and it began to rain. To provide a minimum of light, fire sticks were lit and used to keep the party on the track. After several hours, the silhouette of Naro village could be seen on top of the hill. But in the slippery conditions, a native fell from the log across a ravine, Wilkinson slipped off after him, and three more natives fell on him, sparking a flow of eloquent Australian swearing. This was heard by the watchers above, one of whom recognised Wilkinson's voice, and so contact between the groups was made.

George Mowat noted that they had 'nothing for breakfast. Started walking at daylight. Found apparently deserted native village; police boy found native hiding. OK, families came out of bush. Fed on vegetables to bursting point. This food doesn't last! Sent runner with request to assist with wounded, food. Second runner came with warrant officer and PIB'. Captain Symington was very annoyed to learn of the air drops of food and ammunition that had gone to the Japanese, but there was nothing to be done.

Akira Teruoka wrote that three aircraft attacked them at the Kokoda area, but no record of this mission is included in any official Allied Air Force report of the day's activities; it may have been an ad hoc 'verbal' mission or the supply drops that he mistook for attacks. During the night, his unit ate dry bread for dinner, and listened to rifle shots presumed to come from the Australians. Tomorrow the Japanese would hurry to Owen Stanley Range itself.

As he received more information on 12 August, Lieutenant General Rowell was finding how precarious was the supply situation, relying as it did on native carriers and a few aircraft. The number of carriers was inadequate to maintain the small force built around 39 Battalion in the mountains, and it was only with air drops at Myola, plus carriers, that deployment of a force of four battalions was feasible. The first AIF battalions arrived in the harbour. At 8 am, members of 2/14th and 2/16th Battalions looked at the sun-scorched brown and black hills on the shore. They had been expecting thick jungle growth. By midday, the battalions were coming ashore and on the way to the Itiki assembly area, where they were to have three days before moving off onto the Kokoda Trail.

During the afternoon, observers in the 39th Battalion position at Deniki, watching in the direction to Kokoda, could see parties of Japanese moving towards the main Deniki track. It was obvious an attack was coming. The Japanese would have easily deduced that the Australian force was too small to do more than it had already, and also would correctly have deduced that the lack of reinforcements for their enemy dug in and holding Kokoda indicated that the total Australian force was weak in numbers.

Merritt's E Company 39th Battalion was hurrying up from Isurava to Deniki, slipping on the rocky trail, and enduring the usual afternoon rain. They arrived just as the force at Deniki was 'standing-to' for the evening, and the serious faces were warning enough to the arrivals that silence was necessary. Guides led the platoons to their allocated positions, each man holding on to the bayonet scabbard of the man in front, with the only light a shielded torch at the front of the column, moving through the wet and dripping darkness. Finally the arrivals were in position, and settled down for the night, wondering if the Japanese were already nearby. Don Simonson was a 22-year-old lieutenant, commander of one of the platoons. After the rain, the night became clear, with a starry sky overhead; he could see the area was 'reasonably open'.[13]

Lieutenant Kienzle had ordered that half the carriers on the trail be allowed to rest. They were exhausted and had been used continuously. He was told air drops had begun at Myola, and this shortened carrying task would presumably ease the carrier situation. Far away on the eastern tip of New Britain, at noon, six B17s attacked ships at Rabaul and claimed hits on the airfield, on ships and the wharves, while gunners claimed two destroyed and five probably destroyed from the attacking Zeros.

At GHQ in Brisbane, MacArthur's Intelligence officer, General Willoughby, on this day still believed that the Japanese did not pose a threat to Port Moresby, but only wanted airfields on the north coast. Willoughby was consistently wrong, but was a loyal member of the Bataan clique, which ensured his survival. Two landings were known to have taken place, other ships had been sighted going towards New Guinea, yet GHQ persisted in its belief that the Japanese were outnumbered and that they would go no further than Kokoda.

Captain Symington's company left Naro at 6 am on 13 August, with the PIB carrying the wounded and assisting the sick. Peter Brewer, of ANGAU, was so ill with dysentery that he could not stand without assistance; all were hungry. Jim Cowey brought up the rear. At 10 am, heavy firing could be heard from Deniki, so a detour was made to avoid the most likely areas occupied by the Japanese attackers. At noon, they arrived at the old radio transmitting station, then set off to Isurava, south of Deniki.

Aware an attack was developing, in the 39th Battalion position, Major Cameron had positioned Bidstrup's D Company on his right, Jacob's C Company in the centre, and Merritt's E Company on the left; it had not yet been in action. Lieutenant Don Simonson's 20 Platoon was the extreme left platoon, and had one Lewis gun, with only one magazine. The Battalion War Diary described the attack as beginning at 9.50 am with machinegun and rifle fire from the front and flanks, evidently intended to draw return shots from the Australians and allow the Japanese to gain information on positions, but the battalion held fire, waiting for targets.

A typically Australian incident occurred at the beginning of the action, which must have puzzled the Japanese. Reg Marsh, CSM D Company, had intended to take advantage of a natural cascade of water in the position to have a shower. He had stripped off and just got properly soaped up when the Japanese began firing, with bullets pinging off rocks around him. Marsh grabbed his boots and clothes, and began running back up the slope to the HQ, but the sight of the pillar of company discipline running naked under fire, bare buttocks bobbing, brought roars of laughter from all the Diggers in sight. The Japanese fire ceased instantly. Unfortunately, no record of the incident from the Japanese viewpoint survived. Then many Japanese were seen, only some 40 yards away, but they were shooting and so were other Japanese, placing a heavy volume of fire onto the Australian position.

2nd Lieutenant Onogawa's unit left at 5 am to attack and made their way through the jungle to the base of the hill. Two scouts crept up, and returned with the news that it was not held by enemy. 2nd Lieutenant Sasai, of No. 2 Company, was told to advance along the path to the hilltop. Onogawa believed the Australians were really there, and sure enough Sasai was shot dead. Then the companies advanced through the Australian rifle, grenade and machinegun fire.

I/144 came up the hill onto Merritt's company, with Simonson's platoon taking most of the pressure. The Japanese came up en masse, four or five abreast, but were hurled back by automatic weapons and grenades. The fighting continued, and the Aussies learned another lesson: automatic weapons had to be shifted quickly after firing, before accurate return fire killed or wounded the crew. Also present was Akira Teruoka and 55 Division Medical unit. They too had reveille at 5 am, advanced, and waited while the fighting went on only 70 yards away 'in the jungle of a mountain at Sakogo'. He noted that the Australians also attacked, but did not open fire until 30 yards away, and their sniping made things difficult for the Japanese.

The attacks on 39th Battalion at Deniki continued, and E Company lost nine men in the first hour. There was a pause at about midday. Lieutenant Simonson heard the noise of mess tins from the direction of the Japanese, so crept out to investigate. Only 20 yards away, he saw a group of Japanese sitting around eating, apparently confident they could do so undisturbed. Simonson determined to show that the Australians could do things to make their presence felt, and his grenades destroyed two machineguns and killed or wounded the picnickers. Jack Boland, from the AA Platoon, put this and other examples of Japanese nonchalance in action down to the fact that they had not been attacked before by opponents; they were always on the offensive, their foes defending and inept in jungle warfare.

After lunch for the Japanese, the probes and attacks continued, into evening and night. With darkness came rain and more mist, adding to the problems of the defenders. Simonson's platoon lost 10 killed or wounded, and one missing for some days, but who later rejoined the unit. The platoon position had to be tightened and the forward section pits abandoned. The platoon Lewis gun had been supplied with two more magazines. Firing continued in the darkness until after midnight, and there was quiet for some hours. All knew the Japanese would continue pressing next day.

Meanwhile, Captain Symington's A Company had begun arriving at the Isurava Rest House, where a signals section was looking after the telephone line. Dehydrated mutton was available, and to the starved soldiers it was the finest of foods. Some tinned salmon had been distributed from supplies brought up by Chaplain Earl and some natives, but the people in charge of carriers had left for the rear when the sound of firing at Deniki was heard.

It was then that the soldiers with Jim Cowey realised just what the previous days had taken from that brave man. He was so exhausted that the physical effort of eating was almost beyond him. He had stayed behind to make sure that as far as possible no

Australian was left behind, had taken command of those he did find, had led them and continued to teach them while bringing them out from the midst of numerous Japanese, had set a high standard of personal coolness and courage in action, had endured hunger, cold and rain; he was more than 50 years old. Jim Cowey received no medals for his service and exploits on the Kokoda Trail, but is well remembered by the unit survivors.

George Mowat, A Company, described the day's travel through the jungle, everyone listening to the sound of battle, but tiring due to lack of food. On arrival at Isurava, there was the 'bumper hot meal ready. Hash and vegetables, hot tea and biscuits. Delicious. First hot meal for 7 days. No blankets or ground sheets'.

While 39th Battalion was defending Deniki, the air war continued. At 11.30 am, B17s attacked the *Nankai Maru* convoy 75 miles (120 km) north-north-east of Gona; no hits were claimed. Ten B17s were attacked by fighters, which damaged three bombers, and one B17 salvoed its bombs due to engine troubles, while six did not bomb because of the fighter attacks. At 3.15 pm, three B26s attacked the ships, now only 20 miles (32 km) north of Gona, despite interception by seven Zeros, but none of their bombs scored a hit, though gunners claimed one fighter probably destroyed. All three were hit, and one crash-landed at Porlock Harbour. Two other B26s turned back with mechanical problems. At 6.15 pm, three B17s bombed a cruiser five miles (eight km) north of Gona; all 23 bombs missed. Crews saw three transports off Gona, and three warships steaming north.

Seaman 1st Class Shunji Shin, No. 2 Company Sasebo 5SLP at Buna, recorded the arrival of nine Australians: five men, three women and a child, brought in by local natives. These people were Lieutenant Louis Austen, and Anglican missionary civilians: the Reverend Henry Holland, the Reverend Vivian Redlich, Mr John Duffill, two half-caste mission workers, Mr Anthony Gors and Miss Louise Artango, with Gors's six-year-old son, and Miss Margery Brenchley and Miss Lilla Lashmar. They had been betrayed by the people of Perembata village while trying to make their way to Tufi, further east along the north coast. They had been beaten and threatened, stripped naked and abused, though the women later were given back their pants, and herded along to the Japanese.

Describing the air combats over the beachhead, Shunji Shin noted that one Japanese fighter made a forced landing, and two planes were shot down, but gave no other detail of the combat. He made no distinction between the combat with the B17s or with the B26s, and his figures may be a total for the day's actions. Another diarist wrote that the ship arrived at Basabua at 5 pm, and that a bomb hit the starboard side of *Nankai Maru*.[14]

Aboard ship, diarist 'Uchida' was excited when he thought of the fall of Port Moresby, after the troops had landed, and estimated it would take eight half-hour trips by motorised landing craft (MLC) to land the 850 Koreans on *Kenyo Maru*. He could see part of sunken *Ayatosan Maru* nearby, and after landing noted the extensive signs of bombing. He was told there had been many casualties in the initial landings. 15 Pioneer Unit was busy unloading the ships, and continued to work despite the presence of enemy aircraft; there was no stopping for air raid alarms. No. 2 Company of the Takasago Volunteer Unit arrived at Basabua off *Nankai Maru*. The company of 264 men was commanded by Terao Yamanaka, began marching at 2.15 next morning, and arrived at Soputa at 12.15 pm.[15] On the opposite side of the island, ships were unloading at Port Moresby, as Brigadier Potts's 21 Brigade went ashore.

On this day, MacArthur's GHQ sent to Lieutenant General Rowell a suggestion by US Major General Hugh J. Casey, Chief Engineer at GHQ, that explosives be placed in the passes of the Owen Stanleys, and detonated to block the passes to the Japanese. Such was the level of knowledge of the battle area by senior US officers at GHQ, five months after arrival in Australia and three weeks after the Japanese had landed at Buna. Rowell politely wrote back describing the conditions on the trail and suggested that explosives be used to assist his advance, rather than deny the enemy progress.

Merritt's E Company again was attacked as the Japanese came on at dawn on 14 August, gradually working their way behind him.

His platoons were holding a knoll, some 250 yards by 60 yards, company strength had gone from 78 to 65 men, but they were still holding. The Japanese eased pressure, and firing slackened.

At that time, Major Cameron decided to withdraw, and the order was given so suddenly that when it arrived and was executed, some of the Dalby and Pentland platoons, plus personal equipment, were left behind. The Japanese resumed the attack; E Company was under pressure, with enemy passing by their position; C Company was being mortared. The superior numbers of Japanese were threatening to swamp 39th Battalion if it remained in place. Cameron realised that if he was to continue to block the path to Port Moresby, he would have to move back to another position and force another delay on the Japanese there. He signalled NGF at 8.30 am of his intentions and the withdrawal began. Soldiers were told the battalion was leaving, and to take as much food and ammunition as they could carry. With vivid memories of recent days, the men obeyed. One man carried 1100 rounds of .303 ammunition in bandoliers.

17 Platoon D Company went first and held the radio transmitting station position, about 20 minutes walk from Deniki. C and E Companies moved back past them, then 16 and 18 Platoons. Cameron's orders to Captain Bidstrup were to ambush the enemy at the transmitter, but not to stand and hold, then move back to join the battalion.

Cameron was outstanding in many ways. One of the things he made time for, as he advanced and retreated along the trail, was to draw a series of accurate sketches of the terrain along the route, and copies of these were used later. No maps existed, and those soon to be issued were simply inadequate, but Cameron's accurate sketches, made with his talent 'for getting the lie of the land', as a battalion commander put it, were of great value.[16]

The Japanese did not follow up their success. The combined remnants of A and B Companies already were taking up position in the Isurava area as the other companies passed back to Alola. Akira Teruoka's squad from the medical unit had climbed the mountain to bring down casualties. They took one dead and six wounded to the battalion medical unit, went back to their camp for breakfast, and later carried the wounded to the hospital at Kokoda. He saw one dead Australian.

Again the relentless rain poured down, and the wet, tired and ill Australians made their way along. Hungry, suffering from dysentery, malaria and dengue fever, sometimes all three, the Diggers were told to light fires and try to dry out as well as heat some food. All were aware that they were the only force holding the enemy, that there was no immediate prospect of relief or assistance, that medical attention was very basic and evacuation for the ill meant a greater burden on the supply system and on the humans tasked to carry casualties. All knew only too well that every man less meant a greater load of responsibility on his mates in the section, platoon and company. Another miserable night was spent on the dank jungle trail.

Cameron's breaking contact and withdrawal may have been done so smartly that the Japanese did not realise it, and were slow to do so, or had more respect for the Australian ability to wait in concealed position for the Japanese to approach, before firing. After the Aussies had gone, 2nd Lieutenant Onogawa's unit made a general attack, supported by machineguns and grenade-throwers. After 20 minutes, they had secured the objective, immediately reorganised and attacked 'No. 3 Hill'. There was no opposition.

At Buna, Sasebo 5SLP beheaded the nine 'Europeans' brought to them the previous day by natives. The execution took place on the beach, witnessed by many Japanese and natives. Left to last was a person described as the 16-year-old daughter of one of the families. This was the estimation of the age of the youngest woman and her relationship with the other prisoners made by the Japanese diarist. Her execution was bungled, and the Japanese had to hold her down, screaming and crying out while they finished the job of cutting off her head. This incident, in varying degrees of detail, was recorded by several spectators, and also referred to later by prisoners. Conveniently, the Japanese officers responsible were said to have been killed before the end of the war, and no war crimes trial was held for the murders. After the war, Sub-Lieutenant Komai was blamed for this by surviving Japanese, but Komai was killed in action. He also was reputed to have murdered Flight Lieutenant Bill Newton, 22 Squadron RAAF, in March 1943 at Salamaua.[17]

Except Father Benson, all other European civilians and military personnel who fell into Japanese hands during this campaign were murdered. Miss May Hayman and Miss Mavis Parkinson, from the Gona Mission, also were betrayed by local people, and were murdered with bayonets at Popondetta after being forced to dig their own graves.

The supply situation for the Australians depended on the carrier force, and Bert Kienzle was fully occupied with keeping supplies going forward along the trail, evacuation of wounded, and coping with the increasing number of desertions from the carriers. He would be busy with this problem for the next four days.

Recorded air attack for 14 August was confined to one bombing raid. At 9 am, six B17s attacked the ships unloading off Gona. From 4500 feet, through rain, with cloud base at 1500 feet, visibility two to five miles (3.2 to 8 km), under attack by Zeros, they aimed at a ship and cargo now unloaded on the shore. No hits were seen on the ship, and results on shore were not known. Six Zeros attacked, damaging four bombers, but gunners claimed two destroyed. Shunji Shin noted that two Japanese fighters made forced landings, so the bomber claims for two destroyed may have been quite accurate, but the fighters only had to land on the nearby new Buna strip to be repaired.

General Kenney must have been dissatisfied with the performance of his air units, even when bad weather was taken into account, and he resolved to have low-level attacks made on such targets. High and medium level bombing missions, as described above, were inflicting little damage on ships. If the senior officers of his bomber units were reluctant to diverge from the high-level precision bombing so beloved of the bombardment prophets, he knew of at least one officer who agreed with him – Bill Benn. Kenney had a great knack for picking the right man from the gathering of eccentrics and intelligent, aggressive men with initiative. He decided to give Benn a squadron command, to develop tactics for the B17 in a role that had never been considered by its designers or the military leaders who ordered it into production. The four-engined Flying Fortress of the stratosphere was to attack ships from below mast-height.

Only two reconnaissance missions were flown from Port Moresby on 15 August, with a B17 to the Buna–Gona area, and another to Rabaul and Kavieng, but it turned back when the bottom door of the ball turret fell off, making it unserviceable.

The members of 2/14 and 2/16 Battalions at Itiki were briefed on the situation at the battlefront. The brigade was tasked to secure 'The Gap' and recapture Kokoda from the Japanese. Since arrival, the battalions had been preparing for the move to Kokoda. All possible weight was discarded, but it was still impossible to reduce the load carried by each man below a minimum of 45 pounds (20 kg). Maps were issued, but all were aware of the inadequacies of the printed sheets. Compasses were in short supply, but instruction was given in the method of using a watch to determine north.

Brigadier Potts spoke to the battalions and told them that their task would be to wipe out the Japanese at Kokoda, force them back to the Kumusi River. The Japanese were said to number only about 1200 soldiers. Potts was addressing a gathering of fit, confident men, sure of their superiority, proud of their status as AIF. There were no dithering British generals, nor units of other nationalities to give way on the flanks, as was believed to have happened in Malaya. 2/14th was to lead the advance next day, followed by 2/16th the day after.

2nd Lieutenant Onogawa wrote in his diary that No. 3 Company was ordered to defend the area between battalion HQ and the hill captured the day before (Deniki). Four Australian prisoners said they doubted the Japanese could successfully cross the mountains. These men probably were from the platoons that were left behind or became separated during the quick withdrawal ordered by Major Cameron the previous day. The prisoners were not named or identified in any other way, and there was no other detail of their fate, but as nothing more seems to have been recorded of them, they were obviously murdered.

Meanwhile, 39th Battalion, at Isurava, began to dig in with helmets, bayonets, tins, and whatever was available. The Japanese short entrenching tool was a prized possession. Captain Bidstrup, ambushing at the radio station, sent Jack Boland on reconnaissance towards Deniki. When close to the position, he climbed to the top of some high ground and looked across, to see parties of Japanese foraging around the old location. There was no sign of movement towards D Company, so Boland's patrol collected tins of rations conveniently dumped by the track and returned to report. Bidstrup then ordered Boland to take his entire section out some 200 yards towards Deniki, as a standing patrol, and also told him that the company was only to ambush and delay, not hold the position. When Boland passed this on to his Diggers, there was not a lot of enthusiasm. No one looked forward to engaging what certainly would be a superior number of enemy, and be faced with covering 200 yards back to the company, especially if there were wounded from the clash.

Boland selected a position where the track curved around a huge round rock on the slope. The hill fell away steeply on the right, but was fairly level on the left. He decided to place his men on the left, with the Bren having a good field of fire along the track to the curve and the big rock. This position was only some 60 yards forward of D Company HQ, but below a crest. Boland reported to Captain Bidstrup, who repeated that he wanted 'you' 200 yards forward. Boland, in best Aussie fashion, took the order literally, left his men in place and intended to go forward with one other man to the 200-yard distance, then return if and when the Japanese arrived, and open fire as he originally intended.

Boland carefully began to go past the rock when he saw a bush move towards him, and while he was looking at this spectacle, another bush came into sight and moved across the track, at which moment Boland realised he was watching the two scouts of a Japanese unit. This was Lieutenant Hirano's platoon. The scouts were dressed in green, with shrubbery fixed to parts of their uniform; when they halted they were almost impossible to recognise. Boland also realised that he was standing there in khaki shirt and shorts, the foremost Australian on the Kokoda Trail. As he ducked back towards the other man with him, on the far side of the rock, he knew the Japanese must have seen him.

Halting next to the rock, Boland signalled to his section to warn Captain Bidstrup that Japanese were coming, then he and the other man, Andy McCullagh, took a position behind a very large fallen tree behind the rock. One of the Japanese scouts cautiously peered around the rock and scanned the slope, then must have seen sign of Boland's section, for he waved forward the second scout and another man, presumably the squad leader; all three peered towards the section positions. Boland and McCullagh were only feet away, but out of the angle of vision of the Japanese, who did not expect enemy to be so close.

The Japanese were out of sight of the Bren gunner due to the curve of the track. Another tall Japanese with fixed bayonet came forward and went into the bush on the downhill side of the track, quickly followed by three men. It was obvious to Boland that these soldiers knew what they were doing and were experienced. He wondered what would have happened if they had gone around the other side of the rock – they would have stepped on him and Mc-Cullagh. Then the Bren opened up on three Japanese who walked up the track, around the rock and into its field of fire.

All three Japanese fell or rolled into a water wash that had formed between the log and the track. The Bren stopped. A Japanese light machinegun team came around the rock and set up their gun in the middle of the track, but had trouble extending the bipod legs to get enough elevation to fire on the Australian section position. Boland and McCullagh were watching all this from just a few yards away, and did not dare talk. McCullagh was watching the wash where the Japanese had disappeared from sight.

Silently, Boland signalled to McCullagh to take the Japanese in the wash, while he would deal with the LMG team on the track, after which both men would go for the high ground behind them, and return to the rest of the section. The shrubbery was so thick that although Boland could see the Japanese on the track, he could not sight his rifle on the gunner, so aimed at the body of the gun. He fired, McCullagh fired the Tommy gun at the Japanese below, Boland pulled the pin on a grenade and threw it among the Japanese in the wash, then both were up and struggling away through the vines and saplings to get to the top of the rise.

The grenade explosion frightened both men, and they kept on, making little progress in the thick growth, and collapsed exhausted after only 20 yards. They lay there and listened to yelling and screaming from the Japanese, to the Japanese firing, and realised that there was no pursuit, that in fact the enemy were leaving. Boland stood for a better view and, through a gap in the greenery, could see a different Japanese, quite broad-shouldered, behind a LMG pointing at the position they had occupied. As he watched, the man started to crawl back to the big rock, Boland aimed and shot him, then with McCullagh leaped out onto the track and ran to the top of the rise, collected personal gear they'd left there and went back to D Company.

The Japanese unit can be identified from Onogama's diary, in which he noted that 2nd Lieutenant Hirano went 1800 metres (2000 yards) on patrol during the morning, was contacted by Australians and lost three killed and others wounded.

Later in the day, Lieutenant Dalby's 19 Platoon, which had been separated in the quick withdrawal from Deniki, arrived in Isurava. They had circled the area and came onto the track at Captain Bidstrup's ambush position. Elsewhere in the 39th, George Mowat 'had first shave for a fortnight. Had a beautiful fringe'.

No aerial attack missions were recorded from Port Moresby on 16 or 17 August, but B17s reconnoitred the Vitiaz Straits, Rabaul, Kavieng and Kieta, without reference to combats. By this date, New Guinea Force HQ believed that air drops at Myola had delivered 25 days supplies for 2000 men, with adequate small arms ammunition. It seems that this assumption was based on figures of quantities dispatched from Moresby, and not on reports of items received in Myola. The problems confronting the air supply organisation, such as existed, were that regardless of the number of aircraft available for operations at dawn, flights had to cease when

the weather at Myola denied access to the dropping area. However, weather at Moresby was not necessarily the same as at Myola; no weather reports were available from Myola – the only way
to find out was to fly there; planes often brought back loads if the
weather was too bad for dropping; fighter cover was necessary.
These adverse aspects were not identified until it became obvious
that there were serious faults in the system, and a conference was
held at Port Moresby at the end of August to find solutions to the
problems. The problems were large, and there was little previous
experience or knowledge to consult. Navigation aids did not exist;
the performance of aircraft, the bad-weather instruments and
training of crews all were low by later standards; such factors as
the aircraft's dropping height and speed, protective wrappings and
devices to slow the falling speed, or lessen the impact of the cargoes were matters for experiment as actual drops were made.
Always there were weather, terrain and the enemy – all three
unforgiving.

There was no significant ground action in the Kokoda area on
this day. Having captured the location, Horii's advance force was
waiting for further orders, whether headquarters at Rabaul decided to order them to push on or remain. This was fortunate for
the Australians, as 39th Battalion was suffering badly, and the
nearest reinforcements were 21 Brigade, still at Moresby. At Kokoda on 17 August, the Japanese force woke at 5 am. Akira Teruoka's medical unit cleaned their equipment in relative peace as the
Australians had retreated and there were no attacks planned.

At midday, Lieutenant Colonel Honner arrived at Alola to
assume command of 39th Battalion and Maroubra Force. Ralph
Honner was a schoolmaster, then a lawyer, and a citizen soldier
with the rank of captain when war broke out. He joined the West
Australian 2/11th Battalion, being appointed as a company commander. His service record in Libya, Greece and Crete was outstanding, and since returning to Australia he had commanded a
training battalion in Western Australia. On the death of Lieutenant Colonel Owen, Honner was promoted Lieutenant Colonel and
flew to Port Moresby. There he was told to hold the enemy on the

other side of the mountain ranges until relieved by 21 Brigade. When he arrived to take command, B Company 53rd Battalion was following closely, with C/53rd a day behind. Honner conferred with Major Porter, and decided to leave the PIB and 53rd Battalion elements at Alola to patrol the tracks that converged there, and so that Brigadier S. H. W. C. Porter, commander 30 Brigade in Port Moresby, and who was coming across the mountains, would have a fresh force at his disposal. 53rd Battalion was not to perform up to expectations of the AIF commanders arriving, and the history of this unfortunate unit provides a case study of how not to form a unit for overseas service and how not to employ it on arrival.

The battalion was formed on 1 November 1941, and it was to be sent to New Guinea for service there. Just prior to the departure of the ship *Acquitania*, 104 conscripts of about 18 years of age were selected from the personnel depots and pools in the Sydney area, given one night's leave and put aboard ship next day. Another group of young men were taken direct to the ship, with no opportunity to farewell their families and relatives. The only humanitarian feature of this allocation of bodies was that married men were separated from the gatherings before selection was made. The whole incident is what members of the Western democracies believe is normal in totalitarian regimes, not in our own armed forces. While aboard ship, the soldiers received training in some of the military basics. But the 53rd's problems only began on arrival at Port Moresby. The batches of strangers could have been absorbed into the battalion and become efficient soldiers after proper individual and unit training, but that was not to be. The battalion went ashore, but all their cooking equipment was still on the ship, there was no anti-malarial clothing or medicines, and the unit was placed in the worst malarial area from which to defend the town and area. Defensive positions had to be dug endlessly, and there was a constant requirement for work parties on the wharves, roads and elsewhere, resulting in no training being done. It was only at the end of July – after the Japanese had landed – that B and C Companies went off to begin training in jungle warfare. The rest of the battalion continued with work parties. As with the 39th, platoons were first given a Bren gun on the march to Kokoda. However, the 39th had the benefits of several months' training at Darley before they went to New Guinea. As usual, the junior ranks paid in blood for the shortcomings of the staff.

During the afternoon of 16 August, Lieutenant Pentland's 14 Platoon, separated at Deniki, came back to 39th Battalion at Isurava, after making its way along Eora Creek valley. George Mowat wrote of the day: 'A good night's rest. Hot meal. Digging in. Forward company still retarding enemy. Plenty of rations. Had first wash for 10 days.'

Meanwhile, the Japanese were committing their force for the capture of Port Moresby. Major General Horii's South Seas Detachment main body began to arrive off Buna. *Ryoyo Maru* began to unload 1345 men of 144 (Kusunose) Regiment, including regimental headquarters and regimental troops, plus II Battalion, (II/144) commanded by Major Horie. Also aboard for use by the force were 303 Rabaul natives.[18] Colonel Kusunose had issued Operation Order 113 aboard *Ryoyo Maru*. Units were ordered not to wait for their horses, but go inland some two and a half miles (four km) and prepare for the advance. The II Battalion was to land on the beach at Basabua and move inland before concentrating for the move to Soputa, while the signals and other units were to place themselves to the rear of II/144, with 100 yards between units. After radio communications had been established, they could be used to keep Kusunose informed of progress before going on to Soputa. Kusunose himself would land with the first wave and when II/144 had moved two and a half miles (four km) inland, he would move to the head of the battalion. In his turn, Major Horie issued his orders, reflecting those of Kusunose, and allocating specific duties to subalterns for the landing and move inland.[19] Warrant Officer Sadahiro began a record of 'The military operation for the occupation of Port Moresby', and started with a description of the last hours at Rabaul: 'After seven months preparation and training, at last the time has arrived to rise and strike dauntlessly with an iron maul. Completing preparations for departure, we lined up in files at 09.20 [9.20 am] and bowed to the Palace, marching afterwards to the embarkation point.' On the way, the unit paid compliments to the spirits of three soldiers who had died in action, presumably in the invasion of Rabaul, and at 10 am boarded 5960-tonner *Ryoyo Maru*. Sadahiro had the high honour of carrying the standard aboard. At 4.30 pm the inspection was completed and at 6 pm the ship left harbour. Sadahiro wrote into the record a prayer to the Rabaul volcano for 'ever-lasting good luck'. 1st Lieutenant Horibe, of 6 Company in the same battalion, also embarked. There were 163 men in the company aboard the ship when she sailed from Simpson Harbour. Lieutenant Noda kept a diary in which he recorded his doubts and fears. Rather than being a death-defying samurai ready to die for the Emperor, Noda did not seem overjoyed with the situation. After boarding, he found the inside of the ship 'unspeakably hot and humid. If this goes on for another day I shall be ill'. He wrote of an air raid that did not hamper proceedings and by 4 pm all were aboard, with the force commander coming onto his ship. 'The rain came down and the wind rose, and having spent my time on deck in charge of the natives I know I shall catch a cold.'

From Port Moresby, Brigadier Potts's 21 Brigade began the advance to Kokoda, and the experienced AIF staff realised the information they had was inadequate: some information from ANGAU, one air photo and a track report that was soon found to be inaccurate. 2/14th Battalion was driven to the start of the mountain trail. The unit historian said that no one who saw them forgot the sight of the tanned, fit, laughing young men in shirts and shorts who epitomised Australian manhood as they set off into the hills to meet the Japanese.

Roy Watson was a lance corporal in the Battalion Intelligence Section. He believed the unit was well-equipped, with good morale, but woefully misinformed about enemy strength and about the terrain. The battalion had only the one map, scale 1:500,000, on which there were no contours or trig points. All maps used later were sketch maps drawn on the site. The AASC truck drivers, including Ray Royal, believed that these AIF soldiers would cope comfortably with the enemy. As they slogged along the beginnings of the trail, some of the 2/14th saw high-flying Japanese bombers, with tiny silver fighters around them, and other men heard them pass, on the way to Moresby. None knew what a drastic effect those aircrews would have on the future of 21 Brigade.

Meanwhile, in the Kokoda area, Akira Teruoka's unit had captured a local native and were taking him back to camp, but the man tried to escape, so was shot and killed. Teruoka noted the flight past of Japanese aircraft, the first such notation since his movement into the jungle. Twenty P39s and P400s took off from Moresby as the raid approached, but warning time was so short that interception was not possible; the fighters could not climb quickly enough to meet the Japanese, who bombed and flew away unscathed. This was the first raid since 5 August, and 24 bombers with 24 fighters as escort passed over the target, leaving 11 aircraft destroyed on the ground. Though there was no combat reported, Japanese records list Petty Officer 2 Nobuo Tokashige, of Tainan Kokkutai, lost in operations over Port Moresby this day.

General Kenney thought that here again was an example of the basic inability of the Japanese to use air power correctly. He believed that if they had made a second, low-level attack an hour later, they could have really wreaked havoc in the target area. However, the long-term effects of this raid were severe, regardless of whether or not the Japanese returned.

Kenney had seen fit to give an opinion on the land battle, the Kokoda campaign, to MacArthur, but did not say much about the effect on the ground campaign of this raid, possibly because his US air units suffered needless loss. Three B26s were destroyed or damaged beyond repair, two others were damaged and one was badly damaged landing at 12-Mile. Far more serious was the destruction of the transport aircraft needed to supply the forces on the Kokoda Trail. These aircraft were next to fully loaded bombers. Lieutenant General Rowell had noticed this, and the day before asked that they be dispersed, but General Whitehead's staff failed to do so before the air raid. 7-Mile airfield was controlled by a US unit, which began operations on 15 July. When Raid 78 came over, the five available transport aircraft still were lined up in the open, wingtip to wingtip. All were destroyed or damaged. Each aircraft was priceless, far more so than fighters and bombers at this stage of the campaign. Through what seems almost criminal incompetence, the available supply-dropping aircraft were left bunched together to present the Japanese with a target they could hardly miss. There was no question of surprise, as there had been 77 earlier raids in 1942 on Port Moresby. Once more, it was the frontline soldier who had to pay for the stupidity, mistakes and bloody-mindedness of those in the rear.

It is reasonable to say that because those transport aircraft were not dispersed as requested, and were destroyed, then supplies were not delivered to Myola, so Brigadier Potts was not able to deploy his battalions as a consolidated force, but had to feed them one company at a time into an adverse battle situation, with the result that several hundred young Australians died when, perhaps, they need not have done so, and the Japanese reached Ioribaiwa.

An AIF unit, 2/4th Company AASC, had arrived in New Guinea on 14 August, camped near 21 Brigade headquarters some 35 miles (56 km) from Port Moresby, and work parties from the unit arrived at 7-Mile at 7 pm on 16 August, to begin work next day sorting and packing supplies for delivery to Myola. The aircraft were destroyed, but work began: 1 million rations in case lots, to be broken into 40 stacks of 25,000 rations each.

At sea, en route to New Guinea, 1st Lieutenant Horibe, 6 Company, II/144, saw the dawn arrive, the rain and wind increase, 'and the waves started to roar', so he knew there was no need to worry about air attacks. Warrant Officer Sadahiro was a little more philosophical, remembering that friendly and enemy ships were at the bottom of the seas they were now crossing. Lieutenant Noda still was not too happy, and described the 'dreadful weather'. He was told that three officers of I Battalion (which had been fighting 39th Battalion) had been killed, and thought the battalion was becoming low in strength. Colonel Kiyomi Yazawa's 41 Regiment, destined for service in New Guinea, issued Intelligence Report No. 3 on this day. Readers were informed that on arrival in Rabaul,

the regiment would come under command of the South Seas Detachment (Nankai Shitai); already the Yokoyama Advance unit
had captured Mt Bellamy in the Owen Stanley Ranges; Allied air
strength in the Moresby area was powerful, and there were 20,000
troops of all types based there. The paragraph dealing with the
Japanese situation stated that the regiment, less one battalion, was
making preparations to go to New Guinea, that more elements of
the South Seas Detachment had left for Buna, the Kawaguchi Detachment (Major General Kiyotake Kawaguchi's 124th Regiment
Group) at Palau was preparing to advance, as was the Aoba Detachment, and that on 16 August the Japanese Navy opened the
Buna air base. The enemy was thought to be a brigade of 8 Australian Division (sic), some 4000 men commanded by the brigade
commander, and prisoners taken at Kokoda had spoken of 39 and
49 Battalions, plus the Papuan battalion. It was expected that there
would be many airfield construction, supply and medical personnel 'including American troops, who show no offensive spirit' in
the Moresby area. The report went on to say the following about
the Australians expected to be met in battle: 'Compared to English, American and Philippino [sic – Filipino] troops, the Australian troops have greater fighting spirit, and obey their officers with
willing enthusiasm. In close-range combat during the actions at
Rabaul, Kokoda and Mt Bellamy, they skilfully used the turns of
long forest roads and sniped with automatic rifles at short range of
30 to 40 metres [yards]. They were also skilful in throwing hand-
grenades from strong points. The native troops sniped from treetops at long range and then immediately ran. However, against all
this, our grenade attack is very strong and the Australian troops
cannot make an assault. Although the enemy's precautions are
careless, we must exercise vigilance.' The report then described
the terrain features, and gave a brief account of the fighting so far
in New Guinea, including the actions at Oivi and Kokoda, the capture of Captain Templeton and death of Colonel Owen.[20]

On the Kokoda Trail, the new commander of 39th Battalion,
Lieutenant Colonel Ralph Honner, checked the rifle companies
and took over from Major Alan Cameron. In their discussion,

Cameron recommended that as B Company was worn out and with low morale, and was where the Japanese attack was expected to be pressed home, it should be disbanded and split up among the other companies. Honner agreed that the survivors were physically worn, after the stress of combat, little food of poor quality, not enough sleep, and the continual rain, mud and general jungle conditions; that morale was low after losing two commanders killed. The uncompromising Cameron had a low opinion of some B Company men who had become separated during battle, and made their own way to the rear, but now were back with the company. Honner decided that disbandment was tantamount to destruction, and he wanted to reconstruct a fighting force. He put Lieutenant French in command of the company, and told them all quite clearly that their position was the most dangerous, 'the post of honour'.

In the afternoon, Lieutenant Colonel Honner went forward to the D Company position, where it was waiting in ambush some 45 minutes walk forward of Isurava. He decided that the task could be accomplished by one platoon, and after a C Company platoon arrived there, D Company moved back to the main battalion location. During the day, five more men came in from the bush, after being separated from their platoons in the withdrawals from Kokoda and Deniki. Privates Bromley and Gallagher were from 8 Platoon A Company, missing since the action at Kokoda, and brought news that five more men, with one other wounded, were waiting for help. Next day, Warrant Officer Wilkinson, with the tireless Lance Corporal Sanopa, went to find them.

During 17 August, 2/16th Battalion began its approach march up the trail, 600 strong, each man carrying a minimum of 45 to 60 pounds (20-27 kg) weight. On 18 August, B17s flew to Rabaul and Kavieng; again there were no attack missions recorded flown from Port Moresby.

2nd Lieutenant Onogawa noted that the main body of 144 Regiment was to land at Buna that night and go on to Kokoda. After disembarking, Warrant Officer Sadahiro of II/144 recorded his arrival at 5 pm, and noted the protection given by the bad weather against air attack. Like other arriving soldiers, he saw the wreck of *Ayatosan Maru*, silent warning of Allied effectiveness. The battalion began unloading at 5.30 pm, with Sadahiro in charge of 120 men moving cargo. Apprehensive of air attack, he fretted over the slowness of the work. The rest of the unit landed and set off inland, with Sadahiro going ashore in the final barge. He thought the bomb damage around the area beyond description, particularly in the coconut plantation. Each of his men was carrying a 100-pound (45 kg) load, and he knew he had to catch up with his parent company. Also ashore, 1st Lieutenant Horibe was in charge of the cargo landed from *Ryoyo Maru*, and was very conscious of the danger of air attack, despite the bad weather. As soon as the companies landed, they set off inland, but Horibe was busy until the last of the cargo was delivered at 3 am next morning. The adjutant ordered him and his men to catch up with their parent companies, and they set off towards the distant mountains. Noda was ashore by 6 pm, and set off at once for Soputa. For the first half hour of marching the breeze was refreshing and the road good, but as the platoon entered the jungle, the road deteriorated and travel became harder. He kept going through the night.

Probationary Officer Shunichiro Yano, a veterinary officer, landed with 50 horses for use in the campaign. The headquarters of Tomita Butai, the supply organisation, was established at Papa-ki, and on Buna airfield, six Zeros landed safely.[21] Major General Horii had brought to New Guinea his South Seas Detachment main body: the other two battalions of 144 Regiment with the signals, gun and ammunition elements, the balance of 55 Mountain Artillery and 47 AA Battalion, a company of 55 Cavalry Regiment as HQ guards, additional companies of the Sasebo 5SLP, other support elements, 700 Rabaul natives and 170 horses in all. To follow in two days were the second and third battalions of the Yazawa 41 Infantry Regiment, with artillery and mountain gun detachments, more Sasebo 5SLP, 175 Rabaul natives and 230 more horses. These two convoys would bring Japanese numbers to some 13,000 combat, combat support and logistics troops. The Australians in 39th and 53rd Battalions actually opposing this force had nowhere near any part of it in strength. Even with the advancing 2/14th and 2/16th Battalions, total Australian strength would have been about 1700 men.

Not all the convoys had been located by air reconnaissance, and the 'Ultra' signals intelligence information of such value later was not yet available to MacArthur's GHQ. He and his staff still insisted that the Australians outnumbered the Japanese, and that the Japanese did not intend to advance across the mountains to Port Moresby. The Bataan clique, supposedly leaders of the great fighting defence of the Philippines, had failed totally to estimate enemy strengths, capabilities and intentions. Since the war, armchair critics have compared the numbers of Japanese ashore with the numbers of total Allied troops in the Port Moresby area, and agree that the Japanese were outnumbered. What these people easily overlook is the fact that many of the troops in the Moresby area were not in combat units, but in administrative, supply and construction units, and that some infantry had to be retained for the defence of the Moresby area. The ability to supply battalions committed to the Kokoda Trail was the limiting factor, something not always understood by comfortable critics presented with a few statistics. Lieutenant General Rowell was confronted with the unyielding problem of supply along the Kokoda Trail, which dictated the size of any force he would deploy. Due to the circumstances prevailing before his arrival, four of the nine Militia battalions at Moresby were not fit for operations, because they had not been allowed to train, but had been employed as work parties. The 39th and 53rd were at the end of the line of carriers, opposing a far superior force, and the first AIF battalions could not be committed until they could be supplied. All this was obvious to Rowell and those with him, yet MacArthur's headquarters in Australia persisted in believing its own flawed assessments.

Making his own contribution to the solution of the supply problems was Lieutenant Kienzle. From 18 August to 4 September, he was fully occupied with 'avoiding desertions and keeping the carriers together'. Native morale was lowered by the sight of Australian wounded, and by the exhausting effort needed to transport each man. The number of carriers was never sufficient, but eight men had to be allocated to each stretcher case.

On 19 August, nine B17s attacked Faisi, but only five arrived at the target, bombed with no appreciable result, and flew back to Mareeba. One B17 reconnoitred Choiseul and Bougainville, and there were no other recorded attack missions. Similar missions were recorded for the next day.

After breakfast in the mountains around Kokoda, Akira Teruoka's medical platoon carried wounded to the field hospital located four kilometres (two and a half miles) 'to the rear of Kokoda', arrived at 11 am, then went further back and received more rations and forage, spending the night at the airfield before returning to the front lines. At Buna, Toshio Sato watched the landing of Horii's force, plus Japanese aircraft activity from the newly-built airfield, and deduced that the big offensive to Moresby would soon begin. Lieutenant Noda, who had begun marching once he was ashore, found that it took 12 hours to cover the 10 miles (16 km) to Soputa. A company was detached to operate with the forward troops, and his unit was taken by truck to Sambo, where they slept in the open.

Hurrying along to catch their parent companies were 1st Lieutenant Horibe and Warrant Officer Sadahiro. Horibe and his party finally arrived at the battalion at 11 pm, but were to be allowed only a short rest. Sadahiro's group, struggling along under their loads of 100-pounds weight (45-kilograms), tried to camp for the night, but were ordered to keep going. 'Scolding and shouting at confused subordinates, I again led the march,' wrote Sadahiro, and they arrived not long after Horibe. 2nd Lieutenant Shigeru Ebuchi arrived at Soputa, noting that troop morale was high. II Battalion 144 Regiment reported that all 50 horses had been landed, and were moving to Butemu (sic). Meanwhile, ahead of the new arrivals, Toshiaki Sugimoto, Takasago Volunteers, was hauling provisions and forage up to Kokoda.[22]

The ambush-standing patrol forward of the Australian 39th Battalion position on 19 August was provided by 15 Platoon. Private Hourigan came back to the platoon position to warn of approaching Japanese, went back out and was killed. When the Japanese withdrew, the section commander asked for volunteers to go out and bring in Hourigan's body, but no one was keen to do so. He went out alone and carried Hourigan in. Later, Chaplain Earl arrived with a spade, and Hourigan was buried alongside the track. The battalion now adopted a policy of placing lightly equipped patrols forward on the tracks, to remain in position for 24 hours and change at first light in the usual mist, when it was unlikely the enemy would be present due to the difficulties of night movement. The relieved patrol moved back some 200 yards and waited until 11.30 am, in case the forward patrol became engaged. After that time, the patrol next for duty stood by, already dressed and equipped, until they actually moved out to begin their own 24 hours ambush on the track.

In the Deniki area, Warrant Officer Jack Wilkinson and Sanopa had been unable to find the six missing Aussies. They spent a cold and wet night in the mountains, and were fortunate in arriving at one location just after a Japanese sentry had left. A cigarette butt was still aglow on the ground and his footfalls could be heard receding into the distance. Wilkinson spoke to local natives who told of seeing Australian boot prints and of six men travelling towards Isurava. In fact, the six men had succeeded in avoiding the Japanese and existed on vegetables from native gardens, the owners of which had gone bush to safety. When they arrived at the battalion position, they did so at the time and place where the Brigade Commander, Brigadier Selwyn Porter, was inspecting the front lines. The arrivals were greeted appropriately and the commander's staff carried the soldiers' haversacks back, something that does not happen every day in any army! After two nights' rest at Isurava, the men returned to A Company. Brigadier Porter had recognised George Mowat from prewar days, and shaken his hand. Mail also arrived for the battalion, and with it news of more troops arriving in New Guinea. A Company was camped near the river, and the soldiers were able to bathe daily. As Mowat noted, it was 'cold but good'.

On 20 August, the Japanese II/144 began marching at 2 am, with Warrant Officer Sadahiro's men still exhausted after their ordeal of the previous day. His company was the battalion's advance guard, with 1 Platoon leading. He noted that there were many stragglers, and wondered if it was due to lack of daily training or lack of physical energy, adding, 'what we need is spiritual strength'. After 18 hours marching, they camped at Sambo. 1st Lieutenant Horibe also was on this march, and noted that on arrival at Sambo it was cold and he could not sleep. Due to injuries, company strength was reduced to the commander and 159 men.

The Australian 53rd Battalion also was feeling the effects of cold and the altitude. Its HQ was established at the junction of the Alola–Isurava track. No signals equipment had arrived, and patrols were without communications. The young men of the 53rd were in a strange environment, wondering what warfare involved in the choking greenery, in which one could so easily become lost just a few paces from the track. There was some inequality in the distribution of blankets, later rectified, but all men felt the cold and the rain.

On this day, 20 August, Brigadier Arnold Potts, commander 21 Brigade, arrived at Myola, and was dismayed to see the small amount of supplies available, rather than the quantity allegedly delivered by air drops. It was obvious that he could not commit all his force, so he decided to hold 2/14th Battalion and his headquarters at Myola, and send 2/16th on to relieve the 39th Battalion. The Brigade War Diary stated that the supply situation was 'misrepresented', and the facts have never been really established. Lieutenant General Rowell refuted the official history version, that due to incompetent staff work the supplies never really left Port Moresby, and believed that the quantities recorded were dispatched but were lost during the air drops, or perhaps kicked out somewhere between Moresby and Myola. The pilots were inexperienced, and US navigational ability was a long-standing joke among the Australian forces, from which navigators were supplied to the US squadrons. In addition, the prospect of meeting Zeros in a lumbering transport may have dissuaded some pilots from going too far towards the battle area. Moreover, five transport aircraft were lost to Japanese air attack on 17 August. The inescapable result was that Potts was unable to deploy his force as he had intended.

Within the Australian rifle companies coming up the trail, there was no knowledge of the developing supply crisis, and after the initial physical strain of climbing had been endured, the typical high spirits of the young Aussies returned. The battalions did not doubt that they would push the Japanese back to Kokoda and then back to Buna. In B Company 2/14th Battalion was Ted Symonds, a very big man. As the head of the company began to cross each of the streams and creeks along the trail, someone would call out the betting odds on Symonds falling into the water. This would be taken up and passed along the line, so that by the time he arrived at the log, Symonds was psychologically prepared, and always fell in. 'He'd come out,' recalled Tommy-gunner George Woodward, 'shake himself like a puppy, and say, (mock suffering) "Jesus, you blokes are champions to have as mates".'

On 21 August, the only Allied air activity was reconnaissance sorties by B17s, none reporting combats or sightings of note, yet the Japanese had assembled another convoy and brought it to Buna. Two battalions of Colonel Yazawa's 41 Regiment landed at Basabua, and moved at once to bivouac around Popondetta. The regiment report included the travelling time between points on the Buna–Isurava road and track, also including the information that Giruwa base was under water on 21 August after heavy rain that blocked roads to vehicles, making it necessary to man-pack supplies.[23] III Battalion 41 Regiment (III/41) diary recorded the battalion movements in the month: 5th, left Dariyaon; 17th, arrived at Rabaul; 21st, arrived at Basabua. On *Yasukawa Maru* the transport commander was Colonel Yazawa, and with him was headquarters, II/41, regimental guns and military police. On the *Myoko Maru*, under Major Kobayashi, were III/41, signals, battalion guns and horses. I/41 had yet to arrive. The convoy delivered Yazawa's headquarters, two of his three battalions, regimental guns, signals, ordnance, motor transport, veterinarian, bridge-building and construction troops, more men of Sasebo 5SLP, 200 Rabaul natives, 200 horses, ammunition, food, fuel and forage. Most of the troops for the Port Moresby thrust had arrived.[24]

Further inland, and determined to get to the front as soon as possible, II/144 began marching at 7.30 am. 1st Lieutenant Horibe's company was reduced to the commander and 62 men fit enough for the fast pace under the heavy loads, and these set off in what Horibe described as 'refreshed spirits', but some began to fall out by the roadside. Only 21 arrived at the camping place at 10 pm, though another 21 came in later. Warrant Officer Sadahiro also described the day, and reasoned that excessive marching with little rest combined to cause the large number of stragglers. At Kokoda, Akira Teruoka's unit was waiting for orders. There was a rumour that Major General Horii was to visit them, and another about an increase in soldiers' pay.

The heavy rain also had made life miserable for those in the mountains. George Mowat, A Company 39th Battalion, noted it in his diary, followed by the news that he was issued with a set of new clothes, which were dirty, and needed washing in the creek. He was issued with a towel – he had been making do with a dishcloth and handkerchief. Eight two-man tents were also received. The heavy rain continued all afternoon, and the new clothes had to be dried by a fire. On 21 August, Brigadier Potts's 21 Brigade HQ arrived at Myola, and recorded the supplies available there: two days rations for the brigade, 117,000 rounds of small arms ammunition and 400 grenades; there had been no air drops for the past five days. HQ 7 Division, at Moresby, was informed of the situation. The brigade did not know the transport planes had been destroyed on 17 August at Port Moresby. Of further importance to the Australian troops was the discovery of a second lake near Myola, promptly titled 'Myola 2'.

General Kenney had flown back to Brisbane, and briefed General MacArthur about his visit to the northern areas. He had ordered the A20 attack bombers of 89th Squadron 3rd Attack Group modified to carry parachute-retarded 23-pound fragmentation bombs he had found in storage in the United States. On 22 August, 16 planes from the Tainan Kokkutai at Lae landed on Buna airfield. The water had drained away, but the surface was still unsuitable.

Meanwhile, 2nd Lieutenant Onogawa was told Major General

Horii was in the Kokoda area, and also that other members of his regiment had arrived to take staff and command positions, with 1st Lieutenant Hatanaka appointed to command No. 1 Company. Hatanaka was the third commander for 1 Company in a month. Onogawa was told also that his promotion to 1st Lieutenant was effective as of 1 August, and that soldiers' pay had been doubled. The rumour had been based on fact. Nearby, Akira Teruoka, in the medical unit, was waiting for the arrival of the main body. The weather was cloudy, and he wrote that jungle fighting was very interesting, and they were recuperating in the present temporary camp. Since soon after 10 am, he noted continuous enemy air raids and reconnaissance. However, these sorties are not recorded in Allied reports; perhaps the diary date was incorrect.[25]

Japanese II/144 again began marching on 22 August at 7.30 am, with 2 Platoon leading, and reached Papaki at 9.30 am. They set up camp to rest after the forced marches and to allow stragglers to catch up, as only 85 men were present. Warrant Officer Sadahiro saw the scene of 'desperate fighting' by I/144, prayed in silence and pledged revenge for his friend Sakamoto who had been killed there. Ahead of Sadahiro, Noda was moving to the front, and now his unit began meeting personnel of the advance force as they neared Kokoda. He was told of the death in action of Lieutenant Fukuraku and 10 soldiers with him. The company marched on, resting on a rise a few miles past Kokoda. He was told that 'the enemy are young, vigorous and brave. We have this terrain (to add to difficulties). It will be necessary for us to put forth our utmost endeavour and uphold the prestige of our Imperial Army'.

Of more immediate importance to one of Sadahiro's enemies, George Mowat, was the task of drying clothes by a fire, and he was able to enjoy the feeling of putting on clean, dry clothes, and have a set to change into if necessary. It was his first change of clothing since 29 July.

At 4.25 pm, a B17 bombed Lae and counted seven Japanese bombers on the airfield. Over Lae visibility was unlimited, but there was overcast to the west and north-west. That night, four B17s went to Rabaul, but only one arrived; the others returned with problems. After bombing the airfields, the B17 went down to strafe and two Japanese aircraft were destroyed, recorded so in Japanese documents.[26]

General Kenney had gone to Tocumwal in Victoria, and was not impressed by what he found there. A great modern base was being constructed, some 3000 miles (4800 km) from the combat zone. All the supplies so desperately needed by the flying units were collected at Tocumwal, but would not be released unless correct paperwork was delivered. The commander was quite proud of his inventory system, and his only unhappiness was caused by units requesting items, so messing up the neat statistics on stock holdings. Kenney told the inhabitants to begin packing everything for a move north to Townsville. He noticed also that while combat units were operating with officers and men lacking the appropriate rank, the rear echelon staff wore the highest ranks possible, and enjoyed quite comfortable living and working conditions. Kenney determined to change this imbalance.

The Japanese junior ranks around Kokoda on 23 August were well aware of the arrival near Buna of the battalions and other units, and knew the offensive on Port Moresby was imminent. After 5 am reveille in the battle area, Akira Teruoka's platoon carried sick and wounded back to the field hospital, where he was told that 41 Regiment was moving to Kokoda. 1st Lieutenant Onogawa noted that some of his unit (I/144) went back for rations, and he was told that the main body of the regiment had landed, and that Japanese troops were said to have landed 75 miles (120 km) east of Port Moresby. A short distance away across the jungle, 39th Battalion was holding church services on this Sunday, officiated over by an unofficial chaplain, Jack Flanagan. The service lasted an hour, hymns were sung, but all present were alert for Japanese action. None occurred.

Brigadier Arnold Potts assumed command of Maroubra Force, and sent Major Alan Cameron back as liaison officer to 7 Division, to stress the needs of the campaign. Brigade HQ had moved to Alola, where one plane load of supplies was dropped. It is on this day, 23 August, that the first reference to problems at Myola appear in the war diary of the Supply and Transport organisation at HQ New Guinea Force. Notification of 'unbalanced delivery' resulted in Major Henry being tasked to organise the Supplies and Transport end of the air delivery service. Henry would go to 7-Mile strip next day to begin this task.

Moving up to the front in easier stages after clearing the dangerous areas close to the landings and coastal supply dumps, the Japanese II/144 set off at 6 am and halted again after five hours, at Ipou. At 4 pm, 1st Lieutenant Horibe went back along the track with 11 men, collecting stragglers, and returned to the company at 10 pm, by which time strength had risen to 124. With him was Warrant Officer Sadahiro, who noted that more than 40 men were collected, and taken back to the pleasant campsite by the creek, where clean washing water was available for the first time in a long while. Lieutenant Noda had already left the location of HQ I/144, and began advancing towards the Australians. He could see the ridge top and trees in the distance where his enemies were waiting. He remarked, 'I don't know if it is because I Battalion has had so many casualties, but all ranks of commanders seem to have lost some of their offensive spirit'. He went as far forward as Deniki, then returned to his company, which was to replace a company of 15 Engineers at Kokoda. Colonel Yokoyama intended to leave a force to secure the place before he pushed on again. Noda thought that if the enemy used 'guerrilla tactics' then the Japanese should do the same and attack the Australian supply lines and base camps, but 'Captain Horita would not listen to me'. How fortunate for the Australians; they had enough problems as it was, without worrying about Japanese long-range circling movements to attack the lines of carriers and the precious supply dumps established at such cost. The ANGAU staff overseeing the carriers would have been unable to retain control of the hundreds of natives strung out along a track if the Japanese had attacked them.

Allied air activity recorded for 23 August was three B17 reconnaissances over the usual areas. At Buna airfield on 24 August, the diary of the Japanese 15 Pioneers recorded the return of 16 Zeros from Milne Bay, claiming destruction of 16 Allied planes, but no losses in combat were recorded by the RAAF at Milne Bay for this day. Fourteen B17s set off for Faisi and Rabaul, but poor weather negated the mission. One from Mareeba had to land at Horn Island after the crew could not find Port Moresby. Three attacked Faisi, and four others made reconnaissance flights to the Solomons.[27]

By midday on 24 August, the Japanese II/144 had reached a point just over one mile (two km) south of Kokoda, where they camped. Warrant Officer Sadahiro found it was the place where fighting had taken place, and 2nd Lieutenant Fukuraku and '10 brave soldiers of Takasu Tai fought fiercely'. This was probably scene of the D Company 39th Battalion fighting on the Oivi track on 8 August; at least 11 Japanese were killed in one engagement there. Overhead were Allied aircraft, searching for signs of Japanese presence. 1st Lieutenant Horibe had 48 men in his 3rd Platoon, making it the largest in the company of 131. At Deniki, the company log of Nose unit, I/144, included the notation that the regimental and detachment commanders had arrived. Colonel Kusunose and Major General Horii had come forward to the battle area. Also at Deniki was 1 Battery of the Mountain Artillery. One gun had been broken down into man-pack loads, and was carried along with 261 rounds of ammunition and 30 days rations for the battery.[28]

The newly-arrived Australian 53rd Battalion had a patrol clash. Previous patrols under Lieutenants Campbell, Hughes and Raphach had met enemy and exchanged fire, with no casualties; both sides were reconnoitring. But this time, Lieutenant McDonald and 20 soldiers set off to patrol the Deniki track. An hour along the track, they were ambushed, and the forward scout was killed. The second scout, Private Bostock, shot four Japanese who tried to get to the body of Private MacGraw. Meanwhile, McDonald had got the patrol into position, and in the shooting another six Japanese were believed hit. Then the encircling movements began. McDonald saw this, and quickly but safely moved his patrol back, then returned to the company position. Spirits were high. The patrol had inflicted damage, had stood its ground, steady under fire, and reacted to the orders of McDonald and the section commanders, who had handled the men well. In addition, Japanese grenades were seen to be fairly ineffective, with a high number of duds, and those that did explode caused no casualties, and had little effect.

At Kokoda, while the forward units were patrolling and fighting, Lieutenant Noda and his men ate a filling meal of tasty potatoes, trying to save rice. Afterwards, the Japanese platoon sat around talking of home and potato dishes they had eaten there. He was briefed on the coming operation, which was to surround and annihilate the enemy at Isurava. His company was to await the arrival of Kobayashi's III/41, which was to take over defence of Kokoda. Noda was then to follow the attacking force. At 3 am next day, his platoon became colour guard, taking over from the Shibata platoon of No. 6 Company. Horii's plan was for Major Horie's II/144 to advance along the eastern side of the valley, get around to the south of Isurava, cut off the Australians' retreat and annihilate them. The major thrust was to be along the western side, to dislodge the Australians. The commander of 2 Machinegun Company 144 Regiment, Lieutenant Sakamoto, wrote the battalion's mission as 'advance along the (eastern) side of the valley, deploy to the south of Isurava, block the Australian withdrawal, and annihilate them'.

Meanwhile, on the Australian side, one of the imponderables that effect men's destinies occurred. Wounded and sick men of the 39th Battalion, in 'shocking physical condition', were seen by 21 Brigade Headquarters, and it was decided to relieve them as soon as possible with the 2/14th Battalion. Brigadier Potts had intended to retain 2/14th at Myola, and send 2/16th forward to assist the 39th Battalion. 2/14th Battalion thus was to be the first 2nd AIF unit to engage the Japanese in the Kokoda campaign, and so in the defence of Australia. Major D. B. Fargher, from New Guinea Force HQ, arrived at Myola and confirmed Brigadier Potts's report on the severe lack of supplies. Potts placed Captain G. J. Hill in control of all personnel and supplies at Myola. It was estimated that an additional 800 carriers were needed, and 7 Division was informed.

Meanwhile, back at 7-Mile strip, Major Henry, of Supplies and

Transport, HQ NGF, had begun a survey of procedures and an analysis of the problems. He found one DC3 in operation, and it was able to make four flights before the weather closed in. In Australia, MacArthur informed General Blamey that it had been arranged for six Douglas A24s (light bombers that had been withdrawn from attack missions), one B17 and two transports to be based at Port Moresby, to enable a daily 20,000 pounds (9072 kilos) to be delivered to the forward troops. MacArthur went on to say that air supply was to be considered an emergency means rather than routine, and Rowell was to 'develop other means of supply'. GHQ still persisted in its view of events.

General Kenney returned to Brisbane from Tocumwal, and told his aide, Major Bill Benn, that he was appointed to command US 63rd Squadron, 43 Bomb Group. With Kenney's support, Benn was to show what positive results could be gained by low-level attacks in the B17, which had been designed to operate at the lower edges of the stratosphere.

As ordered, on 25 August, Noda brought his Japanese platoon to 144 Regiment HQ to assume duty as colour guard at 3 am. He may not have been at his best at such an early hour, and 'became exasperated at 2nd Lieutenant Shibata's random chattering'. At 4 am the HQ began moving forward and later stopped for breakfast at Kokoda. On this day, Toshio Watanabe, who had landed at Buna on 21 July, noted that for a month the only food had been rice, miso flour and 'shoyu', adding that everyone was feeling run-down. Coming along the trail was veterinarian Shunichiro Yano, who had landed with 50 horses, going to Kokoda.[29]

Making an early start at 2 am, II/144 began its advance, with No. 5 Company leading. Shibata's platoon had rejoined them. 6 Company commander had spoken to his men before the move out, and Warrant Officer Sadahiro saw that 'the faces of the warriors were tense'. At 2 pm, while making a detour, climbing what Sadahiro described as 'a breathtaking cliff', enemy were engaged and 5 Company lost four killed and four wounded. This action showed that 'the enemy is not to be underrated'. After the reorganisation, 6 Company became the leaders and continued the advance, cutting their way through the jungle at night, and halted at Kaere.

The Australian 39th Battalion had been in contact. Lieutenant Simonson had the forward patrol duty, and at about midday was attacked. Quickly the patrol standing by, under Lieutenant Sword, went to reinforce them, and a third platoon, led by Lieutenant D. R. Clarke, came to stand-by status. At the same time, Japanese rounds from a mountain gun began to land in the battalion HQ area, making a direct hit in the weapon pit manned by Corporals O'Donnell and Reilly; both were killed. Chaplain Earl came up and conducted burial services while bullets whistled past overhead. Meanwhile, Lieutenant Simonson had pushed the enemy back some 200 yards towards Deniki, and hoped to overrun the artillery position, but realised that it was about another 300 yards distant. He went back to the original patrol position. The mountain gun again fired, from 3.30 to 5 pm, and more Japanese infantry came along the Naro track, in the cover of long grass. An Australian listening post was 100 yards forward of the front line. The sentry, armed with a Tommy gun, waited until the leading bunch, and bunched they were, of Japanese was only a few yards away, then fired the magazine into them. Magazine empty, Japanese fallen and rolling away in front of him, he saw many more enemy running towards him through the native garden there, so took direct avoiding action. He jumped over the track and down the steep, rocky hillside to the creek far below, eventually rejoining C Company next day. The other two members of the listening post saw that they could no longer assist him, so ran back to the company, over the creek crossing that was already coming under fire.

Lieutenant Clarke's patrol, returning from a reconnaissance of their intended next position when on duty forward, met enemy at the Deniki–Naro track junction and routed them. Clarke and another killed eight Japanese in the native garden and others were killed by the patrol. At dusk they all returned to the battalion position.

53rd Battalion had also been in action on this day. Lieutenant Isaachsen led a patrol that clashed with Japanese. Firing was quite intense, Isaachsen was killed and two soldiers wounded. Despite a radio malfunction, the patrol did as battalion HQ wanted, and began to move back to Missima. Another patrol under Sergeant Meani had gone out to try to recover the body of Private MacGraw, killed the day before. The Japanese had placed the body in view, leaning against a tree, using it as bait. The patrol was only yards away when heavy fire from the ambush forced them back.

Noda, guarding the Japanese colours, arrived at Deniki after 3 pm to the sound of the guns and small arms from the patrol clashes with 39th and 53rd Battalions. The sounds 'made me think of the fury of the front line. I am anxious, as I believe that the detour of II Battalion has become known to the enemy'.[30]

Meanwhile, Australia's 2/14th Battalion, strung out by companies, was struggling forward in the mud and rain. A certain amount of humour was provided by Warrant Officer Les Tipton, the Battalion Regimental Sergeant Major (RSM), who was having a difficult time, tripping, slipping and falling. His language entertained the junior ranks. The staging areas along the track could accommodate and feed only one company at a time, so C Company and Battalion HQ were leading, with the other companies coming along at intervals. The Intelligence Section of 30 Brigade had constructed a sand-table terrain model of the region, showing the area from Myola to the coast, including that on the flanks.

Each platoon was briefed on the region as they passed along to the battle area. Roy Watson was asked by each platoon, 'Where's the Gap, Wattie?' The Diggers were still under the impression that the Gap existed, and that it could be held by 500 men. Watson believed it was due to this terrain model and the briefing for each platoon that so many men were able to rejoin after the events of the next weeks.

The 7 Australian Division issued its Operation Instruction 7 on this date. The division's responsibilities were for: the defence of Port Moresby against sea-borne attack; defence of the airfields against land or airborne attacks.[31]

Early in the morning of 25 August, from Moresby, 17 US P400s set off for Buna, but 13 turned back in bad weather. The other four attacked at 7.45 am, saw Zeros around the airfield, but were only able to leave one burning and two smoking. A second mission was quickly planned and at 11.10 am, seven P400s successfully went through the weather and again strafed Buna. Despite very poor visibility, 10 Zeros were claimed left on fire, confirmed by Japanese documents. The 15 Pioneers Medical Officer wrote, 'enemy planes machine-gunned in the pelting rain'. Three hours later, a single B17 bombed and strafed for 15 minutes.[32]

The weather interfered with other flying activity during the day. Nine B17s from Mareeba flew to attack Japanese ships in Milne Bay, but weather forced them to return to base. Crucial air delivery of supplies was confined to one flight by a DC3 from 7-Mile before weather halted operations. Four long-ranging B17s were out on their reconnaissance missions, and one found a convoy of nine ships and began to circle them. Seven B26s flew from Townsville to Moresby, prepared to attack Japanese ships in Milne Bay, and seven B17s set off at night for Rabaul and Gasmata.

On 26 August, the Japanese tried to continue with their original plans for the occupation of Port Moresby, despite the campaign that developed on Guadalcanal and neighbouring islands, and went ahead with a landing at Milne Bay. This move would have serious immediate results for those fighting on the Kokoda Trail, but even more serious repercussions for the entire Japanese effort in the South Seas. From being engaged on a sector of their choice, Kokoda, and on one of the enemy's choice, Guadalcanal, the Japanese blithely went ahead and committed forces to a third. MacArthur's command was presented with a new problem and location to be reinforced. The state of near panic created at MacArthur's GHQ called for cool heads at Moresby and Milne Bay in ignoring the ill-conceived messages of advice and exhortation that flowed in. The steady command of Major General Clowes at Milne Bay, backed by Lieutenant General Rowell at Moresby, resulted in defeat for the Japanese landing force. Rowell stated he believed MacArthur's decision to fight the Japanese in New Guinea was taken at a conference this day, and Major General Vasey, from Australia, wrote to Rowell on 28 August, informing him of the decision.

The Milne Bay actions have been well described and while they had an effect on the Kokoda operations, it is not intended to devote much space to them in this book. The Japanese had the initiative, and the important morale factor of a string of victories, plus the ability to land at almost any place they chose on the shores of the bay. The two defending infantry brigades, with their engineers and artillery, were restricted to foot-power mobility, and wisely remained at the airfields from which the vital fighter squadrons operated. General Clowes remained calm, the RAAF flew and operated as they had not done before or since, and the invaders were defeated. It is worth repeating that it was the first time a Japanese invasion force had been repulsed, and this victory was sorely needed by all those fighting the Japanese. It gave particular heart to the British in Burma, and Field Marshal Slim later referred to the boost in morale experienced there when news of the victory at Milne Bay, followed by another successful defence at Imita Ridge, was received. It also raises the question, again, of whether the Japanese command really understood the principles of warfare, and really understood the enemies they were engaging. They had occupied huge expanses of Asia and the Pacific at very little cost, but failed to recognise that after the Coral Sea, Midway, the first Guadalcanal land and naval battles, and the resistance on the Kokoda Trail, their cheap victories were a thing of the past. Trying to fight air, land and sea battles in three separate sectors, from a single headquarters (Rabaul) was a recipe for disaster.

Over Buna, fortune favoured the US fighter pilots, who were able to give the vaunted Zeros a thrashing in full view of Japanese on the ground. At 7.25 am, eight P400s attacked, caught 10 Zeros taking off, and claimed six destroyed and two damaged. Tadao Chiba saw three Zeros shot down, but also wrote that 25 of 26 planes on the airfield were destroyed on the ground; one Allied plane was seen to go down. Another Japanese diarist saw four Zeros shot down.[33]

The US pilot shot down was Lieutenant Gerald Rogers, caught by a Zero while strafing. He flew as far as possible from the combat area before ditching, got to shore, was met by friendly natives, hidden for three weeks and later picked up by an RAAF pilot and flown back to Moresby. Rogers was lucky, as many whites had been handed to the Japanese or killed by natives in the Buna–Gona area. In other air attacks, bombers attacked ships in Milne Bay, the aircraft forced to descend through cloud into the mountainous area, and fly under the clouds at the ships. Accurate attacks were almost impossible.

Lieutenant Noda was not enjoying his stint as commander of the colour guard. 'What with anxiety over the fighting, and the rain and cold, I didn't sleep a wink all night. The lull of the opposing guns is broken by the sound of grenade throwers and the powerful chatter of machineguns.' Being close to regimental HQ, Noda was informed of progress. II/144 reported the going very difficult, but were pushing on to their objective. 144 Regiment HQ had not moved from its location.

During the afternoon, after five weeks facing the enemy alone, the ragged and weary 39th Battalion welcomed the first reinforcements. Captain Gerry Dickenson's C Company 2/14th Battalion arrived to replace C Company 39th Battalion, taking over the track and area east of it. Captain Claude Nye's B Company 2/14th was still advancing and reached Alola in the evening. Behind, Captain Rod Cameron's D Company reached Eora Creek and Captain Buckler's A Company arrived at Templeton's Crossing. Horii's attack was about to be launched, and together Militia and AIF were to engage in actions as ferocious as any in the First World War, and in which these Aussies would equal the high standards of bravery, fighting ability and mateship set by the original Anzacs on Gallipoli. The significant difference was that in 1942 the Australians were fighting in defence of Australia.

Brigadier Potts signalled HQ 7 Australian Division to inform them that the 39th was to be relieved, and added that the soldiers were weak due to the continuous exertions, lack of warm clothing, blankets and food, and were wet every night. He also reported that the 53rd Battalion was below the standard required for action and requested 2/27th Battalion move up to constitute his only reserve. Later, while under shell fire, Potts repeated this request for 2/27th Battalion. In response, Major General Allen informed Potts of the

Milne Bay landings, and that 2/27th would be held at Moresby until the situation became clear, adding that 39th Battalion be sent to Moresby as fast as possible. Potts had been ordered to take Kokoda, but now was informed that his reserve battalion would not be available, though he considered the 39th in need of replacement and the 53rd to be below standard. He was forced to commit his force piecemeal in a defensive battle in which the enemy had the initiative. Potts's position was probably under fire from the Japanese No. 1 Battery, which expended 10 rounds on this day.[34]

21 Brigade War Diary included reference to the lack of definite information brought in by patrols, and laid down two principles: patrols must fight for information; if definite answers are required from patrols, definite questions must be asked of them. Air supply operations at Port Moresby had been moved to Kila Kila airfield, also known as 3-Mile strip, and the supply and service corps soldiers worked all night to transfer the necessary items and supplies there, but next day the impartial weather allowed only two flights into the mountains. During the night, the Japanese attacked the 39th Battalion forward patrol position, with close combat taking place in the dark. Wounds were inflicted from close-range firing and bayonet, injuring Lieutenant Don Simonson and two soldiers. A bullet struck a grenade on Simonson's belt, fractured the casing and ignited the explosive; luckily there was no explosion. As far as Simonson was concerned, the wound was 'a bloody nuisance for sure'. The wounded were able to get back to the battalion, despite fears that the Japanese were on the track, waiting in the pitch darkness. Lieutenant Clarke's aggressive action cleared the garden, and Simonson's platoon remained with command going to Lieutenant Sword, D Company, whose platoon was in position there also. A Japanese diary captured later recorded that 'while slowly advancing in the jungle in the dark night, suddenly came across the enemy. Killed in action was Hikari, while wounded were Corporal Takahashi and Rakusaburo'.[35]

The Japanese maintained a steady fire from their machineguns throughout the night, and the distinctive sound of the slow rate of fire of the 'woodpecker' machinegun impressed itself on the memories of the AIF soldiers. Nye's B Company 2/14th had taken over some 53rd Battalion positions, and spent the night listening to the gunfire.

During the night, the headquarters of Horii's formation and various other support elements all gathered in the location of 144 Regiment HQ. Long-suffering Lieutenant Noda, worried about enemy guerrilla attacks, asked if he 'was expected to guard all this congregation', but was informed he only had to worry about the colours. At 7.15 am on 27 August, 14 P400s escorted seven B26s to attack Buna at 1500 feet. Cloud base was at 4000 feet, and visibility was 10 miles (16 km). Light inaccurate anti-aircraft fire came up, but 18 Zeros attacked; US pilots claimed five destroyed; one P400 was damaged beyond repair, but made it back to base. Sato, the Japanese linguist, noted that four fighters were shot down. Tadao Chiba, of 15 Pioneers, wrote that the airfield was 'completely demolished'. US B26s attacked ships at Milne Bay, despite Zero interceptions, and B17s searched for the convoy sighted earlier, but could not locate it. Three others had had flown the usual distant reconnaissance missions. At the Japanese-held Buna airfield, natives brought in a white man and handed him to 15 Pioneer Unit. This was Lieutenant A. A. Smith, PIB.[36]

At first light on 27 August, at Isurava the Japanese had occupied the garden area and high ground north of the creek behind which 39th Battalion was positioned. Australia's forward patrol in position, two platoons under Lieutenant Sword, was isolated, but in good heart. It was impossible to cross the creek in either direction. Lieutenant Colonel Honner decided to order Sword to return by Eora Valley, but the Japanese found the telephone cable and cut it before he could pass on the instructions. Lieutenant Sword decided to go back to the next delaying position, some 200 yards, and contact HQ from there, but the line had been cut. Private Albert Grace was sent to report to the battalion, but was never seen again. A fever patient, Private Woods, was given permission to make his way back, but shortly after he left there was gunfire, and he came quickly back to the platoons. The Japanese were waiting. Sword's force was cut off, and it was decided to go around the Japanese, back to Isurava, by going up the ridge.

Meanwhile, Lieutenant Pentland's platoon from C Company was ordered to go to the top of Naro Ridge, a three-hour climb, to prevent enemy movement along that track. 39th Battalion, already weak, now had three platoons separated. The fittest of C Company went with Lieutenant Pentland and the remainder formed a platoon under Sergeant Kerslake in the reserve platoon position in E Company. There was no force of any size available to fill the empty position allocated to Sword's platoon. However, Lieutenant Colonel Honner was told to send a platoon from C Company 2/14th to replace Pentland's, so Lieutenant Davis's platoon moved off after Pentland. The Japanese were on the far side of the creek and fighting began. Davis was wounded and began to make his way back alone, but was never seen again. Sergeant Buchecker had a shattered thigh and Private J. G. Smith was killed. Reacting at once, Chaplain Earl and Captain Shera, the RMO, took a stretcher out alone, and arrived at the platoon. They carried Buchecker back while the platoon fought a rearguard action against the swarming Japanese. Later, Captain Nye and his B Company 2/14th arrived, with orders as for those given to Lieutenant Pentland. After discussing the local situation with Lieutenant Colonel Honner, Captain Nye decided to start to the west from south of the Isurava position, and catch up with Pentland.

From the Japanese point of view, Headquarters and 4 Company of II/144 engaged the Australians. No. 4 Company lost its commander, 1st Lieutenant Washiye, and two others killed, with another missing, and Warrant Officer Sadahiro prayed for his safe return. Washiye took a bullet through the right side of his chest. Of this action, Sakamoto of 2 MG Company wrote that the battalion HQ party detoured and clashed with the Australians, losing the Adjutant, 1st Lieutenant Yamauchi, Washiye and Sergeant Nishikada. Sakamoto was saddened by Nishikada's death, as they had served together in 6 Company. The Okamoto platoon of Sakamoto's company lost two killed and five wounded. When the Australians were seen to be retreating, the Japanese changed direction and moved east. In the Japanese rear, the headquarters elements, with the colour guard, began moving forward at 8 am, taking position on a height north-east of Isurava, where they remained, listening to the battle and receiving reports. 1 Battery fired 10 precious rounds, carried from Buna.

Meanwhile, Lieutenant Colonel Ward's 53rd Battalion had a disastrous day. Brigadier Potts ordered the 53rd to recapture Missima, some two miles (3.2 km) north-east of Alola, but the attack failed due to the rough terrain, heavy machinegun fire from positions that could not be located, and the poor physical condition of the soldiers, who also lacked offensive spirit. Lieutenant McDonald was sent out to relieve the patrol that had fallen back on Missima after the death of Lieutenant Isaachsen. When he arrived there, he could find no sign of the patrol or the wireless station and the spot was deserted. However, Japanese were seen in the area. One, setting up a mortar, was killed, but it became obvious that many more were close by. Battalion HQ and the companies came under mortar fire, and fears arose for the safety of a 20-man patrol led by Lieutenant Parsons, forward of the 39th Battalion lines. Lieutenant Colonel Ward ordered A Company and D Company (minus a platoon) to move through B Company, attack and recapture Missima. While the force was moving out of the position, aggressive Japanese went in behind the departing A Company, along the track and into B Company, bouncing B Company out of its positions into the jungle. The Japanese also were among the other positions, and had set an ambush on a creek. While Lieutenant Colonel Ward was moving his command group to the new HQ location, at about 3.30 pm he, Lieutenant Logan and Private Foster were killed in this ambush. Meanwhile, D Company 53rd Battalion was being held up by heavy fire and by the very difficult country. A Company was ordered to attack and secure a position into which D Company was to withdraw. Confusion arose as to the exact locations of the Japanese. As the day ended, the battalion was in an unhappy situation, with the CO, Adjutant, CSM B Company, Warrant Officer 2 Spalding, Corporals Hayes and Hayward killed, and one soldier wounded. The Japanese had come around by the waterfall at Abuari, and were pressing on for the creek crossing and for Alola.

In the afternoon, news was received at HQ 21 Brigade of the deaths of Lieutenant Colonel Ward and Lieutenant Logan. Brigadier Potts ordered Major Hawkins, the second-in-command, to hold the area around Abuari until the arrival of 2/16th Battalion. 21 Brigade War Diary noted that by 7 pm, 70 men from 53rd Battalion were still missing. At about 4 pm, the Isurava position of 39th Battalion was subjected to heavy machinegun and mortar fire, indicating a Japanese attack was coming. When it did, the weight fell on the two forward left companies, Merritt's E and French's B. As the attack developed, Lieutenant Colonel Honner and Captain Merritt were washing and shaving in the creek to the rear of the position. Merritt recalled that Honner grinned and politely asked him to finish his shave and go to his company, as the Japanese 'have just broken through your perimeter'. In Merritt's opinion, Honner was the coolest man he ever met.[37] Behind B Company's positions were more prepared positions in a slightly better location, and after firing, the platoons fell back and held there, shooting down the Japanese who came on across the open ground. However, in E Company the Japanese got through and were able to turn and attack some platoon positions from the rear, forcing Dalby's out of their pits. More Japanese came through the gap, threatening the right-hand platoon. Then Sergeant Kerslake's platoon put in a counter-attack and closed the gap, while from A Company Sergeant Murray's platoon also came up and pushed out the Japanese in the left platoon position, allowing Dalby's platoon to make contact again. But Japanese pressure increased on B Company, on the left, and came in on Dickenson's C Company 2/14th on the right. Then Lieutenant Colonel Honner called back Captain Nye's B Company 2/14th, which had only covered a short distance. B Company informed Honner that it would have to give ground, to which Honner replied that B Company had to hold, as only battalion HQ was behind it. By now it was beginning to get dark. B Company 2/14th rapidly turned around to assist, and Honner was impressed by the confidence and conduct of the 2/14th men as they passed. He also noted the quiet efficiency of the unit, as two mortar platoon men stood on either side of the track, calmly lifting mortar bombs from the haversacks of the passing riflemen, who did not need to slow or to stop walking. The 2/14th brought up the 39th Battalion three-inch mortar that had been air-dropped at Myola. John Dawes, John Sands and Hedley Norman were 39th Battalion Mortar Platoon soldiers who volunteered to accompany 2/14th across the mountains. They were called back to man the mortar, commanded by Lieutenant Bevan French, formerly the Mortar Platoon commander. The Japanese by now were sure that the Australians had no heavy support weapons, so were confidently moving about outside small arms range. In the distance, the small mortar team could see a group of Japanese, and smoke from the fire where they were cremating dead. Lieutenant French gave the necessary orders and the first bomb was fired – scoring a direct hit; three more followed, and even in the mortar position, angry Japanese could be heard screaming. As darkness fell, Captain Rod Cameron's D Company 2/14th arrived, and despite the night and rain, took over from E Company 39th Battalion and held temporary positions to prevent infiltration between B and C Companies.

During the night, the usual tricks of calling out and making noise were used by the Japanese, with little success. However, one was able to creep forward and bayonet a Digger of C Company 2/14th in the arm. The Australian never saw his attacker. At 7 pm, the Japanese III/144 began moving forward to launch a night attack along the main pass, but 'due to a steep ravine and heavy enemy fire, two were killed and the battalion advanced along the ridge', wrote Lieutenant Noda at the headquarters. The 2/14th Battalion had arrived in the proverbial nick of time, as Horii's battalions moved forward onto the weakened 39th Battalion. But for the arrival of the AIF rifle companies, the 39th would have been overwhelmed in place, or probably shattered while trying to withdraw. On the other hand, without the 39th holding a firm position on which the arriving 2/14th could consolidate, the advancing Japanese battalions could have retained the initiative and dealt with each company in turn. 21 Brigade had been advancing up the trail with the mission of throwing the Japanese back, retaking Kokoda and going on to Buna. Within a very short time after engaging the

Japanese, 2/14th Battalion realised their assigned mission had little to do with reality, and they would be fighting hard, defensive actions to hold the Japanese from Port Moresby. Some of the 2/14th realised this within minutes of making contact with the enemy. Held back at Myola by lack of supplies to sustain them further forward, 2/16th Battalion sent forward A, B and D Companies to Eora Creek during the day. The track had become 'a treacherous mass of moving mud with protruding roots that reached out hidden hands to bring the laden troops heavily to the ground', wrote the battalion historian. Captain G. McGee and A Company reached Eora Creek before night, but B Company, commanded by Captain Frank Sublet, was forced to continue in the dark, under a heavy downpour, each man feeling his way through the night. After 15 hours on the track, the last section of Sublet's company came into Eora Creek. There they dined on cold bully beef and biscuits, tried to find shelter in the dark, dripping trees, and get some sleep. No fires could be lit, as it was not known if Japanese were near or not.

Back at Kila Kila strip, on 27 August the Army Service Corps soldiers had three planes available and the pilots managed a total of four flights before the weather prevented more. For the soldiers themselves, there was no food or accommodation provided at Kila, and this was the third day of operation there. On Friday 28 August, there were the daily B17 reconnaissance sorties from Port Moresby, to Buka–Kieta–Milne Bay, the Trobriands–Buna, and to Rabaul. A special resupply sortie was flown by a B17 taking urgently needed .50-calibre ammunition to Milne Bay – the RAAF Kittyhawks were firing thousands of rounds during attacks on the invasion force. Six B26s attacked targets in Milne Bay and eight B17s attacked Rabaul. Only four supply flights had been possible from Kila Kila.

On 28 August, the Japanese 15 Pioneer Unit, at Buna airfield, decapitated a captured white officer: Lieutenant A. A. Smith. Another member of the unit noted that natives had brought in a 'white 2nd Lieutenant' and added, 'Natives have shown goodwill and respect for the Japanese Army. This feeling must be kept up'. Owing to destruction of the aircraft at Buna, it was decided to fly out the pilots, and Tadao Chiba noted that the transport planes were busy carrying luggage out.[38] At Horii's headquarters, there were matters for concern, which led to 'Provisional Order No. 1'. Stragglers were known to be throwing away ammunition in their move forward, as well as eating more than the daily ration of polished rice, and had consumed biscuits and other preserved food. It was necessary for all in positions of authority to keep check on this situation, as resupply was extremely difficult. In addition, food and fodder for handlers and horses going to the rear was to be only the barest minimum, so that as much as possible remained at the front. The climate and weather made it necessary for the Japanese headquarters to issue another order on this day. Continual rain had penetrated rice and fodder, starting putrefaction in the bags and bundles. The following measures were to be observed: rain covers were to be placed on all such items; wet rice was not to be carried with dry; at halts, wet rice was to be spread out to dry; wet rice was to be cooked and eaten first; wet rice was to be roasted and made into hard rice balls; Takasago unit volunteers were to be given about the same ration as soldiers, but if possible be given less; natives were to be given one-third a soldier's ration. Because of Allied air activity, the instruction continued, all units were to observe precautions when cooking, with unit commanders to issue orders as the situation demanded, while exercising control and supervision. Rice was to be washed in the afternoon, if possible, during rest periods, and boiled at dusk or early morning, to be completed by 5.30 pm with all traces of the fire removed or obliterated, but definitely no cooking to be done in daytime.[39]

Japanese No. 5 Company II/144 continued as advance force for the battalion, moving off at 4 am. At 11 am, signs of Australian positions were seen, so the battalion began to swing around to the south, to continue the outflanking move. Behind them, Horii's force of infantry and engineers, with artillery and heavy machine-gun support, was moving forward to wipe out any opposition and get through to Port Moresby. Mountain gun shells, mortar bombs and machinegun fire lashed the Australian positions, where the

Diggers strongly regretted their lack of an important infantry weapon – an entrenching tool. Using helmets, bayonets, clasp knives or whatever was available, they tried to gouge out holes for protection. The first assaults, by the Japanese 41 Regiment, came out of the trees against the 2/14th's C Company, then D and B Companies, and the Diggers were surprised at the size and physical development of the Japanese. Some were later measured and found to be six feet three inches (190 cm) tall. However, big as they were, they fell when hit by the controlled fire of the infantry sections. Successive attacks went in on different places around the perimeter, as the Japanese tried to find a weak spot. Their casualties were heavy, but inevitably the Aussie defenders were losing men killed and wounded. The Japanese tried coming in through smoke, from pyrotechnic candles, but this also failed. Nye's B Company 2/14th was in an area called 'the canefield', and fierce successive attacks went in on Lieutenant George Moore's 11 Platoon. In one attack, a bugler on the Japanese side sounded the charge, and it seemed also sounded retreat, but a rifle grenade fired at the noise must have been effective, as the bugle was not used again. The platoon joked that Bluey Simpson had lobbed the grenade right into the horn of the bugle. Almost every Japanese in this charge was killed, but Moore also was killed and others wounded. Lieutenant 'Mokka' Treacy, second-in-command B Company, came up and assumed command of 11 Platoon. Later, Lieutenant Butch Bisset's 10 Platoon relieved 11 Platoon, but 11 seemed to have a magnetic quality, and heavy fire fell on their new position, wounding four more men. In the D Company position, 17 and 18 Platoons had some field of view across a creek, and shot down Japanese who appeared on the far side. 16 Platoon was in dense jungle, and the Japanese managed to advance through this, in a mist that formed, and split the platoon sections apart, though they could not seize the area. A counter-attack by 8 Platoon A Company then went in and cleared out the Japanese.

At midday, Lieutenant Colonel Key, 2/14th Battalion, arrived at Isurava, and Lieutenant Colonel Honner relinquished command to him. The 39th was to move back to Port Moresby. With almost all of 2/14th in position, there were about four times as many men in position as there had been the previous day. Honner believed that the Japanese attack the previous day showed they still greatly outnumbered the Australians, and intended to launch more assaults. Honner told Key of his belief, and said he was not going to leave the 2/14th alone. Together, the battalion commanders convinced Brigadier Potts that the 39th should stay. The 2/14th took over active forward locations and the tired 39th, rightly enough, occupied the quieter rear positions. Lieutenant Colonel Key had a reserve force of his own A and HQ Companies, plus E Company 39th Battalion. The 2/14th was attacked heavily, and the Japanese broke through the position's northern sector, threatening the main track through the two battalions. The reserve was committed and counter-attacked, restoring the situation. By night, 2/14th estimated that 350 Japanese had been killed or wounded.

Guarding the Japanese colours, Lieutenant Noda heard reports from attacking units, and formed an opinion that although the Australians were being outflanked, 'his resistance is strong and our casualties great. The outcome of the battle is difficult to foresee. Regimental HQ has not moved its position'. Among those killed was 1st Lieutenant Kitamura, OC 3 MG Company, of III/144.

The 2/14th Battalion Intelligence Section was constantly active, going up to the rifle companies and platoons, collecting information and returning to battalion headquarters, where the 'Battle Map' was continually brought up to date. Lieutenant Stan Bisset was tireless. Meanwhile, off to the left flank, the 39th Battalion platoons led by Lieutenants Pentland and Sword had met and continued their detour around the Japanese. At dusk, they sighted what they thought was the main track, but did not know where along it they had arrived, so settled in for the night. All were hungry.

During the day, 40 of the missing 53rd Battalion men had made their way back to friendly lines. They had 'gone bush' after the sudden Japanese attack the day before. The 21 Brigade Quartermaster report stated that the work done by the natives 'cannot be too highly praised'. But the report went on to say that the carriers were overworked, so sickness, desertion and jettisoning of loads 'increased to alarming proportions'. Desertions from the carrier parties were estimated at 30 per cent, but it was pointed out that few deserted because of proximity to the fighting. Myola received 14 plane loads of supplies, but they then had to be carried forward to the fighting units. An indication of problems with the carriers is that of 32 boxes of ammunition sent forward from Myola, only eight arrived at Templeton's Crossing.[40]

Two more transport aircraft had been allocated to the air-dropping operation, and had arrived without notice. The Supply and Transport staff pointed out that this was not the best way to accomplish an increase in delivered supplies. An aircraft required men, at least one truck, and prepared supplies so it could be loaded and despatched quickly. The situation had been met by improvisation, but the staff needed warning of the number of aircraft that would be available next day.

Coming up to the battle area was the Australian 2/16th Battalion, but it was strung out along the track. A Company had left Eora Creek at 8 am, and arrived at Alola at 11.30 am. Standing by the track was Brigadier Potts, with Lieutenant Colonel Caro, the battalion CO. Firing could be heard ahead, as A Company had a meal of the usual biscuits and bully beef. Captain McGee and his men saw that Alola was a hilltop village; two miles (3.2 km) north-north-west was Isurava; two miles north-north-east was Missima; between them was a valley and the fast-flowing Eora Creek. The valley between was thick jungle, and it was obvious problems of command and control would arise if operations were conducted down there. From the viewpoint standing at Alola, it was soon evident that the Japanese were holding 2/14th at Isurava, and also were near Abuari village, astride the track to Missima, on the brigade's right flank. 2/16th had to get into position quickly to counter this threat from the right. Originally it had been intended for 2/16th to take Missima and then advance on Kokoda along that ridge. Coming along an hour behind A Company was B Company, and further back was the rest of the Australian battalion, moving up from the night halt at Templeton's Crossing. Lieutenant Colonel Caro sent A Company to occupy Abuari. This journey involved travelling along a dangerous track down to Eora Creek, and a hazardous crossing of the rushing waters over a simple bridge of two saplings laid across a rock in the centre of the river. Anyone who fell would be swept away into rapids that cascaded and swirled among large boulders; certain death. It was the only crossing. On the far side, the track passed along cliffs, but the going was eased somewhat by native scaffoldings, through flat garden areas and under a waterfall. All this was described as 'The scenery was lovely. The terrain was frightening'.

After reaching the waterfall, Lieutenant John Blythe and 7 Platoon were sent forward to clear Abuari and remain the night at the track junction. B Company had arrived as A Company left. Alola itself had to be secured, and Lieutenant Colonel Caro ordered the B Company commander to position the newly-arrived platoons to defend the track, bridge and village from flanking attacks. C, D and HQ Companies were at Templeton's Crossing, intending to move forward to Alola next day.

In distant Rabaul, the Japanese 17th Army produced its Intelligence Record No. 13. In the paragraphs dealing with eastern New Guinea, it said that Kobayashi's battalion, (III/41), was to leave Samboga next day, advance to Oivi, and be responsible for transportation of supplies to Kokoda; ships had returned safely from Buna to Rabaul for the fifth time. Other sections reported on the events at Milne Bay and Guadalcanal. On 29 August, the Japanese had enough force in the battle area at Isurava to press the Australians on both left and right flanks. The attacks came in to close range and casualties on this day were heavy on both sides. Australian and Japanese officers and NCOs, by the nature of their tasks in infantry combat, were killed and wounded in substantial numbers. Taro Yamamoto, who landed with the battalion gun platoon of III/144, later said that a Japanese rifle company and the battalion machinegun company were almost wiped out, and 10 of the 70 men in his platoon were killed in this action. At dawn on 29 August, fire from mountain guns, mortars and machineguns fell on the Australian areas. Then ground assaults began, with pressure maintained on all company positions of 2/14th. In the canefield, attack after attack went in on Bisset's 10 Platoon. Later, some 250 Japanese dead were counted by a patrol from 2/16th Battalion, and also from a later combined force called 'Chaforce', which swept in front of this vital position. Weeks later, hundreds of Japanese graves were seen here. 10 Platoon lost five killed and 11 wounded.

Lieutenant Noda, with the Japanese colours, was told that the III Battalion commander, Kuwata, personally had taken command of his (Noda's) company and the unit was 'fighting with energy. 2nd Lieutenant Tsutsui and Warrant Officer Matsuyama have been killed. Casualties are heavy. Battalion HQ has not changed its position'. Tsutsui was a platoon commander in 8 Company. Also killed was Captain Kamiya, OC 7 Company, and 1st Lieutenant Hatanaka, OC 1 Company. Lieutenant Hirano was promoted 1st Lieutenant and given command of 1 Company, as the fourth commander in five weeks. That morning, Hirano and Hatanaka had shared a cup of sake. 'How cruel and miserable this life is,' wrote Hirano after the action.

Earlier, at dawn on 29 August, the whole of A Company 2/16th concentrated on Abuari. Corporal Joe Prior took a patrol from 8 Platoon to check a steep spur that overlooked the village, and became the first of 2/16th to engage the Japanese. Creeping forward, they saw a lone Japanese chopping wood near a native hut. He left hurriedly amid a volley of sub-machinegun rounds, followed by two others. 7 Platoon was sent to support the patrol, and soon after, the advancing force was fired on by machineguns in Japanese defensive positions on both flanks. Blythe's platoon had encountered at least one enemy company; the volume of fire was heavy. 9 Platoon, moving on the left, killed a lone sentry, but in return another great volley was fired at them, and the fire was sustained. 9 Platoon attacked, killing an unknown but significant number of Japanese, and captured two light machineguns. NCO casualties were heavy: one sergeant and two corporals killed. Two soldiers were also killed, and Lieutenant Blythe and a Digger wounded.

The Japanese II/144 began to move forward against the Australians, contact was made, and the machinegun unit with headquarters was engaged. 2nd Lieutenant Shigeru Ebuchi noted that the machinegun company commander was wounded in the back, and 2nd Lieutenant Yamanaka was in a serious condition, plus 'our casualties were rather heavy'; 6 Company went to assist. Captain Frank Sublet's two-company force from 2/16th Battalion at Abuari noted the presence of at least two heavy machineguns with the Japanese.[41] It was Warrant Officer Sadahiro's initiation to combat. 'The enemy counter-attacked several times while retreating. I stood under the shower of bullets and shrapnel for the first time and experienced the feeling of danger.' The platoon commander of 1 Platoon (Lieutenant Yamamoto) and four men were killed, with 13 wounded. Sadahiro went on, 'although it is a common experience on the battlefield, I was indignant to see my comrades and subordinates with whom I had chatted together until this morning, falling under fire. The fire was so intense that collection of our dead and wounded could not be immediately accomplished'. In fact, the dead were not collected for two days.

2/16th casualties at Abuari were seven killed and 23 wounded, for an estimated 40 Japanese casualties. Of this action, 1st Lieutenant Horibe simply wrote that his unit of II/144 attacked the Australians from the left, losing four killed and 11 wounded on a hill east of Isurava. Another diarist wrote that, 'in endeavouring to cross the river in face of the enemy at night, Sergeant Nishigawa and a few others were wounded. 2nd Lieutenant Yamamaka was seriously wounded and many others were killed'.[42] Despite Japanese reference to themselves attacking, Captain Frank Sublet, commanding the Australian force, did not know of any such definite action, and believed the Japanese only defended themselves. At no time did he feel threatened by Japanese moves, and later II/144 reported that it had been attacked by 1000 Australians – Sublet had less than 200 men. While the fighting was raging, at 9 am B Company 2/16th arrived in the area of the waterfall below, but continued climbing and established itself near Abuari. Both companies were out of communication with 2/16th HQ at Alola. 11 Platoon 2/16th, under Lieutenant Jack Gerke, had earlier taken up a position on the track. They discovered the bodies of 15 Australians of 53rd Battalion in the scrub. Investigation showed they had been killed by a Japanese machinegun post at 20 yards range. The Japanese had moved the bodies out of sight to retain the innocent appearance of their killing field. At about 11 am, 2/16th established communications with the Abuari force, and Captain Sublet was placed in command of the operations around the village. Sublet informed Lieutenant Colonel Caro that he was taking casualties, and could not commit more troops to the action without leaving flanks and rear open. All Caro could do was promise to send HQ Company to Sublet, but warned that the men would be tired, and anyway could not be expected until late afternoon. By this time, it was obvious that there was little to be gained by pressing frontal attacks on the Japanese positions. More stood to be achieved by sending a flanking force to attack downhill into the Japanese, in conjunction with another flank and a frontal assault. But this could not be mounted until next day, and HQ Company was needed to be a reserve, and to hold the tracks below the waterfall and to Missima. This plan was approved by Lieutenant Colonel Caro and Brigadier Potts.

Captain C. J. King's D Company 53rd was allocated to attack the Japanese left flank next day. However, coordination was difficult. Once the 53rd company left Alola, there was no communication with it, so it was decided that the 2/16th companies would be in position by 10 am, and attack as soon as they heard the 53rd go into action. A guide from 2/16th was to take the 53rd company into position. Brigadier Potts realised the situation was bad, and considered the following courses of action: first, deal with the threat on the right flank; second, hold on the right, while putting in a solid attack around the ridge to the left of 2/14th, to take the enemy in their flank and rear; third, withdraw 2/14th and 39th Battalions. He believed the pressure on the right [on Sublet and McGee, 2/16th] to be a diversion, and the main threat was posed to his front. However, the Japanese pushed 2/14th off the high ground for the fourth time, then encircled 2/14th on the left and were on the high ground between the rest house and Brigade Headquarters. 39th Battalion reported that the ammunition party had been ambushed 100 yards north of the rest house at Alola, and a message in the 21 Brigade War Diary reflected an order that the 53rd Battalion escort for the ammunition party be placed under open arrest. Brigadier Potts obviously had reached the end of his patience with the 53rd. Continuous and heavy Japanese pressure fell on 2/14th Battalion. In Nye's B Company, 10 Platoon was now holding the canefield position.

George Woodward, Tommy-gunner, was on the right of the platoon, sharing a position with Lindsay Elphinstone, the stretcher-bearer. During the night the constant Japanese machinegun fire had shattered nearby tree trunks, scattering pieces of bark and moss, which glowed with phosphorescence, startling George until he became used to it. Elphinstone, a Tasmanian farmer, put things into some sort of perspective by saying that, 'It's got to get better; it can't get any worse!' As Japanese pressure began at first light, George could see them flitting across a native track that ran past his position, so he called to Lenny Meade, the Bren gunner, who came up and together they began to put fire along the track and its sides, hitting Japanese who were trying to get onto higher ground, where 12 Platoon was located. The Japanese turned on this source of fire, and George Woodward recalled that 'the first Jap I actually saw (clearly) was an officer. He came charging down this track and Lenny Meade gave him a full Bren mag, almost cut him in half'. The officer fell very close to them, and they saw that he had binoculars slung across his chest, and his sword was upright, stuck into the ground as he fell. Quickly, George went over the log they were using for cover, grabbed the sword, and returned. It was too heavy, and two days later he threw it away. They were engrossed in their own little world, and did not know what the rest of the section was doing, let alone the platoon, company or battalion. Attack after attack came onto 10 Platoon through the sugarcane, the Japanese charging in to only a few yards before falling. In George Woodward's words, the defensive small arms fire would 'chop 'em up. The Thompson makes such a mess of a bloke when [the .45 calibre bullets] hit him'. Despite its many possible causes of stoppages, he preferred it to the lighter Owen gun. 10 Platoon held through the day, but by late afternoon, the tall sugarcane had been levelled, as though it had been mown. Piled through it were dead, dying and wounded Japanese.

Dickenson's C Company, on the right of the track, was heavily attacked by repeated assaults. Lieutenant W. P. Cox, from A Company, brought up his platoon to assist, but he was killed and the platoon suffered more casualties. Accurate and sustained Bren gun fire from Corporal L. A. Bear held the Japanese and at least 15 were killed by him. Bear took command of 9 Platoon, though wounded twice, and as soon as the attack wavered, Bear volunteered to go out with another platoon after them in a counter-attack. He pressed on until weak from loss of blood. (Bear was awarded the Military Medal (MM), and as a sergeant in 1943, he won the Distinguished Conduct Medal (DCM) and was later commissioned, topping his Officer Cadet Training Unit course.)

Charging in elsewhere in C Company, the Japanese got into the positions held by Lieutenants W. G. Boddington and J. G. Clements, killing Boddington and four others, wounding more, but two private soldiers rose to the occasion. A. J. 'Snowy' Neilson and L. J. Bowen, a Bren gun team, held their part of Clements's position, allowing the rest to reorganise and counter-attack to restore the position. Alone, the team broke up a Japanese attack that began before the platoon counter-attack came in, and Sergeant R. N. Thompson brought up a group from Headquarters Company to help. Neilson received the Military Medal, while Bowen was Mentioned In Dispatches (MID).

The Japanese break-in area threatened the whole battalion position, and at about noon a counter-attack was made. Lieutenant Clements took his platoon, the remains of Cox's, and Thompson's party in to throw back the Japanese. Private Bruce Kingsbury became the centre-point of the attack, using his Bren from the hip, clearing Japanese from position after position, regardless of 'terrific machinegun fire' and created a path for the rest of the attack force. Kingsbury had broken through the enemy when a lone Japanese was seen on a large boulder, aiming his rifle; he fired before anyone could react and killed Kingsbury, then escaped into the shrubbery. But the counter-attack was successful and the position was cleared. At least 12 other Japanese were killed by Sergeant Thompson's party of seven men, and the ground was recaptured. Only one Australian was wounded, by grenade fragments. Bruce Kingsbury, from Melbourne, was awarded a posthumous Victoria Cross; the first won by 2/14th Battalion, the first in the South West Pacific, and the first won on Australian territory.

Meanwhile, Captain R. W. Cameron's D Company, on Dickenson's left and extending from the track to the left, also had been under heavy pressure. Help from Buckler's A Company arrived to throw back the Japanese with grenades and bayonets. Further around to the left, Nye's company was being attacked at all three platoons, but held.

The Japanese were suffering many casualties, and for them Isurava was soaking up enough blood to be important enough to be regarded as a battle honour. There had been nothing like this in their earlier campaigns. Toshiaki Sugimoto, Takasago Volunteers, who had hauled forage to Kokoda, and had gone forward on other duties, wrote that the unit was under heavy fire and unable to advance.[43]

Brigadier Potts ordered C Company 53rd Battalion forward to the battle, to assist 2/14th. The company failed to arrive, Dickenson had to give ground to the assaults, and Japanese got through Cameron's company position at about 3 pm, threatening the rear of Nye's company. In Cameron's position, Private H. C. Wakefield used his Bren to great effect against the swarming enemy, but still they pushed on past. At 5 pm, another assault fell on Nye's area. Most pressure went in on Lieutenant Harold (Butch) Bisset's 10 Platoon, which had withstood 11 company attacks during the day, and now Bisset was hit by machinegun fire. He was badly wounded, and was carried out at great personal danger by some of the soldiers, with another wounded man, but died later, with his brother at his side. The Japanese pressed on and came up against Lieutenant L. F. Mason's 12 Platoon. During the afternoon alone, Mason's Diggers had put in four counter-attacks, each time retaking their position on high ground overlooking the supply line track. Fighting raged around the section positions, and then at 5.30 pm the Japanese put in another attack that forced back the platoon.

Now another man performed feats that are simply described but, perhaps, really can only be appreciated by other infantrymen. Corporal Charley McCallum had been prominent in the fighting, had been wounded three times, and as this attack surged in, pushing back the Australians, he stood among the Japanese, holding them so the rest of the platoon could go back and reorganise. McCallum had a Tommy gun slung on his left shoulder and a Bren on the other. Alone, he covered the withdrawal of the platoon, shooting down the enemy, at first with the Bren. When the magazine was empty, the Japanese surged forward, and McCallum swung up the Tommy gun and shot them down while he replaced the Bren magazine. He brought up the Bren again, and continued firing, knocking down many more Japanese as they came at him, one so close that he managed to reach out and tear a pouch from McCallum's waist belt before falling dead. Witnesses estimated that he shot at least 40 Japanese in this single, furious combat. Then, as always, calm and steady, he made his way back to the platoon. Charles McCallum was recommended for the Victoria Cross by 2/14th Battalion, the award was endorsed by the Brigade and Divisional commanders, but he was eventually given the Distinguished Conduct Medal.

In the fighting, Lieutenant Mason, two corporals and six soldiers were wounded, and another man was missing. Sergeant Matthews took command and reorganised the platoon, under fire, in the new position. It was estimated by Lieutenant Colonel Key that 550 Japanese casualties had been inflicted. 2/14th at this stage had known losses of 12 dead, 48 wounded and many missing, after some elements had been cut off by Japanese attacks. The remnants of the platoons commanded by Pearce and Gardner from Cameron's company were last known to have been fighting in a position forward of the main body. The isolated platoons fought an epic action of their own. They held the position for another two days, after the rest of the battalion had withdrawn, and even went out in search of a troublesome machinegun. Eventually, the group evaded the Japanese and returned to friendly lines. Lieutenant Pearce brought back his small rearguard element on 5 September, while the remainder with Sergeant Irwin trekked for 22 days through the mountains before arriving at Uberi. Irwin used his watch as a compass, and listened to the sounds of battle as a further guide.

Some fighting continued in the rain, which made evacuation of casualties that much more difficult. Stretchers were made from saplings and vines, then the nightmare journey began back along the muddy, wet trail, down the mountainsides, over the creeks and up the far slope, onwards to the distant medical stations. Those at all able to walk did so – only badly wounded were carried. 10 Platoon 2/14th found itself cut off at the canefield, low on ammunition, with Lieutenant Bisset and Private J. A. Ferguson, both badly wounded and requiring stretchers. It was decided to go uphill to where 12 Platoon had been, with the platoon Tommy-gunners leading, to blast a way through any Japanese encountered. Japanese were met and a furious firefight followed, both sides using automatic weapons, in the dark and rain. George Woodward was simply standing erect, firing, aware of shouts and yells all around him, the calls for 'Elizabeth 12!' – which the Japanese supposedly could not pronounce, until the platoon was forced back downslope. He had no ammunition left. Creeping up the main track, they saw shadowy figures – 'Is that Elizabeth 10?' – and found 11 Platoon.

Potts had been fighting at a disadvantage since his brigade began arriving. Instead of consolidating his battalions and meeting the enemy en masse, he had been forced, initially by the poor supply situation, to bring the brigade up in daily packets. As they came to the battle area, he had to feed them company by company into the action to assist 39th and 53rd Battalions. The Japanese had been able to take high ground with little trouble, mainly due to the poor performance of 53rd Battalion. The wasted days and weeks at Moresby that should have been spent in training, but were consumed by work parties, now were paid for with lives and blood of men of all four battalions in the three days 27, 28 and 29 August at Isurava.

Night was falling after a day of intense fighting. In the 2/14th, morale was high. They had arrived at the scene of battle, met the

Japanese, and held them. It was obvious that Australian casualties were far fewer than Japanese. However, the battalion was in a serious situation, with enemy now on higher ground to the left, and Potts intended to counter-attack there with two companies of 2/16th at dawn. The arrival of 21 Brigade had been crucial to the success of the campaign. 39th Battalion was about to be overwhelmed by sheer weight of numbers in Horii's four attacking battalions, when 2/14th came up first and held the Japanese on the track. Then 2/16th came up and was placed out to the right (the Japanese left), and held them there. Horii's South Seas Detachment dashed itself against the impromptu positions held at Isurava and received a wound that fatally weakened it. The Australians possessed only small arms and had only one weapon – a single mortar – capable of sustained fire or delivering high explosive, nor had they entrenching tools, but they fought a successful day of defensive actions against a numerically superior enemy who possessed a substantial firepower superiority.

If a single day in the Kokoda campaign is to be selected as the decisive day, it is this Saturday 29 August. If Horii's force had not been held, and expended much of its strength, the Japanese battalions may well have been unstoppable further down the trail. Anzac Day, 25 April, is honoured throughout Australia and deservedly so. The Battle of the Coral Sea anniversary also is observed each May, mostly with appropriate ceremonies in Canberra. A strong case can be made for nomination of a day to commemorate the actions on the Kokoda Trail, when Australians fought alone in defence of their homeland.

The Isurava position unexpectedly was reinforced by three 39th Battalion platoons that had been separated since the enemy advance on 27 August. After spending a hungry night on the slopes, the platoons moved closer to people around an area recognised as near Alola, and found themselves looking down the barrels of some of the 2/16th Battalion. Identities established, the AIF Diggers welcomed the Militia with cigarettes and tea, then soon after Chaplain Earl and Captain Shera arrived to check them. The platoons set off back to Isurava. The 2/16th were impressed at the sight of the ragged, tired, worn platoons, on bleeding and swollen feet, going back into battle. The Militia, the 'Chocos', were winning the respect of the elite Australian Imperial Force volunteers in the only way that Australian soldiers can do so: by living up to the standards set by the AIF themselves. Other 39th men were returning. Lieutenant Johnston, on his own initiative, led forward a party of unfit but volunteer members of the battalion from the rear. On arrival, he told Lieutenant Colonel Honner that they'd heard the battalion was in trouble. These men could have gone on to the rear, but turned around to go into battle again, well knowing what that entailed. Lieutenant Colonel Honner has described the return of Sword's tattered platoons, looming up in the dusk, and Sword's simple statement that he was reporting back from patrol. Honner returned Sword's salute with 'more than mere formality'.

In recent years, people wishing to make a name for themselves have tried to prove that 'mateship' in the armed forces never existed and was a myth originally created by Dr C. E. W. Bean for the Anzacs, since perpetuated by other writers and historians. How conveniently do these people ignore examples such as the return of the 39th Battalion men to battle.

At 5 pm, Major General Horii's Japanese headquarters was on a hill 1100 yards north of Isurava, and issued the following: 'The Shitai, by its operations since the 24th, has completely surrounded the enemy and since this morning has been making repeated attacks within his position. Annihilation of the enemy is near, but there are still some remnants in a section of the position, and their fighting spirit is extremely high. The enemy's defeated 39 Battalion has been reinforced, and, taking advantage of the ruggedness of the terrain, they appear to be determined to put up a serious resistance. The Shitai will make night attacks and will be expected to capture the enemy positions confronting them during this night and make preparations for further action.' The following paragraphs ordered 144 Regiment to continue the night attacks and capture the enemy position, while 41 Regiment was to prepare to attack from 'the road area' [sic], keeping in mind the movement of a force in case the enemy retreated, the field hospital was to be established, and all other units were to be ready for whatever orders would be given as the battle developed.[44]

The Japanese still appeared to believe that a proper road linked Moresby and Kokoda, and hoped to fight a conventional advance along it.

The 2/14th Battalion was menaced from the high ground to their left, and eventually Lieutenant Colonel Key was forced to ask Brigadier Potts for permission to move back to Isurava Rest House, about halfway to Alola. Lieutenant Colonel Honner and Lieutenant Stan Bisset, Intelligence Officer 2/14th, went back to reconnoitre the position onto which the force would retire. By 2 am, the withdrawal had been completed, apparently without the enemy noticing.

At the end of the day, 29 August, 21 Brigade recorded 39th Battalion strength as 16 officers and 235 other ranks, with 2/14th suffering eight killed, 43 wounded and 41 missing, and 2/16th two killed and 23 wounded in the day's actions. In A Company 39th Battalion, George Mowat had been unable to keep up his diary, but combined several days' notes in one entry. 'Heavy fighting. Held enemy, pushed him back in places. Fighting very fierce, casualties heavy. 21.00 [9 pm], ordered to make a complete withdrawal before daylight.' At 8 am that 29 August, 17 P400s attacked Buna, claiming two Zeros and a twin-engined bomber set on fire, and six B26s bombed, claiming one Zero destroyed on the ground, and that bombs fell among others. Visibility was 10 to 12 miles (16-19 km). Tadao Chiba saw the attack, and noted that two transport planes were destroyed, while Lieutenant Masaji Komori was told one plane was shot down. Three Japanese were killed and eight wounded in the attack. Toshio Sato saw this air battle, adding, 'Tainan Kokkutai has been annihilated. The commander went back to Rabaul'.[45] Five Catalinas harassed Buka during the night, and a total of 17 B17s attacked Vunakanau and ships in Simpson Harbour. Four of a formation of nine turned back for various reasons, but the other five claimed one of the attacking Zeros. Six others flew reconnaissance missions to Rabaul, Faisi, Milne Bay and one important mission was flown by the US 8 Photo Squadron, tasked with coverage of the Kokoda area so accurate mapping could be done.

On 30 August, the Australians attacked the Japanese II/144 at Abuari, but did not succeed in dislodging them. From Abuari, Captain Sublet's force of A and B Companies 2/16th Battalion moved into position for the attacks. At 10 am, the time for the attack if the company from 53rd Battalion was in position, a Japanese machinegun above opened fire. The 2/16th thought it signalled the 53rd troops attacking, but instead distant Brigade HQ informed them that they were receiving the fire and casualties had been suffered. Eventually, the gun was temporarily silenced by rifle grenades. After an hour's wait, word came that the 53rd troops could not advance further, having come up against cliffs. Captains Sublet and McGee decided to attack anyway. Fighting went on till mid-afternoon, with little progress, and it was obvious a strong force of Japanese was in position. Japanese casualties were believed to be considerable, and again 9 Platoon captured a light machinegun. Aussie humour was evident: Private Bob Wilson was hit in the buttocks, and in the midst of action lowered his trousers and asked the nearest Digger, 'Are you sure that is blood?' The 'yes' in reply pleased Wilson. Lieutenant Ron Christian sent Private Leo Bracegirdle to company headquarters, which meant Bracegirdle had a dangerous trip down the slope under heavy enemy fire, and an equally dangerous return. When he arrived back, his first remark to Christian was, 'By Christ, if we ever get out of this, you'll buy me some bloody beer'.

Meanwhile, Gerke's 11 Platoon had moved into its attack position, and was awaiting word. It was known that strong Japanese positions were close by. At about midday, Gerke decided that they might as well have lunch, and in the act of eating saw a sniper about to fire on the Australians. He and Sergeant George Morris fired together, killing the sniper, but losing all element of surprise. Gerke's immediate attack came up against a prepared Japanese position. A light machinegun killed three men, including Corporal Clarke, and wounded another as they crossed a track. Private George Maidment was on the track. He dropped his rifle, picked up Clarke's Thompson sub-machinegun, and standing 20 yards from the Japanese, emptied the magazine at them, and followed up with his own and Clarke's grenades. The Japanese were killed and the gun silenced. The platoon was able to fight its way around the right flank of the Japanese, through enemy who were thought to have dropped from trees behind them. Maidment was wounded in the chest, but made his way unaided to company headquarters, and later was awarded the Distinguished Conduct Medal. He died of wounds a few days later. Sergeant Morris took the Tommy-gun, used it to clear the way to the high ground for the platoon, killed several Japanese riflemen and silenced another machinegun. He was awarded the Military Medal. By the time 11 Platoon broke contact, a heavy mist settled, and as the rest of the force was out of communication, the platoon moved south, around the enemy positions, eventually rejoining several days later.

10 Platoon also had gone into the attack when sounds of firing were heard. At once they encountered a defensive position and heavy fire. All three section commanders were wounded and one soldier killed. John Myhre, a former member of the Norwegian Merchant Navy, and first aid expert, attended Corporal Ting Pearce while both were under fire; he received the Military Medal. While all this was going on, Captain Sublet had been ordered to bring his 2/16th force back through Alola; the brigade was to withdraw.

Horii's Japanese headquarters issued the following at 9.30 am: 'In last night's action, we seized the enemy's "Summer" position, but did not seize his "Spring" and "Autumn" positions. We are making preparations for further attacks. The Horie battalion (II/144) yesterday evening pressed on to the area south-east of Isurava, and defeated an enemy force numbering several hundred and armed with machineguns. The battalion is now preparing to attack the enemy's rear at Isurava. The Shitai will resolutely carry on its offensive in accordance with its previous plan.' Kusunose's 144 Regiment was ordered to become the left flank unit, to attack and take the two uncaptured Australian positions, then go on to the south of Isurava; 41 Regiment was to be the right flank unit, taking under command III/144, but coordinate with II/144 to destroy the Australians at Isurava.[46] At 11 am, the Japanese were able to collect the bodies of 1st Lieutenant Yamamoto and those killed the day before in the fighting, though five minutes later the Australians attacked again, but were repulsed.

As described earlier, Lieutenant Colonel Key had intended counter-attacking on his left flank with two companies of 2/16th Battalion, but instead used them to cover the moonlight withdrawal. After settling in at the new position, the most unfit of 39th Battalion were selected and sent off to the rear, to go to Myola. The battalion was reduced to about 150 men, B Company having just 13 soldiers. Soon Japanese moving around to the high ground to the west attacked B Company, and succeeded at first, but A Company and 2/14th held the enemy. 39th Battalion lost six dead on this day.

At 3 pm, Brigadier Potts ordered Lieutenant Colonel Honner to go back and reconnoitre positions for 2/14th and 2/16th Battalions at Eora Creek, as well as positions for 53rd and 39th Battalions to cover the withdrawal of the AIF units. At 4 pm, with D Company and the wounded, Honner set out across country to avoid the Japanese, who were on the track to the rear. 2/14th was to endure a severe experience after the Japanese secured the higher ground on the left, which Lieutenant Colonel Key did not have enough men to hold. He decided to put his C and D Companies in to clear the high ground along the track to Brigade HQ, but as they began the Japanese attacked A, B and HQ Companies. The unit historian described the roar of firing, as all involved went into action, as the most intense in the history of the unit. The Japanese 41 Regiment continued attacking, and succeeded in penetrating the Australian position, despite acts of bravery and feats of arms. One Australian and two Japanese battalions were all firing at once. The fighting developed into close quarters shooting, but 2/14th was split by the attackers, and 172 members of the battalion were separated from the rest. At the time, Lieutenant Colonel Key was ready to move along the track, and the intense fire that swept it forced him and the HQ party off it and downhill to the creek. The Japanese were swarming across the area. Among those cut off were Lieutenant Colonel Key and members of his headquarters, the adjutant, IO, RSM, OC A Company and five junior officers. The intended withdrawal became somewhat disorganised, and the Japanese exploited their advantage. Their 41 Regiment was pressing hard through the positions, forcing a way to the rear.

Mick Fielding was a member of the Battalion Intelligence Section with Key. 'Battalion Headquarters came under very heavy fire from above and below the track, and Lieutenant Colonel Key decided it was best to move off the track to the low ground, bypass the enemy, and rejoin the rifle companies,' he recalled. The group also had with it Lance Corporal I. G. Leask, wounded in the chest. A stretcher had to be made for him, and carrying him slowed the party, which rested after darkness fell; Leask died in the night. Lance Corporal Roy Watson, Intelligence Section, found himself behind a fallen tree, with Bill Bartlett, firing uphill at the Japanese. Return fire had a drastic effect on the fallen tree, and it began to disintegrate – it was rotten. There was no point in remaining, and Watson said, 'I'm off, Bill. Coming?' The last he saw of Bill Bartlett that day was 'his backside disappearing over an eight-foot [2.4-metre] native fence'. When Watson stood to follow, he 'looked down in horror' as successive Japanese bullets hit each of the bulging side pockets of his shorts – crammed with tins of bully – the impact literally tearing the pockets off and reducing his shorts to tatters, held together only by the waistband and fly. 'In a split second,' said Watson, 'the induced acceleration had me well out of range.' He joined about a dozen others, who decided that their best choice was to cross the Oivi track at first light and make their way to the Alola track, and the 2/16th Battalion.

Other members of the Intelligence Section also brought groups of men back to the brigade position next day. C and D Companies of 2/16th, commanded by Captains Goldsmith and Langridge, held around Alola for the passage of the embattled 2/14th. The battered companies came back, but many were missing. It was a bad day for the 2/14th, with another 10 killed and 18 wounded; two days of battle had cost 48 killed, 28 wounded and 44 missing. The high ratio of killed to wounded shows the intensity of the combat. The battalion was reduced to about one-fifth its strength at the beginning of the campaign: A and HQ Companies, 30 men; B, 54; C, 42; D, 34. Captain Buckler, with two officers and 41 men, was cut off, and began an odyssey that would take them through the jungles for another 42 days before they rejoined friendly forces. After three weeks, seven wounded, two sick and B Company medical orderly Private Tom Fletcher, MM were left at the village of Sengai 2 while the rest pushed on to find Allied units. When help came, all were dead – the Japanese had found them first.

Les Simmons, 39th Battalion Band Sergeant, was commanding 7 Platoon A Company. As the platoon went past, he stood by, checking to see he had everyone. He noticed Bob Nimmo was missing, ran back and found him badly wounded, with the Japanese in sight and advancing. Simmons turned after the platoon, and caught sight of the last man passing around a corner in the track. It was the redoubtable J. D. McKay. When Simmons called out that Nimmo was wounded and needed a hand, McKay instantly returned and they ran back to him, grabbed an arm each and set off with the Japanese in pursuit, firing at this clumsy target. Nimmo had been badly hit in the buttocks, and as his rescuers were dragging him over every obstacle and rise in the ground, it must have been agonising, as well as which his trousers were being dragged off, but he told them not to worry about that. Eventually he was brought to relative safety and evacuated. Nimmo recovered and went back into battle with 2/2nd Battalion later in the war.

A sharp counter-attack, in which Captain A. S. McGavin, of A Company 2/14th, played a major part, with C Company 2/14th, 30 men of D Company 2/14th and a platoon of C Company 2/16th went along high ground on the left. It became a bayonet charge that swept all before it. The historian of 2/16th described it as the man-to-man encounter in the open that Australians understood, rather than skulking in the dim jungle. The Japanese fled from the bayonets, but such an opportunity was available only rarely.

It became obvious that the Japanese assault troops coming forward this day were far from the accepted idea of the short, bespectacled Nipponese with comical front teeth. Many of them were quite tall and muscular, coming from the northern island of Hokkaido. One AIF officer later said he could not believe it when he saw the big fellows coming at him, and at first thought they were Germans in disguise!

Brigadier Potts realised that he would have to fight another delaying action, and decided to do so with 2/14th and 2/16th Battalions, while 39th and 53rd Battalions went on to Eora Creek. As the troops passed the medical posts in the rear, Captain Steward, RMO of 2/16th, had his first sight of members of 39th Battalion, describing it in his book *Recollections of a Regimental Medical Officer*. He saw the 39th men as scarecrows with gaping boots and ragged uniforms, expressionless faces and deep-sunk eyes, weakened by malaria, dysentery and lack of food, but still used in rifle companies against a numerically superior enemy enjoying heavier support weapons. As the units went back through Alola, Bluey Jardine, of 14 Platoon C Company of the 39th, was ordered to take a Bren and hold the track for half an hour to allow the sick and wounded to get clear. Along the track came a procession of 39th Battalion men, stragglers from the 53rd, the stalwart Lance Corporal Sanopa and some police boys, then a party of PIB. When these had gone by there were only six minutes left to wait, but the Japanese had already arrived. There was muttering in the grass, then a machinegun burst hammered into the bush where Jardine first had been in position. He cocked the Bren and fired a magazine into a party of 20 or so Japanese rushing him in a group. All were hit or went to ground except one who continued coming with fixed bayonet; Jardine threw the empty magazine at him and went. Successfully escaping, Jardine put on a full magazine and reached company headquarters, trembling with reaction from the encounter. He caught up with the platoon, ate an emergency ration, but found sleep would not come.

During the withdrawal, Captain Jacob, of 39th Battalion, was killed. Though suffering from malaria, he had been carrying the rifles of some of the sick, but stumbled, and one of the cocked rifles discharged, severing the femoral artery. George Mowat wrote,

'Afternoon. Enemy broke through new position suddenly. Fought until nearly surrounded. Withdrew through jungle in darkness'. Again, the rain streamed down, and in the total blackness, holding on to the man in front, stumbling in the mud and wet, the units struggled back to Eora Creek. It had been withdrawal after withdrawal in the unforgiving hills and the repetitive misery of the rains and cold, short of food and ammunition, and even the elite AIF battalions seemed unable to stop these Japanese. 21 Brigade War Diary recorded that all available carriers were used for evacuation of the wounded and some three-inch mortar ammunition, 2000 rations, 50,000 rounds of ammunition and 500 grenades (useless without fuses) were lost when Alola was evacuated. All rations at Templeton's Crossing were destroyed, and about 1000 more at an intermediate dump were lost also.

In his diary, Tadao Chiba, at Buna, noted that a plane came to take the remaining pilots, and that the airfield was no longer to be used, but Japanese Pioneers unloaded 700 drums of petrol from *Shinko Maru* for use at the airfield. The unit commander gave orders to take shelter when under air attack, and Toshio Sato moved into the jungle with his unit, forced to disperse by the air raids.[47]

There were no air support missions flown over the Kokoda zone on 30 August, as emphasis was on Milne Bay and Rabaul. Two B17s arrived over Rabaul, clouds obscured the targets, so attacked a cruiser and transport at sea, making no hits. Eight B17s attacked Milne Bay, another six attacked Rabaul, and seven more arrived at 7-Mile from Mareeba, to prepare for missions next day. Only one supply flight had been possible from Kila Kila, and that dropped ordnance stores. More importantly, a conference was held at which all the problems of air supply were presented (as on the above pages) and possible solutions discussed. Necessary action was taken to have supplies for the next day's drops ready at Kila Kila at the end of each day, for loading and despatch at dawn. Even when all the factors of manpower, supplies, vehicles and weather were suitable, sometimes the transport aircraft were held on the ground if no fighter escort was available. This final factor was beyond the authority of the Australian Army staff and commanders.

On 31 August, in 15 Pioneers at Buna airfield, the Japanese diarist Tadao Chiba wrote that a telephone message was received about an enemy pilot who was captured by natives but escaped, and it was believed the natives then killed him.[48] Aboard *Myoko Maru*, orders were given for the imminent landing at Basabua. The ship was expected to anchor at 5 pm, and troops were to disembark at once. Five small and 13 large motorised landing craft (MLC) would be available.[49]

At Eora Creek, Lieutenant Colonel Honner found that 53rd Battalion had not arrived, so selected positions to be held by 39th Battalion alone. The battalion was so small in numbers that it had been reorganised into two companies: No. 1 Company comprised the survivors of A, B and C Companies, while No. 2 contained D and E Companies. No. 1 Company, under Captain Merritt, with the three-inch mortar, was on the high ground straddling the Templeton's Crossing track to repel attacks coming up the eastern side of Eora Valley. Captain Bidstrup had 2 Company, and positioned it on the edge of the village to cover creek approaches from Alola. The battalion rear elements and the casualties moved back to Myola. Survivors of A Company 39th Battalion now were two officers and 35 other ranks. They enjoyed hot tea, butter and jam, the first for a week, when they arrived at Eora. 2/14th Battalion was about a mile (1.6 km) south of Alola; brigade headquarters was halfway between Alola and Eora Creek; 53rd Battalion was moving back to Myola, having been sent out of battle, but its C Company was attached to 2/14th Battalion, coming under command of that unit.

Early in the afternoon, 2/14th moved back across Eora Creek, with brigade headquarters. Private Bluey Jardine of the 39th was to take two platoons back over the creek, after making contact with 'a Gerry Dickenson of the 2/14th'. Repeated queries of passing 2/14th soldiers merely brought the response that Dickenson was coming along, and what with the strain of the past days and weeks, Jardine was becoming a little short of equanimity. A scruffy looking chap with a Tommy gun came along and Jardine asked if he'd seen 'that bastard Gerry Dickenson?' It was Captain Dickenson, who politely introduced himself, the two shook hands and discussed the situation, then moved back to their respective locations. Jardine explained that he was only a private, helping out. Meanwhile, trying to rejoin the 2/14th was the group led by Lieutenant Colonel Key. He decided to split his party into two, and gave command of a group of nine to Mick Fielding, who set off into the jungle, with Key's group to follow later. Fortunately, Fielding knew a little of the topography, as he had accompanied the civil engineer who had searched the area of Myola Lake for other suitable landing or air-dropping zones. It had been this party that discovered Lake Myola 2, and the engineer explained to Mick that the lakes were old volcanoes, which had become lakes when extinct, but which had later burst their sides to form Eora Creek. Fielding realised that if he followed the Eora Valley, he would arrive at Templeton's Crossing or Myola. Eventually, his party arrived safely, but Lieutenant Colonel Key was not so fortunate.

Lieutenant Noda, still guarding Japanese 144 Regiment colours, had an unhappy experience. As the attacks had pushed back the Australians, regimental HQ decided to move forward. The thoughtful Noda had not seen any Japanese soldiers along the trail they were following, and said that it was too early to go forward. His advice was ignored. 'Unwillingly we pushed forward with No. 3 Platoon leading. As expected, when we reached the ravine, Corporal Komatsu and five men were killed and Corporal Yamamoto and two men wounded.' Soon after, an infantry battalion arrived and the HQ resumed the advance behind them. At 12.30 pm, they reached the three huts at Isurava. 41 Regiment pushed on as pursuit party. By 4 pm, the Japanese HQ was nearly two miles (about 3.2 km) south of Isurava, and all ate well on potatoes and biscuits left by the Australians. Noda wrote, 'our food supply is quickly diminishing'. Kentaro Fujiwara included in his diary that the unit totalled 105 men; they were climbing the Owen Stanley Ranges. Toshiaki Sugimoto, of Takasago Volunteers, 'encountered many corpses of both sides' as his unit was struggling forward with supplies. It was his final diary entry.[50] At Isurava, 6 Company II/144 reorganised into two platoons, and at 2 pm Sergeant Sorimoto and 10 men left to reconnoitre the road to Port Moresby. The company was carrying 15,760 rounds of ammunition and 267 grenades. Warrant Officer Sadahiro noted that another man was killed, and the advance was to be south, towards a large hill. The Japanese reconnaissance patrol returned at 3.30 pm, and found the unit camped on a river bank, building a bridge. Sadahiro made no more entries in his record of operations, and it was captured on 20 October, north of Templeton's Crossing.

Veterinarian Yano saw wounded retreating from the front, and learned Lieutenant Hamada and the adjutant of III Battalion had been killed. The machinegun unit of 144 Regiment was moving back to Kokoda, and 2nd Lieutenant Ebuchi stopped overnight at Deniki. For the past week, Akira Teruoka, of the medical unit, had been involved in daily arduous work evacuating casualties, despite illness and exhaustion among stretcher bearers of all sections. Natives in the various units were beginning to desert. The Takasago Volunteers had been bringing up ammunition, and a member of its 2 Company wrote that 'the enemy is becoming stubborn. Our troops are attacking from both flanks. Had two air raids today'.[51]

The 2/16th had little contact with the enemy on 31 August, but it was obvious that Japanese were active around them. The battalion had taken up position some 2000 yards south of Alola, astride the track. Captain Frank Sublet's force from Abuari rejoined, after moving along Eora Creek without contact with enemy. Observation posts reported movement, and smoke from fires rose above trees on the flanks. One corporal of 8 Platoon was last seen under accurate fire, separated from the rest of his unit. It was presumed he was killed later by the Japanese. The battalion position could be bypassed very easily, and at 5 pm a further withdrawal began, assisted by heavy mist. At 6.30, the battalion was in new positions. The Japanese could be heard yelling and firing as they attacked the locations just vacated. But at 2 am, again the battalion moved back to better positions.

At midday on 31 August, B26s attacked Lae airfield, resulting in fires and smoke visible from 30 miles (48 km) away; visibility was unlimited. Six minutes later, achieving surprise by coming down the Markham Valley, 10 A20s attacked the airfield at 30 feet or lower, and crews reported four big fuel fires behind the dispersal area, ignited by bombs from the B26s. At 12.35 pm, three B17s bombed Mission Point, Buna, went down strafing, then returned to Mareeba. Three P400s managed to attack the Wairopi–Kokoda trail, after three others turned back, and six A20s trying to attack Alola–Isurava turned back because of weather. B17 reconnaissance flights went to Kavieng, Kieta and Milne Bay. No supply drops were made from Kila Kila.

The Japanese 17 Army compiled Intelligence Report No. 16, and in it stated that it was expected the advance party of 41 Regiment had reached Isurava four days before, on the 27th, with other units arriving later. 10 Company (III/41) was employed as carriers on their advance from Kokoda and on arrival at Isurava it was to take up a guard position. The battalion artillery and mountain artillery of 144 Regiment had reached Isurava on 30 August. The Takasago Volunteers arrived at Isurava on 29 August, commended for excellence in litter-bearing. Other sections described the Milne Bay and Guadalcanal operations, and from an Australian radio broadcast the Japanese learned Allied air headquarters had moved from Melbourne to Brisbane.[52]

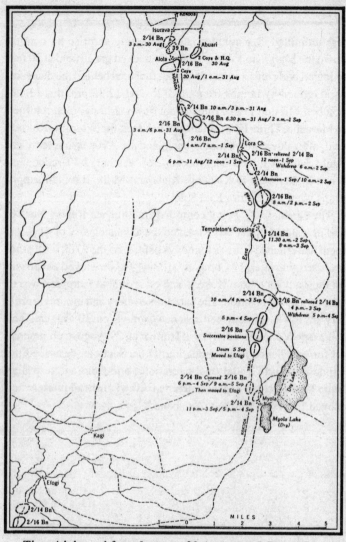

The withdrawal from Isurava, 30 August to 5 September.

Chapter 4
TEMPEST
September 1942

On 1 September, four RAAF Catalinas harassed Buka, and B17s set out for the distant areas. Bad weather foiled two medium bomber attacks planned for Lae and Isurava, but three P400s strafed what was reported as 'Kokoda Pass'.

The Australian 2/14th Battalion now was badly reduced in numbers available for action. Strength was 160 all ranks. The rest were dead, wounded or missing, separated from the unit and making their way back through the jungle. The battalion was commanded by Captain Phil Rhoden, with Lance Corporal Roy Watson acting as Intelligence Officer. The battalion was ordered back to Eora Creek.

At 2 am, 2/16th Battalion had begun to move back again. In the darkness and pressure of circumstances, some section posts were not informed and found that they were alone as dawn broke. One such section caught up with the battalion in only half an hour, covering a distance that had taken the others three hours at night. Another section was near the trail, and had noticed nothing unusual. As light crept through the foliage, Sergeant Gordon Higgs needed a cigarette, but found that he did not have a match. He heard someone close by and stepped in that direction to ask for a light. He found himself standing among a group of Japanese. Higgs pulled the pin on a grenade, threw it into the Japanese, who scattered, while the Australians seized the advantage, left, then quickly caught up with the battalion.

Meanwhile, in the new light, Lieutenant Colonel Caro found that the position occupied by 2/16th was not a good defensive location, so moved C Company to a small ridge some 200 yards forward. Here 13, 14 and 15 Platoons engaged advancing Japanese, and killed five. This force was Lieutenant Colonel Koiwai's fresh II/41. The Japanese reaction was to push through on the right, forcing the platoons to move to higher ground, and 14 and 15 Platoons were temporarily cut off. They rejoined the battalion next day. The aggressive Japanese II/41 got in between C Company and the remainder of the battalion, and D Company fought a series of rearguard actions, with platoons leap-frogging. The company crossed Eora Creek and took up positions on the spur overlooking the crossing.

By early morning at Eora Creek, Captain Merritt's No. 1 Company 39th Battalion had moved forward to cover the withdrawal of 2/16th Battalion from Alola, and to prevent the Japanese from occupying any position from which they could fire on the creek crossing. The platoons of II/41 were right on the tails of 2/16th, and made things difficult for the 39th.

Three logs resting on boulders were all that provided a crossing above the swift-flowing stream. Lieutenant D. A. Paterson's 17 Platoon 2/16th was last, and Merritt's men had to wait for the platoon to cross before destroying the crossing. But the Japanese outflanked the rearguard and arrived at the crossing before Paterson's men, who were engaged in a separate fight anyway. Merritt's force came under fire, and a Juki machinegun was placed to dominate the track and crossing. Merritt had no weapon to counter this, and he and his company were forced to climb a steep slope through the scrub while Japanese across the ravine tried to pick them off. Merritt and Alex Lochhead were the last, with Merritt coming along as absolutely the last man. Japanese fire pinged and thunked around them, as Merritt urged Lochhead to greater speed. In the Aussie fashion, this was looked back on as quite funny – later. Of the task, George Mowat wrote, 'Went forward to cover withdrawal of 2/16th. Suicide job. Japs right on their heels'.

Paterson had been killed, the platoon sergeant wounded, and the firing behind them, at the creek, informed the platoon that they were cut off. Eventually, they and two A Company 2/16th platoons found other crossing places and rejoined their battalion.

At 10 am, Brigadier Potts ordered 39th Battalion to go to Kagi and hold it until 2/27th Battalion arrived to assume responsibility for the location. Lieutenant Colonel Honner signalled the rear echelon at Myola to assemble all ranks capable of marching and meet him at Kagi. The echelon did so and arrived there at 5.30 pm, but the rifle companies had to make an overnight halt before reaching Kagi next day.

Holding the creek crossing was the battalion's last engagement in the Kokoda campaign, and, appropriately, the action was of some historical importance. The Militia unit that had first engaged the Japanese and fought alone against the invaders was also first to secure the withdrawal of an AIF unit, the volunteers proud of their inheritance of the traditions of the original AIF of 1914-18.

Down the mountain slopes from Isurava, 1st Lieutenant Horibe and a group began carrying wounded back from the battle site. He reported that four enemy fighters flew over without seeing them, and north of Isurava his party stopped to build a bridge and do some necessary roadwork. The four fighters he saw were almost certainly the P400s escorting transport planes, and at 9.15 am strafed Kokoda; no ground activity was seen. Cloud base was 6000 feet, visibility unlimited. Under the strafing were members of the Takasago Volunteer No. 2 Company, but no damage was done. At 11 am, P400s escorted transport planes to Kagi, then strafed Kokoda; one aircraft was missing. The ever-changing weather now was visibility 10 miles (16 km), cloud base at Kokoda 10,000 feet.

Lieutenant Sakamoto had been moved to command 2 MG Company 144 Regiment, and listed the officer casualties he knew of: killed were Hatanaka, OC 1 Company, Kamiya, OC 7 Company, and Kitamura, OC 3 MG Company; wounded were Hamada, OC 9 Company, Uyeno, OC 2 Company, and Yanagise of III/144. He added that there were no officers left in 1 and 3 Companies.

Hurrying forward again were Akira Teruoka and his unit, which set out at 6 am. They reached the battle area, and he commented on the number of dead scattered around, both Japanese and Australian. At 11 am they caught up with the rest, and continued marching. In his 'observation and suggestion book', Lieutenant Colonel Kobayashi wrote: 'The Shitai will attack the Australian regulars – approximately 1000 men – in the vicinity of Isurava. The battalion will serve as a rearguard between Kokoda and Isurava, as well as try to transport supplies to Isurava'.[1]

Struggling towards the Japanese was 2/27th Battalion, finding the mountain paths and weather every bit as hard going as all those who preceded them. The 2/27th was proud of the fact that only two men dropped out during the exhausting marches.

The *Kazuura Maru* had arrived off Buna, and among those disembarking was Shigeru Kuniyasu, who also was to record his advance in his diary. Next day, they set off for Kokoda. Forty-seven surgical patients were prepared for evacuation to Rabaul from the Buna area. The convoy was undetected by Allied aircraft, and delivered another 1500 men of Major Miyamoto's I/41, rear elements of Horii's headquarters, transport troops and 300 horses.[2]

GHQ in Brisbane still persisted in its belief that the Japanese only wanted airfield sites, not Port Moresby, and could not understand why they continued to advance. General Willoughby considered himself a strategist, but failed to grasp the immense value to the Japanese of airfields around Port Moresby, rather than Buna.

Any excuse was used by MacArthur to request more US forces for his theatre, and he was convinced he was being starved of resources by those in the army and navy who hated him. The day before, MacArthur had asked for more forces, without which he predicted another defeat. The actions at Milne Bay were just being revealed as an Australian victory, but the Kokoda campaign was going against the defenders. General Vasey, from Australia, wrote to General Rowell and told him that GHQ was like a barometer in a cyclone, 'up and down every two minutes'. Yet the senior officers of GHQ were the Bataan clique, allegedly battle-hardened officers who had given the Japanese an allegedly tremendous setback in the Philippines.

At Eora Creek, the Koiwai battalion (II/41) began attacking across the formidable terrain. The Australian D Company 2/16th had dug in on the high ground. 16 Platoon, under Sergeant Bill Duncan, had a position giving them good observation over the entire cleared area near the village. 17 and 18 Platoons were dug in higher up. Soon after 16 Platoon got into position, the first Japanese appeared, and as the rest of the afternoon passed, 16 Platoon held its ground. At dusk, 16 moved back and settled in with the other two platoons. Koiwai had been organising his attack, which was to go in after the usual probing and harassment by mortars and mountain guns.

At 3 pm, Horii's HQ issued the following: 'Although the loss of time caused by the difficulties of the range, in addition to the delays caused by enemy action had been foreseen, we are concerned at the small quantity of ammunition and provisions carried now left. Although precautions regarding economy had previously been given, it is regrettable that, perhaps owing to continued action and prolonged marching, these directions have not yet been driven home. All unit commanders and those in authority, of whatever rank, must exercise the most painstaking control and supervision, so that every bullet fells an enemy and every grain of rice furthers the aim of the formation, and, further, that full use be made of captured ammunition and provisions.

'With particular reference to the provisions etc captured yesterday, the 31st, near Isurava, disposal must wait upon instructions from high-ranking commanding officers. Regimental HQ, companies, etc, must once again issue instructions to use these provisions in a consistent manner, reducing the daily ration to less than the present ration.'[3]

Brigadier Potts was fighting a series of delaying actions, making the Japanese deploy and attack to take each feature that could be defended. All this cost Major General Horii time and consumed supplies that had to be carried forward from Buna, but time and supplies were what Horii could not afford to expend. Conversely, each rearward move brought Potts's force closer to its own supply base and made communications easier. Potts was well aware that he could fight a last stand at any place he chose to do so, but that would achieve nothing and leave the track open. He had to buy time for other brigades of 7 Australian Division to be deployed onto the trail.

Throughout the night at Eora Creek, D Company 2/16th held the Koiwai Battalion. Conditions were made much more difficult for both sides by the heavy rain that deluged the area. By now, the Australians were well used to the creeping Japanese tactics, the ruses to encourage firing, the tricks to identify the location of automatic weapons, and the calling out in English. Several Japanese were killed at point-blank range. One actually grabbed a fixed bayonet, apparently believing it was a branch to assist in his climb. Grenades and small arms fire shattered yelling groups of Japanese in front of section posts.

Lieutenant Noda, III/144, was guarding the Japanese colours. He had risen at 4 am and the HQ began moving forward at 5 am, but the day's travel was only a few miles. He had spent a comfortable night at the last halt, in Australian tents, but had been unable to sleep as the night became colder, and the nearby elements of 41 Regiment made lots of noise, calling out in loud voices.

Before dawn on 2 September, having held the Japanese for as long as possible before becoming embroiled in a larger close battle, 2/16th withdrew from Eora Creek. The companies slogged back along a ridge, two miles (3.2 km) of tough travel on a slippery trail on steep slopes. By 8 am, 2/16th was in position, about one hour's march from Templeton's Crossing.

First air attack of the day was at 7.25 am, by A20s who placed 44 bombs in the target areas at Alola and Isurava, but saw no enemy. Their escort of seven P400s each dropped a 300-pound bomb, and despite seeing return fire from rifles and machineguns, found no signs of enemy activity. Over Kokoda, visibility was unlimited, but by 10 am, when four P400s dropped 300-pound bombs on Alola, and 15 minutes later when five P400s strafed and bombed Kokoda, broken cumulus cloud had bases at 17,000 feet.

Under the air attacks was Lieutenant Horibe, but his unit was not damaged in any way. With two NCOs and 16 soldiers, he continued on his way to rejoin his battalion after roadwork the day before. At HQ, he was given another 28 men and went on to camp south of Isurava. The company commander was promoted to captain. The company had landed with 162 men, and since had lost six killed, 13 wounded and six others sent back, leaving 137.

The 39th Battalion gathered in the Kagi area, with No. 1 Company one hour's march away to destroy Japanese advancing from Templeton's Crossing and No. 2 Company with the echelon holding Kagi village.

Meanwhile, working their way upstream, the party of 2/14th Battalion soldiers led by Mick Fielding, part of the group cut off with Lieutenant Colonel Key on the 30th, arrived at Templeton's Crossing. Their rations for each of the past three days had been one army biscuit per man, and one tin of bully beef between the nine of them. They went on to Myola, Mick reported to the officer who seemed to be in charge, and they were fed. Then the officer explained that he was concerned about the lack of troops guarding the track from Kagi, and the nine men mounted a standing patrol there until the Australian battalions arrived.

The 2/16th Battalion contacted the Japanese at 11 am. A seven-man patrol from 11 Platoon was on the track to Templeton's Crossing. Twelve Japanese, in sections of six, rifles slung, came along the trail. They behaved as if no enemy were close. The patrol, under Corporal Jim Willis, let the Japanese walk right into the killing ground, and opened fire. Private Gilbert Wooldridge killed 10 with his sub-machinegun. Other Japanese came forward and deployed to attack. 9 Platoon 2/16th engaged them, and countered a Japanese flanking move, forcing them to withdraw. Attacks on the battalion continued during the day, as the Japanese tried to find weak spots in the perimeter.

News of the Milne Bay fighting was passed to 14 Pioneer Unit, and Sei Tatemachi was told that Rabi (by which the Japanese referred to the operation area, not Milne Bay) had fallen to the Imperial forces.[4]

Meanwhile, having delayed the Japanese for the day, 2/16th Battalion again intended moving back at dusk. Battalion HQ went back at 5 pm, and the familiar withdrawal tactic began in the rifle companies. Somehow, the Japanese became aware of what was happening, and attacked at 6.10 pm, as A and B companies were leaving. A crisis was averted by the action of Sergeant Bill Duncan's 16 Platoon, which was in position to cover the withdrawal. The platoon held fire until the on-rushing Japanese were only 20 yards away, then halted them with a volley of light machinegun and grenades. Two more assaults were thrown back, despite the efforts of two Japanese officers waving swords. About 30 Japanese were estimated to be hit, but Private Tom McAtee was killed. The fight was quite noisy, with firing, grenade explosions and much shouting and abuse by both sides. This engagement allowed the 2/16th to break contact, and the battalion moved away until it was too dark to continue, then settled for the night.

The 160-odd Australians of 2/14th Battalion had arrived at Templeton's Crossing, where a hot stew awaited them, and more food was issued. 20 men from C Company, under Lieutenant McIlroy, went to guard the alternative route to Efogi, via Kagi. Later, the unit moved back to Myola. The rations available at the main dump there were described by Roy Watson (Lance Corporal/ Intelligence Officer) as 'epicurean fare, after not much bully and biscuits and plenty of water'. He was able to acquire a pair of shorts to replace the ragged remains of those shot apart at Isurava.

In air activity for the second half of the day, at 12.05 pm, six B26s attacked Lae airfield through moderate accurate AA, and visibility was out to 20 miles (32 km). Three B26s did not attack because of mechanical problems and all returned to Woodstock airfield near Townsville. The Japanese correctly identified the aircraft type, and recorded loss of 'some fuel only'. A B17 reconnoitred Faisi–Buin–Buka, despite 20 minutes of head-on attacks from a formation of Zeros. Two others had uneventful sorties and at night four RAAF Catalinas harassed Buka.[5] Transports *Kazuura Maru* and *Yasugawa Maru* completed unloading at Buna during the night of 2 September and weighed anchor for Rabaul.[6]

In the early hours of 3 September, three RAAF Catalinas again attacked Buka, and hit a fuel dump, while a B17 attacked flying boats at Faisi. Another B17 went to photograph the north coast of New Britain, but the pilot seized an opportunity and recorded Kokoda instead. At 10.10 am, eight P400s escorted transport planes, then strafed and bombed Kokoda, but no results were seen.

Cloudbase was 7000 feet, visibility nine miles (14 km), but an hour later conditions were cloudbase at 2500 feet, visibility to six miles (10 km), when A20s and B25s bombed Busamo–Mubo; no results were reported. A member of Takasago Volunteers noted these attacks and those of the past days, and wrote, 'fighters and Boeings continued aimless bombing and ground strafing. No casualties'. P400s strafed Kokoda at 12.34 pm, but were not as accurate as they could have been, because 39th Battalion at Kagi reported being dive-bombed by four of this type aircraft, the US national markings being clearly visible. No one was killed and one man suffered head and ear injuries from the blast.[7]

Major General Tomitaro Horii issued Operation Order A-112 at 9 am: 'The formation's advance has encountered renewed resistance from the enemy, but on the whole is progressing favourably. Since last evening the pursuit unit met enemy resistance near Iora, but it is planned to defeat them this morning. I Battalion of Yazawa Regiment and the Lines of Communication Hospital landed at Giruwa on 1 September with the fifth wave, and the hospital is expected to be set up in the vicinity of Kokoda.

2. The formation will alter the disposition of the pursuit unit and then continue pursuit towards the western end of the range.

3. The Yazawa pursuit unit will defeat the enemy in its sector and prepare to be relieved.

4. Colonel Kusunose, commanding 144 Regiment elements, becomes the new pursuit unit. They will leap-frog Yazawa pursuit unit and carry on pursuit towards the heights west of Wamai.

5. The other units under command of Colonel Yazawa will follow the pursuit unit in the following order. [Then follows a list of 41 and 144 Regiment elements and supporting arms.]

6. I/41 Regiment, immediately on landing, will follow the main body [of the regiment].

7. Kobayashi unit of the Engineers will continue its present assignment.

8. Owing to the occurrence of casualties, a field hospital will be established at Iora, or west of Iora, and will take care of wounded.'

The order was to be given verbally to the regimental commanders and commanders of pursuit units, who would in turn pass it on to others gathered for the purpose, and who would write it down.[8]

Horii now had his sixth battalion of infantry ashore. 2nd Lieutenant Onogawa had started moving forward again, despite the air attacks, and was told of the transit through the area by 41 Regiment during the night, so the advance could be continued.

In a Townsville cafe, Lieutenant Harry Staley began writing his diary. He was co-pilot for Ken McCullar, already known as a good B17 pilot, and Staley noted that he was happy to fly with McCullar for a while, as there was something to learn every day about the big B17. The crew had just returned from flying out of Moresby and were back for a rest in Australia. They had gone to the cafe for dessert after explaining away some fracas with the Military Police.

General Kenney went to Brisbane, reported to MacArthur on progress so far, and told MacArthur he did not think the Australians would be able to hold the Kokoda Trail. Kenney thought it useless for aircraft to attack the trail itself, as often it was not seen by the pilots, and best results could be gained by attacking ships, airfields and planes, and supply areas at the beachhead.

While Kenney was discussing his ideas with MacArthur, Tadao Chiba, 15 Pioneers, watched troops and supplies coming ashore from another Japanese ship that had arrived undetected, and was protected by three aircraft. This was *Matsue Maru*, with more supplies and another 300 horses, but because of heavy rain and high seas, only part of the cargo was brought ashore, and horses were still aboard when the ship began its return at 2.30 next morning.[9]

During darkness, 2/16th Battalion had been making its way back. Having broken contact with the Japanese, the battalion made its own track along the top of a ridge. This track had to be cut through the vines and trees to allow passage of the following soldiers. Everyone was tired, dirty, wet and footsore. Direction of march was provided by the Intelligence Sergeant, Jack Knox. Thanks to his abilities, the battalion arrived at Templeton's Crossing at 3.30 pm. Soon after, Lieutenant Colonel Caro was called to Myola for a conference to consider the defensive positions there, left Captain Frank Sublet in command and departed. As night fell, the Japanese began harassing the forward positions.

A party of 2/14th and 2/16th men had come out of the jungle and joined 2/16th about 30 minutes before the Japanese began their attacks. Lieutenant Stan Bisset, IO 2/14th, with the RSM, Warrant Officer 1 Les Tipton, the Intelligence Sergeant, Bill Lynn, and 10 soldiers, including two walking wounded, had been among those forced off the track into the bush by the Japanese assault at Isurava Rest House on 30 August. They had moved back towards Alola during the night, halting at about 2 am on 31 August. The party was some 200 yards below the trail, and Bisset and Tipton crept forward, but found many Japanese gathered around the supply dump, chattering away. Responsibility for the waiting party overcame the desire to throw grenades into the Japanese, so they returned and pushed on. After crossing Eora Creek and collecting Captain Wright and his batman, of 2/16th, on the fifth day the party caught up with the rearguard of 2/16th, just before it arrived at Templeton's Crossing. For the entire five days, food available was one emergency ration per man.

The 2/16th Battalion held the Japanese at Templeton's Crossing during the night, but at midday on 4 September a disturbing discovery was made. A patrol led by Lieutenant G. T. Hicks to the left found a Japanese telephone cable running through the foliage, and signs indicated that at least one company of enemy had passed that way. There was high ground to the rear of 2/16th, and if the Japanese took possession of it, the battalion could be cut off. Immediately a reconnaissance was made to find a better position, and eventually one was located on top of a ridge some one and a half miles (2.4 km) to the rear.

In Townsville, Lieutenant Harry Staley heard talk that some B17 crews were to be gathered to form a squadron of the 43rd Bomb Group. B17s went to the Vitiaz Straits, Milne Bay and Buka, and B25s attacked targets in Milne Bay, but there were no recorded missions on 4 September over the Kokoda–Buna–Lae area. The transport planes, the 'biscuit bombers', arrived early over Nauro, and passed above the thatched huts sheltering 2/27th Battalion. The free-falling tins of biscuits, bully beef and ammunition fell among the soldiers, killing one man and injuring five more. The battalion continued its advance, up the worst parts of the trail, moving against the flow of wounded from the 39th, 2/14th and 2/16th Battalions, and fit men of the 53rd. The 2/27th noticed the low morale of the 53rd soldiers. Some recognised friends and acquaintances among the AIF wounded, and cigarettes were offered; there was little else available.

George Woodward, Tommy-gunner in 10 Platoon 2/14th, was among the wounded. Several remained together, to assist each other, but all knew the available medical attention was scanty. One man from 10 Platoon, who had a hand blown off at the canefield, had it bandaged on the spot and set off to the rear, then proceeded to set what may be a record for the journey, and arrived in Port Moresby five days later. Among the 2/14th casualties were two whose experience epitomises the Australian ethos of 'never leave your mates'. During fighting at Isurava, Corporal L. A. 'Teddy' Bear had been wounded twice in the right leg, once in the left heel and once in the left hand, which combined to make it impossible for him to move forward normally, but only sideways, crab-like; Corporal Russ Fairbairn had been shot in the stomach by a large calibre bullet that lodged near his spine. Together they made their painful way across the cruel ridges, with Fairbairn ignoring Bear's urgings to go on ahead and leave him. Fairbairn pushed Bear up the hills, and stopped him sliding back down in the mud. 'I shall never forget that night going up into Efogi,' said 'Teddy' Bear. 'The rain was pelting down, darkness was closing in and things were rather miserable. Still Russ stuck to me, pushing me up that slope. But for him, I am sure I would have fallen back into the creek below.' At stopping places, Fairbairn would scrounge a meal for both men. Bear was very much aware that behind them the Japanese were coming, that it was a great effort for Fairbairn to walk, let alone look after another person, yet Fairbairn remained with him. As well as the shining spirit of determination in adversity, there was the Australian soldier's sense of humour: wounds were beginning to smell, and in George Woodward's small party, the man with the worst-smelling was sent to the rear of the group.

George will remember to his last day what happened when they met 2/27th Battalion on the trail – he was given a slice of bread by someone.

All were aware that only men immobilised by wounds could be carried, and also that in the battle area such carrying had to be done by fellow soldiers, further weakening the fighting ability of the unit. Yet, the alternative was unthinkable – to leave a wounded comrade to the Japanese.

The Japanese 8 Company III/41 attacked towards Kagi, and captured a man from HQ 2/14th Battalion. He told the Japanese that two Australian divisions, of six battalions, were deployed on the mountain range: 14, 16, 27, 39, 49 and 53rd Battalions, totalling 6000 men (sic). 1st Lieutenant Yoshiyaki Morimoto, in charge of codes, noted the incident in his diary, and also that 'II/41 and 8 Company destroyed the enemy on the south side of the valley at 16.50 [4.50 pm]'.

1st Lieutenant Horibe was at Eora, with the rest of his battalion. At 5 am, they had moved out, in the order of 4, 6, 5 Companies and Battalion Headquarters, reached HQ 144 Regiment at lunch, and prepared an attack on a hill, which began at 2.20 pm, with 6 Company as assault company. The hill was undefended, and the 128 men in the company climbed back down again, ready for a night's rest. Lieutenant Noda had handed over to 7 Company after duty as colour guard, and rejoined III/144. While at regimental HQ, his platoon had been issued rations for two days.

The Australian 2/16th Battalion was preparing to move back to the new location from Templeton's Crossing. As the company commanders were being briefed, the Japanese attacked. It seemed that a small, aggressive force had followed the earlier patrol, which had located the telephone wire. This group of Japanese achieved surprise and penetrated the A Company position, killing three men and wounding two. The situation was saved by the determined action of the Bren gunner, Private Brian Maloney.

The planned withdrawal seemed about to be disrupted, but OC D Company, Captain Bret Langridge, volunteered to take the role of rearguard with his company, which was not involved in the action at the moment. This was successful, and the Japanese were held off at the cost of two Australian wounded. Another man was killed later by the enemy outflanking unit, but 2/16th got back to the selected position. The battalion had held off the Japanese for the last seven days, since 29 August.

Major John Hearman, the battalion second-in-command, arrived to take command of the rearguard, with orders to fall back again, to Myola, passing through 2/14th, who would then become rearguard. This time, it was impossible to break contact cleanly, as many Japanese were only yards away, and as soon as the Australians moved back the enemy followed just as closely. However, gradually the withdrawal continued, and a small rear party from 12 Platoon held the track while the battalion moved away in the darkness.

The first two companies of 2/27th Battalion, A and B, arrived at Kagi, but Brigadier Potts decided on a move back to establish a defensive position on Mission Ridge, south of Efogi, and Lieutenant Colonel Honner made the necessary reconnaissance. At 6 pm, Potts informed 7 Division of a strong Japanese attack on 2/16th Battalion, and that he was supporting 2/16th with 2/14th, but the country was 'utterly unsuitable defended localities', so he was regretfully abandoning Myola, and withdrawing to Efogi. He added that he had no reserves for a counter-attack, the men were weary but full of fight; the 2/27th was too late to assist.

By this time, 2/14th had been reduced to about 160 of their original 544 men, and 2/16th had lost more than 100 from 585 men. A and B Companies 2/27th moved to Kagi and took up position astride the track, relieving the 39th. The foremost element of the 39th, a patrol at Templeton's Crossing, was replaced by 10 Platoon 2/27th Battalion.

Meanwhile, 53rd Battalion was learning that it was not wanted. It had been ordered back to Myola, and there informed that all automatic weapons were to be handed in prior to movement back to Port Moresby. Captain Bryce and three lieutenants were to remain at Myola to command troops used as guards on the supply groups of carriers. There was disappointment, as it was felt the battalion had not been given a real chance to get to grips with the Japanese. On arrival at Efogi, the battalion was met by the new commanding officer, Lieutenant Colonel Alan Cameron.

Forty of the fittest men were picked to remain at Efogi for use as workers to collect and stack the items arriving by air drop. Then, the battalion was told to be at a point near the food dump on the Myola–Efogi trail at first light on 5 September. All were to be armed and issued with grenades and other weapons necessary to hold a defensive position astride the Kagi trail. Through the 53rd would withdraw the 39th and 21 Brigade.

Early on 5 September, some two and a half miles (four km) north of Kagi, Horibe's unit began advancing again, 4 Company leading, but there was no contact that day. Lieutenant Noda wrote that everyone was pleased to find a stream flowing south, at what they thought to be the highest part of the mountains; they were over the crest and on the slopes leading down to Port Moresby.

The 53rd Battalion held its position on the track for the withdrawing units. All day and into the night they waited.

Meanwhile, the advancing Japanese were pressing on in the rain. II and III/144 passed through II/41, and were closing on the Myola area. They knew dumps of all types of supplies had to be somewhere ahead of them, and looked forward to capturing them.

The Australians of 2/16th arrived at Myola at 8 am, weary after the continuous rearguard actions. Lieutenant Colonel Caro had rejoined the battalion during its night march. A hot meal and tea were ready, and fresh clothes were issued to replace the torn and muddy uniforms they wore. Unfortunately for D Company, all that remained for them was lukewarm tea and cold bully beef, an injustice that was still recounted decades later. The other companies regarded this as the fortunes of war.

39th Battalion now totalled 185 all ranks, and arrived at Mission Ridge before midday. Two hours later, 2/27th Battalion arrived and soon began taking over the 39th's automatic weapons, rations, blankets, signal stores and medical supplies. The 39th then marched to Menari, where its parade for an address of praise by Brigadier Potts was filmed by Damien Parer and was included in his famous documentary *The Road to Kokoda*. Then the battalion marched for several days, despite illness and weariness, to Nauro, Ioribaiwa and Koitaki. A newly-arrived AIF unit was there in tents, and they stared at the tattered, dirty, bearded, bloody figures moving past.

The 39th Battalion – ill-equipped, ill-trained, ill-prepared, first Australian fighting unit across the Owen Stanleys – met and held the Japanese, forced them to deploy and delay, learned the basics of jungle warfare the hard way against a trained and experienced merciless enemy, and paid in blood for the lessons. Committed to battle again in the Buna–Gona fighting, the 39th was once more to perform at least as well as AIF battalions, but was disbanded by decision from higher headquarters on 3 July 1943. It was removed from the Australian Army Order of Battle; what the Japanese could not do was achieved by army bureaucrats. This incorrect decision has not been rectified.

The rain was penetrating the punctured cans, and spoiling the food scattered at the Myola dumps. The Japanese II/144 arrived first, and what was usable was quickly gathered up and distributed among the platoons. Sakamoto, the MG commander, was pleased at the discovery of tinned corned beef, jam and milk. However, there was nowhere near enough for the entire force.

Eight B17s that set off for Rabaul were forced to return by bad weather, and A20s trying to strafe and bomb the trail early in the day also were forced to return to Moresby. However, at 10.05 am, 17 A20s got through, and attacked Buna airfield from 1500 feet, then made two strafing runs each, silencing one machinegun, destroying two barges, and destroying two aircraft on the ground. The runway appeared to be unserviceable, and AA came from positions around the field before the bombs dropped, but slackened after that. Tadao Chiba watched the attack on the airfield and barracks, 'causing heavy damage', but with no losses to the attackers. 'Uchida', of 15 Pioneers, recorded the first unit casualties since arriving at Buna: nine killed and 'a few' wounded. P400s strafed Alola, Buna, Sanananda and Kokoda, but one fighter dived into the ground at Kokoda and exploded. Pilots estimated visibility at Buna as only quarter of a mile (400 metres), but saw men running at Isurava and equipment stacked in a clearing between Isurava and Alola. Having suffered no damage from the air strikes, a Takasago Volunteer officer near Isurava checked the men of his platoons, and found that there were 33 malaria cases, four indigestion, two with colds, two wounded, and one with diarrhoea, totalling 42 patients needing medical treatment.[10]

B17s flew on reconnaissance of Milne Bay, Vitiaz, Buka and the north coast of New Guinea, and attacked shipping at Dawson Island. The five surviving B25s that had flown missions to Milne Bay returned to Charters Towers.

In Townsville harbour, 2/25th Battalion transhipped to that already carrying the 2/33rd, the *Cremer*, and to other ships, after theirs had been rammed. The already crowded conditions were further cramped. The holds of the ships were fitted with three-tier bunks in rows with only two feet (61 cm) between rows. The mess queues simply moved along the alleys between bunks to the serving point and each man returned to his bunk to eat. Entertainment consisted of watching the Chinese crew play cards. At first, the ships were to go to Milne Bay, which did not please too many people, who wondered about landing in the presence of the Japanese Navy, but this was altered to disembarking at Port Moresby.

On the Kokoda Trail, all four rifle companies and HQ of 2/27th Battalion joined to form a defensive position on the high ground south of Efogi. C, D and HQ Company assisted in carrying stores back from Efogi. 53rd Battalion were still in position. At 10 pm, Japanese were reported close by, and Captain Bryce was able to watch at close range, in the night, the confident advance of the enemy. Obviously, they believed they were holding the advantage. They were quite noisy and seemed not to worry who was near by; lanterns were used with no apparent concern about enemy reaction. Bryce and the 53rd watched all night, noting as much information as possible.

Early in the new morning of 6 September, Captain Bryce and the 53rd Battalion were ordered back through 21 Brigade's positions, then went back to Uberi and a week later to 30 Infantry Training Battalion, where the men at once were dispersed on work parties, as guards, and as coast watchers in the area. All this made it impossible, just as it had been previously, to plan and conduct any training. Later, 100 men were sent as reinforcements to the 39th Battalion and fought well at Gona.

In air activity on 6 September, B17s attacked a convoy of one transport ship, two destroyers and two launches, but claimed no hits, and another B17 attacked Mubo from 16,000 feet, but low cloud prevented any damage assessment. Six B17s flew reconnaissance missions to the normal areas. At 9.50 am, A20s flew through heavy cloud, found a small opening at the target, and attacked Myola 1 and the Eora Creek position. P400s dropped bombs on the enemy on the west side of Myola, and strafed all visible huts, starting many small fires. Kokoda Pass was completely blocked by clouds. At 10.40 am, more P400s each dropped a bomb on Myola, pilots reporting a large fire burning on the northern edge of the lake, but no activity was seen. By that time, in contrast to the conditions on earlier missions, cloudbase of heavy cumulus was at 7500 feet. Later, more P400s dropped bombs, but again saw nothing. One pilot bailed out, was seen to land on Myola 2, but no word of him was received, and his fate is unknown.

2nd Lieutenant Onogawa, 144 Regiment, was under these attacks, and noted that his battalion CO was wounded, and 'many others killed or wounded'. The regimental CO, Kusunose, was ill. Lieutenant Noda's unit had been distributing food left behind by the Australians when what he termed a heavy air-raid occurred; two officers were wounded. Still making his way through the hills, Akira Teruoka had rested near 'an enemy storehouse', then continued walking. He saw two air-raids, but noted 'nothing occurred', and kept on moving forward with his unit.

Horii's headquarters issued an 'Instruction Bulletin' that stated that any unit finding food or forage would at once inform the supply organisation; consumption of such finds without authority was forbidden. Dispersal in the event of air-raids was dealt with, and the areas suitable for different sized units to scatter into were

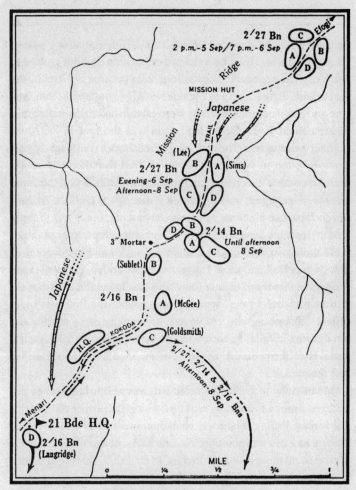

21 Brigade, 8 September.

stated, with an exhortation for all to be continually alert about camouflage, and to take 'minute precautions'.[11]

The Australian 21 Brigade was now together for the first time, but was in poor condition. 2/27th Battalion was fresh, but 2/14th had been reduced to about a company strength and 2/16th had suffered in the recent rearguard actions. The first inwards mail for five weeks was delivered and distributed, and hastily scribbled letters home, written on anything available, were collected and sent out. 2/27th Battalion became the forward battalion in the brigade after the depleted 2/14th and 2/16th Battalions passed through them and took up a defensive position on high ground to the rear. The sequence of battalions then became 2/27th, 2/14th and 2/16th, Brigade HQ in the rear with D Company 2/16th, and line and radio communications were established to the battalions.

Lieutenant F. D. Bell's 8 Platoon was the first in 2/27th to contact the Japanese. The platoon was sent back to the Kagi–Myola track junction to relieve a platoon of 53rd Battalion. Its orders were to contact the enemy, then withdraw. At 2.25 pm, the Japanese were engaged, with 8 Platoon initiating the contact. At least seven Japanese platoons were seen advancing, but it was thought that their scouts detected 8 Platoon in position. Japanese casualties were unknown, but one Australian was killed and two were missing, while Bell and three Diggers were wounded. Private Happy Anderson displayed the qualities here that led to the award of the Military Medal. In the Japanese force countering Bell was Lieutenant Sakamoto, who employed his machineguns, mortar and small arms in holding back what he estimated to be 100 Australians. His Juki medium machineguns harassed Bell's patrol as they left the area.

Meanwhile, at 2/27th position, Brigadier Potts had visited and ordered a move some 200 yards up the slope to further concentrate his forces. Before the move, each man was issued two days' rations and extra ammunition. No one knew at the time, but there would be no more rations issued for 14 days. 2/27th were allocated a position on a grassy spur, above a small clearing near the ruins of the old mission building. Forest-covered gullies (re-entrants) fell away steeply on either side, but the high grass around the battalion limited vision to about 15 yards. Fire lanes were roughly cut, and weapons pits dug with tin hats, bayonets and other improvised digging implements. The four rifle companies were placed in a diamond-shaped configuration across the track, with HQ in the centre. Body holes were scraped out with steel helmets, bayonets and whatever was available. As the move back was being made, large numbers of Japanese could be seen in Efogi, having a meal. As the Japanese were two hours behind local time, operating on

Tokyo time, they probably were lunching. The light weapons available to the brigade meant that the Japanese were out of range, but an air strike at first light was requested.

By 2.30 pm, 2/16th Battalion was in position on Mission Ridge, named for a small mission hut perched on a spur. B Company was overlooking the Mission and Efogi village; A Company was between B and Battalion HQ; C Company was on the right; HQ Company on the left; D Company was to the rear, defending Brigade HQ. Battalion company commanders at this time were: A Company, Captain G. M. McGee; B Company, Captain George Wright; C Company, Captain Keith Goldsmith; D Company, Captain Bret Langridge; HQ Company, Captain Ron Campbell.

Unknown to the Australians, the first signs of sickness from the tainted, captured rations eaten in haste by the Japanese were noticed by them. Stomach pains and other internal complaints struck widely, and officers felt first stirrings of alarm. Sakamoto thought this was due to eating too much rich, captured food, and told his men to be sparing with the items. It was too late. Dysentery was to become widespread, and weaken or kill many Japanese. However, the Japanese had made their assessment of the military situation, decided to attack the Australian brigade, and began moving out of Efogi early in the morning.

Determined to impress on Washington the urgent need for more forces to be sent to him, MacArthur did not refrain from telling untruths. He wrote to General George Marshall and said that the Australians were unable to match the Japanese, and that aggressive leadership was lacking. Of course, the remedy for this was more American formations for MacArthur's command. This allegation about leadership from MacArthur was also sent by General Vasey to Rowell, who had complained about the incorrect impression of the fighting in New Guinea given by the GHQ communiques. Neither knew MacArthur wrote communiques, as he had in the Philippines. In no other Allied theatre of war was information so controlled as to emphasise the importance of one man.

Early on 7 September, the Japanese lit their way out of Efogi with lanterns, obviously aware that the Australians had nothing with which to bring fire down upon them. From the 2/14th observation post, the watchers were amused by the sight of distant lights flying through the air as Japanese lost their footing on the slippery sloping trail down the ridge. Roy Watson's opinion of the Japanese effrontery in using lanterns was, 'Conceited bastards!' By morning, the Intelligence Section watchers had counted at least 1500 enemy passing through Efogi, moving towards 21 Brigade.

At 8 am, eight A20s bombed Buna–Efogi, leaving Efogi village burning, and noted machinegun fire from a hill at the junction of the Efogi–Kagi–Myola track. 2/27th Battalion was much cheered by the event, especially as the planes swept low and fast by the infantry. Particularly impressive were the strafing flight of P39s from the escort. 2/16th Battalion urged on the pilots with usual Australian language.

The Japanese 6 Company II/144 had been leading the battalion since it left Efogi at 4 am, and though there was no damage recorded, the Japanese thought the aircraft attacked them. Lieutenant Horibe was soon to see action. Just after the aircraft left, about a platoon of Japanese was seen near the old mission hut, and were scattered with fire from B Company 2/27th. However, increasingly heavy Japanese fire was returned, with mortars and then the mountain artillery joining in. The grassy area was raked with machinegun, mortar and artillery fire. The artillery was firing from so close a range that the shells exploded before the noise of the firing was heard.

The 2/14th Battalion had been deployed by Captain Rhoden with most strength on the right, covering the alternative route to Menari. He sent a small party to reconnoitre the route, and this was to pay dividends later. The old army saying, 'Time spent in reconnaissance is seldom wasted' again proved to be true.

Lieutenant Schwind, 2/14th, took command of a mortar team composed of men from all three battalions. Three three-inch (76 mm) mortars and 40 rounds had been air-dropped at Myola and carried to Efogi. Schwind found an observation post and a mortar position. The 2/27th mortar team was wiped out when the first bomb failed to clear the tube and detonated. This was the first of such events, and the reasons were not discovered for some time. However, Schwind and his 2/14th team began an effective bombardment of the distant Japanese, until a mountain gun replied, wounding some of the crew. Then the enemy discovered Schwind's position, and turned their attention to him. Eventually, the mortar would be operated by a team who would man it, fire several rounds 'rapid' and then smartly leave the area while the Japanese retaliated. Fortunately, the mortar itself was not hit.

On one memorable occasion, Schwind was actually looking through his telescope at a Japanese officer and saw a mortar bomb hit the man on the head. For some reason, which the unit historian described as 'that peculiar stupidity which went parallel with their cunning', the Japanese persisted in moving through the open area under Schwind's observation and fire.

II/144 engaged an estimated 100 Australians, with Horibe's 6 Company losing two killed and five wounded. Scouts reported the enemy holding a crest position ahead, and Australian mortar fire killed one more and wounded another 13 men. An attack was to have been made, but scouting the position took up the rest of the day. A dawn attack was planned.

Other air attacks were made in the battle area, and at 8.15 am, four P400s attacked Myola 1, then at 8.40 another 11 P400s bombed Myola, starting four large fires. Huts seen previously were covered with brush and shrubbery. Weather was clear, visibility unlimited, but two hours later cloudbase was only 4500 feet when seven P400s bombed Myola–Efogi and reported fires still burning. Pressing on through cumulus that was down to the hilltops, but broken in parts, nine A20s attacked Efogi and Myola 1 and 2 at 11.30 am, bombing what the pilots described as considerable enemy activity. It may have been in this series of attacks that 100 Japanese were killed, as later reported by a prisoner. However, in the 55 Division medical unit, advancing through rain, Akira Teruoka did not hear of this, or make a note of it. He crossed a river and 'entered the jungle' while listening to an air attack, which went on despite the rain, but the unit did not record any damage. Then the clouds sank onto the mountains, preventing further air support for the time being. Lieutenant Noda's unit was hit by the raids, and he recorded company casualties as two killed and one wounded. It was his first air-raid, and he wrote, 'Death is fate. No good being pessimistic. Advance to Port Moresby believing in final victory'. It was his final diary entry. His notebooks were captured next day.[12]

Elsewhere, around the Efogi position, there had been firing and probing by the Japanese, countered by patrolling action from the Australian companies. Captain R. L. Johnson, OC A Company 2/27th, had been wounded by mountain gun shells, and was evacuated. Command was taken by Lieutenant Colin Sandison. Sergeant R. D. Johns, 7 Platoon A Company 2/27th, took out a fighting patrol that engaged Japanese near the mission hut, on the right flank. This patrol was quite successful, killing six Japanese, and capturing a light machinegun and a grenade discharger. The patrol returned without loss, triumphantly, with Johns waving the machinegun and Private Snowy Hill brandishing the discharger. A heavy volume of fire soon fell on A Company, including mortar, mountain gun and machineguns, inflicting a number of casualties. Two NCOs were killed, and one other plus nine Diggers were wounded. It may be that the Japanese followed the returning patrol and observed their progress through the grass. B and C Companies also patrolled to right and left, and the 2/14th observation post reported large numbers of heavily laden Japanese coming up the track towards 2/27th's position.

The day had been very hot and dry for 2/27th, perched out on the sun-heated grassy expanse. A patrol from 18 Platoon brought back some water, and a little more was collected in ground sheets during the afternoon deluge. As night fell, burial parties began work, interring those killed during the day. Ten men were buried. It was obvious that the Japanese were going to attack, and 2/27th settled in to withstand it.

Horii had positioned elements from all three battalions of 144 Regiment, plus Lieutenant Colonel Koiwai's II/41 to attack the top of the hill from front and flanks at dawn. An engineer party, with Lieutenant Sakamoto's machinegun company, set off to find a way around to the rear of the Australians, but progress was halted at dusk by swampy ground.

Meanwhile, another Militia battalion was moving to the front lines. 3rd Battalion, under Lieutenant Colonel A. T. Paul, had arrived at Port Moresby, and also been used for the many labouring tasks that were necessary but cut into training time. On the day the Japanese landed at Buna, 3rd Battalion strength was 32 officers and 751 other ranks. By 6 September, the battalion was arriving at Ioribaiwa. On this day, Lieutenant Colonel Paul was ordered to report to 14 Brigade HQ, as he was deemed too old for the exertions ahead, but Paul himself did not agree with this. Lieutenant Colonel Alan Cameron, ex-2/22nd, 39th and 53rd Battalions, was on the way to take command.

Early on 8 September, one B17 reconnoitred the Buna area, ignored inaccurate AA and bombed barges there, reporting fires started on the barges and fires inland. Three other B17s flew armed reconnaissance in the area. At 8.45 am, eight P400s bombed Efogi. No activity was seen, but many huts burned in yesterday's attacks were noticed, and two machineguns and one AA gun fired with no effect. 2/27th had requested a strike at first light, onto the enemy in the mission hut area; this was the response. Air–ground liaison was still in its primary stages, and not able to respond to rapidly changing battle situations.

At 4.30 am, A Company 2/27th Battalion was attacked, the Japanese advancing through slight moonlight. Using Brens and grenades, A Company repulsed every assault. As dawn came, the entire battalion area was again hammered with small arms, machinegun, mortar and mountain gun fire. Movement in the area was almost impossible, but A Company did receive ammunition and a small amount of water. At 7.15 am, a small attack on B Company was made, presumably the Japanese effort at deception, to induce reinforcements to rush to the newly-threatened area. However, the pressure on A Company was maintained, and kept up until midday, without success.

The unit historian made the point that this action was a rifle section and section commander's war. Each section post, in the grass, was self-contained and self-reliant, unable to call for fire support, conscious that the post formed a link in the battalion defences. The Australians were learning to fight a different style of warfare. No more the trenchlines of Gallipoli, of the Western Front; the battalions, brigades and divisions sweeping forward with the bayonet; no more the vistas of the Western Desert, the hills of Syria. Now it was the tiny world of the section position, each man totally reliant on the others, almost blind in the conceal-ing grass, knowing that there was no artillery support, and that the Japanese were coming, seemingly regardless of casualties. This close combat often demanded more of a man, in trust of his fellows, than the wider scale of battle.

Meanwhile, with 2/27th under pressure, at 6.15 am, Brigade Headquarters came under attack. Concurrently, Menari was evacu-ated, with 3000 rations abandoned. At 7.30 am, 2/27th heard fighting to their left, and later learned that 2/16th had been pushed back, and the Japanese had gained the highest ground on the ridge, between 2/27th and Brigade HQ. Personnel in Brigade HQ de-fended their position, with all ranks in action. The Japanese now dominated the area from their high ground, and the Australian situation was serious. At 10 am, Brigadier Potts contacted Lieu-tenant Colonel Caro and warned him that brigade command might pass to Caro if the headquarters was destroyed.

Captain Geoffrey Lyon, from 2/14th Battalion, had assumed duty as Brigade Major after Major Challen went from brigade to 2/14th. He recalled that after the frontal attack on 2/27th, the Japanese came around on the flanks and got onto the track between the battalions and Brigade HQ. The main Japanese force was west of the track, but two companies attacked Brigade HQ. 'Everyone downed tools and began to fight,' he said.[13]

Horie's II/144 had attacked 2/16th, and Lieutenant Kamimura's 5 Company, II/144, occupied the high point of the ridge and me-naced 21 Brigade HQ. Leaving their position at 4 am, 6 Company II/144 had attacked the Australians (2/16th) at 7.20 am, penetrated their position and held part of it, then drove them off the hill. Those who were worthy of note were the No. 1 Section commander, Private Kiyoshi Fujito, and Private Toshio Kuro. The company lost two killed and eight wounded, bringing the total casualties in two days fighting to six dead and 31 wounded, reducing company strength to 92 all ranks. Kentoro Fujiwara this day noted the casualties in his own company: 11 killed, 17 wounded, bringing company strength to 88.[14]

At 21 Brigade HQ, Brigadier Potts himself was nearly killed by a sniper, and one of his liaison officers, Lieutenant Cairns, was nearly killed in a close action with a machinegunner in the grass. The Japanese was killed by a grenade from Corporal Beveridge, who was himself killed by the machinegunner, but Cairns was only saved from a second Japanese by the other liaison officer, Burnham Fraser, who shot him with the marksman's rifle he carried. Fire from two-inch mortars eased the Japanese pressure on Brigade Headquarters, but there had been two killed and two wounded by about midday.

B Company 2/16th was shelled, and replied with three-inch mortar bombs. However, as the bombs were damaged by water, their range was inconsistent. 2/16th Battalion HQ was attacked by Japanese who had crawled to within a few yards of their position. 13 Platoon under Lieutenant Viv Williams fought a 20-minute action to clear them away. Patrols then found that during the night a Japanese force had dug in across the Menari track, and effectively cut off Brigade HQ from the forward units. There was increasing pressure on 2/16th itself, and it was obvious the Japanese were massing to exploit their advantage. 2/16th was without a water supply and burdened with stretcher cases. Lieutenant Colonel Caro discussed the situation by radio with Brigadier Potts, and decided to attack along the track at 2.15 pm, to clear the way to Brigade HQ for the stretchers and walking wounded.

Caro's orders were for C Company to be on the left; A and B Companies to go down the track; B Company 2/14th under Captain Claude Nye on the right; HQ Company to carry the stretchers following A and B Companies; 2/27th Battalion was to bring up the rear. 17 and 18 Platoons from D Company 2/16th, with Brigade HQ, were to attack from the other side, towards the battalion.

Lance Corporal Roy Watson was acting as Intelligence Officer 2/14th Battalion, and was ordered by Lieutenant Colonel Caro to go to Brigade Headquarters, and report the situation and Caro's intentions. It was known that if the brigade could get out of its present situation, Major Watson, of ANGAU, could guide it along a by-pass into Menari. Watson was to prepare to guide the force back to brigade when he had made the return journey. He asked if he could take Private Gil Ralston with him, it was approved, and off the two men went.

Watson navigated by the sound of the different weapons, the distinctive noise made by Australian and Japanese rifles and light machineguns, naturally avoided the Japanese and steered towards the Australians, and eventually arrived safely. He reported to Brigadier Potts, and returned to the battalions, first leaving Gil Ralston concealed in a position to watch the brigade headquarters battle, so that he could inform the advancing battalions if necessary. On the way in, Ralston had carefully blazed the route, but in a way that only he and Watson knew, which would not be obvious to any Japanese as a blaze mark. Roy Watson then made his way back to Lieutenant Colonel Caro, and there was enough light left in the day for Major Watson to reconnoitre his way to Menari.

All three Australian battalions were cut off from Brigade HQ. The battalion commanders conferred, and agreed that 2/27th would move back to the 2/14th, and together the battalions would attack the Japanese now on top of the ridge, regain contact with Brigade HQ, receive supplies, evacuate the wounded, and continue the rearguard action. Fortunately, to the rear of 2/27th there was cover in the trees and undergrowth, so the battalion was able to move back successfully. The Japanese seemed unaware of the development, possibly because they were recovering from the morning attacks, or had moved away themselves to exploit the success on the flank. Stretchers were made from saplings to carry the wounded and HQ Company was allocated the carrying task. At first, four men were detailed to each stretcher, but soon this was seen to be far too few. Eventually 10 men per stretcher were needed.

The inevitable rain fell as the combined 2/14th–2/16th force began its attack, going downhill into the Japanese. The first shock threw the Japanese back, but they rallied and showed they were well aware of the potential of their position, because they simply moved back onto the track closer to brigade HQ. This was repeated in all parts of the attack, and the casualties to both sides were heavy. Japanese and Australians realised what was at stake and fought fiercely.

Japanese machineguns were very effective in defence of their positions. The close infantry combat, and the leadership required, resulted in many officers and NCOs becoming casualties, as well as many soldiers. At 5 pm, leading an attack by 17 and 18 Platoons 2/16th from Brigade Headquarters position back towards the battalion, to press the enemy from that direction, Captain Bret Langridge was wounded, but continued yelling encouragement to the platoons as he collapsed, dying. Langridge, Lieutenant Lambert and 20 men were killed in this attack from Brigade Headquarters.

The attacks saved Brigade Headquarters, but the area became known as 'Butcher's Hill'. About 40 members of the HQ had been in action, and the only people not actually shooting were Brigadier Potts, Brigade Major, Staff Captain and a signaller. 2/14th and 2/16th Battalions suffered severely. 2/16th lost at least 24 killed and others died later of wounds.

Captain Claude Nye, OC B Company 2/14th, was well aware of the task he and his few men had been given. Not only would they be attacking the strongest Japanese positions, but also their flank would be exposed to attack from Japanese known to be in strength on the right (or west) side of the track. He put 11 and 12 Platoons forward, and 10 in reserve. After two hours of intense action, only eight men, under Warrant Officer Wofty Noble, got through to Brigade HQ; Nye was killed. He had been a popular officer and man, as a platoon commander, staff officer at battalion HQ, and as a company commander. The company now was commanded by Sergeant Jack Matthews. Also among the dead were Corporal Charlie McCallum (Distinguished Conduct Medal) and 14 other men. Seven were wounded, one man dying of wounds later.

Attached to the company for the attack, one signaller was killed and the other wounded.

What had happened was that when Sakamoto and the others had arrived at the saddle, and reported this, Horii sent part of Kuwata's III/144 to exploit the advantage, plus sent in attacks from other sectors. Captain Nye's men ran into some of the stronger Japanese force also making their way to the same area, and the Australians were greatly outnumbered. But, at such cost, the Japanese were fought to a standstill.

With the last light, the Australians began to move back, along the route found by Roy Watson. This move was regarded by some as the most difficult of the campaign. At first, the track went up a gentle slope, but it soon steepened and the stretcher bearers had to make superhuman efforts. Sometimes the track had to be widened; the rain never stopped; night was coming; the Japanese could be anywhere.

Meanwhile, B and D Companies 2/27th moved down the slope and took up a defensive position astride the track. The Japanese picked the time to attack, but were repulsed, and B Company put in a sharp counter-attack at 5.30 pm, flinging back the Japanese, and had the benefit of breaking contact, easing the withdrawal. OC B Company, Captain A. J. Lee, MC, was awarded a Bar to the MC, for his example of courage and leadership, at times under heavy fire and with the Japanese only 20 yards away. Lee and two others were last out, emptying magazines at the enemy.

The 2/27th, with 15 stretcher cases that slowed progress to 'a snail's pace', was able to move away from the Japanese, and kept on going until 9 pm. Unfortunately, the bodies of those killed in the counter-attack had to be left in place, but they were found and buried by 25 Brigade during the later advance.

The two-day action at Efogi cost 2/27th 39 killed and two missing, believed killed. Forty-five members of the battalion had been wounded, for a total of 86 casualties. Later, 25 Brigade counted more than 200 dead Japanese in the area. 2/27th did not give ground, maintained its position, and was forced to leave only by enemy success elsewhere. When it did move back, 2/27th brought all its wounded, weapons and equipment, and forced the Japanese to break contact.

Brigade HQ had heard the outbreak of firing, and deduced it was from an attack by one of the battalions. Brigadier Potts decided to move to Menari, but leave in position a covering force of some 40 men who had been left out of battle (LOB), but brought forward by Captain Russell, 2/14th. Nearby, Bert Kienzle had to post a guard of two armed policemen over carriers remaining with him; the Japanese attack on brigade HQ had greatly unsettled them.

If the Japanese had been able to do so, they could have pushed on to Port Moresby. All that stood between them and their objective was Russell's small covering force. 21 Brigade, its component battalions, was scattered and making its way to Menari. As so often in war, the Japanese commander did not realise what the situation really was in his opponent's camp.

For the Japanese, the cost of victory had been high. Sakamoto wrote of the tragic sight of dead piled high, and the cries from wounded going unheeded. Kamimura's company strength was reduced by 50 per cent. Also killed was Lieutenant Noda, by this time OC 8 Company III/144. His final diary entry was, 'Death is a fate'. 2nd Lieutenant Onogawa had been ordered to assist with evacuation of the wounded, and did so despite air attacks. He wrote down the numbers of casualties: battalion HQ, 47; 1 Company, 53; 3 Company, 43. A total of 143 casualties, some requiring evacuation, would require several times that number of stretcher bearers, so it is reasonable to assume that another 200 men would have been needed to move the wounded back. This evacuation took Onogawa away from his unit for the next week, during which his only diary entries referred in general terms to air attacks, including one severe raid at Kagi on 11 September. A message from Onogawa to the unit adjutant describes the conditions they faced. 'Again held up because of heavy rain, air-raids and lack of personnel. While forming up in rear of the field hospital it became dusk. [Later] Still harassed by air-raids and hindered by bad roads. It is difficult to provide food for 28 stretcher cases and 19 walking men. Perhaps this was the cause of our own men becoming ill.

When six of the wounded died, the medical department warned us. One day's rest taken.'[15]

Interpreter Toshio Sato, at Buna, was told that the Tsukioka Butai (Sasebo 5SLP), 'which occupied Buna caught six or seven Australian men and women and cut their heads off one by one on the beach. There was a young girl of 16. She yelled and cried as they missed her head, but they cut her head by force. He said it was a dreadful sight. The heads and bodies were thrown into the sea'. Probably Sato was referring to the murders of the missionary party and Lieutenant Austen in August. There are several references to the 16-year-old girl in various Japanese accounts, and this may be a mistake in identification or translation, but it is always Sasebo 5SLP that is mentioned as the unit concerned in these and other killings.

In the morning, General Kenney was told that the Japanese were at Efogi, first in a string of items of bad news. His new P38s were grounded due to badly leaking 'leakproof' fuel tanks and other technical problems, and more B25s arrived, but they were totally unfitted for operations, with no gun mounts, no guns, and no bomb-sights. To top things off, when Kenney called General Rush Lincoln in Melbourne to check progress of the move by the supply depot to Townsville, he was told nothing had been done. Lincoln's people were waiting for written orders to confirm what Kenney had merely *said* on 22 August.

In the afternoon, General Kenney went to see General MacArthur and discussed with him Kenney's plan to occupy Wanigela, on the north coast of New Guinea, thus outflanking Buna. Kenney proposed that all troops, weapons, ammunition and supplies be flown in, and that the garrison be supplied by air and sea. This would take the initiative away from the Japanese, who would not be able to ignore the threat to their isolated supply base at Buna –Gona. MacArthur was not convinced that his air arm could accomplish such a feat, and it was obvious that the Allies had nowhere near the number of transport planes to sustain such an operation. Kenney then asked MacArthur to allow him to fly US troops to New Guinea, emphasising the benefits from such speedy movement of fresh troops to the battle zone. MacArthur was not convinced.

By his account, Kenney is supposed to have said to MacArthur that air power was the only thing slowing the Japanese advance. Yet he was also on record as having recently admitted that attacks on the trail were of doubtful efficiency and with little known result. The Japanese themselves were not much concerned about air attacks striking home in the jungle. Akira Teruoka noted in his diary that the Japanese did not fear the aircraft 'because of the jungle zone'. However, next day was to have a different entry.

Six A20s flew from Charters Towers to Port Moresby, as part of the normal rotation of aircraft from Australian bases to forward operating strips, and further south, more AIF units were warned for a move north. Lieutenant Colonel C. R. V. Edgar, CO 2/2nd Battalion, returned from a commanders' conference and told his officers the battalion was to be ready to depart at 10 next morning. As the battalion had been back in Australia for only a month, this was a surprise. 2/2nd, with its sister battalions 2/1st and 2/3rd, was greatly experienced after fighting Germans and Italians in North Africa, Greece, and Crete, with time in Palestine, Syria and on Ceylon (Sri Lanka), which introduced them to jungle conditions. Despite heavy losses in those campaigns, the units retained a kernel of very capable officers, NCOs and men with no illusions about war, but with the confidence and mutual respect that can derive only from such shared experiences. On arrival at the port of Melbourne, 2/3rd had shown the Communist-dominated waterside unions the contempt in which they were held. When the wharfies unloading the ship found that there was ammunition as well as weapons in the holds, they went on strike for more pay, for working with such dangerous items. 2/3rd was unimpressed, as an infantryman normally carried such materials on his person, there was a war on, and finally many of the battalion had been away for two years, but could not go ashore until the ship was unloaded. Some tougher men grabbed a few wharfies, stripped them and coated them in molasses. This led to the waterside unions refusing to work at all, but 2/3rd did their job for them.

Then the similarly sympathetic Victorian Railway Union tried to refuse the battalion access to the train that had arrived, but the soldiers threatened to drive it anyway, so 2/3rd Battalion was delivered to its allocated camp.

Far to the north of the petty attitude displayed by the left-wing trade unionists, in the wet New Guinea night, the battle-weary 21 Brigade endured the dark hours on a steep slope, in full kit, tied to or braced against a tree, waiting for the dawn and the continuation of their withdrawal to Menari.

On 9 September, only one mission was flown over the Owen Stanleys, when A20s flew through broken cumulus and attacked Efogi at 7.50 am. The bombers made three runs each, and silenced a machinegun post. Pilots reported new huts had been built, and many groups of Japanese were seen on paths south of Efogi. Of this attack, Akira Teruoka wrote that his unit had begun walking at daybreak, but at the foot of a mountain had halted as 'movement is impossible because of air attack. The sweeping machine gun fire and continuous air attack is fierce. It seems our damage was very heavy yesterday due to a continuous enemy air attack of one hour and a half. We descended the mountain hurriedly because of signs of rain'.

As morning came at Menari, Brigadier Potts could hear nothing of his battalions. The radio was not working, but there was no firing to give a base for an educated guess at the locations of the battalions. A dump of hats and boots, air-dropped the day before, was assembled, along with rations and ammo for the battalions if they did arrive. At 9 am, Warrant Officer Preece, of ANGAU, arrived, and told of the events of the night, and reported that 2/27th was bringing its stretcher cases out. He went back to guide the battalion. About an hour later, the Japanese began mortaring the village. The supply dump for the battalions was moved to a point 100 yards west of the village, where it was estimated the battalions would arrive. Everyone, including Brigadier Potts, did some of this work, despite machinegun fire from about 1200 yards range. Captain Geoff Lyon fired a Bren back at the gun.

A party of 2/14th Battalion, under Captain Russell, held the log bridge over the creek some 800 yards forward of Menari. With Russell was Lieutenant Rainey and 17 men, mostly transport drivers. Three Japanese dressed in Australian clothes appeared at the far side of the bridge, but were not fired on. Later, the Japanese began infiltrating upstream of the bridge. Private Joe Attard, a Maltese who had served in the First World War, and understated his age to join in this conflict, killed two and dispersed the remainder of the first group.

The enemy presence began to build up, as Horii had five infantry battalions forward, and fire from machineguns and mountain guns began falling on Menari village. Brigadier Potts knew the place would have to be evacuated. Some officers and men made several trips into the huts, under fire, to scavenge tins of food.

The 2/14th came in first, at about 11.30 am, and as there was no time to organise a hot meal, the battalion filed past the supply point, each man being given a block of chocolate, tobacco, bully beef and biscuits, two grenades and 100 rounds of ammunition. Then 2/16th went past, and the small supply party waited for 2/27th. It became clear that Japanese were approaching and had by-passed Russell's force at the river. Roy Watson and George Wild, 2/14th, were on the ridge top out of Menari, guiding parties of withdrawing Aussie who appeared up the slope onto the track to the dump and the rest of the force, and eventually they too came down and joined 2/14th Battalion.

Brigade HQ set off to Nauro, with Brigadier Potts and Lyon last out, stopping to check the positions on top of the hill. At this time, 21 Brigade's effective strength was some 300 men, but 7 Division was ordering Potts to establish a firm base, secure the lines of communication, and attack the Japanese before pushing on to Kokoda. Potts asked Lyon, 'What is a firm base? I haven't got one here. I think they'd better send me one up'. When the HQ had been under attack, a long signal from Division HQ had been received. It requested the return of expendable stores, and the dutiful signaller who brought it to Potts and his staff officers was told in plain terms what to do with the message.[16]

Bert Kienzle sent back all but 100 of the carriers to evacuate the wounded from Menari. For the remainder of September he was fully occupied with problems of acquiring and retaining enough carriers. From the first to the last day of the campaign, there never were enough fit men for the onerous task.

Ahead of the Japanese, 2/27th Battalion still comprised 21 Brigade rearguard, with B Company in that role. The 15 stretcher cases came from all the battalions. One stretcher case died, but the remaining 14 were carried over appalling terrain. Men burdened only with personal equipment were forced to haul themselves up the slopes on hands and knees, grasping trees and branches for assistance. The efforts of the stretcher bearers in these circumstances can be understood only by those who have sweated and struggled over unforgiving terrain in such conditions. A creek crossing took an hour, then the ascent on the far side had to be conquered. It was 1:1. That is, for every foot (or metre) forward, the track rose by that amount. Captain Peter Smith, from Brigade, arrived with a party of 79 native carriers, who took over most of the carrying, but soldiers still had to assist on the worst places, and to give the carriers a rest.

A Company 2/27th, under Captain Sims, followed by Lieutenant Sandison's C Company, moved ahead at 1 pm to check the position at Menari, and to hold it if necessary until the stretchers arrived. They found that it was under fire by Japanese mortars and mountain guns, and in any case was dominated by high ground towards Efogi, from which the Japanese were approaching. Brigade HQ, 2/14th and 2/16th had gone on, and the Japanese were in possession. The companies were attacked near Menari, and as the enemy force was estimated from observation to be at least a battalion, it was decided to go back and inform Lieutenant Colonel Cooper. However, while doing so, 14 Platoon under Lieutenant Caddy, sent out on rear protection, became separated, and the main body of the battalion was missed.

Lieutenant Colonel Cooper and the remainder of 2/27th had arrived on high ground and could easily see the Japanese in Menari. He therefore decided to move to the north, east and south to Nauro, leaving Caddy's platoon to guide A and C Companies.

However, a second patrol also failed to locate the two companies. 2/27th spent the night east of Menari.

Medical Officer 2nd Lieutenant Hiroyuki Hayashi, who landed at Basabua on 18 August, arrived near Menari where he was told 200 enemy troops had been killed. About 330 yards north of Menari was 6 Company II/144, back at regimental headquarters as colour guard, with company strength reduced to 91.[17]

At Buna airfield, Tadao Chiba watched a company of new arrivals install three high-angle anti-aircraft guns and six machine-guns. Nearby was Sei Tatemachi, who had been told on 2 September of the fall of Rabi, at Milne Bay. On this day, three exhausted members of Sasebo 5SLP returned from the operation in a canoe, and said that they had only coconut milk for the past eight days. 'Uchida', of 15 Pioneers, also saw these men, and was told they had covered 100 nautical miles in the canoe. One had been shot by natives. The three determined sailors were Seaman 2nd Class Tomei, Seaman 3rd Class Maezoko and Seaman 3rd Class Tokeiji. They had come to bring news of their unit, and ask for rescue, as the others were marooned on Goodenough Island and the Allies were preparing to exterminate them.[18]

The 25 Brigade arrived at Port Moresby, and began landing from the ships. 2/33rd Battalion had transhipped from *Cremer* to RAN ships that came alongside and took them to the single wharf serving Port Moresby and the Kokoda campaign. If MacArthur really had decided to fight in New Guinea some five months before, he had done remarkably little, with only a single wharf across which to supply the entire island. By 1 pm this landing was completed, and the battalion was taken by truck to the Koitaki area. At dusk, 2/33rd had concentrated at the Ilola campsite, and the men stacked their packs, blankets, greatcoats, getting down to battle order. Lieutenant Colonel Buttrose had gone to a conference at 25 Brigade HQ. Back at Port Moresby, the rear details were still unloading the rest of the battalion stores.

Despite the late hour, the battalion began issuing ammunition, exchanging their khaki drill for jungle greens, and receiving the long US gaiters in place of the short and useless 'anklets web'.

With the evening meal over, the rifle companies tried to sleep, while the battalion headquarters, signals and medical platoons began sorting the items necessary to the functioning of the unit in the mountains ahead. It was realised that they were at the terminal point of made roads, and only paths existed ahead.

Lieutenant Colonel Buttrose returned and held an O-Group with his company commanders. The situation in the mountains was not good: 21 Brigade was retreating and had been doing so for a week; 2/27th Battalion was missing; the location of 21 Brigade itself was not known. 25 Brigade was to move up at once and assist 21 Brigade to hold, then counter-attack and push back the enemy.

The maps issued to Lieutenant Bob Howland, Intelligence Officer, were what can only be called basic. There were two only: an expanse of green colour, with blue rivers and black tracks marked, as well as village names; except for the main mountain heights, no contours, vertical interval, heights or a grid were printed on the sheets. In addition, 24 sketches were available for company and platoon commanders – these showed an area from Uberi to the top of the range, and the officers were required to fill in information as they went along.

The operation orders contained very little, apart from the instruction that when the Japanese were met, their flanks were to be located and pushes into their rear areas made, as in training in Australia. All ranks were to remove rank badges and all ranks would address each other by first names. Eventually, this led to a lapse in discipline and was countermanded at Gona. One order caused dismay: wounded were to be left to fend for themselves. Already it was known that the Japanese murdered any wounded they came across. In plain terms, the Japanese had the initiative and were still advancing as they had for the past 10 months.

The unit historian described the effect of the order that wounded were to be left to look after themselves. It was given to men just awakened, at midnight in a darkened tent, a few hours before departure into the unknown jungles. The AIF prided itself on its medical services and part of its high morale came from the fact that recovery of wounded was emphasised. Yet not one word was spoken by any of the men receiving the order, and they prepared for the move.

When the left-out-of-battle party and the platoons such as Carrier and Mortar that would not be going into the mountains were subtracted, 2/33rd would set off with 29 officers and 550 other ranks. D Company 2/33rd was to depart at 4 am next day, by truck to McDonald's, with the rest of the battalion following.

Each rifleman carried 100 rounds in two bandoliers, two grenades with four-second fuses, an emergency ration, a field dressing, some Bren magazines or a two-inch mortar bomb, and five days' rations; some 55 pounds (25 kg), excluding a blanket or tent-shelter. 2/33rd hoped the packs and blankets would be delivered by the battalion B Echelon, which the unit historian later classed as wishful thinking.

From the time the units of 25 Brigade arrived in Port Moresby, they were told horror stories about the Japanese and the jungle by the Militia work parties at the wharf, by the military police and other rear area troops who knew nothing first-hand and exaggerated the partial truths given them: the Japs came at night and bayoneted you in your sleep, they called out in English for help to trick you, they did things to draw fire, they went around the rear and attacked headquarters and aid posts, they were excellent at camouflage and got close enough to bayonet you before you knew it, Japanese heavy weapons were carried on horses and the Australians had nothing to match this, wounded were tortured and bayoneted, et cetera. Some of the 3rd Battalion (Australian Military Force, Militia) were told that the Japanese fired a small calibre bullet, and you could easily sustain three or four wounds from these, but the Japanese were so good they could not be beaten anyway. Later, it was realised that there was some truth in all this, but it was found also that the Japanese could be defeated and decisively so. Never before and never again did the battalions hear such panic-stricken drivel, and in the long term it did nothing to improve their opinion of the people who manned the rear areas. One veteran of the campaign remarked that all had heard how Australian officers had escaped from Malaya and Singapore supposedly to inform the Australian forces how to fight the Japanese, but no information of value ever reached the battalions before going into action on the Kokoda Trail.

Also arriving in New Guinea were 2/25th Battalion under Lieutenant Colonel C. B. Withy, and 2/31st Battalion under Lieutenant Colonel C. C. Dunbar. On the 4th, 2/25th lost one killed and five injured in a collision at sea, when SS *Van De Lyn* collided with SS *Perthshire*. After a delay and transhipping in Townsville, the entire 25 Brigade had arrived, was kitted out with the new green dyed clothes, and prepared to go forward.

On 10 September, there were no attack sorties recorded over the Owen Stanleys, and only photographic P38s covered the Lae, Salamaua and Buna areas. However, Akira Teruoka wrote of 'a dangerous enemy air attack near the river. The strafing was pretty fierce and I felt bad, but fortunately nothing happened to the soldiers in the vicinity'. He may have made an error in the date, and been referring to a day before. His unit kept marching, despite rain. Japanese troops in the Buna area were told that Tulagi, in the Solomons, and Milne Bay would be attacked by a combined air, army and navy force. Tulagi would be bombarded by 20 destroyers and 50,000 men.

The Australian 2/16th Battalion, after leaving Menari the previous afternoon, were to hold a high hill south of the village until 9 am this day. A patrol early in the morning had engaged the advancing Japanese from ambush, killing about 10 men. Corporal Bill Speed, the patrol commander, then led his men back to D Company along previously selected routes, arriving with no casualties. The Japanese soon arrived at the battalion position, and were fired on. At once they went into their usual practice, trying the flanks, probing for the limits of the Australian position and preparing to attack. 2/16th was well aware of the Japanese tactics, and the soldiers were experienced in concealing themselves. More Japanese became casualties. They retaliated with machinegun fire raking the ridge top, but most of it was too high and no Australians were hit.

At 9 am, 2/16th began to move out and along the track to a

selected position south of Nauro. The track was a mud- and water-filled drain, up to knee-deep in places, but never less than six inches (15 cm) in depth. All had to struggle along it, and the rearguard had to fight and then move quickly as well.

On the slopes near Menari, 2/27th Battalion waited for A and C Companies to rejoin them. When they did not arrive, B and D Companies moved off as advance and rearguards, with HQ and the stretchers between. Movement was slow, and the unit tried to follow high ground parallel to the main track. Ahead went Captains Smith and Fraser, from Brigade, to try to regain contact with 21 Brigade. Their track was followed by the battalion. The main body of 2/27th now consisted of 313 officers and men, including the 14 stretcher cases and three men from 2/16th. Food available consisted of, perhaps, one tin of bully beef per man, left from the issue on 5 September. Only native vegetables were to be found until 21 September.

Meanwhile, A and C Companies were split into small parties that independently made their way, as ordered, back to Itiki and the main Australian force. Their journeys were easier and quicker than that of the battalion's main body.

On the main track, the Japanese had established themselves after crossing the creek. The Australian 2/14th telephone line was cut at 2.30 pm, and the brigade stretcher parties were forced to detour to the east. Sergeants Jack Mathews and Bert Warman went 'missing' at this time, and the battalion believed them killed by the Japanese on the track. Japanese documents indicate that they may have been captured. As no reference to them arriving at Buna exists, nor is there any reference in the many captured diaries, letters or orders to prisoners being sent to the rear, it is reasonable to assume that they were murdered.

The Japanese documents state that just before 3 pm, two Australians were captured by 41 Regiment. At the headquarters, 1st Lieutenant Morimoto noted the results of their interrogation: the men had come from Brisbane, in a three-ship convoy, arriving at Moresby on 10 August; their commander was Brigadier 'Botto' (Potts), and they had arrived at Isurava on 26 August; defensive lines were at Isurava, Kagi and Efogi; Colonel Key, 14 Battalion, was believed killed at Isurava; there were two Australian divisions and many Americans at Moresby.[19]

After the war, a Rabaul mixed-blood man used as a labourer on the trail described the treatment given two Australians who had just been captured. Their pockets were emptied and they were tied to trees, then beaten by the Japanese as part of the interrogation. Later he saw them, arms bound, used as carriers, and later still saw them being fed – the Japanese threw biscuits on the ground and the bound men had to eat from the mud, like dogs.

The 2/14th party under Captain Russell, at the creek crossing, was fired on when withdrawing. The Japanese had ambushed the track and covered it with a hail of fire. Joe Attard and Eric Vial were killed and another man wounded; a fourth had bullets deflected by his equipment. The force was split into two, and made their separate ways back to the unit. Sergeant Thorne and three men arrived at Uberi nine days later, and Captain Russell with the others came into Ioribaiwa in seven days.

The rest of 2/14th reached Nauro about 5 pm. They had slogged on through endless rain, moving along a muddy trough that was the track. On arrival, many men went fully clothed into the Brown River to wash off. At this time, command of the battalion passed to Major Challen, MBE, formerly the Brigade Major. Captain Rhoden was awarded a Mention In Dispatches for his effort in commanding 2/14th after the loss of the CO and much of the HQ. One thousand rations and 20,000 rounds of ammunition were abandoned at Nauro.

The Japanese commander, Major General Horii, issued a series of orders, all with the location given as at Wamai, a place just on the Moresby side of the creek at Nauro. Order A-114 ordered the pursuit unit to defeat the small enemy force opposing them and press on to the heights west of Wamai as scheduled, then take a key (unnamed) position near the road to Moresby. At the same time, a special reconnaissance of Australian positions at Ioribaiwa was to be made. 41 Regiment was to check the area north of Wamai to see if a road ran through the area, and if so to take the high ground overlooking it. The engineers were to assist both units, as required, while the rest of his force waited in their present order of march, in readiness to move forward. Still the Japanese were looking for that road to Moresby.

Order A-115 ordered the medical unit of 144 Regiment to set up a position near Wamai to take care of those who fell out on the march, and the field hospital to leave part of it where it was presently located, but the main body was to pack, follow and join the main formation.

Order D-25 first stipulated that the formation would push on to the objective, the heights west of Wamai on 11 September, and prepare for future operations. Ammunition would have priority in forward movement, followed by food and fodder, then medical supplies. Detachments from all units would go to the rear next day and bring forward the supplies. The estimated times for the round trips were: Wamai–Isurava–Wamai 7 days. Wamai–Kokoda–Wamai 10 days, with extra in the case of casualty bearers.

The order listed the number of men to be detached for carrying duties from each unit in the advance, ranging from 200 from 144 Regiment to 60 from a medical unit, totalling 1050 men. As far as possible, carriers were to be natives, Koreans, Takasago volunteers and Japanese supply unit members, but if necessary men from combat units were to be sent.

Another instruction dealt with the amounts of food to be allocated to each carrying detachment, with the aim of bringing forward the absolute maximum possible, and not have it consumed on the way forward. Another dealt with the matter of escorting wounded with medical personnel until they reached the hospital to be established at Efogi, and asked for the allocation of 300 captured blankets taken at Menari to be given to the hospital. Again, these orders were to be passed verbally to all concerned, who were to write them down.[20]

D Company 2/33rd Battalion, led by Captain Clowes, arrived by bus at the road junction at McDonald's plantation, disembarked and began marching along the dirt road to Ower's Corner, the start of the Kokoda Trail. After an exhausting day, they arrived at

Uberi, and found that the radio could not contact the battalion coming along behind. Already the mountains were imposing their dues on the new arrivals.

At Uberi, a gathering of senior officers of 25 Brigade took place. Lieutenant Colonel Buttrose, CO 2/33rd, had arrived after his D Company, but soon Brigadier Ken Eather also arrived, with reconnaissance groups from all the brigade battalions. Eather spoke to Brigadier Selwyn Porter, at Ioribaiwa, and was told to send forward the 2/33rd to Imita to begin a flanking move on 12 September from Imita to Nauro and from there to attack and cut the Japanese supply line, that is, the track.

Brigadier Potts was informed Brigadier Porter was to relieve him; the axe had fallen. He was to brief the other brigade commanders on conditions on the trail. Meanwhile, 21 Brigade was ordered to hold the present position until 8.30 am, then fall back to the ridge north of Ioribaiwa. It was obvious the Japanese were intending to encircle the small force in its present location.

Meanwhile, 3rd Militia Battalion had advanced along the trail towards Nauro, and halted for the night. All were tired and looked forward to a quiet night. B Company were at the rear of the battalion position, but were not told anyone was outside the location. Unknown to them, a single Papuan soldier was patrolling, and came back to B Company, instead of the intended spot, to HQ Company. A sentry from B Company challenged with, 'Who goes there?' The Papuan replied with the same, 'Who goes there?' This went back and forth a few times, until, keeping in mind the barrage of yarns about Japanese cunning, the sentry decided to resolve the matter, so fired. The Papuan smartly dived into a dip in the ground and discreetly remained there until dawn. When he did come into the position, he was somewhat critical, and suggested he could probably come to a better arrangement with the Japanese!

Air attacks on 11 September began at 11.30 am, when Buna airfield was attacked by six B26s that went down through cloud base at 6500 feet to drop 72 bombs on the runway and dispersals, destroying four aircraft on the ground; AA was light and inaccurate. Sei Tatemachi, of 14 Pioneers, was sent to repair the bomb damage. He noted that the airfield was 'full of holes from air attack. Filled in holes and returned'. A single A20 on armed reconnaissance over Myola–Nauro–Efogi dropped eight bombs and created an explosion in an ammunition dump at Efogi. Ineffective machinegun fire came up at the plane and one conspicuous track was seen north of Efogi; visibility was 10 to 15 miles (16-24 km). At 5.05 pm, under a cloudbase at 3000 feet, 15 A20s attacked Buna airfield with 100-pounders, starting fires, destroying two aircraft, despite AA fire that seemed to be augmented with air-burst mortar explosions in an attempt to create a barrage effect. One A20 crashed 60 miles (100 km) along the coast from Milne Bay, and the crew were seen to bail out. The mapping process was being served, with four P38 photographic sorties over the area.[21]

Struggling through distant mountains was the Australian 2/27th Battalion, burdened with the stretchers, which sometimes were passed along a human chain over the worst of the slopes. By this time, all were feeling the effects of lack of food combined with hard physical labour. The isolation, lack of information and uncertain situation lowered morale. Still they went on.

The 2/14th and 2/16th Battalions were combined to form a composite unit, with total strength of about two full companies. Lieutenant Colonel Caro commanded, with Major Challen as second-in-command, and the unit was allocated a defensive position. They now heard of some of the units coming into the battle: 3rd Battalion, 25 Brigade, 2/1st Pioneer Battalion and 6 Independent Company.

The first Japanese shot here was a very tall fellow, walking along the track with slung rifle, talking to himself. It was presumed that he was sent forward to draw fire. Soon after, at 8 am, the enemy attacked D Company 2/14th, which was 400 yards forward of the main position. D Company's role was to force the enemy to deploy, to lose time, and to suffer casualties. The Japanese attacked from three sides, with fire support, but were held. Some passed by, but were held on the main position. Four Australians, including Warrant Officer W. A. Noble, were killed and five wounded. Sergeant A. L. Sargent and two men were separated and made their way back, rejoining six days later, after travelling with a similar party from 2/16th.

The 2/16th Battalion, in its turn, was rearguard, laid ambushes, and 14 Platoon sprang the first, inflicting about 10 casualties on the Japanese, but the next, by 15 Platoon, had no contact. The Japanese were more cautious. The composite battalion took six and a half hours to make the move, then were disposed in depth along the track between the creek and Ioribaiwa. The positions were: A Company 2/16th forward, then D Company 2/14th, B and D Companies 2/16th, Headquarter Company 2/14th, and C Company 2/16th on the edge of the village atop the ridge. Next day D Company 2/14th and A Company 2/16th moved to the high ground east of the village, where 3rd Battalion was located. 6 Independent Company patrolled to the west. 3rd Battalion, like the other units, had climbed the trail, wondering what the future held, but, unlike the ill-fated 53rd, had been allowed time to train in the Moresby area. At first, they held a position to allow the 2/14th–2/16th force to pass, then went back to Ioribaiwa.

Bede Tongs was 10 Platoon Sergeant, and the sight of the AIF veterans was recalled as the platoon's 'first indication of the severity of war, to see men with blood-stained bandages, emaciated', moving past. 3rd Battalion took up its position, and began digging with bayonets, helmets and dixies – there were no spades or shovels. The sound of firing from 21 Brigade added impetus to the digging.

Two of the B Company 3rd Battalion soldiers were taking their time about crossing the creek and climbing the slope again, and so were last to arrive at the water's edge. They were surprised to see a strange Australian opening cans of bully beef and strewing them along the creek bank, in open ground. As they pondered this unusual sight, the man saw them and delivered a blast of soldier's language that hurried them across and up the slope. They had not gone far when there was a burst of machinegun fire from the right.

A Company 2/16th had positioned an ambush party, commanded by Corporal B. W. Moloney, on the south side of the creek. The Australian scattering bully beef where it would be seen was

The famous 'Golden Stairs' at the beginning of the Kokoda Trail (*RAAF*)

The classic signpost, showing the way to Kokoda (*2/3rd Battalion*)

One of the enduring images of the campaign (*AWM No. 14028*)

Kokoda, photographed one week before the Japanese advance at Buna. At left front is the track to Buna; at centre is the ridge with rubber plantation itself and, on the far side of the creek, the airfield and cloud - covered mountains. A Company 39 Battalion approached from centre left, climbed the escarpment into the rubber trees, defended Kokoda, and then withdrew across the airfield into the jungle. This photo was taken at 12.24 hrs - note the thick cloud on the mountain tops at this time of day. (*RAAF*)

The track near Oivi - ankle-deep mud and water. The soldiers are A.E. Heathcote, J.H. Fowler, T.M. Shores and L. White, all of 2/14th Battalion, in the area as part of CHAFORCE which was not involved in action, though all members fought on the Kokoda Trail (*AWM No. 13620*)

Members of the 2/1st, 2/2nd and 2/3rd Infantry Battalions, comprising the 16th Australian Infantry Brigade, moving up along the Trail in the vicinity of Nauro and Menari (*AWM No 27052*)

Private Jack Scally of the 2/27th Battalion, who had been out of touch for sixteen days after being cut off during a retreat in one of the fierce attacks near Myola Lake (*AWM No. 26723*)

What are believed to be the first three Japanese prisoners captured on the
Kokoda Trail, sitting at left in the truck (*Ray Royal*)

Emaciated and badly-treated horses after over-use by the Japanese,
found by advancing Australian troops near the Kumusi River
(*AWM No. 13647*)

Commanding officers of 2/31st Battalion and other senior officers photographed during the advance to Kokoda. Left to right, foreground: Lieutenant Colonel C.C. Dunbar, Commanding Officer; Major E.M. Robson, Second-in-Command; Lieutenant C.H.D. Birnie and Captain E.T. Beazley (*AWM No 27012*)

Men of the 2/31st Battalion stop for a rest in the jungle between Nauro and Menari - but don't leave their Bren gun too far away (*AWM No. 27013*)

Native stretcher-bearers stop at a river to give a drink to their patient, Private A. Baldwin, of the 2/33rd Battalion (*AWM 26856*)

Unidentified Australian soldiers with a captured Japanese mountain gun (at right), and a Type 99 7.7mm light machine gun (at left) (*AWM. No 13644*)

Supplies can be seen falling from this Douglas C-47 'Biscuit Bomber' as it passes over dropping zone (*AWM. No 55150*)

Buna Airfield. The effectiveness of US and RAAF air attacks is shown by the wreckage of this Mitsubishi 'Betty' Bomber. The Japanese were unable to use the airfield to support their force on the Kokoda Trail (*RAAF*)

Pilot Officer J. Brazenor (pilot), and Sergeant Fred Anderson (observer), in A19-15, coming back through the Owen Stanleys. This plane survived the war, and was disposed of on 16 November 1949 (*RAAF*)

Disaster at 7-Mile Airfield. The vital Douglas C47 transports (left) were lined up with other aircraft, and were destroyed or damaged by a Japanese air attack on 17 August. A US P39 flies low over the scene (*RAAF*)

Another scene from 7-Mile Airfield. This rare photo shows the little-known Douglas DC5 climbing after takeoff. On the ground are B17s nos 19208 and 12659. No. 19208 was destroyed in a crash on takeoffon 12 October, after fifteen reconnaissance missions. At left is the fin and rudder of one of the first B24s to operate in the South-West Pacific Area (*RAAF*)

Sergeants L.A. Bear DCM MM and L. Crilly MM, 2/14th Battalion (*AWM No.65542*)

Lieutenant Colonel A.W. Buttrose, Commanding Officer 2/33rd
Battalion (with stick); and Major G.F. Larkin, Brigade Major, 25th
Brigade, at Menari (*AWM No. 27039*)

10 Platoon 16 August 1942. Rear: E.J. McCauley, D.C. Carland, T.H. Bisset, R.A. Dredge, D.J.
Davies, J.R. Kearney, J.A. Ferguson, L.C. Elphinstone, W.A. Wilson, S.C. Ellery. Third: C.F.
Blume, M.W. Bolitho, R.J. Adams, P.B. Benson, J. Marsh, T.W. Wilson, E.S. Symonds, A.F.
Wilson. Second: C.E. Dillon, J.S. Atkin, J.W. Coy, J.P. Callaghan, C.H. Smith, W.J.G. Jeffrey.
Front: C.D. Dunlop, D.E. Webb, W.J. Fraser, J.F. Benson, M. Kiburn, W. Bray, R.F. Woodward,
R. Powell, L.A. Meade (*AWM No. 89210*)

Corporal Lester ' Tarzan' Pett, who distinguished himself in action with 2/3rd Battalion on the Kokoda Trail, and destroyed four Japanese machine gun posts on 28 October 1942 (*2/3rd Battalion*)

Left to right:: General Douglas Macarthur, Commander SWPA, General Thomas Blamey, Commander Allied Air Forces, and General George Kenney, Commander Allied Air Forces, during a visit by Macarthur to Port Moresby in October 1942 (*RAAF*)

Lieutentant Colonel Alan Cameron, Commanding Officer 3rd Battalion, on the Kokoda Trail, September 1942 (*Bede Tongs*)

Above
Dr Geoff Vernon MC, former Medical Officer with the Australian 11th Light Horse in World War I, was the first Medical Officer to attend Australian military casualties on the Kokoda Trail. He began his service on the mountain tracks at the age of 59, and died in 1946 (*11th Light Horse*)

Left
Major 'Buck' Rogers. Commanding Officer US Attack Squadron, led his dive bombers against the Japanese invasion convoy at Buna on 29 July 1942. Only one A24 bomber returned to Port Moresby - Rogers hit one ship before he crashed (*L. Hickey and Furman Adams Collection*)

Lieutenant Colonel Ian Hutchison,
Commanding Officer 2/3rd
Battalion in the latter phases of the
Kokoda campaign (*2/3/rd Battalion*)

Charlie McCallum (*Mrs D.W.T. Tudor*)

George Pearce MC (*Isabel Pearce*)

H.P. Warman (*A. Warman*)

L. E. Tipton (*Marjorie Tipton*)

Bede Tongs MM (*Bede Tongs*)

M.A. (Mocca) Treacy *(Terry Treacy)*

Sergeant George Sayer, RAAF, killed over
Buna on 23 September 1942 *(Robert Piper)*

Captain Claude Nye *(Mrs M. Briggs)*

J.A. Metson *(Metson family)*

preparing the killing ground; he was Lieutenant Colonel Alan Cameron, now commanding 3rd Battalion. Between 30 and 40 Japanese appeared and came to the creek crossing in a very casual manner, as though no enemy were near. They began searching and checking the tins and after a few minutes, the ambush opened fire with two Bren guns and 20 or so Japanese were killed or wounded. Another group of Japanese had crossed the creek, and fired on what they thought to be the Australian position, without hitting anyone. The survivors of the ambush also crossed the creek and spent some time calling in English to the ambush party, telling it to withdraw. By now this trick was well worn. Lieutenant Ross Watts took a patrol down to the river. A party of seven Japanese were found bathing; all were killed. Watts then bathed himself in the stream, but Sergeant Nobby Walker thought this was going too far, and watched until Watts had finished.

Meanwhile, the two 3rd Battalion stragglers had quickened their pace, returned to B Company, and later found who the chap was down at the creek. The example of Cameron's shrewdness in preparing the killing zone for the Japanese was related and boosted his reputation within the battalion.

D Company 2/33rd set off along the track to Imita, but with a radically lightened personal load of kit. Much had been left at Uberi. Even so, the climbs were exhausting, as they had been for each man who preceded them along the trail. At first, halts were made each half-hour, then every 15 minutes. At all, men would be gasping, some retching, knees trembling. The Brens would be passed from man to man at five-minute intervals. In the afternoon, clouds settled in and it began to rain, then mist gathered around the struggling column crawling up the muddy path along Imita Ridge.

At 1 pm, west of Wamai, Horii's staff issued Operation Order A-115 (though the same number had been used for an order on 10 September). The order stated that the Japanese formation had reached its objective, the western end of the range, at 10 am, after defeating 39th and 53rd Battalions, adding that the enemy was in 'a state of utter confusion, and to a great degree have lost the will to fight'.

The South Seas force, the order went on, was firmly holding key points along the line, and preparations were to be made for an advance, probably on 20 September. 144 Regiment was to hold the heights and reconnoitre with a view to advancing on Moresby, while 41 Regiment was to take positions on the left bank of the Nauro River and prepare to carry out tasks allocated earlier – check the existence of a road, and take the high ground if it was located. Supporting arms were given appropriate orders, and when Miyamoto's I/41 and Kobayashi's III/41 arrived they were to revert to be under command of 41 Regiment. The order exhorted all units to 'replenish fighting strength', report all losses and amounts of captured material, pay particular attention to camouflage and avoiding detection from the air, to soldiers' health, and to live off local supplies to ease the burden on the supply line, which stretched back to Buna. However, Horii well knew that now he was to secure a defensive position and wait, and was not to attack Port Moresby unless specifically ordered to do so by Lieutenant General Hyakutake in Rabaul.

At 9 pm, a bulletin was issued, ordering a reduction in the rice ration from the equivalent of a pint to just over two-thirds of a pint, prohibiting between-meals consumption of captured food, and repeating that all such food was to be reported to headquarters, adding that all units were to try to stretch their present quantity of rations to 22 or 23 September (11 days), and also prohibiting the cutting of signals cable for personal use. The bulletin concluded with a list of actions to be taken to avoid air attack, and for care of weapons and siting of latrines.[22]

The unit log of Nose unit, I/144, noted that four prisoners were taken, including Colonel Key. Two days march forward from Menari, Hayashi the Medical Officer came to another place where he was told five enemy battalions, 5000 men, had been annihilated.[23]

Japanese diaries and documents referred to the capture of Key, and it was noted his group refused to give information. Later, Father Benson, the sole survivor of the missionaries and other Europeans captured, related how he had seen a wounded and exhausted lieutenant colonel. A Rabaul mixed-blood man also reported witnessing an interrogation of a lieutenant colonel, and heard him say that he had no idea where his troops or artillery were. The Kempei Tai reminded him that the Japanese commander (Horii) had said that if information was given, the officer would be treated as a prisoner. The Rabaul man went on and did not see the officer again. Another Rabaul mixed-blood man also reported seeing about half a dozen Australians who looked at him as he passed, but he dared not speak to them.

Keishin Tsuno, from the gun platoon of II/144, was told that the Australian prisoners would not give military information, and this so impressed him that when he was captured later while unconscious, he too refused to give military information.

D Company 2/33rd arrived on the peak of Imita Ridge. Ahead thick swirling cloud hid Ioribaiwa, where Captain Clowes had been told the 300-odd men of the combined 2/14th and 2/16th Battalions were holding, with the 3rd Militia Battalion. He sent forward a listening post and positioned his three platoons across the track on the crest. A gale with cold, drenching rain fell on the unprotected platoons, saturating everything in their haversacks and pouches. The 2/33rd was having a hard introduction to the Kokoda Trail.

Early next morning, 12 September, seven B17s attacked Buna airfield through rain squalls, going down to 1000 to 3000 feet before dropping 84 bombs despite heavy and accurate 20 mm and 37 mm AA. One AA position on the north-west corner of the airfield was silenced. Two B17s were badly damaged by AA hits, and one was shot down in flames, going into the sea 20 miles (32 km) down the coast. Four parachutes were seen 10 miles (16 km) along the coast, and after the plane had stopped in the sea, two men were seen swimming to shore. Supplies were dropped to them and the remainder of the formation returned to base. The pilot survived the ditching with the bombardier, but three others in the nose died. Two of the four who had jumped survived the Japanese search and later found the pilot, then walked to Milne Bay, which they reached weeks later, exhausted and in poor condition. Two parachutists were caught and killed by the Japanese.

At 7.25 am, 11 P400s went in ahead of B26s, below overcast sky at 5500 feet, through rain, with visibility four miles (6.4 km), and again attacked Buna airfield. Ten strafed the airfield and one strafed four barges on the beach, reporting fires and what was probably an aircraft burning. Behind the P400s, five B26s bombed from 5000 feet, dropping 58 bombs on the eastern side of the airfield, and the fires started could be seen for 20 to 30 miles (32-48 km). Thirty minutes later, nine A20s came over at only 70 feet, through light rain and poor visibility, to scatter 320 'parafrags', creating a bomb pattern covering the runway itself and both sides out into the trees. One bomb run and seven strafing passes were made, and the squadron claimed 17 aircraft destroyed on the ground, four of them in flames.

This was the first operational use of these parachute-retarded fragmentation bombs, or 'parafrags', brought out from the United States by General Kenney because no one else wanted them. They were to become a potent weapon in the South West Pacific, and Japanese air units were to be caught time and again with aircraft handily presented as targets for the parafrags. They never learned. On this first occasion, the Japanese thought the parachutes meant an airborne landing, and reacted by firing at the numerous 'paratroops', but soon learned their error. However, the idea of paratroop landings had taken root, and many diaries and documents referred to the probability of such Allied action. A Japanese medical officer who had taken part in the occupations of Guam and New Britain had come ashore on 18 August, and been doing surgical work at Buna. He estimated that 40 aircraft had attacked, and added that air superiority was entirely on the Allied side, as not a single Japanese plane had appeared, then went on to write about the possibility of a raid from the beach or by paratroops, though he had only a few men to defend the position. Japanese sentries were placed to watch for such attacks by night and day, and the local HQ ordered all units to be ready to fight, as well as have five days of food on hand. The results of this series of successive strikes, particularly the use of parachute-bombs, had a great psychological effect on Japanese in the area, and caused the diversion of a large amount of manpower from necessary tasks in logistic support for the mountain operations.

In the mountains near Ioribaiwa, Sergeant Major Tadao Totsuki wrote in his notebook that company strength was 115 men. Two months later, it would be 19. Veterinarian Shunichiro Yano accompanied 25 packhorses carrying food. Still walking on was Akira Teruoka, who had heard few aircraft and thought the bombing had decreased in the last few days. He met many detachments going to the rear for supplies, and noted that it was now 50 days since leaving Rabaul.[24]

At Ioribaiwa, an early Japanese attempt to cross the creek was foiled by an ambush from 2/16th Battalion, and the Japanese remained on the far side until dusk, when a second attempt was also defeated by booby-traps and a counter-attack. At about this time, 3rd Battalion received some canned Canadian salmon, a real delicacy, which was quickly eaten. The more observant had their pleasure lessened when they saw the label: 'Label printed in Japan.'

Lieutenant Colonel Buttrose (2/33rd) arrived at the crest of Imita Ridge, and told Captain Clowes that D Company was to lead the battalion on the right flanking move to Nauro. When the other companies arrived at about midday, a native NCO of PIB took the lead and the battalion began moving along a faint path. But by the end of the day, with the rain pouring down again, the track petered out, little distance had been covered, and no alternate route could be located. 2/33rd halted for the night of 12 September strung out along a ridge that sloped steeply away.

Japanese commander Horii issued Staff Intelligence No. 18, which identified the Australian units as 39 and 53 Battalions of 22 Brigade, with 49 Battalion thought to be at Moresby, and 14, 16 and 27 Battalions of 21 Brigade. The Japanese did not use the AIF unit identification of '2/' indicating 2nd AIF. The report briefly described the previous actions, and stated that the Australians had lost the will to fight and were concentrating on the last heights to defend Moresby. Australian losses were listed: Colonel Owen, CO 39 Battalion, killed at Kokoda; Colonel Key, CO 14 Battalion [sic – 2/14], missing at Isurava; OC A Company 14 Battalion missing, and all his platoon commanders killed, wounded or missing, the company reduced to 50 on 9 September; OC B Company 14 Battalion killed, and all platoon commanders killed, wounded or missing, with company strength reduced to 28 on 9 September. This information was gained from prisoners.[25]

Another reference to prisoners was in Japanese 17th Army Intelligence Record No. 27, which stated that in the 'Battle of Stanley Range' 75 prisoners of No. 8 Company, 16 Battalion, 2nd Brigade, Australian Army [sic] had told their captors in Horii's formation that they had gone from Adelaide to Moresby and direct to Isurava, that the 16th had relieved the 39th Battalion at Kokoda, and 16 Battalion covered the retreat of the rest of the force; eight battalions remained at Moresby.

Another paragraph said that 'the navy' had captured a straggler near Kokoda, who said he had left Brisbane on 8 August, and arrived at Isurava on 25 August, his unit some 300 to 500 strong. The navy unit was probably a company of Takasago Volunteers with Horii's force. Again, there is no record of any of these prisoners, or of any others referred to in Japanese documents of the Kokoda–Buna campaign, surviving. The reference to 75 prisoners is quite obviously an exaggeration. Another order issued on 12 September told of a combat near Kagi between 'enemy remnants' and rear echelon troops, and warned units to mount alert guards.

Horii's Op Order A-116 of 12 September stated that patrols had found the enemy to have retreated to the west of Iroibaiwa, but a small force remained on the western bank of the stream there. 144 Regiment was to capture the Ioribaiwa positions on 13 September, after which Horii would move his headquarters forward.

The Chief Medical Officer of the Japanese 41 Regiment was sent a document pertaining to health matters during this period of inactivity. His attention was drawn to the following points: latrines were to be dug, and relieving of bowels in the open to cease; tents to be provided with floorboards; stream water to be divided according to use for drinking, cooking, and so on; 'the drinking of unboiled water is forbidden'; also forbidden was drinking after eating biscuits and uncooked bully beef; gaps in tents to be covered to prevent draughts; anti-malarial medicines given and anti-mosquito precautions taken; the weak and debilitated to be cared for; captured food and forage to be used according to 'strategical matters'; personal hygiene to be observed; and attention paid to disposal of food remains.

The last battalion of 41 Regiment, Major Morimoto's I/41, arrived in the combat area, thus completing Horii's force of two regiments with artillery and engineer support, totalling about 5000 men. The Australian 2/14–2/16th Composite Battalion and 3rd Battalion had less than one-fifth that number.

General Kenney was greatly disappointed that the food dumps accumulated so laboriously at Kokoda, Myola and Efogi had been lost to the enemy, and made denigrating remarks about the Australian defence of the area. An equal effort would have been necessary to evacuate the amount of supplies, and the aircraft and manpower simply were not available. There was a certain benefit to the Australians from this loss. Available officers and men spent hours puncturing the tins before retreating. The contents quickly became unfit for human consumption, but the hungry Japanese troops gorged themselves on the spot and carried more away. In addition to all their other problems, dysentery soon afflicted them, doing further damage to the battalions' fighting ability.

Kenney believed the Australians in Port Moresby were defeatist, from General Rowell down, and that there were signs of panic. There were no US combat troops in New Guinea, and his air units were in no way capable of military ground action. Evacuation plans were made for the US forces, and in the technical units the trained soldiers were given precedence over junior officers, much to the dismay of the lieutenants. When they queried this, they were told that it took 22 weeks for an engine mechanic to receive basic tuition, and after that he began to gain experience, while second lieutenants were produced after 90 days and could easily be replaced. So were the realities of modern war brought home to certain young officers.

Kenney again began asking to be allowed to send US combat troops by air to New Guinea, partly to spur the Australians to greater effort or else the Yanks would claim they had arrived and saved the Aussies, and partly to counter enemy propaganda that the Americans were making free with Australian women while the Diggers were overseas fighting in the deserts and jungles. In reality, the US Army officers and soldiers were far from ready for war, and were to fail miserably when committed to operations at Buna.

Meanwhile, the formation of Kenney's 43rd Bomb Group was proceeding. Harry Staley and the rest of the McCullar crew were among the first included when their 63rd Bomb Squadron was re-established at Torrens Creek. But there was little ceremony; operations had to go on and the aircraft flew regardless of the unit title. The crew went to Mareeba and then back to Port Moresby.

The isolated Australian 2/27th Battalion, carrying its stretchers, had been reduced to only a daily four hours of travel, weakened as it was by lack of food as well as the work required. Patrols found a little food, saw a few Japanese at Nauro, and met one of the small parties from A Company, making their own way back. This was the first information on the events concerning A and C Companies. Only 19 native bearers remained, and these deserted that night. A stretcher case died.

Arriving at the base of Imita Ridge, 2/31st Battalion, on its way forward, was pleased and impressed to find the Salvation Army in residence. Hot tea was given to troops as they filed past. This was not the only occasion when the 'Salvos' were found well forward, and many units made complimentary references to their efforts.

During 13 September, the Japanese shelled Ioribaiwa village and surrounding area, causing some Australian casualties, but 41 Regiment did not seize the ridge as intended, and there was no major ground attack. The track was still held by the composite 2/14–2/16th unit, but 2/31st and 2/33rd Battalions began arriving to the rear of the position.

On 13 September, Lae was the target for the B26s. One formation of seven was to bomb at 10.45 am from 11,200 feet, and 15 minutes later another seven would attack at 7700 feet. Together they dropped 130 bombs, but due to an error, another 69 bombs were not released by aircraft following a flight leader. Japanese

AA fire hit one plane, and pilots claimed two twin-engined bombers burning on the ground. There were no other attack missions over the Owen Stanleys reported in Allied Air Force summaries. However, Gerald Rogers, shot down on 26 August over Buna, returned to his unit, after friendly natives looked after him until an RAAF pilot landed a light plane to rescue him. Two B25s went from Charters Towers to Kila strip, to operate under orders from 5th Air force Advanced HQ, to fly supplies to advanced bases.

On this day, 13 September, the Kokoda Lines of Communication zone was handed from the Army Service Corps establishment at Moresby to 7 Division. A Division Company AASC was allotted to the trail, but the requirement for officers was heavy, one officer to eight men, and this resulted in a drain on other AASC units in the area. NGF Headquarters began to organise an air supply company, called an Air Maintenance Company. The daily ration at this time was 28.5 ounces (808 grams), of meat, biscuits, tea, sugar and milk. The air supply operations were hampered by bad communications with the forward troops, no information about whether wrappings were successful or not, if recoveries of drops were effective, there was no definite maintenance plan, sometimes changes in priority meant changes in aircraft loads, and aircraft had to become available overnight for use at first light. In addition, there was a shortage of AASC personnel and of suitable wrapping materials.

On the far side of the mountains at Buna, Toshio Sato, a Japanese interpreter, was told that 25,000 parachute troops from Australia might attack them, and no reinforcements would be sent to his Pioneer unit in the Buna area. He wrote, '200 men will have to face 25,000 paratroops'. The paratroop scare was widespread. Diarist 'Uchida' had discussed the situation and the new parachute bombs with other officers, when a runner came in with the startling news that Americans were landing at Basabua, on the very spot where the Japanese themselves had come ashore. After some excitement, it was found to be a false report. Unknown to the Japanese, of course, there was a great deal of nervousness around Port Moresby about the dreaded Japanese landing there.[26]

Having decided that the right flanking move to Nauro could not be accomplished in a reasonable time, Lieutenant Colonel Buttrose had contacted Brigadier Eather on the landline and been told to return and join the force at Ioribaiwa. As dusk was falling, 2/33rd left the track some 500 yards below the Ioribaiwa crest and filed along a track to their allocated position right of 3rd Militia Battalion. However, as dark fell and the rain began again, it became obvious that the battalion would not be able to move into position during the night, and the order was given to halt and wait until daylight. Close by, the 2/33rd could hear the night activity: Brens, Japanese light and heavy machineguns, mountain guns and mortars. In the struggle along the ridge in the night and rain, 2/33rd had become fragmented and small groups were strung out in the jungle, grass and rocks, all wondering what was going on around them. But there was no information. Firing broke out, and broke out again and again during the night.

At 6.30 pm, Horii issued Operation Order D-27, directing 41 Regiment to establish a 'Resource Collection unit' and a 'March Casualties Collection unit', to begin work on 14 September. The Resource Collection unit of 200 men was to be headed by a company commander, and collect foods between Wamai and Efogi, for collection at a depot near Wamai, completing the task by 20 September. The 100-man March Casualties Collection unit was to be led by a company commander, with medical staff, to gather in those who had fallen out on the march from Efogi. At the same time, the area around Wamai was to be scoured by formation headquarters and the cavalry troop that had been acting as guard force.[27]

The serious food situation in the Japanese forces was again reflected in Horii's Operation Order No. 3, issued 'west of Wamai'. As foraging parties scouring the local area had brought in considerable quantities of vegetables and fruits, the rice ration was to be reduced again, to two-thirds of a pint per man engaged in great physical exertion, and half a pint for others. All units were to do their utmost to eke out rations 'under the minute and careful supervision and guidance of executives of every rank'.

The Japanese II/144 was preparing for another attack. 6 Company had returned from its detachment as colour guard, that duty taken over by 5 Company. Order of march south of Ioribaiwa had been 4 Company, 6 Company, Engineers, machineguns, mountain artillery and then the signals unit. From mid-afternoon, reconnaissance and preparations for the attack were being made. Another man died at the medical station.[28]

Rumours continued in the Buna area, and Japanese there were told that 15,000 enemy paratroops were going to land in the area. (The Allied commanders would have been delighted to have such a force and the aircraft to deliver them!) In reality, General Kenney was given permission to fly a unit of the US 32nd Infantry Division to Port Moresby, but he had nowhere near the necessary number of aircraft to do so. It was a challenge, and if successful would be another step forward for air power, so George Kenney applied his considerable talents to the task. However, from the Solomons, Admiral Ghormley asked for assistance from MacArthur's forces, in the form of attacks on Rabaul, for the period 15-16 September, to support his own operations, and despite Kenney's misgivings, MacArthur directed him to assist Ghormley. MacArthur was well aware of the shortage of aircraft in his own command, but as everything for the SWPA had to pass through the South Pacific Area, he no doubt wanted to give Ghormley as little excuse as possible to take and use for himself materials and units en route to Australia. Entire squadrons allocated to Kenney were held in the Pacific theatres on the orders of the local commanders, and released when the situation warranted, or, in some cases, not at all.

On 14 September, Allied air activity relevant to the Kokoda–Buna campaign was confined to nine B17s that set off to attack shipping at sea or at Rabaul, but were forced back by bad weather, and one A20 on reconnaissance got through to Myola at 9.45 am, but there was no sign of activity.

Akira Teruoka at last caught up with the main body of his Japanese unit and was given two letters from Japan, with news of preparations for harvesting and breeding. The unit was to rest for a few days, and he remarked that he would like to return to 'normal physical condition and be strong and healthy'.

The Australian 2/33rd Battalion, on the wet, jungle-clad ridge slope at Ioribaiwa, took stock in the new day of 14 September. A certain amount of the night firing was found to have come from the battalion itself, as well as units on the crest at Ioribaiwa. Lieutenant Barclay, 11 Platoon B Company, was found dead, shot in the head. As soon as possible, Lieutenant Colonel Buttrose had his companies moving and going into position onto the high points of the ridge. To the left, they could hear firing where 2/31st Battalion was in action, and where the composite 2/14th–2/16th Battalion was under attack. No one in 2/33rd dug in, as there were no digging tools. Patrols went out, but found nothing. While 2/33rd may have been less than happy with the events of the night, to the 3rd Battalion they presented 'a magnificent sight, coming in with their jungle greens. Our dress was khaki shorts and shirt'. Sergeant Bede Tongs thought 'They looked as though they could clean the Japs up in no time'.

The 2/31st Battalion advanced from Imita, having listened to the gunfire and explosions of the night before. As the battalion came up to the crest of Ioribaiwa, Brigadier Porter met them. He recognised many faces, having been a former commanding officer of the battalion in the Middle East. 2/31st went forward, order of march being D Company, A, Lieutenant Colonel Dunbar's HQ, B, HQ and C Company, moving west behind the composite 2/14–2/16th, in an attempt to outflank the Japanese.

The battalion began advancing along a razorback ridge that was only 20 feet (six metres) wide on the top, sometimes narrowing to five feet (1.5 metres), with very steep slopes on either side, which would make outflanking moves extremely difficult and time-consuming. It began to rain in torrents. Snipers in trees harassed the platoons, and other Japanese fired on them.

Companies went off to the flanks, but at 4.30 pm Lieutenant Colonel Dunbar called them back. The Japanese pressed in and fired strongly at the ridge top, but failed to shift them. The night was spent in rain on the ridge.

The Japanese 6 Company II/144 had gone into the attack at 1.40 pm, probably against 2/31st Battalion. After advancing, unsure of what was ahead, they made contact. 2 Platoon was leading, with 1 Platoon on the right, but, as Lieutenant Horibe wrote, 'met stiff resistance. The battle did not progress as desired'. He had one killed and four wounded. Japanese HQ II/144 ordered 6 Company to attack from the left of the road, and 7 Company (III/144) was supposed to be attacking from the road itself. Then at 4.30 pm, while advancing along the road, Horibe's unit saw the Australians retreating from the right, and 'inflicted a heavy loss'. Corporal Hosokawa died there. But the Australians held their position, to cover the withdrawal of the main force, and, as Horibe noted, actually became stronger. He reported this to the Battalion Commander, Major Horie, and was ordered to remain in position to fire at the enemy as they retreated.

With the arrival of 25 Brigade, the composite 2/14–2/16th Battalion had hoped to be withdrawn, but when 2/31st could not get forward, the composite unit was again left facing the Japanese for the night 14-15 September. The enemy continued probing and reconnoitring. In 2/14th Battalion; it was Lance Corporal Roy Watson's birthday, fortuitously mail arrived and with it his birthday mail and a gift from his parents, a watch.

Horii informed his force in Order A-117 at 4 pm, that 144 Regiment had defeated a small force of enemy and was advancing towards Ioribaiwa. Smoke visible from Uberi showed that perhaps the Australians were destroying ammunition, and the formation was to advance towards Ilolo. 144 Regiment was to accomplish this, after which the formation was to take the ammunition dump. Further orders would be issued in due course. 41 Regiment was to advance on 16 September to the west of Ioribaiwa, a detachment of 20 men to remain at Wamai to receive air-dropped supplies.[29]

Colonel Yazawa, of 41 Regiment, was given his orders for the capture of Port Moresby. Kila Kila airfield was to be taken first, by I or III Battalion, with the battalion commander to be left to decide how to hold the occupied airfield while the remainder went on. Next, Moresby peninsula and the town itself were to be taken, with one battalion (I or III) to guard it and mop up, while II Battalion continued the advance with the regimental commander, but definite plans had not been decided upon as to whether or not II/41 would move to take the enemy in the rear or would combine with 144 Regiment under direct command of Major General Horii. All units were to expend every endeavour to capture the airfields before the installations and supplies could be destroyed by the enemy. 144 Regiment was to capture 'North aerodrome' (7-Mile), first pushing through to take the high ground west of the runway.[30]

7 Australian Division issued Operation Instruction 11 on this day, and it is interesting to compare it with the Japanese orders. The division was to: establish control of routes leading from Kokoda to Port Moresby, to defend Port Moresby against attack from the north; regain control of routes to Kokoda through Isurava–Deniki; deal with small enemy patrols penetrating to Moresby.[31]

During the night, Lieutenant Horibe was told to be ready to move at any moment, but while assembling his men must have attracted the attention of the Australians, as a barrage of mortar bombs fell among them, wounding five. The platoon at once dived back into their trenches, strengthened guards, and waited out the night. Private Nakao died.

At first light on 15 September, 2/31st Battalion had patrols out, and the battalion mortar fired three-inch bombs at the Japanese positions. Later, a patrol sent to check the results of the mortaring contacted the Japanese, losing one killed and two wounded. This was part of the right arm of a Japanese pincer attack on Ioribaiwa. The returning patrol reported that the Japanese camouflage was very good. Japanese had been seen climbing trees, then pulling up after them on a cord their camouflage materials.

At 9.30 am, an A20 attacked Myola with six bombs, and checked the track to Efogi, but saw no activity. Weather was clear to Myola, but then clouds went right down to the hills. The Japanese had been up and moving for some hours. Akira Teruoka's medical unit woke at 3.30 am and moved off an hour later. As the combat units moved on quickly, 'we sick and weak were left behind,' Teruoka wrote. Despite what he had been told the day before, they were not to rest. He added that Allied air activity lately seemed to be limited to reconnaissance by one plane (the A20), and added that fear of air attack had decreased, 'and we feel more comfortable'. The Takasago officer who had counted 32 malaria cases on 5 September had 39 cases on the 13th, on the 12th had written that many were ill with the sickness, and that diarrhoea was next most prevalent. On this day he recorded that three of his company died in field hospital as there were no medicines. But the unit still was called on to carry supplies and ammunition to the forward troops.[32]

The Japanese, at first slowly and now more quickly, were being defeated by a combination of several factors, quite apart from the stubborn fighting withdrawals of the Australian units. One important factor was insoluble logistics problems. Horii issued Operation Order No. 5 on this day, stating that if resupply and foraging went well, each man could be issued two and a half pints of rice (1.4 litres) on the 22nd or 23rd, and two-thirds of a pint (one-third of a litre) on the 28th. 'This is the best that can be done', said the order, and all commanders were again urged to capture enemy supplies and live off the land. Another aspect of the problem was what amounted to a vicious circle, in that having sent back many troops, labourers and natives to bring up supplies, those remaining had greater difficulty in carrying forward what ammunition, supplies and baggage was needed for the advance. Consequently, personal and unit material not essential to the advance was to be left at a suitable place for later collection. The Japanese made a few parachute drops of supplies, but no real attempt was made to use aircraft to alleviate the problem, in stark contrast to the effort on the Allied side.[33]

At Ioribaiwa, the Australians in 2/14–2/16th Battalion defended the track up from the creek. During this fighting, 2/14th strength was reduced to less than 90 all ranks, with another seven killed and 12 wounded. The forward elements were forced back slightly. Private L. F. 'Pappy' Ransom, of 16 Platoon, remained in his position all day, and was able to shoot four Japanese setting up a mortar and machinegun position close to him. By remaining calm and hidden, carefully observing and waiting until the right moment to fire an aimed shot, Ransom survived the day, though many enemy were close by. At dusk he made his way back to the Australian positions, and exchanged a series of classic Aussie understatements with a sentry, who asked where he had been, was informed briefly, and then told Ransom that he 'reckoned there was someone down there' as the firing during the day had been heard.

A patrol from 2/25th Battalion went out on his information and killed the crews of the weapons without Australian casualties. This force was from A Company 2/25th, led by Lieutenant Jefferson, and claimed 15 Japanese killed, but darkness prevented an accurate count or further action. It was 2/25th's first clash with the Japanese, but already they had suffered two casualties from mortaring. C Company 2/16th came under accurate fire from the mountain gun, which killed four and wounded 10 men. To avoid further casualties, the company moved slightly away from the position where the shells were impacting.

At 2 pm, D Company 3rd Battalion was surprised by Japanese and forced off a high feature overlooking the village on the right. 17 Platoon had cleared a patch of ground, to improve their field of fire, and then began deepening their weapon pits on the heights. Other company members recall that they were eating biscuits and bully when, suddenly, Japanese, later estimated to number 20, were among them, having crossed open ground. The platoon was bounced out of its position, then the company was rolled up.

Up to the time of writing, exactly what happened has not been clarified. Company headquarters was well to the rear, and the company second-in-command was, for some reason, with B Company. A regular patrol had been made, each day, across to C Company, and the slope was so steep that the soldiers had to grab vines and trees to help them along the ridge. One of the patrol survivors believes that the distant Japanese had seen the daily disturbance among the treetops and leaves, and sent a force to ambush them. Of the eight men in the patrol, four were killed and the others wounded. It seems the Japanese continued their assault and overran the D Company position.

It also seems that the D Company sentries may not have been keeping a lookout, and that the weapons of those digging were out of reach. But whatever happened, the fact remained that the Japanese had occupied part of the battalion position. Captain Bert Madigan and his men of 2/16th manoeuvred to bring the Japanese out into the open, and were estimated to have killed or wounded about 30. In the confusion, Private Colin Kendrick, a D Company stretcher bearer, three times crawled forward alone, without covering fire, but being shot at by the Japanese, to bring back wounded Australians. He was awarded the Military Medal, and the citation included the phrase, 'each hazardous trip was made with supreme courage'.

Private Noel Geraghty had just placed his haversack on the ground and was chewing on a biscuit when the firing began and bullets were flying past. He jumped behind a small rock, but at the same instant Lieutenant Bill Woodger dived behind it also and was hit, by what Geraghty believes was a bullet aimed at him.

Meanwhile, on the Japanese side, Lieutenant Horibe's scouts had reported that the Australians had moved back 220 yards, and Private Sasaki brought with him two abandoned Bren guns. Horibe tried a quick attack, but failed and lost six men wounded. His platoon then crept around the Australian position and fired at 'the moving enemy, and inflicted heavy loss'. It may have been his men who bounced D Company out of their position. During the day, another man in Horibe's company died from malaria, another was wounded by a mortar round, and Horibe was ordered to prepare for a dawn attack.

The Japanese who had forced out D Company 3rd Battalion were between Australian companies of different battalions, which made coordination of counter-attacks difficult. Of course, the Japanese were heartened by this further advance onto the peak of a crucial ridge.

Inaccurate maps and poor communications added to Brigadier Eather's problems, influencing his decision to clear himself from the embrace at Ioribaiwa, take a pace back to Imitia and start advancing from there. But there could be no rearward move from Imita. Eather asked permission to go back, but Major General Allen told him there was to be no retreat from Imita; it was to be held to the death. Eather agreed. Allen and Lieutenant General Rowell knew that their positions as commanders were in great jeopardy. On this day, Eather also informed 7 Division of the urgent need for carriers and ANGAU personnel to control them.

From C Company 2/25th Battalion, Lieutenant H. Steele was ordered to take out a patrol to locate and destroy a Japanese work party that could be heard on the slopes of Ioribaiwa chopping trees and making other noise. Steele took 20 men, armed with six Tommy guns, 15 rifles and 42 grenades. An NCO from 3rd Battalion indicated the area where the noise had been heard, and the patrol departed. But from somewhere, Japanese saw them and directed mortar fire onto their area, so Steele withdrew to a position on the track. They were still in danger, for automatic weapons fire began cracking into an area just above them, and Steele believed it was preparatory fire for an attack, so moved again and then returned to the battalion. He later was told that a strong enemy force had been higher than his patrol on the slopes. He reported that it was difficult to judge sound, and though the fire orders for the mountain gun could be heard, its location could not be identified.

In the 2/33rd Battalion position on the right of Ioribaiwa Ridge, there was no contact with Japanese. Lieutenant Colonel Buttrose was told that the Japanese were probing 3 Militia Battalion, and had penetrated its D Company position. Heavy firing on his left confirmed this, then a mountain gun began firing. 2/25th Battalion was to send two companies from their right towards 3rd Battalion while one company from 2/33rd swept in from the left. A Company 2/33rd was tasked for this, and in addition, Buttrose sent Lieutenant Dick Cox with 18 Platoon to patrol the high ground and perhaps distract the Japanese while A Company was moving out.

Cox's platoon swept their ground, and saw their first Japanese: a well camouflaged lookout in a tree, betrayed only by movement. As Sergeant Bill Crooks was about to drop the Japanese with a single rifle shot, other Japanese were seen moving past the patrol. Cox decided not to get his platoon involved in a fight with what could be a larger body of enemy moving forward, but to return and report, and arrived back as D Company was about to move out.

A Company, under Captain Lawson, had struggled on through the jungle and rough terrain for two hours, but saw no Japanese or any sign of Captain Boag's C Company 3rd Battalion. Firing had been heard for an hour, and Lawson was told that the left company from 2/25th was in contact, but still found nothing, so at 4.30 pm decided to go back to battalion headquarters for more information.

Lieutenant Cox was not given time to report his sightings, as events had overtaken them, and Captain Clowes was taking D Company out to sweep along Ioribaiwa until Japanese were engaged. The company was about 80 strong, with half having seen action against the Vichy French in Syria. 16 Platoon led, followed by GHQ, 17 and 18 Platoons.

Meanwhile, in the air war, at 12.10 pm, five B17s arrived over Rabaul but clouds prevented any assessment of the damage caused by the 16 bombs dropped. Ten Zeros from Lakunai intercepted, and one was seen to go down in flames. Ten hours later, four other B17s bombed Vunakanau, but one B17 was lost and another crash-landed at Hood Point, plus another three that set off returned because of bad weather. Over New Guinea, at 12.25 pm, 11 B25s dropped bombs from 3000 feet on barges at Sanananda and stores at Buna, saw nothing to report on the airfield, though AA was medium inaccurate, and cloud base was 5500 feet, visibility eight miles (13 km). The B25s returned to Horn Island rather than to Moresby.

Despite what the aircrews reported about the AA, the Japanese No. 1 Battery 47 Field AA Battalion (I/47 AA) reported shooting down two aircraft on land and one 'crashed to the right of the position'. There were no details of these alleged wrecks, which it may be presumed would have been examined to identify the type, and see what other information could be found in them.[34]

The 15th Pioneers at Buna were relieved when told that the Yokosuka 5SLP was to assist in patrolling the area, and would arrive three days later. The threat of the 25,000 Allied paratroops still hung over Buna. Toshio Sato was told that the Yokosuka unit was the remnants of a force that had been defeated at Midway, in the Solomons and at Rabi (Milne Bay), adding that one-third of the

Pioneers were annihilated by strafing. One of the men was Noboru Wada, who had already seen considerable action in the Hong Kong campaign and in the Netherlands East Indies, in the Solomons and Milne Bay. Yokosuka 5SLP was a battalion-strength unit of 1000 men, comprised of a headquarters, two rifle companies of 234 men each, and artillery, AA, engineers, transport, medical and supply companies or platoons. It was a balanced force for landings or other assault operations as required.[35]

General Blamey flew to Port Moresby and, with Lieutenant General Rowell, went to HQ 7 Australian Division. Here they checked and discussed the plans for the counter-attack to be launched by 25 Brigade next day. Blamey said he was satisfied, and on his return to Australia made a radio broadcast stating his confidence in Rowell and the units in New Guinea.

In Brisbane, General Kenney was told he could fly the US 128 Infantry Regiment to New Guinea, beginning on 18 September, when a sea-borne move of other units would begin. It was to be a crucial test of the air arm, and Kenney was determined to succeed. As well as the transports he did have, he arranged for the loan of 12 Australian civil airliners, and ordered the use of every bomber then in Australia for repairs.

Meanwhile, the isolated Australian 2/27th Battalion, in the hills above Nauro, had made no progress that day. At first, Nauro seemed deserted, but closer inspection showed at least two companies of enemy there. Lieutenant Colonel Cooper considered an attack, but the burden of 13 stretcher cases forced him to decide against it. Nauro could not be passed and the tired men had to make their way back to the night position on the high ground to the east, which they had reached on 14 September.

By 6 pm, at Ioribaiwa, Captain Clowes's D Company 2/33rd was clearing a native track near sheer, bamboo-covered cliffs and rocks. The forward scout came to a track corner and looked out over an open area with part native garden and part kunai grass. He saw two natives, one chopping wood, then about 50 dispersed Japanese, who at once opened fire, and one of the natives also aimed a rifle, but Private Peter Barr dropped to the ground and shot him first. Behind Barr, Lieutenant John Mosely's 16 Platoon came into action, practising the engagement drill, and were firing at the Japanese in a few seconds. Captain Clowes ordered Lieutenant Logan to take 17 Platoon to the right to outflank the Japanese, and Cox's 18 Platoon to the left to try to get above them.

The locale was against them. Logan's men spent 10 minutes struggling through the growth and when they reached the open ground the Japanese brought automatic weapon and grenade fire onto them. Cox's platoon was trying to climb the cliffs. Meanwhile, 16 Platoon was under heavy fire, with men killed and wounded. Captain Clowes decided to break away, and gave the order to retire. As it was now getting dark, he held the company some 200 yards away, went into all-round defence, and sent the attached Battalion Intelligence Section member back to the battalion position with a report of the action.

Lieutenant Colonel Buttrose was thus informed of A Company's failure to engage the Japanese attacking 3rd Battalion, and of D Company's contact with no success to report. He realised that the Japanese were in some strength on his left front. The composite 2/14–2/16th also had been forced to give ground, and had lost about another 40 men during the day. On the far left, 2/31st Battalion had been clambering about on razorback ridges for two days, engaging Japanese.

Brigadier Eather ordered Buttrose to send two companies to the west to drive a wedge into the Japanese along the ridge; D Company was to return to the battalion position, but not become engaged in fighting, rather to ambush any Japanese dislodged by the two-company attack. As Buttrose had no line communications with his companies, he would have to wait until first light to pass on these orders.

Again, there was heavy rain as well as thunder during the night. In D Company, some men had to use rifle slings to tie themselves to trees to avoid slipping down the steep slope in part of the company position. Three men were missing. The first day's action had been less than satisfying. In other probing actions during the night, Lance Corporal Ben Roberts, 2/16th, effectively used grenades against the Japanese. He was credited with killing eight enemy.

The 2/25th Battalion moved its A Company into position between 2/31st and 2/33rd Battalions, and all prepared for the morrow. Ahead of 2/31st, the Japanese lit fires and talked loudly enough to be heard. Suspecting some sort of wily, Oriental trap, the battalion did not react.

On 16 September, weather reduced the effectiveness of much of the air activity. A20s on a mission to Buna were forced back by weather, but the 16 escort P400s did get through and strafed barges at Sanananda, while six B26s flew to attack a cruiser at sea, but could not find it. Five B17s went to Rabaul, found it covered by cloud, so made the long return journey without dropping bombs. The morning reconnaissance A20 mission was flown to Nauro–Efogi, and fires west of Efogi were all that were seen; no track activity was noticed. The next mission was a lone B17 that went down to 1600 feet to bomb barges at Sanananda, with unknown results. There was a break in attacks until 3.55 pm, when ceiling was unlimited, and six P400s attacked barges at Buna, noticing machine-gun fire from the shore. At 6.50 pm, six B17s attacked Vunakanau airfield at Rabaul, reporting four fires and an explosion.

At Ioribaiwa, 3rd Battalion had reorganised, with some Aussies positioned to defend the rear. Ron Seaman and Laurie Britten, 7 Platoon, were placed behind battalion headquarters and told that any movement in that rearward direction would be enemy, so they settled down with the Bren gun. Below them was a creek, and Seaman saw shrubbery moving, then noticed a man camouflaged with leaves crawling up the slope. He realised that 'the moment of truth' had arrived. Laurie Britten readied the Bren and Seaman pulled the pin from a 36-grenade, released the striker lever and saw the smoke coming from the top, so threw it. The crump of explosion was followed by a stream of loud Australian abuse that convinced them there were no Japanese down there! A soldier from headquarters was returning from the creek with water when a grenade thrown by Seaman actually bounced off his steel helmet, flew further down the slope and exploded harmlessly below him. Seaman and Britten were quickly the focus of attention by headquarters officers, but pointed out that they were following their instructions and had regarded any movement as enemy. They never saw the affronted soldier. Years later, Ron Seaman was having a beer with several ex-3rd Battalion fellows, and one was asked if he remembered the time at Ioribaiwa when the grenade bounced off his helmet – after a few more beers, Seaman confessed to throwing the grenade!

Elsewhere at Ioribaiwa, the Japanese 6 Company 144 Regiment put in a two-platoon attack at 7.30 am to clear the ridge before them, and at 9 am, Ito Platoon charged, but met stiff resistance and failed. The charge was put in by Sergeant Ito, Corporal Yokoda and 16 men. As 6 Company Commander was wounded, the commander of 5 Company took over both companies. A separate Japanese document stated that an entire platoon was lost in the charge, and also mentioned the company commander loss. When the wounded had been evacuated, it was discovered the Australians had withdrawn, so a section of 1 Platoon went forward and occupied the position. By the end of the day, the enemy company was on the ridge and in communication with its II Battalion HQ.

This description of an attack coincides with information from the Australian 2/31st Battalion. D Company was attacked at 8.10 am, for half an hour, during which the company had two wounded, and estimated that 14 Japanese became casualties. At 9 am, the company two-inch mortars were fired onto a party of Japanese trying to bring a medium machinegun around to the right. Then the battalion was ordered to withdraw, and at 11 o'clock Major Robson left to reconnoitre positions on Imita. (The time difference is due to the Japanese using Tokyo time throughout the campaign.)

Troops other than Horibe's on the peaks were able to see the distant glitter of the sea that marked their objective. One more ridge line blocked the way, and after that they would be descending to the coastal plain, the airfields, the harbour, the prize of Port Moresby. That last ridge was Imita.

Horii had suffered considerable casualties to take Ioribaiwa, including total loss of the platoon from 6 Company II/144 in one charge. Sakamoto recorded losses in II/144 of 15 killed and 64 wounded, one of the latter being Lieutenant Kamimura, OC 5 Company, his own MG Company losses as two killed and 15 wounded, and that 5 and 6 Companies with the Okamoto MG platoon, were merged under Lieutenant Kihara from battalion HQ for the final charge in the rain to the top of the ridge. The differences in the Horibe and Sakamoto detail of company commander losses may be due to confusion at the time, or to translation errors. Private Watanabe, 1 Company I/144, wrote that every company was at half-strength. At Horii's HQ, Lieutenant Hayashi noted the 'tremendous litter of dead' and 'the great stench from the corpses'.

Some of the Australians facing the Japanese also had suffered heavily. The composite 2/14–2/16th Battalions had to endure one last ordeal. All morning 2/14th was pounded by mortars, machineguns and mountain guns from front and flanks. Some of the strongest men, who had borne the strain of the previous weeks, showed signs of breakdown, and several were ordered back for a short period of rest, but they hung on.

However, this intense Japanese effort, of ground assaults and heavy fire, with penetrations into the Australian positions, forced Brigadier Eather to the decision to go back to Imita, reorganise, and attack from there. At 8.15 am, Eather signalled Major General Allen, and later spoke to him by telephone. Allen urged Eather to hold Ioribaiwa, repeated the importance of the position, but left the decision on withdrawal to Eather. Eather's view was that he would have no freedom to manoeuvre if all his force was committed to Ioribaiwa, that he had to keep his force intact to cover Moresby, and the move back to Imita would help secure his vulnerable carrier supply lines. Allen and Rowell made it quite clear there could be no more withdrawal. No matter what, Imita had to be held.

A Company 2/25th replaced the remnants of 2/14th Battalion, and the other companies of 2/25th waited for their orders to go into action. There was some surprise when the order to go back to Imita was given. Initially, 2/25th was to be the rearguard, later passing this role to 2/33rd. So far, 2/25th had lost four men killed, and two officers and 14 men wounded, but did not consider that it had come to grips with the Japanese.

'Tich' Moore, 2/14th Battalion Intelligence Section, had been going back and forth to the dangerous forward slopes, taking information on the enemy back to the headquarters. When told that he need not go back to the front line again, as 2/25th had arrived, he said, 'Just my luck. Left my haversack in the hole'. Mick Fielding told him not to worry about it, but 'Tich' replied, 'Oh, I can't do that – it's got a tin of bully in it!'

The company commanders of 2/33rd Battalion were given their orders at 6 am, and the isolated D Company received theirs from the Intelligence Officer, Lieutenant Howland, who went out to their position. B and C Companies moved off to the left of 2/33rd's position, met 3rd Battalion and later a representative from 2/25th Battalion, which had been in action for the past day. Captain Tom Archer, OC B Company 2/33rd, turned his company to the north, and decided to advance until he contacted Japanese.

At 10 am, B Company 2/33rd began to go forward through low, dense scrub and kunai, which combined to reduce visibility to nil. Firing and shelling could be heard to the left and ahead, and as they reached the crest of a ridge, a blast of rifle, light machinegun and grenade fire hit them. They went to ground, but visibility was still nil, and all that could be done was to fire low in the direction of the Japanese. A reconnaissance by Sergeant Twentyman failed to locate the Japanese flank, but soon after noon it became evident that the Japanese had gone. B Company was told to hold their position, with C Company in support. There was no more action that day, but at night Japanese could be heard creeping about to the front.

Lower down the slope, Clowes's D Company began moving back to the area of contact at dusk the previous day. Private McLeod had last been seen knocked down and apparently killed by a hit to the neck, but he amazed 17 Platoon by stepping out of the bush. McLeod had spoken to the wounded Lieutenant Mosely during the night, but did not know where Mosely was now. Despite further searches, and with fire from the Japanese aimed at the company again, the two missing men, Mosely and Corporal Bradford, could not be located.

At 11.30 am, Lieutenant Colonel Buttrose was surprised to

receive an order to withdraw, direct from Brigadier Eather on the telephone. The surviving elements of 21 Brigade were at that time beginning to withdraw, followed by the 25 Brigade units, of which 2/33rd was to be the last, fighting a delaying action for four days before going back to Imita Ridge. At midday, Buttrose sent a runner to each company with the orders: B Company to move back to the brigade food dump, take up position there and begin destroying all food not moved away by 4 pm, plus booby-trap what could not be destroyed; A Company to move to a position 15 minutes' travel to the rear of B Company; C Company to move to positions in and around the kunai patch half an hour's travel from Ioribaiwa village; D Company to move to the rear of A Company. No company was to move back until it had engaged or ambushed the leading Japanese elements. Apart from the CO, the rest of 2/33rd was surprised by the order. Casualties had been light, and no one felt that they'd really been in action, and in fact other than 16 and 18 Platoons, no one had seen a Japanese.

At the brigade food dump, Brigadier Eather explained to Lieutenant Colonel Buttrose that the Japanese had succeeded in placing strong groups between 2/33rd and 3rd Battalion, and behind 2/31st. 25 Brigade was thus engaged in holding off attacks, trying to plug these gaps between battalions, and relieve the composite 2/14–2/16th Battalion, the brigade had suffered about 100 casualties, which took all the carriers to evacuate, and really 25 Brigade had been reacting to Japanese moves rather than dictating the course of events. Eather had decided to withdraw to the better defensive position offered by Imita Ridge, reorganise, and attack. His brigade HQ began to move back to Imita at noon.

Meanwhile, also at about noon, the composite 2/14–2/16th had handed over to 2/25th Battalion and moved into a reserve position at Uberi. As the 2/14th slogged up the forward slope to Uberi in the pouring rain, there was the Red Shield of the Salvation Army. Albert Moore had gone as far forward as the senior commanders would allow, to serve hot coffee and biscuits to the Diggers.

For the first time for 18 days, there was no enemy to the front; there was shelter from the rain. The tired soldiers could see the organised preparations massing for the coming counter-offensive.

The withdrawal order was received by Captain Archer at B Company 2/33rd with relief. The 2/25th companies were leaving to follow their part in the orders, and Archer wondered what would happen with no one on his flank. Happily, listening posts reported no movement by the Japanese. Archer got B Company on the move and by 3 pm they were at the food dump destroying clothes, food and setting booby-traps in what remained. The brigade trudged past on the move back to Imita, and at 5 pm the rain began again, with lightning flashing through the wetness, the dark hillsides and cloud overhead.

B Company was then told to move back and leave Captain Lawson's A Company to shoot the Japanese when they began looting the food dump, so Archer's Company moved onto the track behind the rearguard of 2/31st Battalion. Captain Lawson deployed his 7, 8 and 9 Platoons, and all settled down to wait. At 6 pm, two Japanese were seen cautiously moving along the track, then they halted only 20 yards from the entrance to the ambush killing ground. Everyone waited; no more Japanese were seen. Then someone fired, whether by accident or due to nerves will probably never be known, and all in 9 Platoon who could see a Japanese also fired. There was no known result, and Captain Lawson unhappily gave the order to withdraw by sections, as arranged. The rendezvous was 200 yards to the rear of C Company, which was in a kunai crest to the rear of A Company. However, steady Sergeant Tobin, of 8 Platoon, was still holding his position, as no Japanese had been seen to shoot at, and Lieutenant Roberts had to go back to order the disgruntled Tobin to take his men out. There was no further night contact, and 2/33rd wondered what the new day would bring.

Akira Teruoka had risen early, but found he was too weak to move along the track. The unit went on ahead, and two other privates came back for him, carrying his equipment until they caught up with the platoon. There Teruoka was given a physical examination, some medicine, and allowed to rest, before he again set off over the mountains. 2nd Lieutenant Onogawa was told that the general offensive was to begin on 20 September, and determined to return at once to the battalion. In the forward Japanese positions, Lieutenant Hirano was dismayed at the small amount of food issued, and Sakamoto also noted the tiny amount available. In later days, many officers and men wrote of the lack of food, though ammunition continued to arrive. But Port Moresby was almost in reach. That night, the tired Japanese on the heights at Ioribaiwa could see the searchlights at Moresby, and the faint glow in the dark sky of the town lights. They needed one more supreme effort, and success would be theirs.

During the day, in Australia General Blamey had broadcast to the nation on the results and impressions of the situation gained during his recent visit to New Guinea. He said that all concerned were confident the Japanese would not take Port Moresby.

Air attacks on 17 September again had mixed results, mainly due to weather conditions. A B17 attack by eight bombers on Rabaul was foiled by weather, but one bombed Lae, and at 7.40 am another attacked a ship at Salamaua from 1000 feet, scoring a direct hit and leaving the ship burning. Cloudbase was 12,000 feet, visibility 30 miles (48 km). Another B17 crew were last heard reporting they were lost and about to bail out. Two hours later, at 9.40 am, cloudbase had lowered to 5000 feet, and visibility reduced to 20 miles (32 km), when eight P40s escorted 11 RAAF Beaufighters to attack Buna, fires were started in eight barges, and fires started at Sanananda were visible 25 miles (40 km) away. The P40s claimed two machinegun posts silenced, confirmed barges burning and a large fire, believed to have been petrol.

The Japanese No. 1 Battery 47 AA Battalion fired on the attackers, claiming four Beaufighters destroyed and one probably destroyed in 30 minutes of action: 09.40, one Beaufighter with right engine on fire banked left and fell into the coconut grove; 09.45, another fell into the coconut grove; 09.55, one shot down into the sea; 10.00, one disappeared flying low into the jungle south-east of the airfield; 10.10, another with engine on fire fell into the sea. The battery reported that the Beaufighters were manoeuvrable and persistent in low-level attack. The battery's 2 Section was commended for their fast and efficient rate of fire, and 2nd Lieutenant

Uchida was praised for his excellent direction. However, no Beaufighters were lost.[36]

'Wada', the diarist at Buna, was told that of 16 attacking fighters, three had been shot down, for a loss of two large motorised
landing craft and a truck destroyed. A medical officer watched the
attacks and identified the aircraft, adding that the planes 'burned
up a lot of petrol and materials. Barrack area strafed and bombed'.[37]

Akira Teruoka got up at dawn on 17 September. Five men from
each sub-unit went to look for food, could not find any, and 'came
home disgusted'. Major General Horii, with staff and unit commanders, gathered at Isurava 'Six House Height' and surveyed the
battle area. Close by, Lieutenant Horibe was given acting command of 6 Company II/144. His CO, Major Horie, told him to
move from the position occupied last night. The first task was to
evacuate the wounded, and then two dead 'brave warriors' were
buried. He reorganised the company into two platoons, one led by
Sorimoto and the other by Fukumoto. Work began on digging
positions and air-raid trenches, as well as erecting tents. After
another two men were detached to escort the wounded, company
strength was down to 50 men.

With the rest of the Australian 25 Brigade gone past to Imita the
previous evening, 2/33rd Battalion waited in its ambush positions.
C Company, under Captain Larry Miller, had occupied a large
kunai-covered knoll. The main path went across the kunai, along
the ridge, but a detour had been created that looped around the
eastern edge of the knoll before continuing down the ridge, and a
detour sign had been placed at the junction on a stick. Miller's
orders were simple: allow as many Japanese as possible into the
killing zone, hammer them, then withdraw in the order of 15, 13
and 14 Platoon. The final touch was having the three two-inch
mortars available ready to bombard the kunai after 14 Platoon was
past. But there seemed to be no Japanese coming forward. Captain
Clowes sent Lieutenant Cox and three men of 18 Platoon forward,
past C Company, to try to locate Japanese and try to draw them into
the ambush. Lieutenant Cox's feelings are unrecorded, but can be
imagined. Walking briskly and spread out, the four men went

along the track, across the kunai, up the stairs constructed on the side of the ridge and into the jungle. They knew Japanese were watching them. Rather than stick his head too far into the lion's jaws, Cox stopped at a suitable distance and took the patrol back, still in clear view. It is not known what the Japanese made of this.

The Japanese were too cautious to blindly rush down the track after Cox, but came forward to the edge of the jungle and fired in the general area of the company. No one moved or fired back; silence fell. There was movement in the trees, and two Japanese in khaki were seen. Then comments in English were heard: 'They have all gone'; 'Plenty good tucker here', and similar. Nothing happened. Then, their footfalls clearly heard by C Company, a group of Japanese came down the stairs and into view. The leader, an officer with a sword, walked up to the 'Detour' notice, took it from the stick, read it, and beckoned forward those behind. It was 7.30 am.

In double file, bunched together, some clearly seen to be carrying tins of Australian food, the Japanese set out across the kunai in the early morning light. They were chattering and laughing, and no one seemed to be alert for enemy. Captain Miller aimed at the officer and dropped him at 10 yards range as the surprised Japanese were flailed by fire from rifles, sub-machineguns and Brens. They scattered back to the trees, leaving about a dozen visible dead in the killing ground.

From the jungle, light machinegun and mortar fire played across the company position. Captain Miller gave the withdrawal order and 15 Platoon, under Lieutenant Warne, moved back. The Japanese saw this, and tried to advance, but were repulsed by Lieutenant 'Heck' Davies's 13 Platoon. Another Japanese machinegun was firing from the low ground, and the Kelly brothers put it out of action with grenades. Sergeant Rowe was checking the edge of the drop away from the kunai, looked down and saw a Japanese in camouflaged clothing only 20 yards away. As Rowe sighted on him, the man looked up; it was the last thing he saw. Other enemy were down there, and Rowe reported the flanking movement. Grenades were flung over the lip of the gully. Miller ordered 13

Platoon out, and as they went threw more grenades among the Japanese below. The flanking movement ceased.

Miller's headquarters then followed 13, and Lieutenant Bill Innes remained with 14 Platoon, to move back when he considered it time to do so. Innes used a whistle to signal his sections, under Sergeant Storey and Corporal Jeffreys, to go. He then sent out Corporal Smeaton's section, and came back himself, telling Private Friend to signal the mortars to open fire. Twenty-eight rounds of mortar fire exploded in the target area, and the company was clear. It was estimated that some 50 Japanese were killed in the action, but no records to verify this, or to give the Japanese side of this engagement, were later captured. C Company came back through Clowes's D Company, exultant at their success after hours of waiting. By 8 am, the jungle was quiet again, the sun shining, with only birds breaking the silence. D Company waited in the rear of a kunai patch on the reverse slope of a wild and overgrown razorback ridge that would allow the Japanese little room for manoeuvring. Lieutenant Colonel Buttrose ordered withdrawal by companies to the flatlands along Ua-ale Creek, with only 18 Platoon remaining in the D Company ambush. Three hours later, 2/33rd was positioned with companies 15 minutes from each other along the track and creek crossing. The Japanese had learned their lesson, and 18 Platoon was not able to spring its ambush, but Japanese grenades and fire broke the stillness from time to time as they searched for Australian positions. There was no further contact that day.

Major General Kenney received the bad news that the Japanese were now at Imita Ridge, only 26 miles (42 km) from Port Moresby, but also the news that the Australian 25 Brigade was moving to hold the Japanese there. Kenney persuaded General MacArthur to go to New Guinea next day, as a visit by the Supreme Commander would boost morale. Prior to this, MacArthur's headquarters, headed by General Sutherland, had contented itself with sending numerous telegrams from Brisbane to New Guinea and the Australian commanders on the spot. No one in authority at GHQ had visited the front to gain personal knowledge of conditions and the situation, but this did not prevent the veterans of Bataan and Corregidor, in Brisbane, working from inadequate maps and hearsay, from trying to tell the commanders in action what they should be doing.

During the day, the Japanese destroyer *Mochizuki* evacuated 98 patients from the hospital at Giruwa. Up until this time, Japanese casualties were taken from their unit to Kokoda, and then carried by natives, labour troops and Takasago volunteers back to the coast. From now on, only walking wounded arrived at the hospital. An officer told Lieutenant Ebuchi that Lieutenant Noda had died in action.[38]

Buna area itself now came under command of (Japanese Navy) Captain Yoshitatsu Yasuda, who brought with him 280 men of the Yokosuka 5SLP. Yasuda began construction of the formidable defensive works that were to cause so much trouble to the Allies in later fighting at Buna. Word was received by Japanese in New Guinea of 'sizable damage at Rabaul as a result of bombing'.[39]

Far away in Canberra, General Blamey had reviewed the New Guinea situation for the Australian Government Advisory War Council, gave detail of the Allied forces available, and concluded by saying that Generals Rowell and Allen and their troops were confident of holding Moresby. However, Prime Minister Curtin was telephoned by MacArthur that evening and informed that in MacArthur's opinion, an inferior force of Japanese was pushing back a superior number of Australians and had been doing so since the Japanese landing. Therefore, MacArthur was going to send US troops by air and sea to halt the advance. Then MacArthur said that it was necessary for Blamey to go to New Guinea to 'energise the situation', for Blamey to meet his responsibility to Australia. Mac-Arthur went on to say that while he did not have the authority to send Blamey, he would speak to him in those terms and asked if Curtin also would persuade Blamey to go. Curtin agreed.

MacArthur succeeded in a masterstroke. Blamey was responsible for all Australian land forces in the SWPA, and New Guinea was only a part of this difficult and widespread task. He allowed commanders in the field to get on with their jobs without interfer-

ence from him, but realised that when the inexperienced Australian political leaders had been manoeuvred by the Supreme
Commander SWPA into requiring this return to Port Moresby of
him, he would have to obey. In the event of the Japanese flooding
out onto Port Moresby lowlands, and any sort of disaster developing, a convenient scapegoat would be to hand. And with Mac-
Arthur controlling public information communiques, there would
be no great fighting defence, as supposedly happened on Bataan,
attributed to the forces under Blamey.

Just after midnight, on 18 September, a B17 bombed Salamaua
Isthmus from 3000 feet, and two Catalinas harassed Buka. Early
in the daylight hours, a B25 on reconnaissance of Andemba–
Wairopi–Kokoda reported supplies stacked in shacks, groups of
ponies going towards Kokoda, and in the Buna area, the crew
counted 27 burnt out barges on Sanananda Point, and four 37-mm
AA guns in a field five miles (eight km) inland. In the Buna–Gona
area, ceiling and visibility was unlimited, but it was cloudy over
the mountains. Seven Beaufighters set out to strafe the Buna–
Kokoda track, six were turned back by weather, but one got
through and attacked trucks at Popondetta; there was no AA fire.
The weather by that time was visibility three miles (4.8 km) and
closing in, ceiling over Buna 7000 feet. The Japanese No. 1 Battery 47 AA Battalion claimed to have inflicted serious damage on
a reconnaissance P38.[40]

Under the mountain trees, Akira Teruoka's unit was woken at
5 am, and again men were sent to look for food, this time returning
with a large quantity of small sweet potatoes. Though improved,
Teruoka thought it would take a long time for him to return to good
health. He also heard that sick and wounded were to be evacuated
next day. The constant passage overhead of enemy aircraft had
made it difficult to cook during the nights. Formation orders had
already laid down that cooking was to be done at certain times, and
certainly not attempted at night.

Lieutenant Horibe, with his company's strength now 55 men,
assembled his platoon commanders and inspected the Ioribaiwa
position. His orders from II/144 were to send out scouts to seek

information and also forage for food, while those in camp were to continue work on sleeping and cooking installations, deepen air-raid trenches each day, not walk about with lights at night, only walk on the road, and not cut down trees or branches near tents. At Buna, Tadao Chiba welcomed 200 men of the Yokosuka 5SLP as they landed, and at the same time, 2 Company Takasago Volunteers left for the mountains 'on an important mission to deliver ammunition to the South Seas Force'.[41]

A patrol of six men from the isolated 2/27th Battalion, Potts's 21 Brigade, sent forward by Lieutenant Colonel Cooper, made contact with 2/16th Battalion. Their message, giving the location of 2/27th, finally reached 7 Division HQ 36 hours after it left the battalion. The 2/27th slowly moved forward, with D Company detached to bring along the remaining stretchers. As a last resort to care for casualties, Captain Keith Viner-Smith, the RMO, had allowed maggots to remain on the wounds of walking wounded and stretcher cases, as the simplest and best prevention of gangrene.

Brigadier Eather instituted a policy of active and aggressive patrolling out to a good distance from Imita, to keep the Japanese off balance. Each patrol was to be of 50 men, with rations for five days, a minimum of seven Tommy guns, a Bren and grenades, to create disruptions on the Japanese side of the valleys. So far, 25 Brigade had lost eight officers and 84 men as battle and sickness casualties.

The 2/25th Battalion sent out a fighting patrol to Ioribaiwa, under Captain R. Dodd, with two sergeants and 48 men selected from HQ, C and D Companies. The patrol left at 10.45 am, and as they closed on the Japanese, could hear them talking and chopping wood. Cautiously, the Australians advanced, and from the amount of noises, coughing and so on, deduced an enemy company was in the old 2/25th A Company location. While manoeuvring to assault the outpost, then exploit the attack advantage, a steel helmet fell off and the distinctive noise alerted the Japanese sentries, who gave the alarm as they were rushed and killed with Tommy gun and bayonet, but then the patrol had to withdraw. Captain Dodd moved away for the night.

The 2/33rd Battalion waited in its delaying position, but no Japanese were contacted during the day. Nine men from the 2/27th came in, were fed and sent on their way to Imita. At 7 pm, Lieutenant Colonel Buttrose gave orders for the move next day into the Imita position, where the battalion location had been reconnoitred already. From 2/31st Battalion, a strong patrol was sent out to harass the enemy in the area west of the Ioribaiwa–Imita track. Lieutenant Upcher, Lieutenant Gardiner and 50 men, with 10 Tommy guns, grenades and five days rations, set off into the jungle.

None of the Allies knew that Imperial GHQ in Tokyo decided Guadalcanal was to have priority, and on this day ordered South Seas Force to go back and hold Buna–Gona until the Solomons operations had been brought to a successful conclusion, then again advance over the ranges and take Moresby. Once more the ineptness of the Japanese high command is evident. Only a group far removed from reality could issue such an order, apparently believing that nothing had changed since July, and that their enemy could be bundled back once more. All was ignored: the Australian battle experience, knowledge of terrain, reinforcements, the ability to provide supplies, and the important increase in air strength.

Four Catalinas harassed Buna during the early hours of 19 September. Weather at Lae was clear, visibility maximum, at 8.10 am, when it was attacked by six A20s striking the plantations and runway, and crews saw bombs from the B26s immediately after them hit east and south of the runway, as at 8.11 am eight B26s bombed from 6100 feet. At 10 o'clock, a B17 on reconnaissance strafed a ship, and at 11, four B17s took off from Waigani to attack a 5000-ton cargo ship in the Dampier Straits, and at 2.15 pm, a 3000-ton vessel was attacked from 1000-1500 feet. No direct hits were claimed, but four near-misses were scored and the squadron was credited with sinking the ship. At 5 pm, two other B17s attacked a ship from 1500 feet, again there were no hits, but the closest bomb exploded 30 feet away, and the gunners strafed the decks. Cloudbase was 8000 feet, with haze to 2500 feet, visibility 5-10 miles (8-16 km).

Though not reported in Allied Air Force (AAF) documents, it

seems Beaufighters attacked Buna, as the Japanese I/47 AA Battalion described a series of sightings and engagements at about 8 am local time. One Beaufighter was reported to have crashed in flames in the western jungle, and one other 'disappeared into the jungle'. Two gunners were wounded in the strafing, and the report clearly described the RAAF markings. An officer in 2 Company Takasago Volunteers, carrying ammunition forward, noted that at '07.40 [7.40 am] they bombed and machinegunned last night's camping place'. Lieutenant Morimoto, cipher officer, noted that 'enemy aircraft failed to find the ammunition dump, which was well hidden by the jungle'.[42]

Akira Teruoka had been on guard duty during the night, and after assisting in evacuation of the sick early in the morning, went to wash his clothes. He was assigned to assist the anti-aircraft sentry during the day, and noted that it was difficult to 'perform satisfactory duty day and night after my long illness'.

Australian night patrols had been fired on by Japanese sentries of III/144, so II/144 strengthened their own guards, but no attack developed. Lieutenant Horibe sent a five-man scouting party out to locate the Australians and find food. The party returned with no information and no food. Later, word was received that three of the wounded died, and another man was still missing.

Not far from the Japanese positions was Captain Dodd's patrol from 2/25th Battalion. The Japanese detected his position in the early light by movement in his location, and turned heavy fire on him, so he moved away. He had sent back to the Australian lines 15 sick men from his force. There was further firing from unseen Japanese, but Dodd avoided them, moved to a safer location and decided to remain there and rest his men before harassing the Japanese on the morrow.

Across the valley on Imita Ridge, 2/33rd Battalion moved into its positions, and were served a hot bully beef stew, the first 'cooked' meal since 10 September. For the next five days the battalion rested, aired their feet and slept reasonably well at night; meals were cooked and tea brewed, with companies rotating through a forward position. Patrols from 2/31st Battalion, in the valley below, returned and reported that while no smoke could be seen above Imita, plenty of noise could be heard. On the battalion right, an observation post of 14 Field Regiment was established. 2/27th Battalion main body was pushing on to rejoin the Australian forces, and left 16 wounded, seven stretcher cases and nine walking wounded under the care of Corporal John Burns and Private Alf Zanker. They were to remain there for 13 long and worrying days.

Generals MacArthur and Kenney arrived at 7-Mile airfield, Port Moresby. Kenney was pleased at a successful fly-in of the US 128 Infantry Regiment, and hoped that this display of air mobility would persuade MacArthur to allow similar operations, particularly to occupy Wanigela, on the north coast of New Guinea, and outflank Buna. To Kenney, MacArthur seemed unconvinced.

During the day, 2/14th and 2/16th Battalions resumed their separate identities. The weakened condition of these two battalions, which had set off up the Kokoda Trail so full of confidence, clearly shows the cost of holding the Japanese at Isurava and Efogi. 2/14th comprised 101 all ranks: Battalion HQ plus remnants of A, B and C Companies, 40; HQ Company with part of A Company, 30; D Company, 19; Lieutenant Greenwood's stretcher party, 12. 2/16th had a total of 142 all ranks: Battalion HQ, 20; A Company, 36; B Company, 30; C Company, 20; D Company, 37. The ratio of killed to wounded in warfare, in general, is 1:4. The ferocity of the actions involving 2/14th can be judged by the following figures of losses suffered by the battalion rifle companies in the Kokoda actions. A Company, 12 killed, 23 wounded; B Company, 31 and 38; C Company, 19 and 24; D Company, 31 and 20. In addition, there were dead and wounded in the Headquarters and specialist platoons. 21 Brigade's battle casualties in killed, wounded and missing on the Kokoda Trail had been 248 in 2/14th, 163 in 2/16th and 88 in 2/27th Battalion. The number of sick men, in addition to battle casualties, was estimated at about 900.

The brigade, hobbled by the supply debacle, had been attacked by three to four times their number, and by an enemy with the advantage in firepower. They bought the priceless commodity of time, and sowed the seeds of Horii's defeat. Brigadier Arnold

Potts had been forced to commit his battalions piecemeal, and never was permitted to fight as he would have preferred. 39th Battalion also had gone into action as companies arrived up the trail, but they were 'only Chocos' and the AIF had not been too perturbed at the news that Chocos were in retreat. However, 21 Brigade was 2nd AIF, and expected to stop the Japanese smartly, then bundle them back to Buna. Instead, each battalion had been roughly handled. 2/14th, fighting fiercely and exacting great payment from the enemy, had been reduced to a fraction of its strength and had lost its CO, only the second AIF battalion commander to be lost in action since 1939, but the third of his rank lost in New Guinea in six weeks; 2/16th also had been greatly reduced in numbers, while 2/27th had been shattered and forced off the battlefield, with two companies split into small parties to avoid the Japanese and make their own way to safety, while the rest of the battalion also sought to avoid contact and bring its wounded back. All through the mountains were parties of stragglers making their painful, hungry way to friendly territory.

If such a situation had been brought about in a Japanese regiment, it would have been classed as an Australian victory. While the remnants of 2/14th and 2/16th continued to resist, and the soldiers did not consider themselves beaten, the sad fact remains that 21 Brigade was eliminated temporarily as a fighting formation.

Horii, facing supply problems, concentrated his units at the decisive point and, despite great cost, shattered 21 Brigade, then maintained pressure. But 21 Brigade had forced on him consumption of items he could least afford: food, time and young leaders.

The attitude of 21 Brigade is best expressed by George Woodward, 10 Platoon, B Company 2/14th Australian Infantry Battalion: 'At no stage was I ever beaten. We were not beaten by the Japanese, we were beaten by lack of supplies. If we'd had our three battalions together, and our mortars, the Japanese never would have got past Isurava.'

21 Brigade submitted recommendations for the following awards for the period 16 August to 20 September: three Victoria Crosses,

one Distinguished Service Order, four Military Crosses, one Bar to the Military Cross, four Distinguished Conduct Medals, sixteen Military Medals, one Order of the British Empire, one Member of the British Empire, 68 Mentioned In Dispatches. Inevitably, this list was reduced by higher headquarters, where staff officers were (and are today) placed in the unenviable position of conducting such reviews.

Low-level air attacks began early on 20 September, and at 7.15 am, eight P40s and four P400s strafed Kokoda airfield and the track to Wairopi, and the pilots saw a large fire at Kagi. Visibility was three miles (4.8 km), with haze to 5000 feet. Twenty minutes later, six A20s attacked supply lines from Buna to Wairopi, fires were started at Popondetta, there was an explosion at Sangara Plantation, black smoke rising from Arehe, and hits scored in the clearing at Andemba. By this time, visibility was only half to one mile (800 to 1600 metres), with thick haze below 1000 feet. The Japanese Takasago volunteers carrying ammunition forward were below the planes: 'While marching, enemy planes dropped bombs in the rear, then machinegunned us. After this, planes attacked without let up.'

At 12.40 pm, five Beaufighters attacked Lae after failing to find a schooner reported off Cape Waria. Barges and a tug were strafed, as was a heavy AA position on Mt Lunaman, and pilots reported visibility between one and two miles (1.6 to 3.2 km), with cloud-base at Lae 13,000 feet.

Japanese diarist 'Wada' noted that the general attack on Moresby was to start this day. However, it was not to be. The real situation at the front was known or suspected only by officers in positions of authority. A medical officer at Buna had sent forward medical supplies as requested by Horii's formation in the mountains, and wrote that 'I and III Battalions have suffered great damage in frontline engagements up to the present, and II Battalion is the only one that can be used now'. From nearby Giruwa, 100 Japanese soldiers were evacuated to Rabaul on *Kazuura Maru*.[43]

On the slopes of Ioribaiwa, on 20 September, Captain Dodd's

patrol from 2/25th Battalion had left its position and again advanced towards the Japanese, who once more could be heard chopping, talking and making noises. Dodd's men observed the Japanese as best they could, and on one place on a spur, where the track was visible, counted 100 Japanese passing in five minutes. There was no indication to the Australians that the Japanese intended to retreat; they seemed to be improving their positions, and were as quick to fire as ever. Dodd decided to return, bringing the information he had gathered. He reported that both enemy and friendly troops could be detected by coughing, as many men were affected by the cold and persistent wet.

Japanese 6 Company II/144 had been inspected for 30 minutes by Lieutenant Horibe, who was not satisfied. 'Camouflage was insufficient and construction rudimentary.' A three-man patrol returned without finding signs of enemy activity to the position's front, and two more men arrived, bringing strength to 59 men. Still tired after long illness, Akira Teruoka felt much better after dinner, and wrote of the evening return of the men who had carried away the wounded.

Major General Horii issued a message to his troops, which broke the news that there would be no assault on Port Moresby in the immediate future:

'1. After the departure of our Detachment from Rabaul, it is now over one month since we took over from the Yokoyama Unit, which, sent here ahead of us, put up a brave fight. We first reduced the strong position at Isurava, and continued on crushing the enemy's resistance on the heights north of Isurava, at the Gap, Iora, Efogi, etc, and repeatedly carried out rapid pursuits of the enemy. We smashed his last resistance in the fierce fighting at Ioribaiwa, and today we firmly hold the line on the heights in that area, the most important point for the advance on Port Moresby.

'2. For more than 20 days of that period, every unit forced its way through deep forests and ravines, and climbed over scores of high peaks in pursuit of the enemy. Traversing mud more than knee-deep, clambering up steep precipices, bearing uncomplainingly the heavy weight of artillery ammunition, our men overcame the shortage of our supplies, and we succeeded in surmounting the Owen Stanley Range. No pen or word can depict adequately the magnitude of the hardships suffered. From the bottom of our hearts we appreciate these many hardships and deeply sympathise with the great numbers killed and wounded.

'3. We realise that the enemy in the Tulagi and Guadalcanal Islands has not yet been annihilated, and we have not yet won back the Samarai and Rabi aerodromes. Therefore, we are staying here and firmly maintaining our situation so that during this period we can perfect our organisation and replenish our fighting strength, and then strike a heavy hammer-blow at the enemy stronghold of Moresby. However, in front of us, the enemy still crawls about. It is difficult to judge the direction of his movement, and many of you have not yet fully recovered your bodily strength. I feel keenly that it is increasingly important during the present period while we are waiting for an opportunity to strike, to strengthen our positions, reorganise our forces, replenish our stores and recover our physical fitness.

'4. You will all bear in mind how vital are the situation and character of the Detachment in the South Pacific, and how increasingly heavy are your responsibilities. You shall strengthen your morale, replenish your vigour, and having perfected all your preparations for battle, you shall, when next we go into action, ungrudgingly throw in the whole fighting power of the unit.'

Horii had yet to tell his men that they would withdraw, and go all the way back to the coast. However, the inflated claims from Japanese headquarters at Rabaul helped sugar the pill a little. 17 Army Intelligence Report No. 34 informed readers that:

• Between 25 and 31 August, 144 Regiment had found 300 Australian dead in the Isurava area, and captured 73 weapons of all types.

• Between 31 August and 5 September, 41 Regiment had found 91 dead, and captured 39 weapons, three radios and a generator.

• Between 6-8 September, Major Horie's II/144 had cut off the enemy's retreat, resulting in 320 enemy dead being found by 144 Regiment.[44]

While Australian losses had certainly been serious, particularly in 21 Brigade, there were not 700 dead from the five battalions engaged.

Earlier in the day, 3rd Battalion had sent out a large patrol of 60: Captain W. J. S. Atkinson, Lieutenant W. A. Dullard and 58 men, to sweep out, find the Japanese lines of communication, then harass them. The battalion had been patrolling, with little result, close around its own positions. Lieutenant Colonel Cameron called for volunteers for the patrol, and Sergeant Bede Tongs had gone up with other men from B Company to put their names down. When they were told who the proposed patrol commanders were to be, they went back and crossed their names off the list. Cameron queried this, but changed the commanders to Atkinson and Dullard, who was a very popular and respected officer. The patrol was issued with five tins of emergency rations for the five-day patrol, but some men acquired an extra tin or so of bully beef. Such was the ration situation. They set off for the Japanese.

During the day, General Kenney had been with two enthusiastic supporters of his low-level attack ideas. The recent low-level attacks on two ships had shown that bombs could be placed quite close to, if not into, vessels at sea, and Major Benn and Captain Ken McCullar had flown skip-bombing attacks on the Moresby wreck, the SS *Pruth*, conveniently placed for such tests. No. 521 'Black Jack' was the test aircraft, and 10-second fuses were tried, but actual bombing showed the fuses functioned closer to five seconds. However, it was obvious that this low skip-bombing method was necessary if the aircraft were to score hits on ships. The rest of Benn's 63rd Squadron was on alert at Waigani.

Lieutenant General Rowell sent a letter to HQ in Australia, making the following points: a. Japanese success had been due to their concentration of superior strength at the right place and time; b. simpler requirements of Japanese soldiers; c. better Japanese clothing and equipment; d. lack of Australian reinforcements at the scene of action; e. better-trained enemy; but, f. the Japanese had reached the limit of their advance.

Rowell also referred to the necessary development of Port

Moresby as an air base, and its defence against sea attack. His own offensive actions would be limited by the administrative and supply problems existing in the theatre at the time. Important factors for immediate consideration and action were recognition that jungle and mountain warfare exacted a high rate of manpower wastage, and that training so far conducted in Queensland and the Moresby area was not realistic enough. Reinforcements for the combat units, especially AIF, would be required in some numbers, or the units would simply waste away.

Rowell was informed by personal signal that one of Blamey's aides would be arriving next day with a letter for him. Rowell was curious, and waited for its arrival.

General Blamey assured Kenney that there was to be no further retreat, and in fact he was going on to the offensive in a few days. In addition, the arrival of the US 128 Infantry Regiment was going well, with about 600 men being delivered every 24 hours, in a very basic but smoothly-running operation. When the US infantry commander arrived, he went to Headquarters NGF to discuss the route his unit was to take in walking over the mountains. This route had been selected for him by officers at GHQ in Brisbane, and it did not take the US commander long to find that the GHQ proposal was useless and bore no relation to the true conditions.

The long journey by 2/27th Battalion was coming to an end. A reconnaissance patrol discovered a chocolate wrapping, first sign that the area was patrolled by friendly forces. The unit camped for the night, hopeful of better news on the morrow.

During the night, into 21 September, a RAAF Catalina had battled through rain, severe turbulence from cumulo-nimbus, tropical rain clouds with base at only 3000 feet, to attack Buka. Weather over the Kokoda Trail was better, and at 8.05 am, six A20s swept over Menari–Efogi–Nauro–Yodda–Kokoda at 1500 feet, dropping 20-pound bombs on likely targets, and hits were scored on huts; crews reported the Efogi–Myola track showed much sign of use; south of Isurava, ceiling and visibility were unlimited, but north of Isurava cumulus was down to the hilltops in places. RAAF P40s with 500-pound bombs flew to attack Wairopi Bridge, pilots reported the road itself had been greatly improved, their bombs scored four partial hits on the bridge, four hits within 50 feet (15 metres), and the centre was sagging when they left at 9.20 am. East of the mountains were high clouds and 10-15 mile (16-24 km) visibility, but to the west was solid overcast at 5000 feet.

2nd Lieutenant Ebuchi was told Yazawa Butai (41 Regiment) was retreating. For the past several weeks, most of his diary entries had consisted of notations of the death, wounding or sickness of other officers of 144 Regiment. The average Japanese soldier was well aware of the hardships facing his unit. Toshio Watanabe had landed with I/144 on 21 July, and been in the fighting around Kokoda. On this day he wrote of the many mountain crossings necessary to bring up supplies, adding, 'we are very much distressed by shortage of food'. About the combats, he wrote, 'in the fighting between Kokoda and Isurava, our company was reduced from 180 to 80 men. Our company commander Ogawa killed at Kokoda; next commander Hatanaka killed at Isurava; third commander is Hirano. Every company reduced to half strength'.[45]

In 55 Division Medical Unit, Akira Teruoka seemed to be on the way to recovery from his illness. He had risen early, felt much better, and had eaten his food. He prayed for a quick recovery. The food ration for the day was dry bread, beans, mash, oil and meat, of which Teruoka wrote, 'I was happy because supper was very tasty'.

From 6 Company II/144 position, Lieutenant Horibe sent out a five-man patrol. They returned with an Australian light machine-gun, and had heard the sound of trees being felled on the other side of the river, but sighted no enemy troops. A ration of rice and other food arrived – two-thirds of a pint (third of a litre) of rice, soy sauce and wheat paste, to last two days. It was not enough, but Horibe wrote, 'life is tenacious'. Company strength rose to 60 men. Takasago volunteers arrived with more ammunition, and were given a day to rest before going back. Thirty-six of the 238 men in the party had malaria.

The Japanese 17 Army issued Intelligence Report No. 35, and it stated that:

• Between 6 and 14 September, 144 Regiment had captured 187 rifles, 23 LMGs, 35 pistols, one mortar, and quantities of ammunition.

• The commander 14 Battalion [sic – 2/14th] had been captured.

• The Papaki bridge had been washed away on 10 September, and not replaced until 20 September.

The Japanese were told of more battles in the Solomons and in the Coral Sea, and some dutifully transcribed the claims into their diaries. Three US carriers were claimed sunk, and 2000 planes destroyed, for a loss of 400 Japanese aircraft. There had been no such battles. The most recent in the Solomons had been on 25 August, when Japanese carrier *Ryujo*, destroyer *Mutsuki* and transport *Kinryu Maru* had been sunk, plus 90 aircraft lost, for a US loss of 20 planes. USS *Enterprise* and Japanese Navy ships *Chitose* and *Jintsu* had been damaged by air attack.

At noon, 2/27th Battalion arrived at the Jawarere supply camp, and tea, biscuits, chocolate and cigarettes were available to a pleased group of Diggers. A patrol with rations and medical supplies was at once sent back to D Company and the stretcher patients. Later, a stew and sweets were served, the first proper meal the battalion had enjoyed for 14 days.

General MacArthur, with General Kenney, returned to Brisbane. During his visit, MacArthur's personal sighting, if any, of the jungle battleground had been from a window of the B17 transport used by Kenney, as the plane circled before landing at 7-Mile. His time had been taken with inspecting engineering works in progress and in talks with various US commanders. MacArthur also had met some of the first P38 pilots, in the area on a training flight, and awarded medals, visited units, and been seen to be in Port Moresby. The astute Kenney had played on the MacArthur ego and more or less paraded around the location so that personnel of all ranks would know or hear that the Supreme Commander was with them. It did little good, because most junior ranks saw through MacArthur's posturing, and he was detested by them.

Lieutenant General Rowell was, in his own words, to face a problem more difficult than that of fighting the Japanese. The letter delivered to him by Lieutenant Porter, one of Blamey's aides, informed Rowell that Blamey was to arrive in New Guinea and conduct operations from there. However, Blamey was not bringing his own headquarters with him, but only a small personal staff of four officers. Accommodation and messing was to be provided by Rowell's HQ. Blamey assured Rowell that this move did not imply any lack of confidence in him, but was due to pressure from the inexperienced politicians who were inclined to panic.

With Rowell was MacArthur's chief of intelligence, Major General Charles Willoughby. Rowell asked if he knew anything about the matter, and Willoughby replied that it was all political. Willoughby then signalled MacArthur, informing him 'situation entirely in hand', that Rowell enjoyed the confidence of all command echelons, and that little was to be gained from imposing an extra headquarters level at that time. But, having been associated with the loss of the Philippines, MacArthur had manoeuvred to have the senior Australian commander in place if a further disaster occurred and Port Moresby was captured by the Japanese. Blamey and whoever else was necessary could then be sacrificed, but the Bataan clique would be relatively immune. In the event of an Australian victory, MacArthur would still be in position to accept kudos, as his GHQ staff controlled what could be released to the media. Lieutenant General Rowell was a small marker on MacArthur's board. MacArthur was astute enough never to criticise Blamey before Australian members of the GHQ staff, but there was room for only one great star in the South Pacific sky, and there were more effective ways to have Blamey's light dimmed.

Also on 21 September, the fresh 16 Brigade 2nd AIF began to arrive at Moresby. For the next 10 days they were to remain in the area, on local defence tasks, before being committed to the Kokoda campaign. Green clothes and equipment were issued or dyed, weapons were painted green, and in light of experience on the trail, decisions made about the numbers and types of weapons to be carried, the amount of ammunition and so on. It was noticeable that in comparison with the earlier units, these battalions now carried shovels, torches, folding saws and similar items.

By 22 September, the Japanese had been ashore at Buna and in the Kokoda campaign for two months. Strafing attacks by fighters were made on visible targets on this day. At 8.10 am, four P400s strafed barges, huts and AA positions in the Buna–Sanananda area. Pilots reported heavy AA 500 feet (150 metres) north of the runway at Buna, a large petrol fire at Andemba, and an ammunition fire at Menari, with clear weather over Buna, but at Wairopi it was overcast at 5000 feet. At 8.15 am, 12 US P40s, each with a 300-pound bomb, took off to attack the Wairopi Bridge, claiming two partial hits, making it unusable, after which the P40s attacked bridges and stores at Kokoda and Yodda, set launches on fire and hit an AA position at Buna, despite light Bofors and machinegun fire that damaged two fighters. On the Moresby side of the mountains the weather was hazy to 5000 feet, and on the far side there were broken heavy clouds at 4000. Six A20s attacked targets in the Nauro–Kokoda area with nothing to report.

From the ground, the Japanese I/47 AA Battalion recorded the Buna attacks, claiming one P39 shot down in flames at 8.20 am, but noting one range-finder destroyed by strafing. Weather was clear, 'no hindrance to observation', and 4 Section was credited with the destruction of the P39, as their firing 'was always accurate and correctly distributed'. Lieutenant Morimoto noted that the rear unit in the main force area was heavily bombed for an hour in the morning.[46]

An officer with 2 Company Takasago volunteers also referred in his diary to the second battle in the Coral Sea, as the reason for the Japanese Navy being unable to attack Port Moresby from the sea, and was told that no other force could be organised until November. He believed that the great fighting power of the enemy was because of the many Australian soldiers in the 40,000 troops (sic) opposing the Japanese. Of more immediate importance to him was the matter of food and medicines. He had nothing available for those suffering from colds, wounds or malaria, and the men had to wait for natural healing or death. A party had gone to get food, but at least a week must elapse before their return. However, his commander said that 9000 bales of rations had arrived at

Basabua on a ship. Closer to the front, Akira Teruoka had enjoyed breakfast from the rations delivered previously, and was told that he would be the permanent guard, day and night. More rations were delivered.

In the rifle companies, Lieutenant Horibe had inspected his unit weapons, and supervised a cleaning session. Another patrol cleared the area to their front. At 2 pm, 4 Company sentries fired, and the battalion stood-to in the fighting positions on 'the resistance line'. From 3.30 pm, 4 Company was shelled, and Horibe put his men into air-raid trenches. Later, one day's dry bread ration was issued.

This was the first use of Australian artillery in the campaign, and came from the 25-pounders of 14 Field Regiment firing from Ower's Corner. The guns had been man-handled into position by the gunners and men of 2/1st Pioneer Battalion. No Japanese appears to have been unduly concerned that they were within range of weapons that could engage them regardless of weather, day or night.

Now, after a few days of rest and time to think about it, 25 Brigade knew that the Japanese were a formidable enemy in many ways, but not the supermen described in the tales they had heard on arrival at Moresby. He could be beaten, he could be outfought, and outmanoeuvred. To add to this, the soldiers could see the supply lines bringing in ammunition and food to Imita; the air formations overhead, with not a sight of a Japanese plane; at last Australian artillery was firing in support. What was not so good was the increasing number of men sick due to breaches of hygiene. 25 Brigade asked 7 Division for hygiene personnel to instruct in and supervise application of correct hygiene measures.

Brigadier Eather met Lieutenant Colonel Cooper and discussed the future of 2/27th Battalion. The companies, except D Company with the stretcher cases, was trucked to a camp in the Sogeri Valley. That night, the Diggers had the unaccustomed luxury of blankets. Their ordeal was over.

Average weight loss was two stone (12.7 kg). The stress imposed by the battle, then the slow evasion through the very rough terrain, burdened with the stretchers, with the ever-present worry that the Japanese might ambush or overtake them, the lack of food, the rain, and the pitiless jungle had been greater than any previous in the life of the battalion. All living wounded, all automatic weapons and almost all equipment had been brought out.

Lieutenant Upcher's patrol from 2/31st returned without contacting the Japanese west of the track to Ioribaiwa, despite five days in the area.

The Japanese 17 Army produced Intelligence Report No. 36, which stated that Horii's formation was now holding its line, but 'making preparations in its rear'.[47]

General Kenney returned to Port Moresby. He later noted that this was the ninth successive day that every available aircraft had attacked the Kokoda Trail. This may have been a good passage for memoirs, but is not borne out by records of the missions. While the attacks on Rabaul, Lae and the Buna area were well-documented by the Japanese, there is very little record to confirm claims of much damage along the trail itself. This was later observed by the advancing Australians, who found many installations untouched by air strikes. Twenty-five years later, in Vietnam, the US Air Force was to expend an unheard of tonnage of bombs against jungle targets for very little positive result, except impressive statistics in the Pentagon.

More importantly, Kenney spoke to Generals Blamey and Rowell about his plan to airlift the force to occupy the proposed Wanigela base, while supplying by air the force fighting its way back across the mountains. Blamey was impressed by the airlift of the US 128 Infantry Regiment from Australia, and agreed to the Wanigela mission, but asked that it wait until he had advanced far enough across the mountains to believe that the offensive there was going well. MacArthur had listened again to Kenney expound on the idea, and sent him back to talk to Blamey, to see if the Australian commander on the spot agreed. Happy with the result of the talk, Kenney set off again for Brisbane, to meet General Hap Arnold, chief of all US air forces.

The night bomber attacks continued on 22 September, and nine B17s attacked ships at Rabaul and Lakunai airfield at 8.35 pm, claiming two probable hits. The AA barrage was 'very thick', and the bombers were only at 6000 to 8000 feet, illuminated by the moon; three were hit by ground fire and another hit in the nose, with the lower hatch shot away, all instruments except the pilot's compass destroyed and the RAAF navigator badly wounded. On a moonlight reconnaissance at 11.15 pm, a B25 passed over Buna–Gona at 2500 feet, dropping six bombs on the airfield. The crew saw burnt-out barges below, though dense haze in the target area cut visibility to three miles (4.8 km). Three Catalinas from Bowen and Cairns attacked Buka.

Getting off to an early start, at 6.50 am on 23 September, two P40s on a 'verbal orders' mission attacked Taupota Mission by strafing. Eight P400s were over the Kokoda–Wairopi area strafing targets at 7.30 am, but there was little to see. The Buna–Kokoda road was in good condition, the weather clear but hazy, visibility to nine miles (14.5 km). Six Beaufighters, escorted by eight US P40s, made a sweep of coastal areas at 10.10 am, to attack and destroy small boats and dumps in the Sanananda–Wairopi area. Despite light and accurate AA, the Beaufighters attacked seven barges and a camp at Soputa. There were broken clouds over Buna, bases at 3000-4000 feet, and suddenly the RAAF pilots saw, coming down through the clouds, six Zeros escorting nine bombers, apparently intending to land at Buna.

The P40s, low on fuel, could not stay to fight. All six Zeros attacked one of the Beaufighters, and the pilot, Flying Officer D. J. Moran-Hilford, with Sergeant W. Clark as observer, turned into them, watching the individualistic Japanese pilots forced to dodge each other as they all tried to attack him, then he was past, flat out down to sea level, reached a speed of 260 knots and at once began to outdistance the Zeros, who nevertheless followed for about 10 miles (16 km). All Allied aircraft returned safely.

The Japanese I/47 AA Battalion had seen all this, having prepared for action when the Beaufighters attacked Giruwa. Their report confirmed the unsuccessful attack on the Beaufighter. Two and a half hours later, seven Beaufighters returned to catch the Japanese aircraft on the ground, but none were there, so they strafed. Three-quarters of the barges seen were under water. One Beaufighter, crewed by Flight Sergeant G. W. Sayer and Sergeant A. S. Mairet, was lost, the first 30 Squadron Beaufighter loss in New Guinea. Sayer was a widely experienced bomber pilot, with many operational sorties flown against the Italians in the Middle East and East Africa, against the Germans with an RAF Wing in the USSR, and against the Japanese in the Malayan–East Indies campaign. He had been one of a party of 12 RAF and RAAF men who escaped to Australia in a small boat, and survived a close inspection by a Japanese submarine, a close encounter with a whale, storms and other adventures, before arriving on the coast of Western Australia. He enlisted immediately after another notable RAAF pilot, the famous Australian Rules footballer 'Bluey' Truscott. Sayer had flown at least 40 operational missions.

The Japanese I/47 AA Battalion reported that at 11.52 am they fired with two-second fuse setting and scored a direct hit on the plane, which fell into the south-east jungle with flames shooting from its fuel tank. The gunners also claimed another Beaufighter from the formation at 11.54 am, and claimed a direct hit on the nose of a third at 12.04 pm, which fell 500 feet (150 metres) from the gun's position, at which the crews shouted 'Banzai!', while another Beaufighter was supposedly hit in the right wing, which fell off, the plane went into the jungle, and at the same time strafing US fighters were driven off by machinegun fire. The Japanese examined the wreck of the Beaufighter close by, and listed the British weapons found in it, as well as noting that there were two men in the crew. Again, Battery HQ praised the work of the various sections for gaining so many victories with so few rounds of ammunition. Immediately behind the Beaufighters came a dozen P40s that attacked Buna, through heavy and accurate AA that lessened as the attack continued, but two P40s were hit. Pilots noticed supply dumps spaced 400 yards apart along the Buna–Kokoda road. Visibility was good, and cloudbase was at 4000 feet. The Japanese aircraft had gone from the airfield, and may have gone on to drop supplies at Kokoda, as 12 were reported to have done so.[48]

The Japanese 47 AA Battalion was claiming a steady flow of

victories, but Sayer's Beaufighter is in the unit records as the first and only one to have been examined. Those shot down into the sea obviously could not be examined, but others supposedly falling close by may be assumed, if they really did crash, to have been visited by the battery members for identification of the type and checking for technical intelligence information. There is no such information in the battalion documents captured later at Buna; the claims were (and are) without confirmation by Japanese inspection on the ground, or from Allied records. As with their fighter pilots, the Japanese gunners were over-claiming to a degree that was laughable.[49]

The Japanese positions at Ioribaiwa continued to be developed, and Lieutenant Horibe sent out another patrol, which heard more noise of tree-cutting from the 5 Company front. Then, at 3.30 pm, his position was shelled for an hour, but no damage was done.

The patrol from 3rd Battalion under Captain Atkinson, to harass Japanese lines of communication, returned after engaging enemy on the western end of Ioribaiwa. Lieutenant Bill Dullard was leading the first section, and Sergeant Bede Tongs the second. At a track junction, they conferred briefly, Dullard went left and Tongs to the right. Tongs's section found and cut Japanese communications cable, heard firing on either side as other sections engaged, then four healthy, well-equipped Japanese came down the trail and were killed. The Japanese were on the high ground, and the action developed, with much firing, Japanese bugle calls, yelling and 'Banzai!' yells. Bede was waiting for the whistle blast that signalled withdrawal, but held his position. Time passed and he sent a runner to the headquarters location to find out what was happening. The man came panting back, and gasped, 'They're gone!' The section rapidly left, and caught up with the remainder of the patrol, when Bede forcefully stated that the whistle blast signal was not very good. Then they were saddened to find that Dullard and three other men had been killed.

The patrol returned to 25 Brigade Headquarters, where a cup of tea was provided, despite the lack of rations. Some empty bully beef tins were to hand, and Tongs was so hungry that he wiped out the fat residue in the tins with his finger, 'and ate it with relish'. They returned to the battalion position, and during the night were pleased to hear the guns of 14 Field Regiment firing on the Japanese. The bang and distant 'crump' of the explosion 'were really music to our ears', said Bede.

The long-range night bombing campaign continued, despite little result, and at 7.55 pm, seven B17s found visibility so poor that they could not bomb Faisi, so returned to Moresby, but three attacked Buna airfield from heights between 4000 and 9000 feet, each dropping a 2000-pound bomb. Below the bombers, as they returned over the mountains to Moresby, were the wet and tired combatants, some planning advance and some withdrawal. At 11 pm, 144 Regiment received Japanese commander Horii's Operation Order Ko-120, and prepared for the move back to Eora.[50]

In Moresby, Lieutenant General Rowell was trying to define his position as Commander New Guinea Force, after General Blamey arrived and imposed himself on Rowell's HQ. Though Blamey would not say so plainly, Rowell felt that he was being supplanted, and the conversation became somewhat acrimonious. Only a week earlier, Blamey had expressed confidence in Rowell. Rowell suggested that the size of the force already in New Guinea warranted establishment of an Army HQ, while he continued in command of offensive operations, and further suggested that First Army HQ in Queensland be brought in. Blamey rejected this, as he did not want General Lavarack assuming such a command. Rowell then said that if Blamey did not do something similar to his suggestion, the Americans would bring in such a headquarters. Subsequently, this is what happened, effectively confining control by Blamey's Allied Land Forces HQ to Australian formations.

At 1 am on 24 September, the first elements of the Japanese 'Stanley Force' began to withdraw, moving back to the coast. The force comprised Horii's headquarters, HQ 144 Regiment, II and III/144, II/41, mountain artillery and engineers, plus other support and supply troops. Horii proposed three positions be held: Nauro: II/41, mountain artillery and engineers; Menari: HQ 144, III/144, mountain artillery; Kagi: Force HQ, II/144, mountain artillery.

Having to start a retreat with the lights of their objective visible on the horizon must have been hard for the Japanese to bear. On other fronts, Axis formations had been held just as the prize seemed within their grasp. Elements of the German 3rd SS Panzer Grenadier Division 'Totenkopf' had actually reached the outskirts of Moscow, and even entered the subway system, bringing back tickets and other souvenirs before being forced away into the winter. Rommel's Italo–German forces had been held only 60 miles (100 km) from Alexandria and the great prize of the Suez Canal. And, of course, the Germans had gazed across the English Channel at the chalk cliffs of Dover. Now, in the dark, wet New Guinea night, the tide of Japanese victories began to ebb as the first parties made their way back along the slippery paths.

When told of the decision to retreat, Lieutenant Hirano felt as if he had been hit 'with a bolt from the blue. It left us momentarily dazed to have to retreat from our present position, after advancing so close to our goal at the cost of enormous sacrifices and casualties'. He included in the privacy of his diary references to Lieutenant Colonel Tsukamoto: an old man who was continually yelling.

A Japanese account of the retreat by a journalist present described the sight of Horii and his staff officer, Tanaka, sitting on mats in a dirty tent, waiting by the light of a candle for the message to arrive. Allegedly, one message from Rabaul arrived, quickly followed by another that indicated the Emperor himself had directed the retreat take place at once. Immediately, the Japanese force is supposed to have begun moving back, and as it was the first time Japanese forces had retreated, there was no training or experience in the operation, and it soon became a rout. As has been shown, planning and preparation had been done, and as will be seen, the withdrawal was well executed. Japanese forces had retreated in China, as well as in the 1939 combats against the Russians in what was called 'the Nomohan Incident'; this journalistic account of events was yet another exaggeration.

In aerial activity throughout 24 September, aircraft from Australia and Port Moresby ranged well out to the east, to the Solomons, as well as attacking New Guinea targets. A Catalina scored four hits in the dispersal area at Buka at 2.40 am, and at 3 am, six B17s attacked ships at Rabaul. One went down to 1500 feet and dropped four 500-pounders on an 8000-ton ship, claimed one direct hit, and reported fires and explosions coming from it, while the other aircraft bombed from 25,000 feet, with no result. On return to Moresby, the bombers found an air-raid in progress, so went on to Horn Island. Eight P40s flew to strafe Kokoda airfield and the Wairopi area at 7.30 am, one truck was left burning, but pilots reported Wairopi Bridge in use. On the Moresby side of the mountains weather was clear, with scattered cloud at 25,000 feet, but on the Buna side clouds were in the valleys, though visibility was 20 miles (32 km). Thirty minutes later, nine A20s attacked Mubo from 1500 feet, bombing and strafing, with ceiling and visibility unlimited. There were no further missions flown until late in the afternoon, at 5 pm, when six B17s, with 15 US P40s as escort, looked for ships reported in the Buna area, could not find them, so bombed the Gona wreck with 500-pound bombs; Buna was overcast. Three P40s, also carrying bombs for the ships, attacked Wairopi Bridge, but the other six P40s with bombs brought them back. Pilots reported heavy cumulus over the mountains and cloud down to 1000 feet. There were no Allied losses or damage to aircraft reported.

The 63rd Squadron spent the day practising Benn's new bombing tactics, and would do so for another day, then be sent to Moresby to use them on bombing missions. At 7.45 pm, the day's bombing cycle was completed, when six B17s attacked Rabaul, dropped 24 bombs on ships, but claimed only one probable hit.

The Japanese at Ioribaiwa were suddenly shelled at 3 am on 24 September, the rounds impacting in the living area of Horibe's 6 Company II/144, wounding three men before the rest got into shelter, and this bombardment continued throughout the morning. With one other man evacuated sick, company strength was 56. Half the Koiwai battalion, II/41, moved up onto the right flank of the Japanese position at Ioribaiwa.[51]

The 2/25th Battalion sent a strong raiding party from B Company to attack a Japanese position. Most of the company was em-

ployed, under command of Lieutenant A. Barnett, with Lieutenant Strachan as his second-in-command. The plan was for 11
Platoon and a section of 10 to assault the selected enemy post, with
12 Platoon following and the force headquarters at the rear.
Corporal Mitchell and four men crept forward at 5 am to remove
the trip wire and dangling tins, and had done so in 20 minutes, but
one wire was missed and the rattling tins sounded their warning;
the Australians charged, the Japanese fired and left. 11 Platoon
was after them, but Barnett was wary of any attempt to close in
behind him, so manoeuvred Strachan and Lieutenant Howe's platoon to the flank. The Japanese put out heavy fire, the Australians
threw grenades, the fire continued, casualties were suffered, then
enemy were seen moving on the right flank. Barnett brought his
force back to a piece of high ground, and broke contact. He had
four wounded, and Japanese casualties were unknown.

Other 2/25th Battalion patrols from Imita for the past days had
no contact, but on this day, 9 Platoon under Lieutenant H. Steele
contacted Japanese in a position where battalion HQ had been
during the time at Ioribaiwa. He was told to attack from the flank
with grenades, and later, at 11.15 am, Lieutenant Walker and 17
Platoon joined 9 Platoon. Artillery fire was controlled from 9 Platoon, and later from a position in B Company.

D Company 2/33rd Battalion moved out on a patrol. They
reached elements of the 2/25th, at the site of Miller's ambush, on
17 September, and were told of the low barricades erected by the
Japanese all along the lower slopes of Ioribaiwa. It began to rain
and mist came up from Ua-ale Creek, making observation difficult,
so Captain Clowes decided to remain in the position he had reached, forward of 2/25th, and try again on 25 September.

After breakfast in the Japanese 55 Division Medical Unit, it was
decided all sick and weak were to be moved to the rear. Akira
Teruoka and the rest began the trek back, resting often under the
trees. The air attacks did not worry them, but behind, in the forward positions, they could hear artillery and mortar rounds exploding. News of the move back now was known in many units,
and No. 2 Company Takasago Volunteers heard it from Captain

Uyama, HQ South Seas Detachment (Horii's HQ), who told them that plans for a frontal attack on Moresby were now changed, all patients were being moved to Eora, in the rear, and the volunteers also were to move back.

In the Buna AA position, the Japanese I/47 AA Battalion reported that its fire had driven off two reconnaissance planes, and in the appearance by B17s got a very close hit in the centre of the formation of the leading three bombers, causing fire from the left wing-root of the leader, and assumed their marksmanship had driven off the planes, as no bombs were dropped. However, a diarist wrote that 15 planes attacked and four were shot down, adding that there were seven or eight raids a day. 'Wada' wrote of 'five strafing attacks in the afternoon', and a fire in the jungle presumed caused by bombs.[52]

Japanese estimation of the capabilities of their enemies continued to be inaccurate. 2nd Lieutenant Ino, 41 Regiment, arrived at Buna on the 20th, and went to Soputa. He was told the battalion was to patrol Giruwa as enemy paratroopers were expected.[53]

On 25 September, Horibe's 6 Company, and the other Japanese front-line positions, stood-to at 6 am, when an estimated 50 Australians attacked the neighbouring 9 Company, III/144, and 'precautions were strictly enforced'. Later, two days' rations were issued – one packet of bread and less than half a pint of rice per man. Again, a single patrol went out, and returned to report that there was no change to the situation in front of the company.

This attack on the Japanese may have been that by Clowes's D Company 2/33rd patrol. After another wet, sleepless and uncomfortable night, they went on and came to a small native store hut and a vegetable garden, which had been dug up by the Japanese. Here for the first time they saw the distinctive mark of the Japanese jungle boot with its separate big toe. Despite knowing well they were in the presence of the enemy, when the Japanese opened fire Cox's part of the patrol was taken by surprise and scattered. Grenades burst and machinegun fire shot twigs and branches off trees. Cox and his NCOs quickly regained control, but he realised that the Japanese greatly outnumbered his men, and were so close rifle bolts could be heard cocking and many voices clearly distinguishable. Leap-frogging back by sections, Cox's men took up a position on the edge of the native garden. No one had fired and no one had seen a Japanese. Now rounds began impacting around them, and one hit the 108-set radio, putting it out of action.

Captain Clowes had taken the rest of the patrol in the other direction, heard the firing, realised it was not aimed at him, and continued. He took two men with him, and cautiously they approached a crest, looked over and saw that the ground had been cleared out to some 30 yards and a log barricade constructed. The three carefully moved on until they could see over the barricade, and watched a line of Japanese some 40 yards away, apparently queueing for a meal. They appeared to be in high spirits and not alarmed at the distant firing. Clowes decided to return with this information, and eventually the patrol returned to the kunai patch where 2/25th was in position and Clowes reported to Brigadier Eather over the telephone line. He then took the patrol back part way to Imita and camped for the night.

Elsewhere, at 5.30 am, B Company 2/25th attacked the enemy in the old Australian battalion HQ and brigade HQ position on Ioribaiwa, held the location for two hours, then were forced to move back slightly out of the beaten zone of the Japanese mortar barrage. Some Australian weapons were found. The company was told to hold on, and at 10 am D Company arrived, then later Battalion HQ moved up to D Company, followed by A Company.

The Japanese HQ 144 Regiment received Operation Order Ko-121, and the main part of the regiment began moving to Wamai. Aircraft passed over, but no damage was suffered by the units strung out along the paths. They were to keep moving on, until they reached Wamai at 11.30 on the night of 26 September.[54]

At 8 am on 25 September, a single Beaufighter reconnoitred Buna–Mambare but found nothing to report, except that the Wairopi Bridge was usable. Visibility was two miles (3.2 km), with cumulus down to 1500 feet. There were no further missions reported flown until midday, when eight US P40s set off for Wairopi Bridge, two lost formation so returned, and the other six, each with a bomb, attacked, claiming one direct and two partial hits, and that the bridge was completely destroyed. There was no activity to be seen. On that side of the range, there was a complete overcast at 6500 feet, and on the Moresby side clouds were down to 5000. An unknown diarist in a Japanese transport unit wrote that the Papaki Bridge was destroyed and was impassable.[55]

Six B17s looked for shipping, found none, so bombed Buna, noting that the runway seemed unserviceable. The Japanese I/47 AA Battalion believed that the B17s were intending to attack them, and that their fire drove the bombers away to the airfield. 'Uchida', of 15th Pioneers, recorded the attack by six B17s, and continued with his opinion that the Buna airfield was unsuitable, the ground was waterlogged and though the bomb craters were filled in and smoothed over, the runway was 'soft like ricecakes', concluding 'Buna base has no utility value'.[56]

The Japanese preoccupation with Allied airborne attack continued, and some troops at Buna searched for reported enemy parachutists, but found only one of their own parachutes with food attached.[57]

2nd Lieutenant Onogawa, having hurried to get back to his unit in time for the general attack of 20 September, had arrived at Isurava. During the past days he had noted the air-raids that did no damage, and news of alleged successes in the Solomons. Now he was told that the unit would take up defensive positions between Kokoda and Isurava, while the others did so on the southern slopes of the ranges, and Yazawa unit (41 Regiment) were to defend Kokoda airfield.

Rabaul was attacked again at 3 am on 26 September by six B17s, but one could not find the target so returned to base. The other five went in at 4500 feet, with 20 bombs, claiming one probable and three possible hits. At 8.25 am and 10.20 am, Hudsons of RAAF 6 Squadron and Beaufighters attacked a 500-ton ship, left it burning, and when it was seen again at midday, it was reported as gutted. Three A20s attacked targets in the Ioribaiwa–Efogi–Menari area from 2000 feet, despite broken cumulus down on the hilltops.

Among the columns of retreating Japanese sick and wounded,

Akira Teruoka, of 55 Division Medical Unit, had been making his way, assisted by a nameless native carrying his military and personal equipment. It had been raining, but he noted he was not cold, as there were enough blankets. During the night he had got up to look for water, but felt weak, so slept where he was. On this morning, when he woke, the party of men had already gone, so he continued on after them. It was his final diary entry. Departing Ioribaiwa, Lieutenant Horibe left one platoon behind, and in compliance with battalion orders, took the remainder of his company along the track to Wamai.

The 2/25th Battalion had endured the harassing Japanese fire during the night without replying. Two Japanese who appeared on the track were killed. During the day, patrols from B Company contacted Japanese who fired a heavy volume of machinegun and brought down artillery before withdrawing; 15 Japanese were counted dodging away. Battalion strength this day was 26 officers and 492 other ranks.

Captain Clowes moved his D Company 2/33rd patrol closer to Imita, and at noon told the men to halt for two hours to cook a meal. Just as the fires were alight, the battalion came up, and Lieutenant Colonel Buttrose called to get the fires out and join on the end of the column, as the battalion was moving to Ioribaiwa. However, D Company did manage to make tea before joining the march. It was to be D Company's third climb up the slope.

With his forces gathering to begin the assault on the Japanese positions, Lieutenant General Rowell was also burdened with the presence of General Blamey. Rowell addressed a letter to Blamey, seeking definition of the powers to be exercised by each man, now that Blamey, during a visit to Milne Bay, had given orders to Major General Clowes. Blamey did not refer to Rowell's letter in his reply, but composed one that stated plainly that he was in New Guinea to 'take control', and directed Rowell to inform his staff that all information relating to operations, administration, logistics, sea and air forces was to be passed to Blamey, who would command through Rowell and his staff. Rowell instructed his staff in writing of the above requirement. Rowell had informed Blamey that he might ask to be relieved of his command, to which Blamey replied that Rowell would go on the Retired List.

Once again, on 27 September the impartial weather prevented effective air attacks on the distant Rabaul area. Two Catalinas attacked Kahili at 12.30 pm, and Simpson Harbour at Rabaul was the target for seven B17s, but solid overcast, storms and lightning forced six to return. At 6.22 am, one bomber arrived and attacked at 8000 feet, into heavy and accurate AA, and claimed a direct hit and a near-miss from three bombs, reporting smoke seen later from the area of the ship. Though good at first, the weather over New Guinea also deteriorated during the day. Over Gona, with cloudbase at 7000 feet, and cumulus coverage of 8/10ths, a B17 dropped seven bombs on buildings at 8.10 am, and at 10.22 am, six Beaufighters swept the coast and Kokoda track, strafing targets, but were turned back from Salamaua by weather, reporting cloud-base at Gona at 1000 feet. Simultaneously, seven A20s attacked supply dumps at Kagi and Ioribaiwa from 1500 feet, despite cumulus down to the hilltops. Pilots saw no Japanese, but noticed more huts had been built and the road showed signs of use. Two B17s had been sent to the Vitiaz Strait searching for ships, but rain and cloud down to 50 feet over the sea forced them back. From 2800 feet, they attacked barges at Buna with 20 bombs, through medium intense accurate AA, which damaged one B17 in the right wing. Buna was reported as overcast and hazy, visibility out to 10 miles (16 km). The hit in the B17's right wing came from a shell with five-second fuse from I/47 AA Battalion, was reported with the information that the B17 turned left and dropped its bombs, then went away low to the south-east. The other B17 also was claimed as driven off, as were other earlier aircraft in the area.

Japanese HQ 144 Regiment began moving from Wamai to Menari. Though aircraft were reported overhead, no damage was done to the unit. At midday, Lieutenant Colonel Tsukamoto sent a message to Horii, informing him that no enemy resistance had been met along the unit path, that transport facilities for casualties to reach Menari were 'not favourable', and that the regiment would try to hold the enemy for a day or two, then ended with a request for rations to be sent at once. At the end of the day, Horibe's 6 Company had stopped near Wamai, after marching all the previous night. In the afternoon, the platoon that had held the Ioribaiwa position as rearguard caught them up. Company strength was 51 men.

Behind them, the Australian 25 Brigade was preparing to attack the old positions. All day the preparations had gone on, and by nightfall all was ready. No one knew the Japanese had left, and patrols had returned with information about the log barricades, and gaps blown in them by artillery. It was thought the enemy main strength was on the reverse slope. A telephone system had been installed by Captain Griffin, and Brigadier Eather was able to hold a commander's conference with all battalion commanders able to hear him and each other clearly; it was a marked success. Eather gave each battalion its instructions, and all knew what the other units were to be doing. Everyone expected a stiff fight.

On 28 September, at 12.50 am, three RAAF Catalinas bombed Kahili. Later, three Beaufighters swept the Buna–Gona–Sanananda coast for barges, but no serviceable ones were seen, nor was there any sign of activity, but a stores dump was strafed, and Wairopi Bridge was reported as usable at 8 am. Keeping up the pressure, at 8.45 am, four P400s strafed houses at Myola, then at 9 am, eight US P40s attacked Buna, pilots reporting four fires in the buildings and that the Buna–Kokoda road had been heavily used, but one P40 was missing. There was a thin layer of cloud at 4000 feet, and visibility was unlimited. The heavy bombers believed they could destroy the troublesome Wairopi Bridge, so 63rd Squadron sent two B17s to bomb it at 8.50 am, but the weather was too thick and they returned to Durand airfield with their bombs. Later the bridge was attacked by eight P400s, which started small fires near the bridge, but were unable to keep them burning, and no results could be seen. The bridge was reported to be 10 feet (three metres) wide, and the weather there was clear, visibility unlimited. At 11.05 am, a B17 reconnoitred Buna–Lae–Finschafen, and reported cloudbase at 15,000 feet, then dropped three bombs on Lae airfield, with two hits claimed on the south-east part of the runway, and the third bomb fell in the water. Two more 63rd Squadron B17s tried for Wairopi Bridge, but weather was unsuitable, so they diverted to Buna. One blew landing barges out of the water and the other claimed hits on two AA positions near the airfield.

Lieutenant General Rowell went to meet General Blamey for the usual morning conference on 28 September, and was told that Blamey had decided to relieve him of his command, and had sent an adverse report to Prime Minister Curtin and to General Mac-Arthur. When Rowell saw the report, he told Blamey the charges in it could not be justified, to which Blamey replied he did not have to justify it to anyone. Rowell prepared to return to Australia that night, which he did in (US) General Robert Eichelberger's plane.

Concurrently with Rowell's removal, the Australian counter-offensive began. At 9 am, 25 Brigade launched its attack on Iori-baiwa. The battalions advanced and soon reports were coming in to headquarters of platoons and companies finding Japanese equipment, but meeting no resistance. By early afternoon the ridge was occupied again. D Company 2/33rd sent 17 Platoon to check the area of the action on 15 September, looking for Lieutenant Mosely and Corporal Bradford. Both were found dead, unburied. Corporal Bradford and a 3rd Battalion soldier were found in Japa-nese positions, not in the area of the action of 15 September. They had been killed, presumably after interrogation. 2/31st Battalion occupied the high ground on the ridge, and assessed the Japanese strength there as two companies, with 'commanding fields of fire'. Australian dead were found and buried. Also found were Japanese graves, and lookout positions in trees. The Australians reorgan-ised and began preparations to continue pursuit of the enemy.

At midday, the Japanese 144 Regiment began arriving at Efogi. The unit had begun marching at 4.30 am, with the regimental head-quarters leading, then the signals unit, and II/144 bringing up the rear. Aircraft flew over, but did not see them. Horibe's 6 Company arrived at 3 pm, having been on the march since 4 am. Another small ration of rice, less than half a pint, was issued, plus seven cigarettes per man.

On 29 September, weather again interfered with the air effort, and little result was gained from the flying. An A20 reconnoitred Japanese camps in the Nauro–Menari area, but all valleys were closed by cloud and at 8.05 am the pilot dropped his bombs above the overcast when he thought Menari was below. A single reconnaissance version of the P38 photographed the Wanigela area. At 11.48 am, a B17 dropped seven bombs onto Salamaua airfield with unobserved results, as cloud reached from 4000 to 24,000 feet. Two B17s were ordered to attack Wairopi, but instead bombed barges at Buna from 3000 feet, claiming six barges and an AA position destroyed. I/47 AA Battalion saw the B17s attack from the south, fired 28 rounds that were claimed to have been close to the bombers, and the gunners believed they had driven off the planes. No damage was suffered by the Japanese.

The 2/25th sent out a patrol under Captain Andrews, ordered to remain out for five days and to contact the enemy. For their part, D Company 2/33rd were surprised to be told that the company would provide a 50-man patrol, to try to contact the Japanese, find another track to Nauro and find any 2/27th men in the area. Having already done most of the battalion patrolling, it was thought that the company should have been spared this task. One day's rations were provided, and another three days were made up of emergency rations from the brigade reserve. Captain Clowes took his men out and began the patrolling, moving through deserted native gardens and villages. On the second day, when the emergency rations were opened, the company was angered to find all had been tampered with. Some were empty, all contents removed and dirt inserted to make up the weight. Others had only the dehydrated vegetable powder left. The perpetrators were never discovered, but as usual the frontline troops bore the cost of the indulgences of the rear echelon personnel. Clowes continued the patrol, but when radio communications failed and no food could be found, decided to return to the battalion. They arrived back on 2 October, rejoining at Ioribaiwa.

There was little else of note in ground actions that day on the Kokoda Trail. At Buna, interpreter Toshio Sato was told that a spy had been discovered at Rabaul, hiding in the extinct volcano with

▲

a wireless set. Allegedly, he had signalled with a torch and been seen by Japanese aircraft. The Japanese had a great fixation about spies, and made life difficult for captured missionaries and local people in occupied areas with their zeal in identifying and arresting spies. There is no record of such an Allied spy signalling from the volcano. In the mountains, 2nd Lieutenant Onogawa now noted that the force 'seems to be constantly retreating. Rations will be distributed at Kagi. Medical, signals and mountain artillery units are descending the mountains'. 144 Regiment had begun marching at 4 am, resting, but pushing on through the day and night. Aircraft flew over, but did not see them. At midday, Major Horie (II/144) was ordered to fortify Eora as a base for a future offensive. The march continued until 1 am, when the force stopped on a grassy hill.

Lieutenant General Rowell arrived in Brisbane and met Mac-Arthur. They discussed New Guinea and Rowell suggested stopping the mountain fighting and attacking Buna from the sea. Mac-Arthur replied this had been intended, but the US Marines nominated for the operation went to Guadalcanal. Rowell went on to Melbourne, out of the New Guinea campaign, but to a continuation of the fighting with Blamey.

For the last day of September, air attacks were flown, but with little result. At 12.40 am on 30 September, three Catalinas attacked Buin and Faisi, followed at 3.05 am by another over Buka. A P400 dropped its belly tank on Wairopi at 8 am, but the fire from the petrol went out. The pilot strafed huts at Myola and Menari, and reported weather had been closing in rapidly. At 11.45 am, three P400s attacked huts at Menari, but there was nothing to report, and at 12.23 pm, a B17 over Buna dropped seven bombs through moderate heavy AA, but results were not reported. For their part, the Japanese I/47 AA Battalion reported an attempted attack on them, but that they drove off the bomber. Six A20s attacked Menari at 11 am and 1.30 pm, fires were started, but there was little else to report. Menari was clear, but cumulus was down to the hills in places. At 12.35 pm, two B17s attacked Wairopi Bridge from 3000 feet with 20 bombs. Visibility was good, with scattered cloud at 4000 feet, crews claimed hits on the bridge approaches, that the bridge was sagging when they left, but they saw no track activity. The two bombers then flew at 250 feet to the coast, machinegunning likely targets, but nothing was seen below them. Two later B17s could not see the bridge through thick cloud.

2nd Lieutenant Ebuchi was at Eora, and was told by Captain Uyama that III Battalion was retreating to Kokoda, so decided to await them. He saw the South Seas Force HQ, Regimental HQ and HQs of I and II Battalions pass by. HQ 144 Regiment began marching to Kagi at 5 am, undetected by aircraft overhead, and at 7 am left III/144 behind to obey 144 Regiment Order No. 141. Kagi was reached at 9.30 am.[58]

At the close of September, the Japanese I/47 AA Battalion claimed 11 enemy aircraft destroyed in two weeks, with many others driven off. It was reported that this was achieved despite a lack of platoon leaders and communication facilities, but all members of the battery worked to the utmost. Although exposed to strafing, the Observation Section on the coast observed the flightpath of aircraft and reported on the effectiveness of firing. 'They worked in spite of heat, storms and strafing, on guard in swamp, jungle and 10 metres [33 feet] up in trees,' said the report. The battalion commander wrote that from the time they took up position, the battery 'fearlessly and calmly drove off enemy planes and displayed the power of AA until the enemy finally abandoned his attacks'.

However, 'Wada' noted attacks to the end of the month: 24th, 'five strafing attacks in the afternoon'; 25th, 'reconnaissance and raids as usual'; 26th, 'eight bombs dropped by Boeings'; 27th, 'attacked with Lockheed Hudsons and Martins'; 28th, 'enemy planes seemed to be attacking Giruwa'; 29th, 'reconnaissance by Boeings and Martins made raids in the afternoon'; 30th, 'raids as usual'. Not far from the gun positions, 67 Line of Communication Hospital (L of C), Giruwa, compiled its reports, and found that in September it had 270 officer and 2640 other-rank patients.[59]

In and around the Ioribaiwa positions, large quantities of equipment, weapons, ammunition, letters, postcards and belongings were found and sent back to Intelligence staffs. Lieutenant Colonel Withy, DSO, MC, CO 2/25th Battalion, was evacuated with a severe skin complaint, and sent back to Australia; Major Marson assumed command. There was little ground action on the Kokoda Trail. Captain Andrews, 2/25th Battalion, pushed ahead, reached Nauro at 11.30 am, and found a single sick Japanese, who was taken prisoner.

General Kenney had been promoted Lieutenant General on the recommendation of General MacArthur. In the eight weeks of his command, Kenney demonstrated his grasp of the air situation, proposed solutions to problems, showed that he meant business by sacking the unsuitable and inefficient, then promoting to command young and able leaders who revitalised the US air units. Despite many claims by his bomber crews, postwar investigation by a Joint Army Navy Assessment Committee (JANAC) could not identify any naval or merchant ships sunk by 5th Air Force operations in August or September. This was a contentious issue, not eased by strike photography that showed ships receiving bomb hits and under bomb explosions. A suggested reason is that Japanese records were incomplete, and some ships lost may have been those captured during their advance through the former US, British, French and Dutch colonies. However, hundreds of bombs and many flying hours were expended on these attacks by heavy bombers on shipping – yet the Japanese had put ashore the Horii force on New Guinea, landed and retrieved the Milne Bay force, and fought the Guadalcanal campaign.

It had taken the Japanese seven weeks to fight their way to Ioribaiwa from Buna. It would take the Australians almost as long to fight their way back to the northern beachhead area.

Chapter 5
TORNADO
October 1942

Early on 1 October, a Catalina harassed Buka, the sole reported long-distance sortie of the night. At 7.45 am, six Beaufighters made a coastal sweep to Salamaua, strafing buildings and barges at Sanananda. One was hit by AA, but returned on one engine. Four P400s escorted the RAAF planes, did some strafing of their own, and attacked Menari with unobserved results. The formation pressed on through rain, with maximum visibility five miles (eight km). Two P400s flew a weather reconnaissance at 8 am, dropped incendiary belly tanks at Wairopi Bridge, started fires that burned the reserve bridge, and strafed 16 new huts at the east end of Myola 1. Visibility was eight miles (13 km), with ceiling at 10,000 feet. At 9.30 am, Wairopi Bridge was attacked again, by two B17s from 4000 feet, 20 bombs were dropped, and hits claimed on the approach and west end of the bridge itself, making it unusable. No activity was seen on the road to Buna, and visibility was good, despite light rain and cloudbase at 10,000 feet. Forty-five minutes later, another B17 unable to locate a ship off Finschafen attacked the bridge with seven bombs from 4000 feet, and damage was claimed to the eastern end. Cloudbase had lowered to 8000 feet, and it was hazy. But by 3.30 pm, the energetic Japanese had laid planks across the hole. Two P400s returned with incendiary belly tanks, saw the repairs, their tanks exploded on the bridge, and the pilots claimed destruction of 18 feet (5.5 metres) of it.

Marching back along the trail, 2nd Lieutenant Onogawa wrote of the constant descent in the rain, and of his arrival at Isurava at 6 pm. Next day, rations were to be issued and further orders given for the defence of Kokoda. At Eora, Lieutenant Horibe rejoined his battalion with a company strength of 54 men. Some 162 had landed on 18 August from *Ryoyo Maru*. 2nd Lieutenant Shigeru Ebuchi, of II/144, travelling back to Kokoda, met another officer who told him the battalion was to form part of the rearguard, so determined to catch up with the unit. On the coast, Japanese diarist 'Uchida' was told that a regiment (41) was to move from Kokoda to Basabua, and informed that the plan was to secure Guadalcanal, then attack Milne Bay and Moresby.

The hardships undergone by the frontline troops were known to those in the rear. An unknown writer left the following: 'According to stories related by soldiers who have been on the extreme frontline in the Moresby battle, our forces lacked provisions and proceeded under difficulties. Due to the fact that the rear units did not come up, and the fact that landing operations against the enemy from the sea were delayed, our forces turned back. Whatever the case may be, they had to climb mountains twice as high as Mt Fuji, and as soon as they crossed one river, they had to face enemy positions. In the meantime, they were strafed by enemy planes countless numbers of times, and compared to the Singapore, Malay and Bataan battles there have been much more hardships encountered here. Out of rice, and short of tobacco, they attempted to requisition things from the natives, but in New Guinea, things have come to the point where there isn't a piece of paper. They used papaya (paw-paw) leaves for tobacco and dug roots at night. Enemy remnants wandered around during the daytime, and even though these groups were small in number, they were dangerous, and our men could not loiter.'[1]

The Australians were still building up the momentum of their pursuit, which also depended on the supply situation. A force of 5000 carriers was needed to sustain the battalions intended for deployment along the trail. On this day, Bert Kienzle had just 1000, and these were not all fit; some had been hauling heavy loads for 14 weeks without a real break.

However, MacArthur issued GHQ Operation Instruction No. 19 on this day, which stated that SWPA forces would attack with the objective of driving the Japanese back north of the Kumusi River, with New Guinea Force to advance to Wairopi, occupy and hold Goodenough Island and the north coast of New Guinea south of Cape Nelson in such strength as to deny them to the Japanese, then all land forces would prepare to secure Buna–Gona on orders from his GHQ.

The usual midnight harassment of Buka on 2 October was made by a Catalina, and four more attacked Buin, claiming eight hits on the runway. Rabaul was the target for six B17s, which dropped 30 bombs on shipping, going down to 3800 to 5500 feet, claimed hits on some of the 30 naval or merchant ships in harbour, and reported intense and inaccurate AA. No claims were verified after the war. Weather was clear over Rabaul, but 60 miles (96 km) from New Guinea the crews encountered a weather front, with icing at 16,000 feet. Over New Guinea, at 10 am, three A20s going under cloud ceiling at 200 feet attacked targets near the Myola lakes with 20-pound bombs, and crews counted 11 fires burning along the Myola–Efogi track, as well as many new huts built, many signs of track activity, and one machinegun firing from Myola 1.

Eight P400s flew to attack Wairopi at 10.50 am, and belly tanks with incendiary bombs attached were dropped, with claims made for three hits on the western end, and two-thirds of the bridge was reported destroyed, with only a part in the middle and a part on the eastern side left. Weather was clear, with only scattered cumulus between 5000 and 10,000 feet. A Japanese transport unit member wrote that 'the Paigi Bridge was destroyed by the enemy'. Kentaro Fujiwara, who had seen his unit of 115 men lose 26 killed in battle, noted that he was on the 'march to Isurava'. The Japanese watched Allied aircraft passing overhead, and many diaries and official documents record flights of aircraft that did not detect them, nor the supply dumps under the trees.[2]

The already serious supply situation was a constant worry to Major General Horii. His staff reported many instances of the following 'violations of transport regulations': Bags of rice had been partially emptied on the journey from Buna to the front; boxes of dry bread had been pierced with bayonets, allowing pieces of bread to be removed, but moisture to enter and spoil the contents; five tins of beef left of a consignment of 33, the rest filled with stones and earth; of 11 bundles of personal equipment sent to Ko-koda, only eight arrived; wasted half-cooked rice was to be seen along the track in bivouac areas; Japanese rice was most often stolen, not foreign rice, and it was notable that less was missing from the supplies carried by the natives and Takasago volunteers than from items carried by the Japanese themselves.

After a conference at Deniki, Horii's HQ issued an instruction that all units were to report the total number of men on strength; rations would be reduced on 3 October to 1.2 pints (680 ml) of rice for those carrying war supplies and for patients, but half that for natives; others to receive .9 pint (500 ml) of rice; natives to receive .3 pint (200 ml) of rice. Takasago volunteers, Koreans, Chinese civilians and natives were to be given foreign rice, and only if none was available would they receive Japanese rice; deserting natives were to be brought back as they were urgently needed and units were to treat them well, within the limits of the above rations; all personnel were to 'spread propaganda to bring natives back in'.[3]

Lieutenant Colonel Cameron's 3rd Battalion reached Menari early in the afternoon, and continued to Efogi. There was no ene-my opposition, but the area through which they passed showed signs of the dysentery that plagued the Japanese, and also signs that they were eating grass, roots and fruits, which the local people and the Australians knew to be inedible. Also the battalion found the bodies of two Australian soldiers, one tied to a tree and bayo-neted, and one beheaded. Cameron sent Captain Boag's company on to Efogi, and the remainder of the battalion began clearing dropping zones at Nauro. This was to take the next two days.

Cameron sent for Sergeant Bede Tongs, and asked if he would volunteer for a patrol to Kagi. Tongs agreed, and was told to take eight men along the Kagi track until they located the Japanese, also act as flank protection for the Barnett–Cox patrol from 2/25th, and look for Lieutenant Colonel Keys or men of the 2/14th who might be in the area. Two men were to be sent back to report after 24 hours. Bede went back to 10 Platoon, selected his eight men and they left. All were in good spirits, despite the knowledge that each step took them closer to the Japanese.

A prisoner was taken by 3rd Battalion. A patrol under Sergeant Burns captured him, and brought him back. He was Jiro Okino, a member of the horse transport unit of Horie's II/144. He had arrived at Buna on 21 August and taken horseloads of ammunition to Kokoda, then been used himself as a pack animal to the front lines. He had been loaded with an 82-pound (37-kg) weight of grenades, but had rapidly tired and was left behind. Eventually, a passing sergeant told him to leave the grenades and get back to his unit as fast as possible. Weakened by diarrhoea, he had been simply taken prisoner by the Australians. He had long realised that the capture of Port Moresby was far more than a three-day journey from Kokoda, as he had been told.

The Australian 2/33rd Battalion prepared to move, the first stage being a crossing of the Brown River. So far, five officers and 135 ORs of the battalion had become casualties. Thirty were to be 'left out of battle', and 55 detached to the Carrier Group, leaving, for the advance, 449 of the 664 all ranks who had landed. Only 11 casualties had been suffered in battle, the others resulting from accidents of various kinds and illnesses, including exhaustion, gastric disorders, skin diseases and fevers.

2/31st Battalion was moving to Nauro, and after being out of communications due to radio problems in the hilly country, made contact again on the heights between Ioribaiwa and Nauro, where again Japanese spotter positions in trees were noticed. 2/25th Battalion patrols reported large quantities of ammunition hidden in the trees, but no food, and again there was much obvious sign that the Japanese were plagued by dysentery. The Japanese had brought up ammunition rather than food, but the air forces had detected neither the carriers labouring forward, nor the ammunition dumps, despite General Kenney's claims that only his air attacks were holding the enemy back.

During the day, the wounded men of 2/27th, who had been left behind under the care of Corporal J. H. Burns and Private A. F. Zanker, were at last located by a patrol with a medical officer and an ANGAU-led carrier party. Another five days were to pass before the casualties reached Port Moresby. Burns kept a diary, which has been reproduced in both the unit history and the official history. It is a testimony to the quality of mateship that recently has been questioned by a few people wishing to build a reputation. An example of truly selfless courage is described when Burns and Zanker knew someone was coming to their camp, but did not know if it was to be Japanese or Australians who would appear. Burns sent the patients able to move into the bush, and then stood by the 'beds' of the others, waiting...

On 3 October, 100 Squadron RAAF flew 10 Beauforts on a strike against shipping at Faisi–Buin, and claimed five probable hits; one aircraft did not return. Eight P40s dive-bombed bridges on the Efogi–Buna track, and strafed likely targets. The road was reported as used, and three of five spans of the Wairopi Bridge were seen to be gone. Kokoda was closed in by cloud at 9.40 am, with overcast at 5000 feet between Kokoda and Buna. Soon after, three A20s dropped 20-pound bombs in the Efogi area, and reported cloudbase at Kokoda as 200 feet, but clear at Efogi. Two B25s attacked Wairopi at 1.30 pm, and claimed three direct hits and three near misses, confirmed by Australian Army observers (long-range patrol in the area), who reported the bridge as demolished. One B17 reconnoitred Buna–Salamaua–Lae–Finschafen, reporting overcast at Buna at 5000 feet, Salamaua and Lae clear with visibility out to 40 miles (64 km), but Finschafen with visibility zero and cloudbase only 200 feet. The gunners enjoyed themselves and machinegunned a Japanese camp on the west side of the Kumusi River. Another B17 reconnoitred Rabaul.

General MacArthur made his closest ground visit to the front line, when he was at Ower's Corner to see the start of the advance by Brigadier Lloyd's 16 Brigade. With MacArthur was the Australian Minister for the Army, Mr Forde. MacArthur made one of his grandiose statements, telling Lloyd that by an act of God, his brigade had been chosen for the task, that the eyes of the Western world were on him, and, 'Good luck and don't stop'.

Lloyd was described as a genial gregarious man, who displayed drive and spirit in action. His manner was that of an English regular officer, he enjoyed a drink, had a sense of humour and was a good leader. He later said that the New Guinea campaign was as hard a physical test as any in the First World War, and that the troops of the 2nd AIF were as good as, if not better than, the original AIF, with officers who were more flexible and versatile. Lloyd took pains to know his officers and as many of the men as possible, and this was repaid with greater efforts by junior ranks, who appreciated their commander taking an interest in them.

Further forward, the Australian battalions were advancing with no enemy contact. However, 2/25th Battalion reported that 'control of the natives was lost' when rumours spread of proximity of the Japanese. The battalion was late starting off, but reached Nauro for the night. 2/33rd had crossed the Brown River on a large tree trunk, being photographed by Damien Parer and George Silk, of the Department of Information. The battalion had been given food for thought as it came forward, when it passed through the positions held by the 2/14th and 2/16th in the Ioribaiwa actions, with the filled-in pits and crosses marking the dead. The smell of decaying bodies, Japanese corpses out in the jungle, was oppressive. The battalion camped at 4 pm, then sent back a party to bring up the rations dropped at Nauro. It became evident that air-dropping was convenient in some respects, but resulted in a great deal of destruction in the contents of bags and boxes.

Meanwhile, on the Japanese side, at the end of a day's digging, and a reconnaissance for platoon leaders and machinegunners along the top of the ridge defended at Eora, Lieutenant Horibe's company was tired, and he noted that cold, lack of sleep, severe fatigue and lack of adequate rest caused beri-beri and malaria. By this time, No. 1 Battery of the Japanese mountain artillery unit had only 102 men available of the 152 on strength. The unit was carrying one mountain gun and 50 rounds of ammunition, plus rations and personal weapons. They had fired 210 rounds of artillery since 24 August, and each one had been carried over ridges and streams.

There was little air activity on 4 October. At 1.50 am, four RAAF Catalinas from Cairns attacked Buka. At 8 am, US P40s strafed the Buna–Efogi road, reported no activity seen and the Wairopi Bridge not repaired. On the Moresby side of the mountains there was stratus at 5000 feet, the other side was clear, but in the valleys there was low cumulus cloud down to the ground. General Kenney's plan to develop an airfield at Wanigela began to gather momentum, and natives started work clearing the strip for the first landings. The Japanese had no idea such an audacious move was contemplated.

In the mountains, the Japanese had successfully broken contact, and were preparing to hold the advancing Australians. There was no ground contact between the ground forces on this day.

Tadao Chiba, with 15 Pioneers, noted the arrival of ships at Basabua. One returning passenger was Major Kobayashi, commander III Battalion 41 Regiment, going to Japan. The food situation in the Japanese positions at Eora was far from good, so Horibe sent 11 men to dig potatoes at Isurava, but another 11 were evacuated with beri-beri, bringing his company strength to 34 men.

Sergeant Bede Tongs's patrol from 3rd Battalion were on the track to Kagi, and passed the area of battle at Efogi. It was 'a very devastating sight. Numerous Australian bodies were there. A very disturbing sight was six stretchers in a line, with skeletal remains in the stretchers. The soldiers in the stretchers had been either bayoneted or shot. We left the identity discs on the bodies for those people moving along behind us'.

As the patrol climbed the steep slope to Kagi, they passed 15 or so dead Japanese by the track. There were plentiful signs of the diarrhoea rampant in the Japanese units, and the bodies were fly-blown. As the patrol neared Kagi, there was a disturbance behind them. A second 3rd Battalion patrol, under Sergeants Hogan and Griffiths, had overpowered one of the 'dead' Japanese who sat up and tried to throw a grenade. They took him back to Menari.

Most of Kagi was burned, but in one hut, Bede Tongs found three Rabaul natives, two shot by the Japanese when they were too weak to work, and the third had deserted to look after his friends. They were handed over to ANGAU, and two men of the patrol went back to report.

At 7 am on 5 October, three B17s arrived over Lakunai airfield, at Rabaul, but six others had been forced back by weather. The three attacked at heights from 2500 feet to 22,000 feet, dropping 20 bombs. Five minutes later, through clouds up to 22,000 feet, eight more B17s attacked Vunakanau, dropping 59 bombs across dispersals and the runway, despite intense and accurate AA. Seventeen fighters came up, attacked, US gunners claimed four probably destroyed, but five B17s were damaged and one shot down. At 8.20 am, two B25s attacked two destroyers and a transport 15 miles (24 km) north of Buna. Six Zeros attacked, and the B25s went down very low on the water, claiming two destroyed, but one B25 was lost. Two hours later, six more B25s attacked the convoy, and this time 12 Zeros attacked, but the B25s closed up and went on, and the Japanese did not press their attacks. One B25 was hit and was unserviceable until repaired.

Kurado Uchida, 15 Pioneers, was one of a party that examined a crashed twin-engined bomber in the area. One body was recovered, and it was presumed others were buried in the wreckage, but it does not seem from his description of the event that any great effort was made to investigate. It may well have been the lost B25 mentioned above.

General Kenney began his airlift of troops to Wanigela, with a battalion from Milne Bay. There were no signs that the Japanese had any information about the activity.[5] At 2.20 pm, a flight of Beaufighters and six B17s, at 4500 feet, attacked the warships north of Buna. The bombers could not find the ships, as cloudbase was down to 500 feet out to sea, but it was clear over Buna, so they bombed AA positions on the north-west end of Buna airfield. Japanese reports indicated ammunition and petrol supplies were hit. Sasebo 5SLP lost its 13-mm ammunition, petrol, its crew quarters and all their belongings and kit. Lieutenant Iwami certified the loss by enemy action of all the above, as well as identifying the time and air-raid. A witness was Tadao Chiba, who experienced his 12th air-raid at Buna, when he saw four Boeings come over and blow up the storehouse of 13-mm ammunition and other supplies. A Takasago volunteer wrote of the heavy attacks, and mentioned damage 'on the bridge behind Kokoda and the supply shed'. However, in an effort to keep up morale, troops were told that three of five attacking Boeings were shot down. At 3.55 pm, an A20 attacked barges at Sanananda, and at 5.07 pm, seven A20s dropped bombs on barges at Sanananda. Pilots reported high cumulus cloud over the ranges, but the northern shore was clear, with 15-mile visibility (24 km).[6]

Meanwhile, at 11 am, Advanced Headquarters 7 Australian Division opened at Uberi. Major General Arthur Allen formed his Command Group, an advanced part of Advanced HQ. The group was comprised of himself, the GSO1, Assistant Director Medical Services (ADMS) and two Liaison Officers (LOs). Major General Allen informed HQ New Guinea Force that air drops were essential at Menari and Nauro. 2/33rd Battalion had begun marching at 9 am, heading for Menari. On arrival, native gardens were found to have been thoroughly cleared by the Japanese. In an effort to gather knowledge of the country ahead, and to make contact with the enemy, 2/25th Battalion sent a strong patrol out for five days, to check the area to Myola. Lieutenant Barnett, with Lieutenant Cox as second-in-command, and 53 men, were at Menari by 4 pm.

The Rabaul natives found by Bede Tongs's patrol caused a great deal of interest. They were the first who had escaped or been left behind by the Japanese to be found alive. They had been badly treated, and their plight made an immediate impression on the carriers employed by the Australians, whose own working hours were long, food and conditions poor, but their treatment had not been as bad by far as that experienced by the men from Rabaul. Bert Kienzle made sure that the local carriers met the Rabaul men.

While Allen's headquarters was settling in and the Rabaul natives were the centre of attention, the Japanese 144 Regiment reached Kokoda, and it was decided to bivouac there. The area south of Kokoda was commanded by Lieutenant Colonel Hozumi, the airfield itself came under Lieutenant Colonel Tsukamoto of HQ 144 Regiment, and northern area came under Major Koiwai, with 41 Regiment units on the eastern side of Kokoda. II/144 was at Eora. The regimental movement log frequently noted that Allied aircraft passed overhead, but did not sight them. Horibe's company at Eora was warned of the advance of strong enemy forces at Kagi, and he was told by his battalion headquarters to take precautions. His company was down to just 28 men.[7]

As the day drew to a close, and after a tiring seven-hour march, the Australian 2/25th Battalion reached Menari. The battalion diary described the track as very difficult in ascent and descent. The battalion spent the night on a steep slope, in heavy rain, with many dead Japanese scattered throughout the area. On the Port Moresby side of the mountains, 2/1st Battalion began the tortuous climb over the trail, struggling up the 2000 steps of the 'Golden Stairs', and crossed Imita Ridge.

GHQ in Australia on this day, 5 October, established the Combined Operational Services Command (COSC), which had all Australian and US supply elements under its authority. At last, an organisation had been created that was of equal importance to any of the combat formations, and that was to be vital in supporting the fighting units. Of all the combatants in the Second World War (and since), the US forces were superior in organising and employing logistics, and the SWPA formations were to benefit greatly.

During the day, General Blamey sent to MacArthur's GHQ a detailed analysis of the supply and communications problems confronting New Guinea Force as it prepared to advance to the Kumusi and to Buna. Some 10,900 soldiers and carriers were to be employed in the forces active on the Kokoda Trail, at Wanigela and at Wau, and all were to be supplied by air, with cargo calculated at 10 pounds (4.5 kg) per man to be dropped daily. The factors of supply by road (which had to be built), by air-landing instead of air-dropping, by sea and by carriers were examined, and it was shown that without air supply, 10,000 carriers would be necessary to support the Kokoda thrust if no air supply was available. The daily requirement of air transport to support the advances ranged from a bare minimum of 61,900 pounds to an acceptable maximum of 102,000 pounds (28,077 to 46,267 kg).

On 6 October in the Kokoda area, 2nd Lieutenant Onogawa wrote that his unit had descended 5600 metres (18,370 feet) along a river and entered the forest, near the airfield to be defended (Kokoda). He was told their plan was still to capture Moresby, and that Lieutenant Colonel Tsukamoto would replace the sick Colonel Kusunose. Horibe's company strength at Eora increased to 43 men, with the return of various parties sent for rations and from foraging, and work continued on the defensive positions, though his soldiers were exhausted and starved.

Yazawa Force was to establish itself around Oivi, and Colonel Yazawa also had under command I/144, plus a platoon of 2 MG Company, two mountain artillery guns, an engineer company minus a platoon, radio and telephone detachments, and field hospital and stretcher bearer detachments. The Murase battalion of 41 Regiment was to hand over defence of the coastal area to local units and move at once to Oivi, coming again under command of its parent regiment. 144 Regiment was to go to Ilimo, to repulse any Australian move on the flank between Oivi and Papaki, and a machinegun company of 41 Regiment deployed to defend the river crossing at Papaki with five guns, including two 13-mm heavy machineguns.

At a supply conference, Horii's staff established a detachment that was to go over the routes taken by the transport units and collect all items of equipment, clothing, weapons and such to be found, then deliver them all to the Kokoda supply dump. All units were to submit by 10 October a detailed report on lost, damaged or unusable equipment, weapons and clothing. All communications wire was to be regarded as valuable formation material, and not as a source of easily available wire for various tasks. The field hospital was to set up at Papaki, and also be responsible for continued evacuation of casualties, while the convalescent unit was to make every effort to aid personnel to return to health and send them back to their units. 'Every possible step must be taken to increase fighting strength,' stated the document. Even non-combatants and civilians must be prepared to fight if enemy appeared in the rear, using captured weapons or those of hospital patients.[8]

The Australian 25 Brigade by this time was well aware that its performance would be limited by supply line capabilities. It was making slow progress in the difficult terrain, hampered by a lack of carriers. Supplies were being built up at Nauro and Menari, and the brigade was to check for possible drop zones at Efogi. Major General Allen, commanding 7 Division, again informed HQ in Port Moresby of the urgent need for carriers. 6 Independent Company came under command and would be used for long-range patrolling and gathering of information behind Japanese lines.

Until the problems with air drops could be solved, and until airfields suitable for use by the DC3/C47s were found or captured, a great amount of supply work devolved onto the carriers. The prewar administration had been well aware of the lifestyle of the population, in which everyone in a village had a certain role. Removal from the area of more than a certain number of able-bodied men would have an adverse effect on food production and other matters effecting the village and tribal groups. The maximum permissible recruiting figure from areas close to the Kokoda Trail was just over 8800, but by this time ANGAU had 9300 and was required to acquire another 4000. Normal recruiting methods failed, and what amounted to press-ganging was used. The natives, already reluctant, tried every means possible to get back to their homes, and the ANGAU staff were continually trying to cope with desertions, not to mention real and feigned illness. The requirements of 20th century warfare were particularly devastating on village life.

2/33rd Battalion reached the southern slopes of Efogi ridge, then enjoyed the second of only three nights of the 56 spent in the mountains during which it did not rain. During the advance, the unit had passed an increasing number of Japanese graves and the unburied corpses of Rabaul natives, left where they fell when they could not carry Japanese materials any longer. 2/31st Battalion arrived at Menari at midday, and air-drops began, continuing all afternoon. A patrol to the high ground to the east found signs of the passage of 2/27th battalion: blankets, stretchers and ammunition. No enemy were met.

General Kenney, with no knowledge of the land battle conditions, previously had denigrated the Australian Army for retreating so fast that food dumps were abandoned to the Japanese, and now made the remark that the Japanese were retreating too fast for the Australians to catch them, adding later that most of the Japanese starved to death anyway, with only a few killed by munitions. Previously he claimed that it was only relentless air attacks that had held the Japanese on the trail. The daily record in previous pages shows just how ineffectual were air attacks on the trail and advancing Japanese. Kenney seemed determined that if US units were not to get credit for the success developing on the Kokoda Trail, no one would. Kenney created a great air force from the units he found in Australia, but seemed unable to resist giving an opinion on something he knew little about, such as ground fighting, and was sparing in praise to his allies. Three B25s reconnoitred the Buna–Oro Bay area, the only combat mission recorded that day.

On 7 October, there were no attack or reconnaissance sorties flown in the Kokoda campaign recorded in the Allied Air Force squadron-level attack and reconnaissance reports, or in the daily operations report from Headquarters Allied Air Forces to General Headquarters SWPA. However, in his diary, 2nd Lieutenant Onogawa noted three attacks at Kokoda about midday. Three A20s did fly an attack mission to Kokoda and Buna, and three B25s flew reconnaissance to the Buna–Oro Bay area, followed by a single B25 sortie. The missions are recorded in the logbooks of Allied Combined Headquarters in Townsville and RAAF War Room. Onogawa's diary, in this case, is more accurate than the AAF reporting system. There are many records of missions flown in one type of report that are not mentioned in another. The RAAF Central War Room record, and logbook of Allied Combined Headquarters Townsville may note these missions, but AAF Daily Reports, AAF Intelligence Summaries or Attack and Reconnaissance reports may not, and for many days all differ in detail and in content. No single source can be considered accurate, and it is known that not all flights were recorded. However, the massive flying effort alleged by General Kenney, which he claimed halted the Japanese, certainly would have been recorded, and also mentioned in the war diaries of the Australian units in action against the enemy, as well as Japanese official and personal documents that were captured. Such regular and numerous references to overwhelming air activity confirmed by other sources do not exist. In fact, it is rare to find reference in Japanese documents to damage suffered by air attacks along the trail.

Major General Allen informed Lieutenant General Ned Herring, Rowell's successor as Commander NGF, that 'the gravest concern' was felt over the air drop program. The air forces could not supply the aircraft necessary to deliver the daily minimum of 50,000 pounds (22,680 kg) in suitable weather, and Allen emphasised that the minimum did not allow for building a reserve. Recent drops had delivered less than half the requirements, as losses had been heavy. Unless supplies could be assured, the number of troops needed to deal with the enemy could not be kept on the trail.

The term 'air drop' meant just that, with all items pushed out of the aircraft door. There simply were not enough parachutes available to ease the descent, and any parachutes that would have been used would not have been able to be recovered for reuse. Much was wasted, as the 'pushers' had to get as much out of the plane as possible on each pass over the clearing, the pilots were concentrating on flying the aircraft safely, avoiding mountain crests and the deadly trees, so accuracy was not always possible. The unpadded tins simply hurtled to the ground and much of the contents were ruined. Up to 90 per cent of biscuits were destroyed on some drops. It was found that the best dropping height for packages was between 300 and 400 feet. Below that height, the speed resulted in cargoes smashing and scattering over a wide area.

Some of these early air drops were quite informal. Ray Royal, a driver with 9 Company AASC, often found himself assisting as a 'kicker-outer'. Sometimes he volunteered, at others he was ordered to do so, after delivering the cargo to the plane door. When the aircraft reached the drop-zone, the crew chief or another person pushed the boxes and bundles along the floor to the open door, at which sat the 'kicker-outer'. There were no safety belts or straps – the man had one foot placed somewhere in secure reach inside the rear of the cabin, and held on with one hand. The other hand guided the box and the free foot kicked the cargo out the door into space. The plane was banked at about 45 degrees as the pilot flew around the clearing or mountain top, and the man in the doorway had an excellent view of the trees. As matters became more organised, the AASC companies provided men for the specialist air-delivery units, safety belts were introduced and parachutes were attached to some of the cargo. The early missions were a time of learning for all concerned, and again it was found that there are few cheap ad hoc solutions to problems in modern warfare.

Toshio Watanabe, of I/144, noted that HQ South Seas Detachment, HQ 144 Regiment and I and III Battalions were assembled at Kokoda, living in the jungle. He had come to believe that the Port Moresby campaign was discontinued. His company, No. 1, was now tasked with guarding the regimental colours. Major Horie, commander II/144 at Eora, inspected his battalion positions, and his thoroughness made this a process that kept the companies involved all day. Some form of raft had been constructed at the coast by Colonel Yokoyama's engineers, and this day was devoted to testing it, with the colonel riding on the contraption.[9]

The long-range patrol of Lieutenant Barnett, from 2/25th Battalion, reported that it was close to Myola. At the battalion itself, busy around the dropping zone, Sergeant Wakefield was killed when hit by part of the air-dropped cargo. Bede Tongs's section patrol from 3rd Battalion, along the track to Kagi, was carefully checking as they went. Morale was high, and all knew and worked according to the practised drills they had adopted. George Webb was the permanent forward scout, by mutual agreement, and moved along, Tommy gun ready. Still no one had found the Japanese.

At Efogi, Lieutenant Colonel Buttrose sent patrols from the 2/33rd to determine the source of smells of unburied bodies noticed when the unit camped. No one realised that they were at the scene of the 21 Brigade battle a month previous. Soon, reports of finding bodies increased to the extent that platoons from all the companies were sent out to search the entire area and bury the dead. For two days the grim work went on, until 99 Australians had been buried.

Diggers were found in trees, in trenches, in the bush, still with weapons in their hands, equipment and haversacks still worn. Captain Nye and his men of 2/14th were found; 10 men around a trio of three-inch mortars; Captain Bret Langridge, killed leading D Company in the attack against the Japanese near Brigade HQ; Captain Ferguson and 32 men of 2/27th at the creek crossing. Ninety separate burial services were conducted by one padre. The Japanese had collected their own dead, making large mass burial mounds, marked with a perimeter of jungle vines and a single, large cut pole, with Japanese characters written on the surfaces.

On 8 October there was no flying activity reported in the morning, but at 1.40 pm, three B25s dropped 15 bombs on Buna while on armed reconnaissance. Crews saw nothing to report. The B25s were followed at 3 pm by another armed reconnaissance mission, three A20s that flew along the Kokoda–Buna track three times, at 50 feet, and saw nothing. In the afternoon, the bomber force from Mareeba began to concentrate at Port Moresby, and that night, the harassing attacks continued. At 8.50 pm, four Catalinas attacked Rabaul, causing a large fire, possibly in a fuel dump, visible for 60 miles (100 km). Two hours later, three more Catalinas bombed Buka targets.

In ground action during the day, the Japanese positions or forward posts were found. Lieutenant Barnett's patrol from 2/25th Battalion engaged an estimated platoon of enemy, and Barnett attacked. He sent half the force with Lieutenant Cox out to the right, to attack when Barnett did so. After waiting 45 minutes, Barnett attacked, but was badly wounded, Sergeant Worland was wounded also and Sergeant Patterson was believed killed. It was imperative to get the casualties back to proper medical attention, but Brigade HQ instructed that the patrol was to remain in contact. However, the patrol had gone off the issued maps, was not sure where the enemy were, and could not find Myola.

Bede Tongs's 3rd Battalion patrol also was in contact. They sloshed along in the rain, knowing they were closing on the enemy, and had gone on for some two and a half hours when forward scout George Webb gave the 'close on me' signal. Tongs went up to him, and Webb pointed out five positions where the Japanese had squatted overlooking the trail. Large leaves had been stripped from a nearby tree and placed on the mud to make a comfortable place to sit. What the Aussies did not know was whether this Japanese standing patrol had seen them, and gone back to give the alarm, or gone back at the end of their duty. However, the Japanese position was probably not more than 150 yards away. Bede did know that he and his six men were two days' travel ahead of the battalion, he had no communication other than on foot, and could not afford to have casualties.

Carefully, the patrol advanced, found the Japanese and opened fire. There were many rounds whistling and cracking past, when George Webb's Tommy gun jammed and could not be cleared in that situation. Bede withdrew his patrol while Webb cursed the Thompson sub-machine gun. 'A good gangster's gun,' was Bede's opinion, 'but not very good in the jungle.'

The patrol had located and engaged the enemy, as ordered, and began to return to the battalion to report. The Japanese did not pursue, and eventually at Kagi the patrol met the 2/25th Battalion. Both sides were very careful about strangers in the bush, and after a certain amount of shouting in distinctly Australian terms, identities were established, just as 2/25th were preparing a three-inch mortar to fire on the patrol. Bede took his men back to the 3rd Battalion and reported.

At Buna, Medical Officer 2nd Lieutenant Hiroyuki Hayashi recorded the Japanese force's casualties for August as 400 killed and 600 wounded, and for September as 200 killed. Other Japanese documents stated that 'due to lack of food and malaria, 300 out of 800 men of South Sea Detachment perished'.[10]

The ninth of October saw a relatively big air attack begin on targets at Rabaul. General Kenney had personally ordered the gathering of a force of B17s for a large blow, and this marked a new stage in overcoming the problems of distance, supply and maintenance. Thirty B17s set out for the target. Seven Catalinas from Cairns were to coordinate flare dropping passes with the B17 bomb runs, and a total of 90 500-pound and 207 300-pounders were carried. The targets were well-lit by the Catalina flares, and the B17s went in at 4500 to 11,000 feet through heavy, intense but inaccurate AA. Fires were visible 80 miles (128 km) from the target. Only one aircraft did not reach the target due to mechanical trouble. Ken McCullar and the crew of 'Black Jack' had worked at nights under floodlights to complete an engine change, and were pleased to be ready for the mission. What co-pilot Harry Staley called 'tremendous amounts' of AA were fired as they passed over Rabaul at 7000 feet, but the aircraft was not damaged. Perhaps going where angels would fear to tread, a single B17 sent to reconnoitre Lae and Rabaul after the attacks was set upon by Zeros, resulting in the tail gunner killed and co-pilot wounded, with two engines shot up and holes in the wings, fuselage, tail, cockpit and turret. By comparison, on 9 October over Europe, the US 8th Air Force sent 108 heavy bombers to the Fives–Lille steelworks, while another seven flew a diversion.

In attacks over New Guinea, at 9.50 am, a combined striking force of nine Beaufighters and 14 B25s attacked Lae. The Beaufighters reported the Japanese warning system was good, as the AA barrage began before the force reached the target. The B25s claimed 70 bombs fell on the airfield and others on the south-west side. The runway itself appeared neglected, and cloudbase was reported as 1500 feet.

In the jungles near Myola, Lieutenant Cox, responsible for the wounded Lieutenant Barnett and Sergeant Worland, plus the other 52 men, was told to remain in the area and that Captain Donnan, the medical officer, was moving forward to him. He could not find Myola, but had located the enemy three and a half hours from the Kagi track junction.

In Horibe's 6 Company, work went on all day in digging and preparing Japanese defensive position at Eora. There was some shooting from the left front, but no definite reports of enemy activity. Rice, sauce and wheat gluten rations for two days were issued to his company of 44 men. One man had died in Kokoda hospital.

Medical Officer Hayashi was told that three Japanese soldiers were killed by natives, but did not record any other detail. In the Buna area, an unknown diarist wrote that at last his stomach was full, though only with green pineapple, which had been collected by one of the unit. The only Japanese food available was soft, boiled rice, and he presumed that 'we will probably have this for quite a while'. He had scrounged two cigarettes, but had been out of tobacco for a week. One comfort was the tent he had erected, which withstood the heavy rain throughout the night, but did not leak. He had been told that three Japanese planes were shot down in actions during which three Boeings and three Allied fighters were lost.[11]

Three deserters from 2/1st Field Regiment joined 2/1st Infantry Battalion on this day, being keen to get a closer look at the Japanese than they would achieve with their parent artillery unit. The three were more or less hidden in the platoons, and accompanied the unit into action.

The demand for native carriers far exceeded the supply, and instead of the thousands required, ANGAU had only hundreds. Bert Kienzle on 9 October allocated his available carriers graded as 'A'-class: 214 to Menari, 225 to Nauro and 227 attached to the forward battalions.

On 10 October the B17 force returned to Rabaul. Seven Catalinas from Cairns began dropping flares at 2.30 am, and 21 bombers, at heights from 4500 to 13,000 feet, attacked through intense, heavy, but inaccurate AA on targets in Rabaul and Lakunai airfield. Catalina crews reported fires visible from 90 miles (145 km). 'Black Jack' was second aircraft over the target, and the aroused defenders caught the B17 in four searchlights, making it a well-lit target for every AA gun in range. Ken McCullar was forced to half-roll the big bomber to escape, but brought the aircraft back with no damage. After that experience, the crew was ready for the return to Mareeba and three days' leave in Cairns. The bombers stopped at Moresby long enough to refuel and got away to Mareeba as soon as possible. There was no intention of leaving a valuable concentration of B17s for any Japanese retaliatory strike. At 9.50 am, three A20s swept the Kokoda–Buna track, bombing a bridge and claiming a direct hit. Though there was little to be seen, the track east of Wairopi showed signs of use by vehicles, and visibility was poor, with scattered cumulus down to 200 feet. At 12.15 pm, looking for a ship off Buna, six B25s attacked a camouflaged ship-like object at the mouth of the Mambare River. Only four bombs were dropped on it, the other 32 going down at Wairopi. Crews saw nothing else to report, though visibility was excellent, with the only clouds on the tops of the mountains. 2nd Lieutenant Onogawa, at Kokoda, was told finally the bridge at Papaki had been destroyed after 68 bombs had been dropped on it.

2/25th Battalion moved forward, and passed Efogi, noting the many unburied Australians from the actions fought there. They pushed on to the Kagi–Myola track junction, arriving at 4.20 pm. Earlier, Lieutenant Cox had reported that he had found the Myola track junction, and 20 minutes later had arrived at the lake. 2/31st also passed through the area, in turn noting many unburied dead, other signs of battle, and particularly hundreds of primed Mills grenades scattered around, plus shells for the Japanese mountain gun that were still in their canisters.

By the end of the day, Australian dispositions were:

25 Brigade: 3rd Battalion AMF (less one company) north of Efogi
3rd Battalion company at Kagi
2/25th Battalion between Menari and Efogi
2/31st Battalion east of Menari
2/33rd Battalion between Kagi and Myola
16 Brigade: 2/1st, 2/2nd and 2/3rd Battalions moving forward in the area of Menari.

Brigadier Eather ordered 2/25th Battalion to clear the track up to Templeton's Crossing, and 2/33rd to clear the crossing. Private Noel Geraghty, 3rd Battalion, was given an unusual and frightening task. Alone, he was sent from the battalion position with a quantity of tea and sugar, about 13 pounds (six kg), for the natives at Efogi. Another soldier volunteered to go with him, but was refused by the company commander, who sent Noel out with his rifle and only six rounds of ammunition, and the proviso that he was to fire only if cornered by the enemy. Geraghty later said that, 'Quite a few times before this run, I thought I was scared, but I realised I didn't know what fright was until I was away on my own, not exactly knowing where I was going or what lay ahead of me'. The story was that the tea and sugar was necessary to persuade the natives to support the Allies rather than the Japanese. Geraghty made the journey safely.

On 11 October the only mission over the Kokoda area was flown at 10.10 am, three A20s with an escort of eight P400s doing armed reconnaissance of the Kokoda–Yodda–Mambare–Cape Waria section of the region. From about 1200 feet, 80 bombs were dropped on Asisi village, three miles (4.8 km) south of Wairopi. The bridge itself was reported as unserviceable, but barges at Sanananda were seen and strafed. Visibility was excellent, with scattered cumulus at 200 feet.

Toshio Sato had definitely had enough of Buna, and wrote that 'technicians, engineers and instructors all desire to go home very much'. Toshio Watanabe wrote that Lieutenant Colonel Tsukamoto was acting regiment commander, adding that for three days there had been no rice, the soldiers had been eating only potatoes, and had 'never experienced so much shortage of food'. It was his last entry, and his notebook was captured nine days later. At Eora, Lieutenant Horibe had a company strength of 43 men. He noted in his diary that 162 had landed, 127 had been on strength at Efogi, 112 for the action at Isurava [sic – Isurava came before Efogi], 88 at Ioribaiwa. For the past few days his men had continued digging, been inspected by the battalion commander, and been alert for advancing enemy. He had taken a part of the company to dig another position on a nearby ridge crest, and overseen an issue of 'a handful of rice' to each man. Shots were heard from 4 Company, but no action developed.[12]

2/25th arrived at Templeton's Crossing without enemy contact, and by noon, 2/33rd arrived nearby. Lieutenant D. Cullen was commanding C Company 2/33rd, as an ill Captain Miller had been evacuated a few days previously. A 14 Platoon force under Lieutenant Bill Innes had been reconnoitring the area since the day before, and had been fired on by Japanese. Innes reported that the Japanese had prepared a strong, narrow but deep position. Lieutenant Cullen began preparations for a company attack next morning at 8 am. He intended sending 14 Platoon along to the left for half an hour's movement, then to get across the track, while 13 and

15 Platoons put in the attack, clearing the track and to the left of it. It was estimated that two hours would be necessary to get the machineguns into position, led by the platoon sergeants. An afternoon patrol lost two men wounded, and no information was gained, except that the Japanese were alert.

A patrol by 3rd Battalion lost two killed. This patrol was to go back to the location where Sergeant Bede Tongs had contacted the Japanese, and he agreed to guide it. As they neared the spot, he told the officer in command they were close, and the scouts should be warned. The platoon sergeant nearby, Lance Armstrong, heard this, and also heard the lieutenant rebuke Tongs, reminding him that *he* was in command. The Japanese fired, both forward scouts were killed, the lieutenant turned and took the following two sections with him, to report. Bede Tongs and Armstrong then extricated the leading section, with much firing and grenading, but the bodies of the scouts were, unavoidably, left in the Japanese killing ground. When they arrived back at the battalion, Lieutenant Colonel Cameron questioned everyone in the platoon, with the result that the lieutenant was sent away from the unit. Cameron already had kicked out an officer at Ioribaiwa. He could not tolerate weakness in his officers.

Brigadier Eather and Major General Allen conferred on the supply situation. Allen issued his orders to the brigades: 25 Brigade was to maintain contact with the enemy by patrolling, to consolidate in the area of Eora Creek–Myola–Kagi, and to secure Alola as soon as possible for use as a drop zone; 16 Brigade was to defend Myola, and be prepared to move through 25 Brigade to take Kokoda. By 5 pm, HQ 25 Brigade was established at Efogi North. The staff had counted the skeletons of 24 Australian along the track. Australian Command Group 7 Division was at Menari, where 2/1st Battalion was tasked to improve the drop zone, and worked at this for three days. They then spent until 17 October at Myola, collecting the items dropped from the many supply flights.

Major General Allen was being pressured by Blamey to advance more swiftly. Blamey reminded Allen that he was to capture Kokoda and had been supplied, then pointed out that there had been negligible Japanese resistance for so slow an advance, and offered to relieve Allen if the personal strain was too much. Allen replied that it seemed his plan to capture Kokoda had been mis-understood at Moresby, that his brigade commanders had been correctly instructed, and that the main barrier to a quick advance was the terrain, plus the lack of carriers. He reminded Blamey that the amount of supplies consigned by air was not relevant to the length of the daily advance, rather it was the ability to deliver to the forward troops. Allen also informed Blamey that the terrain was the hardest yet encountered, 'and cannot be appreciated until seen'. He also pointed out that his units were advancing, but re-maining fit to fight. He assured Blamey that physically and men-tally he was fit, but was disappointed that Blamey was dissatisfied with the progress made by the troops.

At 10 am on 12 October, C Company 2/33rd Battalion attacked the Japanese position at Templeton's Crossing. The Japanese re-sisted strongly, and a fierce action developed with visibility redu-ced to a few paces in any direction. The strip of ground was only about 10 yards wide and 200 deep, with the Japanese firing from holes and the Australians trying to shoot or grenade them. Two Australians were killed and three wounded, but the Japanese were forced out and back. They could be heard shouting and chopping wood further away in the jungle, and other positions could be seen. One dead Japanese was found, and others were known to have been wounded. Cullen had cleared 300 yards of track. C Company settled down to wait for the rest of the battalion.

By the time 2/33rd began moving along it, the track had been well and truly churned into a succession of pools of black mud and water. All traffic into and out of Myola passed along the dirt path, and rain allowed no chance for it to dry out. On either side of the ridge the ground fell away, and the trail followed the top of a nar-row ridge, only a few paces wide. The jungle closed overhead as they moved along a matted, green tunnel, with no sight of sky. The moss, ferns and orchids noticed by George Mowat, of A Company 39th Battalion, also were remarked on by these later travellers.

Inevitably, it began to rain – a fine drizzle. The day was made gloomier with clouds and mist, and at the 7000-foot level it was cold. It was hard to accept that the men were marching in a tropical morning rather than a winter's evening. The only warm clothing was a thin woollen Army pullover, and the groundsheet was kept rolled so as to be dry for the night. None of this did much to lighten spirits as the battalion moved up to attack.

At 10.15 am, three A20s with seven P400s as escort swept the Kokoda–Buna–Pongani area at 2000 feet, bombed Isivita village, but no activity was seen, though the P400s reported accurate 40-mm AA at Buna. An hour later, three B25s reconnoitred Buna–Lae–Vitiaz Strait–Gasmata–Buna. An afternoon flight over the same area was made by another three aircraft.

Japanese diarist Horibe, in position at Eora, noted that air activity had been constant, a day's ration of bread was issued, and he had sent another 10 men for potatoes from Isurava. General Horii issued Instruction 43: 485 men from the infantry, artillery and engineers were to withdraw to the Giruwa Convalescent Unit.[13] In the hospital area at Giruwa, a member of the Takasago volunteers organised a defence unit of patients able to fight. Up to 100 out-patients a day, mainly Korean labourers, would normally attend the hospital, and it was believed that this activity would reveal the location of the hospital to Allied aircraft, so 'from the stand-point of morale and prevention of infectious diseases', it was decided to establish a distant ward for the numerous Koreans. In addition, all cooking was done at a kitchen 1100 yards from the hospital, in case of air attack, and fires were lit only between 2 and 4 am and 4 to 5 pm. The writer noted that anything detected from the air was attacked, and camouflage had to be perfect, with constant work necessary to maintain it.[14]

This determination to fight, even with hospital patients and in the area close to a hospital, led to the obvious result in the battles around Buna – it was deduced by the Allied troops that even in and around hospitals the fanatical Japanese would fight to the death. The Japanese themselves had shown little mercy when overrunning hospitals in Hong Kong, Malaya and Singapore, and escapees had told of cold-blooded slaughter of medical staff and patients. The Japanese had sown the wind, and would reap the whirlwind.

At 1 pm, Lieutenant Colonel Buttrose and the rest of the 2/33rd Battalion arrived at C Company's position. Lieutenant Cullen reported that the Japanese were some 300 yards ahead, in well-camouflaged holes that had logs across the top, in a system of positions that seemed to extend back for 600 yards. While they were talking, Lieutenant Innes was scouting the position, and Corporal Terry Campbell was killed.

Buttrose ordered an attack for 2 pm. There were no maps; the area had never been surveyed; none had been produced. B Company, under Captain Archer, was to pass through C Company astride the track; Captain Clowes's D Company was to pass along the left, go for 600 yards and cut the track there. There was no time to reconnoitre Clowes's advance, and he was simply estimating his progress along the side of the ridge, leading the company over and around the obstacles of terrain and huge fallen trees as quietly as possible to avoid alerting the Japanese. It was still drizzling.

B Company set off with 12 Platoon leading. The platoon commander, Lieutenant Phil Curry, had joined the battalion in the Middle East, but this was his first action. His leading scout, Private Ludbrook, turned a corner in the track and was shot dead; this was another lesson learned. C Company had withdrawn to allow B Company freedom of action, and the Japanese had followed up, taking position much closer than expected. 12 Platoon began firing at what targets could be seen. Two more men were wounded; Ludbrook's body was out of reach.

Captain Archer told Lieutenant Curry to hold his ground, and he would put 10 Platoon on the track, with 11 to the left. This move started at 3.30 pm. Heavy fire drove everyone to ground. Few could see a Japanese, as the visibility was very limited. Men actually got onto the track, but were unable to destroy the Japanese positions. These were holes big enough for a man, enclosed in logs, with only a narrow firing slit, but mutually supporting. It was almost impossible to throw a grenade into the firing slit – it had to be placed through the small gap. With the weapons available to the platoons, the advantage was with the Japanese. Flame-throwers, smoke grenades, mortars and satchel charges were all things that might have been a million miles away. The attack cost two killed and six wounded.

Meanwhile, at 3 pm, off on their own flanking move, Captain Clowes and D Company heard firing to the rear, and presumed it was B Company in action. He decided to find a suitable place and attack. Sergeant Frank McTaggart went to the right, to find the track, and soon returned with the news that he had seen it, and the body of an Australian on it. This was Private Erp, C Company. Clowes pushed on for another 30 minutes, then came on a relatively clear ravine that led in the general direction of the Japanese; on his right was a steep slope. He looked back and could see the entire company, in single file, all looking up at him. Clowes gave the signal for all to turn right and waved them into the advance.

The sounds of firing from B Company were heavier and D Company began the struggle up the rising ground. Soon the physical effort and little gullies and breaks in the ground began to fragment the original long line, but still they clambered upwards, reached the top and stared. Only 20 yards away was the track, and on it were half a dozen surprised Japanese in lean-tos, but at the feet of most of the Australians was a 20-foot deep (six-metre) ravine, though some of 16 Platoon had arrived on the track itself. All platoons began firing and getting the Brens into action, or watching along the track to left and right for approaching Japanese. Rifle grenades were prepared and fired by a team of four men: Sergeant Bill Crooks, and Privates Olly Hawkins, Georgy Wenham and Eddie Ball. The platoon mortars could not be used as the jungle canopy was close, but the grenades were fired almost horizontally into any visible pit.

The Japanese reacted and began grenading and machinegunning in return. This fire, from the flank, forced D Company off the ridge and track, and Captain Clowes ordered a move back into the jungle. The drizzle thickened into a downpour and the company settled into a night perimeter, with Clowes intending to attack again in the morning.

Captain Archer reported the results of B Company's attack to Lieutenant Colonel Buttrose, and the battalion settled down for the night. Corporal Savage's section of 11 Platoon spent all night awake, only 40 paces from the Japanese. 2/33rd had lost six killed and 12 wounded, with little to show for the effort. D Company was out of contact, though firing had been heard. There was communication back to 25 Brigade at Efogi, but little assistance would be available, as everything had to come along the track. After discussion with the company commanders present, Lieutenant Colonel Buttrose decided on another attack at 9 am. Forces would go to the right along the Japanese flank before turning in to attack. The temperature was 45 degrees F (7 degrees C), and some of the battalion tried to keep warm by wearing corn bags that had been dropped in the air supply. The bags kept out some wind, but not rain. During the wet night, Major Cotton, the second-in-command, came forward with food and ammunition, and began carrying back four stretcher cases, with the assistance of some brave local people he had persuaded to make the trip.

While on the track from Menari to Efogi, Bert Kienzle was shown the remains of a white horse in a creek, and told that it was Horii's mount. However, the carcase of every white horse found was said to be Horii's horse.

On 13 October, the heavy bomber force again flew to distant targets, and airfields at Rabaul were targets for 18 B17s that attacked at 4.15 am, from 6000 to 9000 feet. One aircraft could not find the target, so bombed Buna instead. For three hours overlapping midnight, six Catalinas from Cairns attacked Buka. In daylight, over New Guinea, three Beaufighters, with seven P400s as escort, reconnoitred Kokoda–Buna, and below a 100-foot cloudbase, strafed barges at Sanananda. While strafing Kokoda, one Beaufighter was reported as 'on the outward journey, burst into flames 900 feet [275 metres] from the top of the last ridge on the Moresby side of Kokoda', hit the hill, exploded and burned for at least five minutes. Wairopi Bridge was assessed as unserviceable, but another was seen at Ilimo.

Lieutenant Horibe had returned to Japanese battalion headquarters ammunition, grenades and a light machinegun surplus to his company requirements. He had sent a section to reinforce the advanced position, and was left with a strength of 42 men. Fifteen soldiers remained at Rabaul; 27 had been killed since landing and one had died, 60 were wounded, 23 sick, and six transferred. He was the sole officer, with only four of the establishment figure of 17 NCOs left, and 38 of the 157 privates. He made no further diary entries, and the diary was captured at Templeton's Crossing on 20 October, a week later. Into 67 Line of Communication Hospital, Giruwa, came 330 patients from front-line units.[15]

West of Templeton's Crossing, on 13 October, scouts from 2/25th Battalion were fired on, then Lieutenant Strachan was wounded by accurate sniper fire. B and C Companies were forward, D went into reserve, and A moved onto the ridge left of the track. An assault by C Company forced the Japanese off the high ground on the left, and the battalion consolidated for the night.

At Templeton's Crossing itself, in the morning of 13 October, Captain Archer's B Company 2/33rd was to lead the attack again. 11 Platoon would push astride the track, while the other two platoons moved to the right, going along the Japanese flank for about 30 minutes or 100 yards, turn left, and go uphill into the attack. This all took time, it was still drizzling, the Japanese were awake and heard the noise as the platoons began scrambling up the wet, muddy rise. The firing began. Both platoons got onto the track, and some men succeeded in putting grenades into the Japanese pits, but all were forced off again by the heavy fire. In 10 Platoon, Private Jim Laing got to the track and could see a Japanese light machinegun only 10 yards away. He turned and called for the Bren, but in the scramble the magazine was knocked off, and Laing found himself with a useless piece of metal pointing at the enemy. Corporal Cooper, 11 Platoon, had a broken extractor on his Tommy gun as he was about to fire on a pit while his section came up.

Because of the thick foliage, the slope, the heavy Japanese fire from positions that were hard to see and extremely difficult to knock out, Captain Archer again ordered a move back to the original position. The single three-inch mortar had tried to fire in support, but it was stopped for fear of hitting the platoons.

On arrival back at the position, Captain Archer decided to attack again, this time from the left flank, with the aim of destroying the forward Japanese positions. A reconnaissance by Lieutenant Marshall and two men was halted when they met two Japanese, who wounded Marshall before he killed them with his Tommy gun. The battalion now depended on A Company for any gains, and the distant D Company, under Captain Clowes, from whom firing had been heard.

When first light seeped under the misty trees at about 8 am, Captain Clowes gave his orders for the renewed attack, then sent a runner with a written report to the CO; the radio was useless. The runner, Jim Lindsay, set off, was fired on, dived into the bush and became lost, kept going south, and next day met some 3rd Battalion soldiers. He arrived back at 2/33rd to find he had been given up and listed 'missing'. But while Private Lindsay was making his own odyssey, the company was in action. Captain Clowes decided to move past the end of the ravine that had separated the platoons from the Japanese the day before, get onto the track, and attack, taking out the positions from there.

However, Japanese were waiting, and began firing with light and medium machineguns and throwing a hail of grenades. Any attempt to go up into that blizzard of fire would result in heavy and useless casualties, so again Captain Clowes ordered a withdrawal. Individual acts of bravery and leadership were unavailing. At midday, D Company set off back to the battalion position, and five hours later arrived at the HQ Company position, where Lieutenant Colonel Buttrose placed them in reserve.

Meanwhile, Lieutenant Power and 50 selected men, in groups of five led by an NCO, had gone along the left of the Japanese position. Power, a Regular Army officer, now was commanding A Company. At 11 am, he stopped and issued his orders: six groups would attack and three would be in reserve. They were so close that the lean-tos could be seen, and Japanese heard talking. Fortunately, the enemy had been distracted by the attacks from D and B Companies. Power's groups began quietly to climb the slope.

They achieved surprise. Japanese were sitting around eating, and one medium machinegun was covered with a tarpaulin. A Company began shooting Japanese right and left; Sergeant Elliott shot six with his Tommy gun; Sergeant Tobin and Jack Rossiter grabbed the machinegun and began to drag it away; Bren guns were sealing the approaches, shooting more Japanese. Then the Japanese reaction gathered weight, and Lieutenant Power called the groups back. The machinegun was left, and the wounded carried away, under a hail of light machinegun fire, grenades and what was presumed to be abuse from the Japanese. At least 20 enemy were seen dead or badly wounded. By 4 pm, Lieutenant Power was back at the HQ position, and a party of wounded came in later, as he was going out to look for them. For this action, Power was awarded the Military Cross.

Lieutenant Colonel Buttrose had the mortar fire in support, and 18 bombs were sent on their way, but ranging could only be done by sound, and only three bombs were seen to burst among the Japanese positions. Not to be outdone, the Japanese fired 34 bombs into HQ Company, wounding five men. The Japanese were quite alert. As soon as the canopy was cleared for the Australian mortar to fire, they sent bombs into the position.

The day's attacks had cost three dead and 13 wounded, including two officers and eight NCOs. This type of warfare, with the communications equipment and weapons available, in the conditions prevailing, consumed junior leaders at a fast rate. An airstrike was ordered, if the weather permitted, and Clowes's D Company was to go in to follow up this support. C Company was to attack along the track, while Power and A Company were to repeat their style of attack. Again, Major Cotton and his hardworking team, with the natives, made a resupply journey to the battalion and carried out the wounded. The dead were buried in the small cemetery made nearby. It rained on the waiting battalion, and the night was cold and miserable again.

Meanwhile, 25 Brigade HQ advanced to Myola. The battalions reported that the Japanese encountered were not ragged and starved, but relatively clean, wearing good uniforms and rubber boots in good condition. Brigadier Eather decided to send 3rd Battalion in to Templeton's Crossing to assist, with orders to move to the left of the Japanese and attack some 1000 yards along that flank. Further to the rear, 16 Brigade HQ arrived at Efogi, described as 'a bleak spot high above the clouds, with rain beating down'. At Division HQ, on 13 October, Major General Allen made the comment that he 'was more afraid of a stab in the back than I am of the Japanese', referring to the pressures building from Mac-Arthur and Blamey.

On 14 October, recorded air activity in the morning and afternoon was confined to a single B25 reconnaissance of Buna–Salamaua–Lae–Finschafen, with nothing to report, one 500-pound bomb was dropped and hit south-west of Wairopi Bridge. There were no relevant flights recorded until 5.02 pm, when two B25s covered the usual reconnaissance area, reporting AA at Buna as inaccurate, Salamaua airfield seemed unusable, Lae airfield also unusable, with no aircraft sighted. During the day, 670 men of the US 128 Infantry Regiment were flown to Wanigela. At midnight, Colonel Carmichael asked the 63rd Squadron at Torrens Creek to be at 7-Mile strip by dawn, and the squadron began a hurried preparation of all available planes and crews.

At 11 am, on 14 October, Colonel Kusunose visited units of his 144 Regiment for the last time. He was ill, and due to be evacuated to Rabaul. The elements of 144 at Kokoda received orders from Major General Horii to move to Eora, and prepare the area for defence. Two weeks later, Kusunose was replaced by Colonel Yamamoto, whose name was taken by the regiment.[16]

The combination of rain and the valley walls combined to make it dark in the battle area at Templeton's Crossing until about 10 am. The clouds were just above the treetops, and it was not thought air support would arrive in time to be of much use. The companies moved off to make their attacks, and the mortar prepared to fire in support. Lieutenant Power led his A Company 2/33rd Battalion force, now reduced to 40, past the position from which they had attacked the day before, and at midday the first four groups began climbing to the Japanese. This time, the Japanese were waiting, and held the attackers down the slope with heavy fire and a rain of grenades. Private Carr was killed and six were wounded, including two NCOs. Sergeant Elliott could see a machinegun firing, and behind it a mortar, which he realised was the one bombarding the 2/33rd. After some manoeuvring, Power realised that it was useless to persist, and he could see Japanese crossing the crest and going into the jungle to counter-attack. The confident enemy were now calling out in English to confuse the Australians. But Power resorted to Arabic, learned when the battalion was in the Middle East, to order the withdrawal. Taking the wounded, the force made their way back, disappointed.

C Company 2/33rd also got into position, began climbing the steep ridge, and were held by heavy Japanese fire when close to the track. Two were killed and 14 wounded, for no gain, and as the platoons began to move back the Japanese followed for a while, sniping and grenading. Back at his company HQ, Lieutenant Cullen was reporting to Lieutenant Colonel Buttrose, Lieutenant Innes was having his wounds dressed, and Lieutenant Warne asked what was happening. Buttrose rebuked Warne and sent him back to his platoon to harry the Japanese and stop them organising a counter-attack from the left. Warne went back, left his platoon sergeant and a section to hold the track, and took the other two out to the left. As he approached the top of the ridge, Warne was shot dead, having led his platoon in action for a few minutes. A visitor to the battalion at this time was Colonel Kingley Norris, ADMS 7 Division, who assisted at the aid post with the casualties.

Late in the afternoon, Sergeant McTaggart and a patrol went out and crept in close enough to see the body of Private Erp, still on the track. McTaggart saw a Japanese in a pit only five paces away, so threw in a grenade. He fired his Tommy gun at two other pits and turned to give an order to the patrol, but they had gone, thinking he had been killed by a Japanese grenade. This did not please McTaggart at all.

The day had cost 2/33rd four dead and 19 wounded; it still rained; it was cold; the Japanese mortar continued to fire, but caused no casualties. While the overall Japanese situation was bad, it is evident that the defenders opposing the 2/33rd were far from being the scarecrows dying of starvation described by General Kenney. Close by, 3rd Battalion was arriving to assist in the action. 2/25th had patrolled during the day, losing Private James killed in action. 16 Brigade HQ arrived at Myola in 'the usual rain', while Major General Allen's Command Group moved to Menari.

The worsening situation of the Japanese force was evident to many of their officers, and the following was in a file of 41 Regiment documents: 'Officers and men realise the present condition of the formation cannot be helped. However, the men are gradually weakening in their physical condition due to the lack of food and the continuous rain, with no chance of recovery. Malaria and beri-beri patients are increasing; there is insufficient clothing; boots are soaked with no chance of drying. Potato, papaya (pawpaw) and coconuts are taken to make up for the lack, but these are available only in small quantities.'[17]

At 4.40 am on 15 October, reacting to the requirement from Colonel Carmichael to be ready to fly to Moresby, the first of five 63rd Squadron B17s took off from Mareeba under an 800-foot cloudbase, headed for Port Moresby. When they arrived, at once the crews were briefed and sent on reconnaissance flights to the Faisi area. First off was Ken McCullar. At 8.30 am, three A20s and seven P40s searched for enemy from two miles (3.2 km) south of Templeton's Crossing to Popondetta, with nothing to report. Two hours later, three B25s flew the same reconnaissance, again with nothing to report, and bombed Wairopi. At 2.05 pm, in the Solomon Sea, three B17s attacked a light cruiser. After bombing, through heavy and accurate AA, the B17s went down to strafe from 50 feet, while another B17 dropped four 500-pounders on a destroyer. Harry Staley, in 'Black Jack', personally thought that the cruiser sank, as two bombs from the aircraft exploded close on each side of the ship, but they were only credited with damaging it. No cruiser was known to have been sunk by air attack on this day. General Kenney, flying back to Port Moresby, stopped at Townsville and Mareeba to award 250 medals to members of his air units for exploits since he had assumed command.

Before dawn on 15 October, at Templeton's Crossing, movement to attack positions began in the dark. Lieutenant Colonel Buttrose talked with Brigadier Eather over the landline. 3rd Battalion was to be led into position by Lieutenant Power, to attack at 11 am, while 2/33rd pushed up the track from the right. Clowes's D Company was to move up to B Company, then attack the Japanese positions only 40 paces away.

Meanwhile, the Japanese were making their own preparations for coming battles, and at 9 am, the leading elements of 144 Regiment from Kokoda started for Eora, passing through Deniki at 10.30 am. On the trail were I and part of III Battalions, headquarters and communications troops. 2nd Lieutenant Onogawa had been at Deniki for two days, was told that regimental HQ had gone past, and was behind his position. This was his last entry, and the diary was captured on 23 October, north of Eora Creek.

The Australian rifle companies at Templeton's Crossing carefully moved into position and scouts crept forward to the Japanese positions. There were no enemy to be seen; patrols went in and gradually it became clear that they had gone. A few rifles and some ammunition were left, but no sign of Japanese dead or alive were found. In its area, 3rd Battalion reported the enemy had departed.

Later, 2/33rd Battalion compiled a report on this Japanese position, enemy tactics and their weaknesses. The good protection afforded the occupants of the Japanese positions was described, and the difficulty of putting a grenade into the pits or firing slit was emphasised. Other points mentioned were that the Japanese often seemed to put their weapons out of the holes and fire blindly, but the machinegun positions covering the main track were well positioned, with good camouflage; a strong counter-attack force was always available to move to whichever part of the position was penetrated by attackers; the main defensive weapon was the machinegun, with riflemen moving to vantage points relevant to the movements of attackers; the machineguns were often moved to different positions to lessen the effects of reconnaissance and information gained during battle; the Japanese hand-grenade made a lot of noise, but was not very effective otherwise; the Australian three-inch mortar was disliked by the Japanese; when he was driven from his positions often there seemed to be signs of panic, with much running to and fro and wild firing of all types of weapons. It was stated at the conclusion of the report that the Japanese seemed to have found this type of defence adequate against semi-trained troops, but he would give way against trained and determined attackers, the battalion had been attacking uphill against prepared positions, but had inflicted more casualties than it had received.

Clowes's D Company 2/33rd was ordered to keep the Japanese moving, and the rest of the battalion would follow at 2 pm. Also, D Company 3rd Battalion was sent to move through the area and get in behind the enemy holding 2/25th Battalion at Kagi. However, 2/25th found the enemy gone, and went after them, but they turned and killed the forward scout of C Company, and the battalion brought up its mortars. Of 27 bombs fired, eight were duds, and 2/25th, as had other battalions, realised air-dropped mortar bombs were often defective. C Company 2/25th advanced up to a Japanese barricade across the track before darkness. Alternating lead platoons in the advance from Templeton's Crossing, Captain Clowes pushed D Company 2/33rd on and reached Eora Creek. The soldiers looked out at a shallow but fast-flowing torrent swirling around and along rocks. The Japanese had destroyed a bridge, so Sergeant McTaggart took two men across, but they were fired on at close range from the northern bank, and went back to report.

The battalion began to arrive, and Lieutenant Colonel Buttrose sent 13 Platoon to outflank the Japanese post while the companies came into a small perimeter. Soon the Diggers were reporting finding bodies of 2/16th Battalion men, killed there early in September. Lieutenant Dark and 13 Platoon returned to report that he had found no sign of Japanese. 2/33rd settled down for what was a night more miserable than most so far. It was absolutely black at the bottom of the gorge; the creek roared over the rocks; the rain teemed down; it was cold. Few slept, and many meditated on the lonely graves of the 2/16th men in the primitive surroundings.

25 Brigade HQ received reports of the finding of bodies of the

two 3rd Battalion soldiers killed where Bede Tongs had led the patrol back to the scene of his patrol contact. The bodies had been cannibalised; one had both arms amputated. Major General Allen moved his Command Group forward again, to Efogi. Air support had been requested, but was not supplied. 16 Brigade recorded 'another cold wet night'.

Japanese diarist 'Wada', who kept a diary while in the Buna area, daily recorded the reconnaissance and attack flights, along with notations on fever, moving camp to avoid aircraft, and news from the Solomons and Guadalcanal. The tone of the diary was defensive, and there was little record of Japanese successes. In 15 Pioneer Unit, 'Uchida' left a record of the moral failings of some of the Japanese force. 'It is natural that soldiers on the battlefield should live in close comradeship, but many unpleasant incidents occur. There are no supplies on this island of New Guinea. There are no natural fruits or vegetables, etc, just rice and barley and soup and pickles. Aside from these things there is nothing resembling food. Occasionally, one or two units land canteen supplies, and at such times there are horrible incidents. Last 13 August, while a boat was being unloaded at Basabua, 60 cases of beer disappeared, but nobody knows where. On 4 October, provisions for 15 Pioneer Unit came by patrol boat, and even though they were guarded while unloaded, several things, including a box of condensed milk for patients at Buna, disappeared at night. There are among soldiers some who are unworthy of the name. One of the reasons for all this is that enemy bombings force all unloading to be done at night. Another is that there is no warehouse and supplies cannot be locked, while in the jungle things are easily hidden. In other words, it is extremely convenient for things to disappear.'[18]

Aerial activity on 16 October began at 7.30 am when three A20s attacked bridges over the Kokoda–Kumusi area from 1200 feet, with nothing to report, except the bridges seemed to be unusable. Later, three B25s reconnoitred Buna–Lae–Vitiaz Strait–Gasmata, and attacked villages along the Mambare, also with no enemy activity to report. At 3.55 pm, two B17s attacked a ship in the Buin–Faisi area, claimed near misses, and the heavy bomber presence in

the region continued when three B17s left for Kavieng and Lorengau, followed by four more covering the same targets and searching ocean areas. A report of three aircraft carriers and battleships
at Buin had two aircraft diverted there, but as no warships were
seen from 12,000 feet, a 10,000-ton transport was attacked and
claimed sunk. Once again, the Japanese 144 Regiment was under
the passing bombers, safe from view below the trees. The regimental log noted the time of the flight past, and the lack of damage.
At 8.30 am, the troops passed through Isurava, and had a long rest
at 'the Gap'.[19]

The overriding need for airfields drove the Australian command. Bert Kienzle put carriers to work at Myola 2 clearing an
airstrip, and noted that they did three times as much as Australian
soldiers, who should have been more aware of the need to clear a
runway. However, after a personal investigation on this day,
General Whitehead, US commander of the planes that would have
to use the strip, rejected it.

The battalions rotated through the task at Myola found it strange
after the closeness of the jungle. 'It seemed incredible,' said Bede
Tongs. 'You thought you were seeing things. All of a sudden you
had this large, open area.' After the sweat and accumulated grime
of the past weeks, Bede seized the opportunity to strip off and jump
into the clear flowing stream at Myola, but he just as quickly jumped out – it was icy cold. The alternative, water dipped in a dixie and
poured over the bather, was endured. The rain here on at least one
occasion was sleety, and on two of the mornings there was white
frost on the grass.

The soldiers, busy picking up air-dropped items, soon realised
that some penetrated the crust and were in the morass beneath,
relatively unharmed, but could not be found, and presumably are
there to this day. At least one section carried a tin of biscuits found
in the trees back to their bivouac position to supplement rations.

Rumours abounded. The most attractive and optimistic was that
after Kokoda was captured, the battalion would be flown back to
Moresby, to a rest camp, and when healthy again would be sent on
leave to Australia. This gave the retaking of Kokoda a certain

attraction. After several days at Myola, 3rd Battalion again returned to the muddy trail and eventual contact with the Japanese. On the Kagi track, A Company 2/25th was forward company, and made preparations to engage the Japanese, but a patrol from D Company found the positions abandoned, and the battalion resumed the march to Templeton's Crossing.

At Eora Creek, the 2/33rd began to move out after a cold and uncomfortable night. 16 Platoon, down to nine men and Sergeant Jack Audsley, patrolled out to the west and back, and found no Japanese. The battalion began to push on to Templeton's Crossing itself. The jungle now encountered was the thickest seen. The track snaked through bamboo thickets and prickly vines, then at 11 am the files came out into an open kunai area on a crest, and this gave a view to the north, to the clouds over Kokoda. Below was the creek, its rushing waters audible as it swirled on to the Gap; to the right, a great mountain wall towered almost 4000 feet (1220 metres) higher and to the left, but not visible was the left side, going up another 3000 feet (915 metres). Ahead was Templeton's Crossing, and if 2/33rd occupied it, the battalion would be rested and another battalion would take up the lead.

Soberingly, Japanese bootprints were visible on the track, with water still oozing into them; small fires were found, still alight. The Japanese were just ahead. The nerve-wracking task of scout was done by Private Jock Proudfoot. He saw two Japanese on a ridge, and 16 and 17 Platoons alternated in sweeping out to left and right, clearing the small ridges, and the kunai patches; both platoons saw small parties of Japanese. At 1 pm, D Company 2/33rd arrived at the crossing, and as the track junction was sighted, rifle and machinegun fire drove 18 Platoon to ground. Close behind was a company of 3rd Battalion, which was to take the northern arm of the track and go on to get behind the Japanese holding 2/25th Battalion. Captain Clowes ordered a company attack: 18 Platoon to go on up the track; 16 Platoon to go in from the right; 17 platoon to follow 18. To the surprise of all concerned, 18 and 17 Platoons crossed the 20-foot wide torrent (six-metre) on a small bridge without being shot at, then began the difficult climb up to

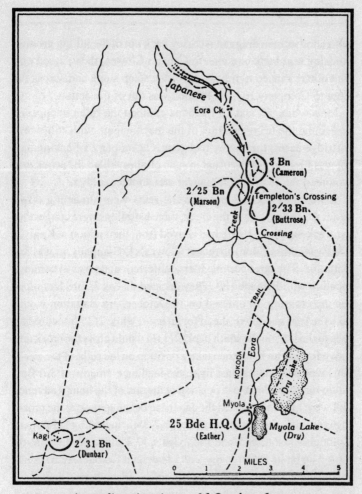

Australian situation on 16 October, 6 pm.

the top of a ridge on the far side. 16 Platoon went up some 200 yards and crossed without any problem, then began to climb a steep re-entrant. All this took time.

After an hour, Sergeant Audsley saw to his left four men, but could not identify them, so sent off three men to do so. As his other six men were crossing a small ravine, they were hit with a volley of rifle fire from about eight Japanese. Audsley was badly wounded in the shoulder. Corporal Goldsborough was the only other NCO left, and was at the rear, as platoon sergeant. He ran forward, and with another man dragged Audsley back out of the killing ground. Audsley sent back one man to Captain Clowes, then passed out. The others carried him back down the steep slope and across the Eora to Company HQ; 16 Platoon was out of the action.

Meanwhile, 17 and 18 Platoons climbed the ridge unopposed and found the firing position of the machinegun, with still-warm cartridge cases; the enemy had gone. C Company's flanking patrol was fired on, and as usual in such clashes, killed the scout, and wounded the section commander and another soldier.

It was now about 3 pm, and the rains were streaming down again. On the far side of the creek, three battalions were congesting the track junction. 2/25th had arrived from their action at Kagi; 2/33rd was coming along in rear of Clowes's D Company, as was 3rd Battalion. The three commanders conferred; none was in communication with Brigade HQ. They decided that as 2/33rd had secured the crossing, as ordered on 10 October, 3rd Battalion would take the lead and move ahead for an hour, while 2/25th secured an area to the left, on the south bank; 2/33rd would cross the creek and move for half an hour, then take a position on the right of the track. This was done, but at last light, the leading elements of 3rd Battalion ran into a Japanese position at the end of the hour's advance and were held there. Then the Japanese began to mortar the crossing area, inflicting three casualties on 2/25th, including Lieutenant Colonel Marson, and one in 2/33rd's 17 Platoon. 3rd Battalion closed up on its D Company, and Lieutenant Colonel Alan Cameron planned an attack for the morning. Elsewhere, Lieutenant Cox's patrol from 2/25th was resupplied at Myola, and continued to Alola.

2/31st Battalion, watching air-drops at Efogi North, saw a C47 lose its rudder, and veer off to crash in the jungle nearby. A patrol was sent, reached the spot, and found three US crew and two Australians dead in the wreckage. Later patrols removed the instruments and sent them back to Moresby. A patrol seeking Japanese was enveloped in fog while on a good track, suddenly found themselves in a Japanese position, quickly killed one and left.

Some members of 15 Pioneers were sent to the Japanese hospital to assist, and 'Uchida' noted that five to eight patients arrived each day in his department, most suffering from diarrhoea, for which there was no medicine left. He added that the enemy were 'fighting desperately' at Guadalcanal, in what both sides realised was a decisive battle. He believed that by the end of the month, Guadalcanal would be taken by the Japanese, Milne Bay operations would begin in November and be successfully concluded by the end of the month, and then in December another drive on Moresby would begin. 'We will stay in Buna until Moresby falls, if it takes all December. We must stay for two months more in Buna.' He pondered his whereabouts at the time of the (Lunar) New Year, accepting that he would not be in Japan. He was most worried about an Allied landing at Buna itself, but 'if there were no such worries, I would be satisfied'. Noboru Wada was told more than 100 planes bombed Moresby and Guadalcanal, combined Japanese air-sea units sank one cruiser and destroyed 37 Allied aircraft, but two Japanese planes were lost and several made forced landings.[20]

Yet another call for help to MacArthur from the neighbouring command in the Solomons came on 17 October. Admiral Ghormley asked for 5th Air Force and RAAF assistance with attacks on Japanese shipping and airfields in the Solomons, and again General Kenney responded. Five Catalinas from Cairns attacked Buka from 1 am, and claimed 14 hits on the runway, resulting in eight big, many small, and three 'huge' blazes, despite low cloud and inaccurate AA. Later reports indicated between 17 and 20 aircraft were destroyed. At 4 am, seven B17s attacked Buin and another reconnoitred the Solomon Sea, claiming hits 100 feet (30 metres) from a transport, and one other claimed hits on an unidentified vessel in Simpson Harbour.

Still employed on Solomons reconnaissance missions, three B17s set off at 7 am to cover sea areas. Flying through AA from two cruisers, Ken McCullar's crew attacked a 15,000-ton ship going into Faisi Harbour, and claimed near misses from 4000 feet. The crew were expecting Zeros to intercept, as the airfield was only 30 miles (48 km) away, but no fighters appeared. At 3.30 pm, three B25s on the usual region reconnaissance dropped seven bombs on the track at Mubo, reported Salamaua AA as intense and accurate, but no ships were seen.

On the Kokoda Trail, on 17 October, the Japanese 144 Regiment arrived at Eora at 9 am, at what the log termed 'the front line', adding that it had been decided the regiment would hold 'the present line'.[21]

Australian 25 Brigade HQ arrived at Templeton's Crossing, and set up in 2/33rd Battalion perimeter. Brigadier Eather congratulated Lieutenant Colonel Buttrose and the company commanders for their work at the enemy positions on the track. At about the time he was doing this, the Japanese landed 30 rounds of mortar and artillery in the battalion area, wounding four men. During the day, and the next, the battalion patrolled the area to the right.

Meanwhile, Lieutenant Colonel Cameron's 3rd Battalion was attacking the Japanese positions ahead. Captain Beckett's D Company had been holding the location where it had encountered the Japanese. Cameron sent Captain Atkinson's B Company up the ridge to the right of D, while A and C Companies under Captain Boag went through a village on the right, getting around into the Japanese rear. Lieutenant Col Richardson had resumed command of 10 Platoon, so Bede Tongs was platoon sergeant. When contact was made, Captain Atkinson ordered 10 Platoon to attack. A runner told Bede the scouts were killed and wounded, then came back and told him Lieutenant Richardson was wounded. Bede saw himself as 'a bit like Charlie Chaplin then. I looked around to see if there was somebody I could say something to, and there was nobody over my shoulder'. He was back in command of the platoon. There was no time for anything but to get on with the action. Captain Atkinson came up and urged him to get on with the attack, but some of the Diggers were making a stretcher to evacuate Richardson, who had been hit high on the left side of the chest. Bede decided to have Richardson moved back, then get on with the attack, despite reminders, 'Sergeant Tongs, this is your attack'. The stretcher was made, Col Richardson placed on it, and the stretcher bearers lifted it, but before it was waist-high the lashings parted and the hapless Richardson thumped to the ground. Frothy, bloody foam began to come from Richardson's wound, and Bede thought he was dying, but Richardson survived when he was eventually evacuated. Atkinson was urging Bede to attack, so he placed the sections with two up and one in reserve, told the Diggers that they would use fire and movement, and before the attack began, himself advanced along a fire lane. Bede took the pin from a four-second grenade, and with his rifle in his left hand, began to crawl down the lane, keeping below the shrubbery that the Japanese had left in it. After some distance, he thought, 'This is a dangerous thing to be doing', looked up and found himself staring down the barrel of a Japanese light machinegun some 10 paces away. The two Japanese manning it were looking intently off to their left, committing the cardinal sin of not watching their own front. Bede carefully released the striker lever from the grenade, holding it close to the ground and allowing the lever to spring into the mud, so that it would not fly away and attract the attention of the Japanese. He waited for one second, threw it into their pit, and followed it with another. Bede did not see the explosions, as he was face down, helmet rim embedded in the mud, with bullets flying over his back from a Japanese flank position. He looked up, saw smoke over the gun position, and ran back to the platoon.

Captain Atkinson was there, 'Get on with this attack', and Bede called to the platoon, 'Get stuck into the bastards', at which the sections advanced, firing from the hip, grenading, giving covering fire so that one section advanced in turn. There was 'terrific morale, calling them all the bastards under the sun, cooeeing and yelling'. Then a runner from the third section came up, calling, 'The bastards are at the back of us!' Bede told him the section would have to handle it, as the two others were going forward, and the man ran off to pass on the message.

The attack rolled on, leaving Japanese bodies in its wake, and Bede saw one man carrying his .303 rifle in one hand and a Jap machinegun in the other. When questioned, the man said he was going to use it, 'as soon as I get the right opportunity'. The assault pressed on into a Japanese headquarters area and found some scattered documents, and something of even more interest – food. Rice was cooking, and some men took a handful as they passed. Also in the position were bags of dried fish and uncooked rice.

So far, the attack had pushed on against light resistance, but inevitably heavy Japanese fire was met, and the assault halted. There had been no Australian casualties. Bede told the men to prepare for a counter-attack, and these came in, but were held. The rear section had killed four Japanese, and rejoined to take part in the defence against the Japanese attacks. Eventually the enemy were held some 25 yards away, and through the night tried sniping and grenading. However, the Japanese rifle made a tinny rattle as the bolt was worked, and the Japanese grenade was activated by thumping it on a hard surface, so the Aussies always knew when the Japs were about to do something. The grenade throwers were urged on with, 'Come on you yellow bastard, let it go,' and answering calls in Japanese came from the darkness, but Japanese pressure lessened as the night wore on.

By this time, it was realised that unless the Japanese had a machinegun firing down a track, most of their fire went high. The fire coming into the 10 Platoon position was somewhat accurate, and Bede Tongs noticed that there were very obvious patches of white tree trunk visible where the Japanese had removed sections of bark. These patches were close to some of the pits occupied by the Aussies, and after he told his men to cover the white areas with mud, the Japanese fire eased.

The B Company 3rd Battalion attack had pushed the Japanese back, and the platoons advanced to a spur 100 yards forward. Japanese weapons, equipment and documents were captured. Private G. Dwight was the stretcher-bearer, and soon built a reputation for fearlessness, going up under fire to bring back the wounded regardless of danger. On one occasion he carried another man 150 yards under fire. By late in the day, Atkinson and Beckett had lost seven killed and 11 wounded. Later, A and C Companies, having reached the enemy flank, attacked a Japanese post, killing 30 without loss, but as the position was not good, the combined companies withdrew to a defensive location.

From 2/25th Battalion, Lieutenant Howes took out a patrol to try to locate the Japanese mortars, but returned without success. Major Millroy was now in command, and the battalion numbered 25 officers and 401 other ranks. Despite intermittent enemy mortaring, no more casualties were suffered by 2/25th. 2/31st sent out its own patrols, and arranged its company commanders: Lieutenant Upcher commanded D Company and Lieutenant Phelps C Company, while Warrant Officer 2 Cameron had 2 Platoon.

In his diary, Monoru Wada noted on 17 October that Japan had been successful at Guadalcanal, sinking a destroyer and setting fire to a tanker, while bombers from Rabaul made a night attack on Port Moresby.

Major General Allen, at Myola, received another message from General Blamey that showed how the wind was blowing. MacArthur, said Blamey, believed the 'extremely light casualties' suffered by the Australians indicated that no serious attempt was being made to throw back the Japanese, therefore Allen was to attack with energy and speed at all Japanese positions; it was essential Kokoda be taken as soon as possible and the Japanese apparently were gaining time by holding Allen with inferior numbers.

Allen immediately replied that the brigade had been in action all day and at the time was holding Japanese counter-attacks, having lost 50 killed and 133 wounded. Allen 'respectfully' informed Blamey that the success of the campaign could not be judged by the scale of casualties, that although 16 Brigade would begin advancing next day, the supply situation dictated that only three battalions could be maintained in action. Allen also reminded Blamey that no commander senior to himself had seen the operating conditions, and suggested a senior staff officer come to 7 Division HQ for discussions. As a final point, Allen included the figures for men unfit for operations because of sickness: 25 Brigade, 730; 16 Brigade, 39. Lieutenant Colonel J. P. Minogue, liaison officer from NGF Headquarters, was moving along the track and arrived at Allen's HQ next day, 18 October.

Later, Allen said that Blamey had two courses open to him after receipt of Allen's message: have confidence in Allen's judgement, or come forward himself or send a general officer forward for a personal appreciation of the situation. Allen emphasised that his troops understood the importance of taking Kokoda, and were more keen to do so than Blamey. Allen did not inform his brigade and battalion commanders of Blamey's message. He had confidence in them, and did not wish to cause unnecessary loss of life among the forward troops.

General MacArthur had sent another message to the US War Department in Washington, asking for more men, planes and ships, despite recent Japanese retreats at Kokoda and Milne Bay, as the Japanese Navy was still very strong and the other enemy forces were far from beaten. However, the 'Germany-first' policy was not to be changed.

Again on 18 October, the B17 force from Australia was targeted on Buin–Faisi, in the neighbouring Solomons theatre. The attack opened at 3.35 am when nine B17s dropped 44 bombs on Kahili airfield and ships, the nearest exploding 100 feet (30 metres) from a ship. At 5.10 am, six more B17s dropped a dozen 1000-pound bombs through heavy, intense and accurate AA, claiming damage to a heavy cruiser and two other possible hits. Three of the big bombs were duds and another three were jettisoned. Immediately behind them were five more B17s, which dropped four 1000-pounders and 14 500-pounders, to claim four near misses. Four Zeros attacked Ken McCullar's B17 during the bomb run, and co-pilot Harry Staley thought the end had come. He looked up and a Zero was coming head-on, flashes twinkling from the wing cannon and cowling machineguns, four streams of tracer seeming to fly right at him in the cockpit. They missed, though Ken McCullar maintained his steady run. As soon as the bombs were gone, McCullar took the big bomber right down onto the water, just high enough to keep the propeller tips out of the waves, and flew for home. The Zeros circled, but did not go down to attack again.

Two other B17s flew sea search missions, ending with attacks on Faisi seaplane base. One claimed hits on five four-engined flying boats, and that bomb blast knocked out eight float-planes nearby, and the other came in a few minutes later, claiming a direct hit on one flying boat. The first also claimed a successful strafing attack on a 500-ton ship, which caught fire. After returning to Moresby, the B17s flew to Mareeba for two days' rest and maintenance. Over New Guinea, at 8 am, three B25s flew the usual reconnaissance of Buna–Lae–Vitiaz Strait–Gasmata–Buna. A small ship was seen near Buna and promptly attacked with two bombs and machineguns. Unfortunately, it was friendly. The US 128 Infantry Regiment was using two 20-ton luggers to ferry men and supplies to a newly-established Allied position at Pongani. Four hours later, another B25 on reconnaissance dropped five bombs on Paiva Bridge, missing by 100 feet (30 metres) at either end. At 2.40 pm, a B17 on reconnaissance went down to 2000 feet to strafe four schooners at Manus Island. The afternoon B25 reconnaissance of the Buna–Salamaua–Lae–Gasmata area saw some action, with bombs hitting a single-engined twin-float aircraft (probably an Aichi E13A 'Jake') at the village on Pilelo Island, more fell on the track near Mubo, troops seen 14 miles (22 km) south-east of Mubo were strafed, and some of the men were definitely hit by machinegun fire. 'Uchida' heard the air-raid alarm sounding continuously, and 'the sound of bombing was heard all day'. Noboru Wada wrote that Japanese planes shot down 20 Allied aircraft over Guadalcanal, and that enemy planes had attacked Giruwa, but caused no damage.

At Eora, 144 Regiment noted the times of the passing flights, but the Japanese were not detected or attacked. In I/144 was Fumitoshi Yasuoka, who had joined the regiment on 10 October 1941, taken part in the Guam and New Britain landings, and arrived at Basabua on 21 July. Yasuoka was in 2nd Lieutenant Hiroshi Nakamoto's platoon, Captain Naoma Fujisaka's company of Lieutenant Colonel Tsukamoto's I Battalion. He kept a diary with few entries, but on this day wrote, 'No provisions. Some people are said to be eating the flesh of Tori. It is said to have a good flavour'. 'Tori' was an abbreviation of 'toriko', a captive.[22]

In the wet 2/33rd Battalion position at Templeton's Crossing, it was decided to retaliate against the persistent Japanese mortars, which were inflicting a steady toll of casualties in both 25 and the newly-arrived 16 Brigade. A mortar position was made on the banks of the Eora at the crossing, and a 2/2nd Battalion mortar was also emplaced. Captain Power went forward as observation officer and a 2/2nd officer was at the firing position. During the advance, a second mortar crew had been trained as understudies by the 2/33rd mortar team. The second team asked for permission to fire this mission, and were allowed to do so. The first three bombs were fired, but the fourth exploded in the barrel with tragic results; all three men were killed. An hour later 2/2nd Battalion's mortar also was destroyed in the same way. At this stage, no one knew why the explosions occurred. Throughout, the Japanese fired their own heavy weapons at the crossing area. 16 Brigade was tasked to take over the fighting and 25 Brigade was given 'rest', which for 2/33rd consisted of moving back to Myola and on to Myola 2, clearing the area for air drops and cutting the grass with bayonets to make a landing strip! This activity went on until 24 October.

3rd Battalion remained in the leading positions, and patrols from both sides inflicted casualties. A and C Companies rejoined after their successful action the day before. A and D Companies of 2/25th were placed under command of Lieutenant Colonel Cameron, and set off, with their own Captain Blundell as commander of the two-company force, to join Cameron's 3rd Battalion. However, no guides were provided, and they could not locate 3rd Battalion. They did bump into some Japanese, killing three, for the loss of one man in A Company 2/25th.

The wry humour of the Australian soldier came to the fore, creating anecdotes that would be retold for years. In 3rd Battalion, in the mud and rain, few rations, no fires, Japanese artillery fire and snipers an ever-present danger, when Emmett Francis was asked 'How goes it?' he would invariably reply, 'Could be worse'. One day, someone took in the situation, and asked, 'How could it be worse, Emmett?' Back came the answer, 'Just you wait and see'.

For 19 October, apart from the usual reconnaissance sorties over the Vitiaz Strait and to Faisi, there were no missions recorded flown in the Kokoda area. At dawn, Lieutenant Colonel Tsukamoto, acting commander 144 Regiment, went to the forward positions to inspect I/144 defence works. It was thought the Japanese intended attacking on the right of the Australian positions, so Lieutenant Colonel Edgar's 2/2nd Battalion went to the right of 2/33rd. 2/2nd Battalion sent 11 Platoon, under Lieutenant W. Ryan, to patrol to the right. In a contact, the platoon lost three dead, whose bodies could not be recovered until the Japanese had been forced out of their positions. Meanwhile, Lieutenant Colonel Edgar had been to a conference at Brigade HQ, returned, and gave his orders for the battalion attack next day. 2/2nd Battalion was using the new Australian Owen gun on operations, and there was interest from the other battalions in the unit report on the sub-machinegun.

At 11 am, for an hour, three Australian mortars bombarded the Japanese position, inflicting casualties among communications and mountain artillery members of the regimental headquarters, and finally the headquarters moved back 300 yards, out of the beaten zone of the three-inch bombs. In the Australian positions, some satisfaction was derived from the shouting and screaming heard from the enemy positions during the bombardment.[23]

Lieutenant Sakamoto, commander 2 MG Company, 144 Regiment, wrote that rations had been issued, a few ounces per man in the headquarters section, and slightly more with bean paste for the platoons. He added, 'Because of the food shortage, some companies have been eating human flesh [Australian soldiers]. The taste is said to be good. We are looking for anything edible and now are eating grass, leaves and the pith of trees. These don't agree with us, but can't be helped'.[24]

This statement, because of the implications, was translated separately and independently by three different Allied translators when the document arrived at the offices of the Allied Translator and Interpreter Section, GHQ SWPA. It was the first indication accepted at headquarters level that the Japanese had resorted to cannibalism. Forward Australian troops had several times found their dead with evidence of large pieces of meat carefully removed. Incidents such as these tended to make the Allied soldier regard the Japanese as little more than beasts, sub-humans to be exterminated. But the above diary entry, though not available until

Sakamoto's documents were captured early in November, was the first documentary evidence from the Japanese to arrive at Allied headquarters.

The Japanese 41 Regiment submitted a report on health matters to Horii's headquarters. The report described the unhealthy and unsanitary conditions in which the units were forced to live and operate, just as did similar reports on the Allied side, and stated that effective strength was 1163, with 282 patients treated in the regimental medical unit, and another 445 ill and not fit for battle. Sub-unit strengths were given as: HQ 105; I/41 260 all ranks; III/41 324 all ranks.

Their opponents were not much better off. Strengths for 25 Brigade (on 23 October) were: 2/25th 416 all ranks; 2/31st 471 all ranks; 2/33rd 388 all ranks. By 20 October, the brigade had lost 68 killed, 135 wounded and 771 sick. On both sides, illness inflicted several times the casualties resulting from battle.

The Australian 3rd Battalion was active. Two platoons of A Company, under Captain J. S. Jeffrey, attacked a detected Japanese position to the right front of B Company, killing 15 Japanese and taking four machineguns, but lost four killed and six wounded. However, the well-concealed Japanese continued to hold the position. Sergeant Bede Tongs had cause to regret his attempt to look after one of the Diggers. Harry Kennedy was suffering from the dampness, and coughing a lot, so Bede pointed out a spot where sunlight came through the jungle canopy and warmed a place near platoon headquarters, with the suggestion that Kennedy go there and take advantage of the sunlight. But no sooner had Kennedy done so than a Japanese mortar bomb came through the gap, and wounded him. Where possible, 3rd Battalion used the two-inch mortar, and Bede particularly liked the rifle-launched grenade as a way of placing high-explosive into enemy positions.

In 2/25th Battalion, the detached A and D Companies returned after failing to locate 3rd Battalion, and when finally the battalion moved up onto the right of 3rd Battalion, it was replaced by 2/3rd.

Very early on 20 October, seven RAAF Catalinas attacked Buin –Faisi with 58 bombs, claimed several near misses and reported that six bombs were duds. At Buna, the Japanese diarist 'Uchida' observed that enemy air attacks had greatly decreased, with only reconnaissance flights going overhead. He wrote of many patients along the Giruwa road, and in the front lines. 'Very many have reportedly died of illness. About two or three days ago, I had my first diarrhoea.'

In the mountains, 2/2nd Battalion was to attack the Japanese positions from the right, supported by 2/1st from the position held by 3rd Battalion. The Militia soldiers watched the AIF coming up to battle, bayonets fixed, and to some they 'looked like the greatest specimens of soldiers we'd ever seen'. Captain Fairbrother's A Company 2/2nd was led by guides from 3rd Battalion to the position from which the company was to attack and secure the right flank. At 10 am, the guides said there was another 90 minutes of travel, but 18 minutes later the forward elements were fired on, and Smith's 8 Platoon was under light machinegun fire. Hodge's 9 Platoon went well around to the right, getting into the enemy's rear, were themselves pinned, but forced the Japanese out of their original position holding 8 Platoon. The MG Platoon under Sergeant Lacey also circled out to the right, to get to 9 Platoon, but was met by enemy and held. Now it was 2.30 pm; movement through the jungle and across the terrain could not be speeded up, no matter what the urgency. At 4 pm, two sections of Lieutenant Coyle's 13 Platoon went up to the left of 8 Platoon, inflicted casualties on the Japanese, but darkness fell before more could be done.

B Company 2/2nd, commanded by Captain I. B. Ferguson, was almost on top of the Japanese before it was fired on, and suffered casualties at once. 10 Platoon went to the right and, despite light machinegun fire, pushed the Japanese out of their position. The company went on, but again was fired on, though by now B Company had reached the end of the feature it was to clear. Among the dead Japanese behind it were two officers, one of whom was Lieutenant Hirano, the diarist, plus a medium machinegun and mount, rifles, clothing and rations. It had been the position of 1 Company, I/144. B Company went into reserve, and waited out the night.

Captain Swinton's C Company 2/2nd was to protect the right

flank, and had sent platoons and sections to assist as necessary, losing four killed and four wounded. Captain C. F. W. Baylis commanded D Company, to attack in conjunction with B Company along two spurs. With 16 Platoon on the right of the spur and 17 on the top and left, while 18 came along in the rear, the company began the attack in platoon files with scouts well forward by 100 yards to allow manoeuvre when contact was made. As soon as the Japanese fired, the platoons went into open formation and began advancing by fire and movement using light machineguns and grenades, despite heavy Japanese machinegun fire.

16 Platoon was held, with Lieutenant Tanner wounded, so Captain Baylis sent Lieutenant Goodman and 18 Platoon to maintain the assault on that flank. Corporal Roberts's section of 18 Platoon destroyed a medium machinegun and crew with grenades, and the momentum was maintained with fire at the base of trees and likely enemy positions as the force advanced, bouncing the Japanese out of their second position. But 150 yards on, another position was waiting. The battalion mortars fired, but communications were bad and the bombs did little good. B Company, mauled by fire on fixed lines, withdrew to the D Company area. Captain Baylis was told that no assistance was available, and he then sent Captain Blamey with 16 Platoon around to the left, which forced the Japanese to withdraw. The company went on for another 110 yards, and spent the night in positions below the Japanese. It rained, and in the dark and cold, with Japanese and Australian dead scattered through the silent dripping jungle, the Diggers could hear their enemies chattering and moving around the nearby positions.

In the 2/1st, tasked to give fire support, Captain Sanderson's A Company was astride the track, with the river on its left. Captain Basil Catterns's B Company was to the right on a ridge, Barclay's C Company was higher still as the right flank, and when it arrived Simpson's D Company was to fill in behind A Company.

The Japanese were only about 60 yards away, but could not be seen, so fire support had to be given with care, as mortars and machineguns were to be used. Nothing could be seen of the success of 2/2nd Battalion, which attacked down the slope from the right.

2/1st could not keep up the rate of fire, as the battle went on all day. Japanese retaliation was by mountain gun, and tree bursts in C Company 2/1st wounded five, including one officer.

It was decided that Captain Catterns's B Company 2/1st would attack at first light next day, passing through 2/2nd's company in front, and continue down to the track at the foot of the valley. Catterns made a detailed attack plan, including fire support and a diversion, to be provided by the CSM, WO2 McIntosh. During the day, 3rd Battalion had been relieved by 2/1st, and moved back to Myola, coming under command of 25 Brigade on 31 October. In 2/25th, one man was killed, and Lieutenant Steele and a Digger wounded by Japanese mortar fire.

At Eora, 1 Company I/144 was recorded in the regimental log as having 'suffered heavy losses from the enemy's attack and was almost annihilated. Lieutenant Hirano was among the casualties'. At midday, the headquarters began retreating to Mt LeHunte. Lieutenant Morimoto, of the HQ, also noted Hirano's death. Hirano, with Superior Private Doi and four men, was the captor of Lieutenant Colonel Key, CO 2/14th Battalion, in September. At 2 pm, 144 Regiment HQ reached Mt LeHunte, but soon after word was received that the Australians had broken through 'on the left flank of the second battalion' (II/144, Horie), and the HQ moved to a new position on the peak of the mountain.[25]

From Myola, 574 carrier loads were despatched to Station 1, en route to Eora Creek, and despite US refusals to have aircraft operate out of Myola, an Australian Hudson landed there during the day. After consideration of the tragic mortar bomb explosions, Brigadier Lloyd informed Major General Allen that fuses delivered by air drop were faulty, and that they should be examined by a specialist.

On 21 October there were no attack missions recorded flown in support of the Kokoda campaign, though the usual three B25s on reconnaissance over the coastal areas strafed a boat, and overlapping midnight into 22 October, seven Catalinas attacked ships at Faisi, scoring no hits. From Mareeba, at 3 pm on 21 October, nine B17s flew to Jackson's (7-Mile), and were prepared for a mission, but continuous rain had made the runway very soft and it was not advisable to try take off with a fully loaded B17. Noboru Wada, however, noted in his diary that the B17s attacking Buna were driven away by AA fire. No such mission is recorded in the Allied Air Force mission reports, but Wada may have used an incorrect date. 'Uchida', of 15 Pioneers, wrote: 'Today, for the first time in a long while, good news came in. Following message was received from the commander at Guadalcanal – "Rest assured victory is ours. Good news from Guadalcanal in the Solomons, where for some two and a half months a vital battle has been fought, brings tears of happiness".'[26]

On the Kokoda Trail, the dawn attack by B Company 2/1st Battalion found the Japanese had gone during the night. B Company continued the advance as leading company. As the Diggers filed through the Japanese position, they noted the fortifications and living areas, and deduced that they had been opposed by a battalion. Fifty-eight Japanese had been killed by 2/2nd.

In 2/2nd Battalion, A Company was to have patrolled to protect the right flank and link with a company of 2/3rd coming up. 7 Platoon reported the Japanese gone, and counted 14 dead Japanese in the immediate area. The company moved to the next night position; it had lost six dead and 10 wounded. Ferguson's B Company 2/2nd cleared downhill to the creek, arriving at midday. The company reported it had passed through the Japanese battalion position, companies set out from central HQ, into which eight telephone lines ran. The company also lost five killed and 10 wounded, but counted 12 dead Japanese in its area. Another 11 dead Japanese were counted in an area on the right. Captain Baylis reported that his D Company had 'worked and fought extremely well' in the action. The battalion diary noted that the campaign was the most strenuous in the history of the unit, and at the end of the action strength was 30 officers and 463 other ranks. The battalion lost 34 killed, including three officers and seven NCOs, plus 52 wounded. Some of those killed and wounded had low enlistment numbers: NX906, NX1007, NX1291, NX1427, NX1746 and NX1764, indicating that this was at least their third or fourth

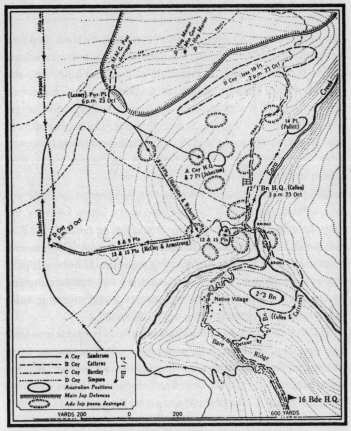

Eora Creek, 22-23 October.

war campaign, since enlistment in 1939, in North Africa, Greece and Crete. Recommendations for awards in 2/2nd Battalion were: the Military Cross for Baylis, Fairbrother and Ferguson; the Military Medal for Corporals Bates, Devine and Pennycook, plus Private Blackford; Mentioned In Dispatches for Private S. E. Evans. Five men had been commissioned, including Sergeant Blain, who had been killed on 20 October.

The pursuit was taken up. While 2/1st moved along the track, 2/3rd followed, parallel and 2000 feet higher (610 metres), along the ridge. Then the track swung away from the river and up to the ridge top. The Japanese were found again. As usual, they had selected a good position for their purpose. A piece of steeply rising ground gave them a view of some 300 yards of the track, and they covered it with fire. 2/1st's B Company went into an outflanking move, but the Japanese had thought of that, and killed two and wounded four. Then it started to rain again. Captain Sanderson's A Company 2/1st was to climb the steep slope on the right, get above the Japanese and attack from that side. The combination of rain, slope, heavy packs and thick jungle prevented A Company from carrying out the attack before dark, so the battalion settled where it was for the night.

2/3rd Battalion also had encountered Japanese on the flank, killing a machinegunner. However, late in the afternoon, they too were held by fire from a gun that could not be located. It killed Private D. J. Fernance and wounded two other men. The Japanese were only 10 yards away, and his sling swivel could be heard clicking, yet he could not be found. It was getting dark and the company had to wait until morning. During the night, a platoon commander went up and brought back one of the wounded.

2/25th Battalion moved back to a dump area for a rest, and time was spent with issue of new clothes, washing, repairing the track in the area and preparing a battalion bivouac site. The battalion stayed for two days, then moved to Templeton's Crossing on 24 October. Much of this new issue came on the backs of native carriers, and 591 went from Myola to Station 1 on this day. A sign of better things to come was the landing of the first Douglas DC3/C47 transport at Myola 2. 2/31st Battalion noted that the day was, 'Exceptional – no rain'.

The Japanese 144 Regiment decided to move back to the vicinity of Kokoda Gap, at midday headquarters handed over to 41 Regiment arrivals, started the walk, and three hours later the Gap was reached. At Buna, 'Wada' wrote that there were reconnaissance flights, and the fifth plane, a B25, was shot down. There is no record of this loss in Allied Air Force records. A Japanese intelligence report of 21 October stated that Colonel Kay [sic], CO of 14 Battalion [sic] said the Australian force was composed of the 7th Division's 18 Brigade, with 9, 10 and 12 Battalions, and 21 Brigade, 14, 16 and 20 Battalions, with in addition 27 Brigade, with 25, 31 and 35 Battalions. The report did not give the date when Key was supposed to have given this information.[27]

The usual reconnaissance missions were flown on 22 October, with nothing to report. At Moresby, General Whitehead ordered the B17s be dispersed, so at 8 am the 63rd Squadron flew from Jackson's strip to Durand, then at 5.30 pm to Ward's, where it was found that Ward's was not suited to B17 operations, and it would take 90 minutes for the squadron to take off, so they flew back to Jackson's. The weather over the mountains was so bad that the afternoon reconnaissance by three B25s was cancelled. However, two RAAF Hudson bombers landed at Myola. During the night, the Japanese bombed Jackson's and Ward's strips at 8.20, but no damage was done to the assembled B17s. General Kenney spoke to MacArthur about the award of a medal to Major Bill Benn, who had been commander of 63rd Bomb Squadron for two months, and had done much to show that the low-level attacks with B17s could be successful. Next day, Benn was brought to Brisbane, and the medal was pinned on.

A report was received in the Japanese positions at Buna that 30 to 40 'white men' raided Eda village, 25 miles (40 km) away. This may have been a reference to 2/6th Commando activity.[28]

During the night, the Japanese holding 16 Brigade had slipped away, undetected by the Australians. When Simpson's A Company 2/1st attacked the position early on 22 October, it was empty. The battalion found a position prepared for more than 300 yards along the track. Behind was a company position and the body of a young Rabaul native, dead of starvation or exhaustion. The battalion pushed on. The Japanese were waiting not far ahead.

Just after 11 am, 2/3rd Battalion took over the task of advance companies, to the relief of two of the gunners from 2/1st Field Regiment who had attached themselves to 2/1st Battalion and were at the time the forward scouts. It was assumed that the Japanese would be intending to make a stand at the Eora Creek crossing as the terrain was well suited, so Brigadier Lloyd earlier had told Lieutenant Colonel Cullen to send a (2/1st) company well out to the left, avoid Eora Creek village and advance to Alola. Captain

Simpson's D Company was given this task, but did not have enough rations for the time they would be away; supply was still not adequate. In an example of 'one of those things', part of HQ Company followed the 70 men of D Company off the track and on their journey, and it was hours before the mistake was noticed. The strayed elements of HQ Company did not rejoin until next day.

Just before the track reached Eora Creek crossing, it followed a naked, open spur as it descended. The spur came to an abrupt end then went down steeply to the village itself some 100 yards below. 2/3rd Battalion came under fire from mortars and machineguns positioned on the mountain slope across the creek. 2 Section, 1 Platoon A Company was leading the 2/3rd, and as they were strung out on the edge of the creek, and paused, Bill Langham called not to stand too long, as it could be a trap and then the Japanese opened fire. Four men were hit, one dying of wounds, and another wounded during the evacuation of these men. Other men were hit as Japanese fire swept the village area and the spur, and more casualties were suffered by the stretcher bearers. This platoon was led by Sergeant Arthur Carson, who was then about 50 years old and who had won the Distinguished Conduct Medal in 1917, as a stretcher bearer at Bullecourt. More were killed and wounded among the combined medical elements of 2/1st and 2/3rd, including the medical officer for 2/3rd, Captain Maurice Goldman.

As A Company 2/1st reached the bare spur, Lieutenant Colonel Cullen ordered Captain Sanderson to move left and outflank the Japanese. This easy to read phrase in reality covers an exhausting expedition so typical of the physical effort requiring much time, before battle could be joined, that was not even vaguely understood by distant headquarters, particularly MacArthur's GHQ SWPA. To carry out this order, Captain Sanderson's men had to go back out of view of the Japanese, cut their own track down 100 yards to the swiftly flowing creek, then climb a 3700-foot (1130-metre) slope on the far side, follow it along for the requisite distance, alert for Japanese outposts on the curving mountain, make contact and attack before night if possible, if not, in the morning. It was about midday as they turned off the main track. They were then out of contact with the battalion, unless runners were used.

The Japanese were firing at all who crossed the bare spur and went on into the village. Captain Catterns sent 11 Platoon (2/1st) along the left side of the trail, and the company second-in-command and CSM were chased into an old pit dug by 21 Brigade, then machinegunned and mortared for three hours as they lay there. WO2 McIntosh was wounded by a bullet and also hit his head on the mortar base-plate in the bottom of the pit. A detour was made to the village.

The open spur was known and ranged upon by the Japanese, but Lieutenant Colonel Cullen and Lieutenant Colonel Stevenson were there, with some HQ personnel, and men of rifle companies of both battalions, totalling more than 130 men. Mortars and a mountain gun fired on this obvious target, causing many casualties, including Lieutenant Colonel John Stevenson, CO 2/3rd, hit in the ear and side of the head by shrapnel, but remained in command. 2/1st lost five killed. 11 Platoon (2/1st) was pinned down in the village.

At 5 pm, Brigadier Lloyd arrived. Earlier messages received by his staff gave the impression that things were going well and that the battalions were securing favourable positions, but by the time he was there in person it was obvious that this was not so. This came about as the maps were of little use, the ground in reality was quite different to that portrayed, and in fact the Japanese had the best positions. Brigadier Lloyd ordered that in the morning the first bridge over the creek was to be captured by 2/3rd Battalion, immediately followed by 2/1st taking the second bridge. 2/3rd would provide guides to take 2/1st on to the bridge. Reconnaissance for these attacks by the commanders was hampered by continuous mortar and medium machinegun fire, but some idea of the terrain was gathered. There were no accurate maps or air photos.

By the end of the day, the Japanese defenders had demonstrated their ability to bring down accurate fire on any target seen below them. 2/1st was moving to outflank them, with its A and D Companies struggling along the left-hand slopes, and a platoon of B Company also was on a patrol to the left. Part of 2/1st HQ Company, by mischance, had also gone to the left and was making its way back. To attack the bridges next morning, Lieutenant Colonel Cullen was left with his C Company, two platoons of B Company, and some of his own HQ.

The 2/1st plan was for C Company to take the second bridge at first light after 2/3rd Battalion secured the first. What the unit history described as a vigorous protest by 2/1st was raised about whether or not 2/1st was to go ahead if 2/3rd failed to secure the first bridge, but it was decided 2/1st would attack in any case.

Meanwhile, the A Company 2/1st force had been split up. When crossing the creek, the platoons had done so at different places, and after several hours' climbing, Captain Sanderson halted 7 Platoon to wait for the others. The platoon commander, Keith Johnson, had been commissioned that day, and had been the sergeant. A corporal was platoon sergeant, and the sections were commanded by a corporal, a lance corporal and a private. The climb up the sodden slope had exasperated the Diggers, who were not made happier when Sanderson decided to go on and attack as planned without the other platoons: there were only 17 men. To quieten the mutterings, Sanderson said that they were going to attack as it was expected of them by the CO, 'now get going'. After travelling along the ridge, the platoon turned down to the creek again. Going was difficult, as they had to descend steep rock faces by lowering each other. It was then discovered that Company HQ had become separated from 17 Platoon and was somewhere back along the ridge. Sanderson's runner, 'Sandy' Rayward, was left alone to wait for them while the rest went on. As dusk fell, the trail was seen some distance away, and then a single unarmed Japanese saw them, stared in surprise and fled. Sanderson decided a night attack could not be made and waited until morning.

8 Platoon, under Lieutenant Stewart Blakiston, had been behind 7 Platoon but found them gone from the ridge top and were unable to track them. Blakiston decided to carry on with the given mission, the attack, but assumed Sanderson would send someone back for them. No one arrived, and the force spent a cold night in the rain at 8000 feet (2440 metres).

▲

On the Japanese side, at 9.30 am, reinforcements arrived for 144 Regiment, and at 11.30 am headquarters issued regimental Op Order 155, giving instructions for guarding the Gap area.[29] Horii's headquarters at Kokoda, at noon issued Order 130A:

'1. The Stanley Detachment has been attacked daily by the enemy since the first part of October, and on the night of the 20th yielded the position in the vicinity of Iola and retreated to the vicinity of the Gap. The enemy suffered very great losses, after which the pursuit became slow.

'2. The Yazawa Detachment shall relieve the Stanley Detachment. The organisation of the Yazawa Butai (newly become the Stanley Detachment) is as follows: 41 Infantry Regiment (less 1 battalion, less one company), a Company of Mountain Artillery, a platoon of Engineers (Takamori), two sections of No. 3 Wireless Unit, Field Hospital evacuation squad. Relief may be expected about the end of October.

'3. The present Stanley Detachment shall firmly defend the present position in the vicinity of the Gap, and shall make it the key position for the next offensive. After being relieved, it shall reform at Kokoda.

'4. The main infantry strength of the Yazawa Butai shall commence to move immediately, proceed to the vicinity of the Gap, and relieve the Stanley Detachment. All other units shall be under supervision of the Yazawa Butai commander upon his arrival at the Gap. The staff officer shall point out the details of organisation and equipment.

'5. Colonel Yazawa shall assign the main strength among the remaining forces to defend strongly the key position at the rear, in the vicinity of Giruwa, and shall appoint a unit, consisting of a machinegun company, as a nucleus for aerial defence near the river crossing of Papaki. The latter unit shall be under my supervision after departure of the main strength of the regiment.

'6. I shall remain at the present location. The detachment commander:

Horii, Tomitaro'.[30]

As well as the Japanese enemy, Major General Allen was in

jeopardy from his superiors. General Blamey again had signalled about the slow advance, and urged Allen to move more boldly rather than attack with a single battalion or company. This was followed by another from MacArthur, in Brisbane, stating that progress was '*not* repeat *not*' satisfactory, in MacArthur's opinion because of faulty tactical handling of the Australian troops. The distant Supreme Commander pointed out that only a small portion of the available force was engaging the enemy, the supply situation and troop condition was better than the enemy's, and 'weather conditions are neutral'. He concluded by urging a prompt capture of Kokoda.

Allen replied that he had been hurt by MacArthur's message, adding that operational difficulties in New Guinea were not understood by those further back, or, as he tactfully phrased it, 'not fully realised'. He repeated that the country was not suitable for wide quick encirclements, that lack of carriers had confined him to one line of advance and to employment of only one brigade, that the units had done well and all realised the need to capture Kokoda, but his force was now in 'the roughest and most precipitous' part of the track.

On 23 October, once more the B17 force attacked Rabaul. From 2.45 am, 20 B17s attacked from as low as 200 feet up to 8000 feet, dropped 149 bombs on ships, claimed at least four direct hits, and at least 33 near misses, resulting in one cruiser, one destroyer and two transports sunk, three other transports damaged and a tanker on fire. Despite heavy AA fire, only two machinegun hits were made on a B17. Six other B17s turned back or could not find the target. Bad weather was encountered off the northern coast of New Guinea, but over the target cloudbase was 5500 feet.

These heavy bomber attacks made at night on ships in distant Rabaul harbour were intended to assist the forces fighting in New Guinea by sinking or damaging ships before they could deliver cargoes to Buna. The B17 crews fought a war entirely different to that endured by the infantry battalions waiting out the sodden, cold nights on the mountain slopes, and the following account of one of the low-level attacks into the harbour is provided to illustrate that aspect of the air war waged in support of the Kokoda ground forces. From the 63rd Squadron, Captain Ken McCullar, already credited with sinking or damaging four Japanese ships, on this mission claimed the destroyer sunk, with two direct hits amidships. He had in the bomb bay four bombs fitted with skip-bombing fuses, so flew around looking for a suitable target. Outside the harbour he saw what was at first thought to be a light cruiser, later identified as a destroyer. Diving to low-level, he attacked at 150 feet at 230 mph (370 kph), releasing two bombs. One flew into the hull and the other hit the deck and rolled off. The explosion almost rolled the ship over, and it was claimed as sunk. McCullar was recommended for a Silver Star. Captain Green claimed hits on the cruiser, a medium and a small transport, while Lieutenant Carl Hustad hit a 10,000-ton transport, leaving it on fire. The squadron was jubilant at the success of the skip-bombing tactic, calling it 'jackpot night'.

But again, postwar investigation could not identify any shipping losses that could be credited to 5th Air Force attacks on this date. Over New Guinea, in the early morning, six A20s attacked the enemy at Deniki, and strafed the Kokoda trail, but there was little to be seen.

While the B17s had been on the Rabaul mission, 2/1st Battalion had been busy at Eora crossing. The cold penetrating rain had ceased at 2.30 am, and the moon came out. This opportunity was seized by Lieutenant Colonel Cullen, who took Captain Cox, the adjutant, on a reconnaissance. They went through the village to Eora Creek, and across the first bridge without being fired on. This was a surprise, and they crossed back to discuss the situation. Cullen decided that C Company (2/1st) should move forward at once to get across the bridges in the moonlight, which was not bright enough to allow the enemy good shooting, but did let C Company see where it was going. Hopefully, C Company could be among the Japanese positions before dawn, and then deal with them in daylight.

While Cox remained near the bridge with a telephone, to pass back any later information, Cullen struggled back up the muddy slope to organise C Company's advance. Moving quietly along a sloppy, but level piece of track, then down a mud-slippery slope to the creek, laden with weapons and equipment, was a difficult task that would soon be confronted by C Company. Most of the time lost by the travelling back and forth was due to the problems of communications. The radios were useless in the mountains, and there was not enough line available to link the companies with HQ. Once the flanking companies moved away, they were alone.

However, this piece of initiative paid off. C Company moved down and crossed the first bridge without incident, and the leading platoon crossed the second before the Japanese reacted. Following platoons dashed over the bridge between bursts of fire. However, Captain Barclay was on the Japanese side of the creek, though almost literally and figuratively in the dark. The moon had gone, and dawn was some two hours away; he had little knowledge of the terrain over which he was to fight. The Japanese had made many tracks through the area, and cleared away all the undergrowth in a basin between two spurs. The track itself left the second bridge, swung back over a small creek, went west up a spur, then turned back north and recrossed the small creek, in effect, forming a half-loop over creek-spur-creek. The Japanese, of course, knew the ground well.

In the darkness and with little information, confusion became widespread, with the Australian platoons simply going towards the sound of Japanese guns and attacking. Lieutenant Bill Pollitt's 14 Platoon found themselves back in the main creek after turning right from the bridge, then in a pocket with Japanese all around the top grenading them. Lance Corporal John Hunt went back, around the slopes and up to the top, then worked his way along, killing the grenadiers. Pollitt credits Hunt with saving the platoon from complete destruction; only seven were unwounded. One of C Company, 'Legs' Eagleton, was hit in the head, and was asked if he could get back to the aid post alone. He got to his feet, waded the river under fire from every Japanese who could bring a weapon to bear and disappeared into the jungle, making it safely.

McCloy's 13 Platoon went left after crossing the bridge, followed by C Company HQ, and was at once in heavy contact. Many Japanese were killed on the slope, including an officer, who may have been Miyaji, commander of the defending force there. Mc-Cloy tried to attack north, as ordered. However, advance was impossible in the face of the Japanese fire that dominated the cleared floor of the basin and lower slopes, and a firefight went on for more than two hours. Then firing from the left was heard; A Company was attacking.

Sergeant Bob Armstrong commanded 15 Platoon, last across and into the action. He sent his sections over between bursts of machinegun fire raking the bridge. As day was breaking, he went left as ordered and found Lieutenant McCloy. As Captain Barclay could not be found, McCloy took 15 Platoon under command also, and sent them to the right to link with 14 Platoon. Armstrong's men were halted by accurate machinegun fire on an open slope, losing three killed, so McCloy brought them back to a better position. Barclay, commissioned from the ranks in 1939 and a veteran of Middle East battles, popular and fun-loving, had been killed.

Captain Sanderson and 7 Platoon had checked in a full circle to find a sign of the other two platoons, with no success. Japanese could be seen not far away, and the trail. The Australians then attacked with grenades and Tommy guns, and 1 Section pushed on to the riverbank. Intense fire cracked and thumped around the other two sections on the slope, and the Japanese reacted strongly; wounded and dead began to increase. Sanderson had been using a German machine pistol, the MP38, commonly called a Schmeisser, a trophy from the Middle East. Then he too was hit, and only four of the platoon were left alive on the slope. A Japanese had called out in English, asking if the Aussies had had enough, but Sanderson called back in defiance. More than 300 empty cartridge cases were counted around his body; bullets from a light machinegun had hit him from behind.

Private Ron Grout, the last section commander, called to the others to join 1 Section at the creek, but only one man made it with him. One more was lost, drowned, as they crossed, and eventually the eight survivors of 7 Platoon arrived back at 2/1st HQ. When the dead eventually were recovered, it was found that their boots and some items of clothing were gone, and a piece of flesh had been cut from one of them.

Meanwhile, back at the spur on the far side of the bridges, B Company and battalion HQ were to follow along the track as soon as it was light, but the machinegun and mountain gun fire, as on the day before, halted this move. An alternate route, going down to the right, through the jungle and over the creek was made, but all this took time, and it was not until 11.20 am that the company reached a point between the bridges. Then, linked by telephone cable to the positions behind, they advanced. On the far side, they found the survivors of the section from 2/3rd Battalion: one dead, one wounded, and two others. Battalion HQ of 2/1st was established east of the second bridge. Lieutenant Pollitt and the survivors of his 14 Platoon appeared and the wounded were evacuated.

B Company 2/1st pushed ahead, led by Lance Corporal Hunt from Pollitt's platoon, who had remained. Tragically, Hunt was killed soon after. B Company in turn was held by the intense fire from machineguns and rifles from the ridge-top positions from which the Japanese commanded the slopes. 2/1st had no other elements to commit, and a request for assistance was made to 16 Brigade HQ. At 4 pm, 17 men of Pioneer Platoon crossed the bridges, reached B Company and were sent west, to the left, to climb above the Japanese and attack downwards onto them. B Company was ordered to advance.

Members of 2/1st believe that if the Japanese had attacked, the battalion would have suffered greatly, but the Japanese were fighting a delaying action, and did not know the situation of those opposing them. At 10 am, the Japanese HQ 144 Regiment issued Op Order 156, which 'ordered the position to be held with desperate courage'. Yoshiyuki Morimoto, the Codes Officer, wrote in his diary that '3rd Company engaged in a fierce battle. 2nd Lieutenant Miyaji, commander of the force occupying along the river, was reported killed'.[31]

The 2/1st Battalion Pioneer Platoon, under Lieutenant Leaney, reached the top of the ridge after two hours of climbing. A section was sent each way along the track. There were no Japanese to the left, but on the right Corporal J. A. Stewart came on a bunker position in a small clearing. With one man, Stewart crept up across the clearing and looked into the firing slit. Inside was a Juki heavy machinegun, and the crew, about to eat dinner. Stewart killed the men with his Tommy gun and tried to wreck the Juki, but nearby Japanese attacked, killing the man with him, then another man, and Stewart and one more were wounded. Lieutenant Leaney brought up the rest of the platoon, put them into a defensive position, then went forward and brought back the wounded man. The Japanese contented themselves with holding their position and did not attack, but later it was found that there were several hundred on that part of the ridge. Probably the local Japanese command was assessing the situation, and considering all the 2/1st attacks against the requirements of their mission to hold the ridge as ordered by General Horii.

While these actions had been fought, Simpson's D Company 2/1st had been struggling on to Alola. 17 Platoon was leading, followed by the HQ, then 16 and 18 Platoons. There was no contact until mid-afternoon of 23 October, when Hollingworth's 17 Platoon engaged Japanese, with all weapons firing in that direction very quickly. At least five enemy went down and the Japanese left the area. Captain Simpson decided to move the company to a higher piece of ground, but 18 Platoon did not get the message and stayed in place. When Lieutenant Dyer realised the others had gone, he sent two men to locate the company, but the Japanese had got in between them, and both were fired on; neither was seen again. One man's paybook was later taken from a Japanese corpse at Soputa.

Dyer rejoined the company. Captain Simpson realised that he would not be able to reach Alola, as his rations were almost gone, the enemy was alerted, and evacuation of casualties would have been a tremendous problem for the isolated company. Also, a 4000-foot descent (1220-metre) remained between him and the objective. He took the company back to the main battle along the 8000-foot ridge line (2440-metre), and met Captain Lysaght's 2/

3rd Battalion company, then the McCloy and Blakiston platoon groups of A Company 2/1st.

These platoons had experienced their own adventures. Blakiston had started down the slope, after the cold, wet night, towards the firing, and met McCloy and Armstrong working their way upwards. It was decided the three-platoon force would combine in a downhill attack. Unfortunately, they were where the enemy had constructed their bunkers, in depth, and the volume of machine-gun fire and small arms fire was enough to hold the platoons. It was decided that without support it would be foolish to press the attack against automatic weapons in defensive positions, and a return to battalion HQ was best. A corporal sent back to warn 2/1st of their return was never seen again. On the way back, the platoons met Simpson's company. Simpson sent Sergeant Armstrong back to Lieutenant Colonel Cullen. The lone journey was something Armstrong said he'd never forget, following Simpson's track back along the ridge, down slope and across the creek.

By the end of the day's fighting, the Japanese outposts and forward defence positions had been destroyed or driven back to the main network of bunkers along the ridge-top. B Company 2/1st had worked its way close to the positions, using what cover was possible on the slopes. The Japanese bunkers and fighting positions were well-constructed, well-camouflaged and well-sited to inflict casualties on attackers. To their left were Leaney's Pioneers and further to the left was Lysaght's company of 2/3rd. Lysaght, and Fulton's company, had similar experiences, fighting against well-prepared bunkers. Lysaght's men had captured two machine-gun posts and Fulton's men had killed many of a Japanese patrol, scattering the survivors.

Back on the spur above the village were battalion mortars and machineguns, ready to give fire support. Close by were B Echelon. After dark, Major Baines and the main part of HQ Company arrived at the battalion HQ area. Rations came up during the night, but ammunition arrived only at dawn next morning. These deliveries were made by the HQ Company platoons, who made two trips. The men had to dig in and be prepared to defend their positions during the day, as well as carry out whatever tasks were allocated, then bring up rations and ammunition at night. It was exhausting work, and resulted in a high rate of real sickness. Four men were killed and seven wounded on daylight carrying parties over the next few days. During 23 October, an Australian company commander was relieved of his command, and told to go back to HQ 7 Division, for movement back to Australia. In the close combat conditions, the highest leadership was demanded from all ranks and no concessions could be made.

Major General Allen gave orders that envisaged the advance being resumed next day, with both brigades on the move. As usual, the enemy did not comply. 7 Division orders to the brigades were: 16 Brigade to secure the drop zone at Alola, pick up the dropped supplies, secure a drop zone in the Kokoda area, secure the high ground at Oivi, and mop up between Kokoda and Oivi, and with 25 Brigade secure bridgeheads over the Kumusi River at Wairopi and Asisi; 25 Brigade was to capture and hold Kokoda, prepare Kokoda for aircraft landings and extend the runway, protect Kokoda, collect and guard all supplies delivered there, and with 16 Brigade mop up the enemy. Carriers were allocated on a basis of 40 per battalion, 90 to each brigade HQ and 110 to division HQ. Bert Kienzle did not agree with this arrangement, as he had few experienced overseers, but realised that operational necessity overrode other feelings he may have had. 25 Brigade was to concentrate at Templeton's Crossing, ready to move on to Kokoda as soon as 16 Brigade cleared Eora Creek. 25 Brigade members were not too pleased about this, as they had not really had a rest at all. However, the situation did not allow for anything else. At Port Moresby, Brigadier Potts was replaced by Brigadier Ivan Dougherty, and Potts left to command 19 Brigade in the Darwin area.

An unknown Japanese at Gona wrote that saki was necessary in warfare, but on this operation there was neither saki nor food. In his diary, Noboru Wada noted that natives reported 50 Australians advancing at a point 15 miles (24 km) south-east of Buna garrison area. 'Uchida' had been waiting for good news from a battle he thought was raging off Guadalcanal, but also spent a nervous day, as it was reported that Allied troops were preparing to attack Buna. When this was found to be a false report, he was 'very relieved when the day passed without mishap'. He did think that raids and attacks might be made by torpedo boats and such forces, and realised that the garrison had to be alert. Other Japanese also were told of a landing by Allied troops at Buna, and there was a certain amount of apprehension as units began to guard their positions. Just as several weeks earlier the Japanese had seemed to some on the Allied side as bogeymen able to appear anywhere in considerable force, so now to the Japanese under continuous air attack did the Allies seem able to make offensive moves to any location.[32]

The first B24s of United States 90th Bomb Group arrived in Australia, but also a message arrived from the US warning of cracks in part of the nose-wheel assembly, so none were able to be used for some weeks. Earlier, General Kenney had decided to replace 19th Bomb Group and its tired B17s with the arriving 90th, and the first 12 crews and planes from the 19th left on arrival of the B24s. In effect, despite reinforcements, Kenney was less stronger.

In the dimness of dawn on 24 October, at Eora Creek, Lieutenant Colonel Cullen, 2/1st Battalion, went forward to visit the forward platoons of B Company on the slopes under the Japanese guns. The Diggers had listened to the Japanese reorganising and strengthening the positions above them, and also had to endure mortar bombs from a position placed to bring the bombardment down onto the close Australian pits. The mortars were exploding in the treetops, a very dangerous matter. Other mortars also fired into the general battalion area, inflicting casualties, but a high proportion of the Japanese bombs were duds. These were cause for fright anyway, as they slipped through the leaves and branches, into pits, close alongside soldiers. One man was actually hit by a bomb that did not explode.

The steepness of the slope can be understood by the following incident: Lieutenant Frew, the commander of 12 Platoon B Company 2/1st, was patrolling to gain exact knowledge of an enemy position when he was fired on by a Japanese on top of a large rock; the first bullet just missed Frew's head, but passed through his foot; the second bullet hit his other foot; Frew killed the man.

Lieutenant Colonel Cullen advised 16 Brigade that he believed a two-company attack from the left would be necessary to dislodge the Japanese, and was informed that a second company would be sent to join Lysaght's, of 2/3rd, already in position. Gradually, the 2/1st force at Eora Creek was increasing in size as the platoons and companies returned from patrols and flanking movements. The third B Company platoon was at once put into position on the slope, linking B Company and the Pioneers.

2/33rd Battalion began to move to the crossing, only 16 officers and 340 other ranks strong. More men had been taken sick during the 'rest' period. The battalion moved along a new track to the area of the first crossing over Eora Creek, took up positions on the left of the track and waited. Also there was 2/25th Battalion. An ill Major Millroy was evacuated, and Captain O'Bryen assumed command, but later Major Marson rejoined and took over. HQ 25 Brigade arrived at Templeton's Crossing at 5.30 pm. The day closed with the ground forces gathering closer to the scene of action, and those units in contact preparing to attack next day.

Lieutenant Morimoto was told 2nd Lieutenant Onogawa was killed in action. Onogawa's diary had been captured by Australians the day before at Eora. The Japanese hospital system was still crowded, and Giruwa 67 L of C had 748 patients. These were men able to get to the hospital; others remained in the mountains.[33]

Aerial activity over the Kokoda area on 24 October had no influence on the battle, and began in mid-morning, when at 10.30 am three B25s flew the Buna–Lae–Finschafen–Gasmata reconnaissance at 1100 feet. They bombed Lae, making two passes from north-east to south-west, claiming two twin-engined bombers destroyed, two more probably destroyed, and silenced the AA there. Much barge and canoe activity was reported on the Kumusi River. A landing ground for DC3s was prepared at Pongani, and US troops began to arrive. General Kenney wrote to General Arnold, commander of all US air forces, asking for more aircraft and that they be sent as soon as possible, as the Japanese had only a two-day flight from their homeland to the battle front and could reinforce their SWPA units quite speedily. Beginning at 10.30 pm on 24 October and going into the next morning, seven Catalinas from Cairns attacked Kavieng, claiming three direct hits on fuel dumps, and a four-engined flying boat destroyed. Fires were visible 60 miles (96 km) away. Bad weather during the day had foiled all B17 reconnaissance flights to the Rabaul area, but bombing missions were to go ahead. Crews waiting for orders knew they would have to battle the night storms before facing Japanese defences at the target.

In the early hours of 25 October, pushing on through the storms, eight B17s attacked Rabaul at 2.35 am. Going in at heights of 200 to 7000 feet, the bombers dropped 67 bombs, claimed hits on three ships and shore targets, and lit fires visible 100 miles (160 km) away. The heavy, intense and accurate AA damaged three aircraft, one having 50 holes discovered on its return to base. Captain Ken McCullar, and Lieutenants Anderson, Hustad and Wilson claimed the hits, from low-level 'skip-bombing'. McCullar had dropped two bombs from 7000 feet, dived to attack from low level, picked a 5000-ton transport, and went for it. Harry Staley believed that the Japanese did not see the blacked-out bomber approaching, and two near misses were scored. But then the defences switched to them, and on the next run a bullet exploded in the nose, wounding two men and missing Staley narrowly. Carl Hustad claimed a gunboat destroyed; it was firing in all directions at the low-flying bombers. The Japanese retaliated with an attack on Port Moresby, and destroyed three aircraft.

General Kenney's heavy bomber strength now was concentrated in the 63rd Squadron. The 19th Bomb Group was returning to the US, the 64th Squadron had nine B17s, but was inexperienced and the other 43rd Group squadron, the 403rd, had eight bombers but also was inexperienced, and some of its crews had been flying with the 63rd. At the same time, Rabaul's Simpson Harbour was crowded with enemy ships, and returning crews were claiming a good proportion of hits with the new tactics. This damage should have been confirmed by photo-reconnaissance and Japanese radio traffic, but was not. However, Kenney and his staff chose to accept the claims. He was still trying to nurture his air forces, yet was forced to divert the most powerful element to the distant Solomons targets as requested by the US Navy command there. As already shown, intermediate US commanders could hold transiting air formations for their own use, and Kenney had to accept the lesser of two evils.

During the night, while B17s had been flying to their own war, in the darkened mountains of the Owen Stanleys, the 2/1st Machinegun Platoon had dug in on the spur above Eora Creek village. They emplaced the only Vickers medium machinegun and looked forward to bringing fire down onto the Japanese. The weapon had been carried all the way from Port Moresby; it was the sole Vickers available. But luck was with the enemy. The very first round of the morning fired from the Japanese mountain gun hit a nearby tree, part of which fell on the Vickers, bent the barrel and rendered it unusable. Major General Allen told all commanders to conserve ammunition, as all carriers were being used on the line of communication from Myola and there was a limit to the quantity of food and ammunition that could be brought forward.

Air attacks in support of the ground troops on the Kokoda Trail began at 9.30 am, when six A20s attacked targets at Kokoda and searched the area, but there was nothing to be seen. Two bombed the Eora Creek area, but the bombs were too far ahead of the combatants to have any effect on the situation for 2/1st Battalion.

The 2/1st Battalion Pioneer Platoon made a sortie, killing two Japanese and wounding others. Elsewhere on the slope, it was suicide to approach the enemy, as machinegun fire started at the slightest sound and raked the slopes. All that could be done from lower down was to harass the Japanese by firing and grenading from different positions. Throughout this time, with the Australians in their pits, bodily functions had to be obeyed, but the Japanese were not sporting enough to allow this to be done in peace. Any movement, any sign of life was fired on, so the Aussies on the slopes had to attend to these needs as best they could, using tins, leaves, what paper there was available in the sodden conditions, and carefully dispose of the waste without drawing fire. So the day

passed, while 2/3rd prepared to attack on the left. 16 Brigade casualties to date were 56 killed and 115 wounded.

Back at Templeton's Crossing, 2/2nd Battalion on this day officially submitted statements made by those members of the unit
who had found the bodies of the three men killed on 19 October.
The men's bodies were stripped, and flesh sliced away with a razor; a razor was found on one of the bodies; some flesh was found
wrapped in leaves and in utensils in the nearby Japanese positions.
The battalion medical officer verified the statements, after he had
inspected the bodies. Tsukamoto's I/144 had opposed 2/2nd Battalion. Sergeant Kennedy, A Company 2/25th, also made a report
on evidence of cannibalism.

Apparently believing some good news, or wanting to believe it,
'Uchida' was of the opinion that 'Guadalcanal Island has become
very profitable to Japanese forces. The enemy cannot use the island base, and the number of planes has decreased considerably'.
There were no further entries, and the diary was found in the Gona
area six weeks later; how 'Uchida' met his end is not known.[34]

During the night of 25 October, in the inevitable rain, 2/1st Battalion at Eora Creek became concentrated for the first time in some
days, when A, C and D Companies finally reported to Lieutenant
Colonel Cullen and were deployed. They had lost 20 killed and 26
wounded. D Company was to go to the left of the Pioneers and attack from there. In the darkness, A Company 2/31st had been working with 2/1st mortar men and machinegunners to take casualties
across the swollen river. The rain had flooded the Eora, and the
bridge had been washed downstream, precariously lodging against
two rocks, but under water. The Diggers had to brace themselves,
in the dark, against the bridge or rocks and pass the stretchers to
the next man, all the while enduring the rain and freezing rush of
turbulent water. The enemy fired mortars into the area, on the correct assumption that the Australians would be busy there. Twenty-
seven stretcher cases took six hours to be carried over the river and
up a 1000-foot (300-metre) climb on the far side. It rained the
whole time; no lights could be used; the identity of the wounded
was unknown, except that they were fellow Australians; no reward

was offered, was requested or was possible, not even a mug of hot tea for drenched, cold men in the darkness, under sporadic fire, coming out of an icy river. The latter-day academics who deny the concept of 'mateship', the Anzac legend, ignore bonds formed in this and innumerable other incidents by Australian soldiers at war.

The persistent Japanese mortaring had been used by the 2/1st mortar teams to try to identify the weapon's position, and by the morning of 26 October, they believed that they were ready to fire on it. The three-inch mortar and 10 bombs had been carried from Ower's Corner, over the great ridges and mountains; now it was to be used. The mortar pit itself was well-concealed, but Lieutenant Reardon moved forward to the crest of the ridge to observe fire. Reardon was worried when Major Baines joined him there, and sure enough, two men was a suitable target for the Japanese, who sent a mortar bomb to them. Reardon was wounded, and bandaged at personal risk by Sergeant Madigan, the mortar sergeant. The mortar attack was postponed.

Again the day passed with fire exchanged between the forward companies and the Japanese, but no ground was gained. The Japanese continually fired blindly down slope and rolled grenades onto the Australians only some 20 to 40 yards away. Even rocks were rolled down, and Captain Catterns, already wounded by a grenade fragment, was badly hit on the knee by one. He visited his forward pits, encouraging the Diggers to keep up pressure on the enemy. A steady trickle of casualties was inflicted by Japanese fire and grenades.

Further to the left, on the higher ground, Lieutenant Colonel Stevenson's 2/3rd had been working around the Japanese flank, but when Lysaght's company attacked, it was held by fire from medium machineguns, and though Gall and Fulton took their men even further around, the Japanese successfully held on. A patrol under Sergeant J. Copeman pushed into Japanese positions and cut the telephone wire, and the Japanese then counter-attacked Gall and Lysaght at dusk, but themselves were held. The Japanese commanders must have realised that these enveloping moves would continue next day.

The constant rain had interfered with the air transport aspects of the supply system. Now the airfield at Myola was unusable, with a creek running through its centre, and in addition, the native carriers were feeling the effects of the constant work, and the cold, wet conditions. By this time, Myola 2 had become a hospital and air-dropping area, with some 700 patients under canvas or thatch, who were to remain for many weeks. Air evacuation failed, with the loss of four valuable aircraft, due to a combination of altitude, aerodynamics, pilot inexperience and less than adequate runways.

At 7.35 am, three B25s flew the Buna–Lae–Vitiaz–Gasmata reconnaissance, bombed and strafed Lae airfield, the radio station at Salamaua, but apart from inaccurate AA, there was nothing to report. The weather was 'good'.

An officer of the Japanese Pioneers at Buna wrote that the Tsukioka Butai (Sasebo 5SLP) on Goodenough Island had successfully crossed to Wellin Island. Shunichiro Yano, a veterinarian, noted that Yazawa Butai (41 Regiment) was waiting at Papaki. The day before, he had 150 horses available. News was received by the Japanese of an action off Guadalcanal in which two US battleships were claimed sunk, with severe damage to three US carriers and four cruisers. Actual results in the Battle of Santa Cruz, fought 25-26 October, were USS *Hornet* (carrier) and USS *Porter* (destroyer) sunk, 74 planes lost, with damage to USS *Enterprise*, *South Dakota* (battleship), *Smith* (destroyer) and *San Juan* (cruiser). Japanese losses were 100 aircraft, damage to carriers *Shokaku* and *Zuiho*, to cruiser *Chikuma* and destroyers *Terutsuki* and *Akikaze*. Major General Horii visited 144 Regiment at the Kokoda Gap position, to personally assess the situation, and returned to Kokoda at 10 am. The Koiwai II/41 battalion arrived at the Gap and moved into position.[35]

At Eora Creek, the ever-present matter of rations dictated that 2/33rd Battalion send 200 men back to Myola 2, from where they carried forward five days of rations for 16 Brigade. This meant physical labour for these men for the three days 26-28 October. Despite the recent time out of battle, the battalion had been busy, and necessary internal reorganisation had not been attended to.

The unit historian pointed out that the strength of platoons varied from eight to 20; there was an imbalance in weapons held; some companies had seconds-in-command, some did not; some platoons were led by sergeants; some had no NCOs at all. It was here that Lieutenant Colonel Buttrose sent in the names of five NCOs for promotion to officer rank ('battlefield commission'), and here that Major General George Vasey visited the battalion on taking over command of 7 Division from Major General Allen. Vasey had flown to Myola, and while walking across the grassy clearing, was seen to be carrying a carton of Ardath cigarettes under his arm. The egalitarian Aussies working on the clearing asked their general if he could spare any, and Vasey soon was handing out cigarettes to the smokers nearby.

The pressures from higher headquarters had continued to mount on Major General Allen. Again, General Blamey sent a message that was unsympathetic, claimed that the difficulties referred to by Allen also confronted the enemy, that attacks still were made by small numbers, that Allen's superior strength was held by few Japanese, 'negligible progress' had been made, and all commanders were to control the situation, not let it control them. Allen tried to explain again, described the well-built Japanese defences, the tenacity of the enemy, the extreme difficulty in movement across the terrain, and the moves he had ordered to cope with all this. He also tried to convince Blamey of the large number of enemy opposing him. It was to no avail, and Major General George Vasey was sent to take command of 7 Division.

On 27 October, at Eora Creek, Lieutenant Colonel Cullen had decided to bring his 2/1st Battalion HQ up to the position held by the Pioneer Platoon, to organise the outflanking move by the battalion. When he reached C Company, Cullen was told by telephone that B Company had discovered the Japanese were gone. He then quickly ordered the rifle companies in pursuit and returned to the bottom of the ridge to continue the advance.

However, the Japanese had withdrawn only some 500 yards to stronger positions. They had prepared an ambush, which was avoided. The companies pressed forward and in a series of actions inflicted and received casualties. Later it was known that C and D Companies were operating at the junction of tracks used by the Japanese to take supplies to the forces resisting 2/3rd Battalion. These patrol clashes continued, with both sides persisting. The Japanese wanted the area open for their use; the Australians wanted it to close the tracks to them. At the crossing, 2/6th Field Company (Engineers) arrived to rebuild the bridge, and 2/1st Battalion was able to concentrate, as a whole, for the first time in a week. Simpson's D Company moved past Burrell's C Company, trying to find the Japanese right flank. Night fell, and it rained. Simpson went on in the trying conditions.

Lieutenant Colonel Stevenson, in pain from his head wound, finally relented and handed over command of 2/3rd Battalion to one of the battalion originals, Major I. Hutchison. Also under command of 2/3rd was Captain B. Brock's company of 2/2nd. The plan of advance was to do so in three columns, each about 300 yards from the other, and go forward about 1000 yards into the rear of the Japanese, in fact, roughly paralleling the positions held so closely to the Japanese by 2/1st. At 8.50 am the advance began, and at 11.30 the first clashes began. The rest of the day was taken with fighting in close bush on the northern slopes, but the Aussies were prepared to push on again on the morning of the 28 October.

The 2/1st mortar was again about to engage the enemy, with Sergeant Madigan commanding at the base-plate position. A telephone line had been laid to an observation post, occupied by Major Baines. The original 10 bombs carried from Ower's Corner were fired quickly, and the team was happy as the Japanese counter-fire was not anywhere near them. They prepared to fire some bombs that had been air-dropped at Myola, but the second of these exploded in the barrel. Three men were killed and Sergeant Madigan had to be evacuated with heavy concussion.

Patrols, constant small arms fire and grenades kept the battle going at a steady rate for both sides, but with little ground gained or lost. As well as enemy action, the problems caused by the environment continued. The field telephones began to deteriorate after constant waterlogging, and the linesmen tracing faults were often at risk from enemy patrols and snipers. During the day, from 2/25th, Lieutenant Jefferson and 23 men moved out to patrol the track to Alola. Coming along behind them was the battalion, with five days' rations, to follow the track and cut the Japanese withdrawal route from Eora Creek. 2/2nd Battalion reported on the Owen sub-machinegun, calling it 'very effective' and 'most satisfactory', but pointing out that it needed more care than other weapons when being cleaned, as there was only a little blueing on the metal.

Meanwhile, the Japanese 144 Regiment made preparations to move from Kokoda Gap to Oivi. For the past week, 6 Independent Company had been reporting from deep in Japanese territory, with its component patrols placed widely across the area of interest. D Patrol was only one hour's march from Oivi, and believed its main danger came from treacherous natives. A Pioneer officer at Buna noted that 260 men of Tsukioka Butai (Sasebo 5SLP) were picked up by *Tenryu* with a loss of one man. Noboru Wada also noted this, but also that Buna airfield runway had not yet been completely repaired after being put out of action by repeated bombings. An officer with the Takasago volunteers wrote that '50-60 per cent of the unit has malaria due to lack of preventive medicine'.[36]

Air activity on 27 October again was of little assistance to the Australian units in the ground battle. Six Beaufighters attacked small boats, barges and AA positions at Lae, leaving fuel drums burning and three barges on fire; smoke could be seen 40 miles (64 km) away. AA was intense and accurate, two aircraft were hit, and one, trailing smoke, went into the sea. Other crews saw it hit the sea, recover, go on for 400 yards, then dive 800 yards from shore, with no sign of the crew seen. Flight Lieutenant E. A. Jones and Flight Sergeant E. R. Richardson were killed. No serviceable aircraft were seen on the airfields, and cloudbase was 5/10th cumulus at 1000 feet. At 12.40 pm, three A20s with four P40s as escort swept the Alola–Isurava–Abuari area, dropped bombs and reported visibility fair through broken cumulus, but no enemy activity. No further flights were recorded for the afternoon and evening, until 11.15 pm, when five Catalinas from Cairns attacked Buka, lighting three fires. Nine B17s enjoyed good weather all the way to Rabaul, then attacked shipping at 3.05 am on 28 October, bombed from 5000 to 9000 feet with 69 bombs, and claimed one hit despite accurate AA. In daylight, three B25s flew to attack Gasmata, but there was only a single twin-engined bomber on the airfield there; one B25 was damaged. A B17 on reconnaissance to Kavieng was attacked by four Zeros, which made 20 firing passes. These four were good, and it was as well the Japanese had not mounted heavy armament on their fighters, as the German Luftwaffe was doing, because they put 193 holes in the B17. Fortunately, there were no casualties and it returned to base.

During the day, Admiral Ghormley asked General MacArthur for more help in the Solomons, and requested attacks on Buin–Faisi and loan of a P38 squadron. Kenney suggested Rabaul would be the better target, but was told to attack the target Ghormley wanted hit. The P38s were still not operational, requiring much work on leaking fuel tanks and intercooler systems, but MacArthur directed Kenney to provide the fighters as soon as they were ready. At 11.35 pm on 28 October, once more the daily bombing cycle was completed, when nine B17s attacked ships at Buin–Faisi with 30 bombs, and claimed one explosion on a ship and other near misses.

Meanwhile, at Eora, Captain Simpson's D Company 2/1st Battalion had pressed on through the night of 27 October, in the rain, trying to get around the enemy right flank. Visibility was nil. A Japanese telephone cable was found and followed to the north. When the cable turned sharply, it was assumed that the company was behind the Japanese lines. The cable was cut, but the rain and dark were so intense that it was repaired by a Japanese patrol without battle being joined; control would have been impossible if an action began. D Company waited out the night and the downpour. As dawn on 28 October came, Simpson moved D Company back, 17 Platoon leading. Japanese were seen in defended positions on the ridge, but it was obvious the Australians were behind the enemy defence line. Despite some urging to attack from the platoon commanders, Simpson decided to return to the battalion. Gradually they crossed a track on the ridge, but were engaged by enemy coming from the other direction, and moved back in a hail of fire.

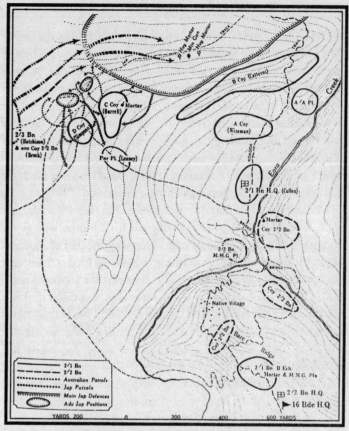

Map labels:
- B Coy (Catterns)
- A'A Pl.
- C Coy (Barrell)
- Mortar
- A Coy (Wiseman)
- D Coy (Simpson)
- 2/3 Bn (Hutchison) & one Coy 2/2 Bn (Brock)
- Pnr Pl (Leaney)
- 2/1 Bn H.Q. (Cullen)
- Mortar Coy 2/2 Bn
- 2/3 Bn M.M.G. Pl.
- BRIDGE
- Coy 2/2 Bn
- Native Village
- Coy 2/2 Bn
- Bare Ridge
- 2/1 Bn B Ech. Mortar & M.M.G. Pls
- 2/2 Bn H.Q.
- 16 Bde H.Q.
- How Mortar
- 8 Hv Gun
- How Mortar
- CREEK
- TRACK
- TRAIL
- KOKODA
- Eora

Legend:
- 2/1 Bn
- 2/2 Bn
- Australian Patrols
- Jap Patrols
- Main Jap Defences
- Adv Jap Positions

YARDS 200   0   200   400   600 YARDS

Eora Creek action, 27-28 October.

Lieutenant Hollingworth decided to use his two-inch mortar, but the first bomb exploded in the barrel, killing or wounding all platoon HQ, a total of six, including the commander and sergeant. Only one man had been killed by Japanese fire. With the rest of the company gone, Hollingworth had to get his platoon down a very steep slope with aroused Japanese on the heights. In an epic of courage and endurance, the wounded walked or were brought back. Private Jack Porter had a split thigh bone, and after evacuation had his leg in plaster for nine months; he walked down the hill, assisting others. Hollingworth reported to Lieutenant Colonel Cullen and Brigadier Lloyd, who decided that air-dropped mortar ammunition was not to be used. After a rest, Hollingworth set off, with stiffened leg wounds, to the aid post on the far side of the creek. The unsympathetic Japanese fired a mountain gun into the bridge area, and a machinegun tried to shoot him off the bridge. Almost immobile due to wounds, using two sticks as crutches, Hollingworth made it back to D Company instead of across the river. The Japanese had been aggressively probing the area between Simpson and Burrell, but were thrown back, despite cutting the Australian telephone line. Visibility was restricted to 10 yards and a nerve-wracking deadly search went on in the ground between the 2/1st companies as the Diggers hunted their enemies.

Meanwhile, 2/3rd Battalion had prepared to renew the advance from their overnight positions. Captain I. C. Fulton was given command of a force made up of his company and that of Lieutenant L. McGuinn. A barrage of rifle grenades was fired at 5 pm, and the assault force attacked down hill, pincering the Japanese position. The forward scouts, as usual, were shot, but the rest of the force kept on advancing, past the outposts, into the central Japanese position. Quite suddenly, the Japanese broke and ran, throwing away their weapons, chattering and gibbering, while the attackers killed those in sight. Sixty-nine dead were counted, and others were believed to be out in the bush, in the unchecked jungle ravines. Some of the dead wore Australian wrist watches. Most were privates, with worn clothing, physically thin, and no food was found on them, only a fish paste. Investigation of the Japanese position showed it was built around a central position that was some 300 yards across, radiating from a central hub. For the first time in the campaign, the enemy had not held the highest ground, but instead the area around the only water supply, a spring on the lower slopes. This had allowed the Australians to get above them, and attack from a more advantageous height. Just as 2/33rd had shown the enemy could be panicked and thrown out of a defended position, so now 2/3rd proved it could be done. Corporal L. G. 'Tarzan' Pett, though only five feet tall (152 cm), alone destroyed four machinegun posts in the attack. It was thought he should have received a Victoria Cross, but instead he was awarded the Military Medal. Australian casualties were 11 killed and 31 wounded.

An ammunition resupply for B Company 2/3rd was made by the RSM, the Intelligence Sergeant and two men, but they were ambushed by a party of Japanese who had already cut the telephone cable. The RSM was killed, the sergeant never found, one man badly wounded and one escaped to take news of the action. 14 Platoon C Company was sent to repair the wire and destroy the Japanese party, who wisely had gone.

During the actions, 2/1st lost 44 killed, 88 wounded and three missing. Initially, 2/1st had been opposed by I/144, then by all three battalions of the regiment. The brigade casualty figure was six officers and 75 other ranks killed and nine officers and 145 men wounded. The ratio of dead to wounded – about 1:2 – indicates the intensity of the close fighting.

The Japanese HQ 144 Regiment was marching to Oivi, but was redirected by Horii to Isurava, and arrived there at 9 pm. Moving to try to cut the withdrawal route was 2/25th Battalion, who were to spend the next four days struggling through very difficult country, going west, then north-west, and finally east to the Kagi–Alola track. The jungle was so dense that at one time only 600 yards of progress was made in two hours. No Japanese were found, and the battalion moved in its own little world of green, wet jungle.

Captain Grahamslaw, ANGAU, was District Officer for Mambare, and reported that the Orokaivas were under the influence of the Japanese, that tribal warfare had broken out with weapons formerly held by the Papuan Infantry Brigade, but the Japanese had intervened to halt any violence. An intelligent native named Amboga was the leader, and was trying to establish himself as head of the region.

On this day, having been replaced by 'Bloody George' Vasey, Major General Allen visited the wounded before he moved to Darwin as GOC Northern Territory Force. The units were sorry to see him go, and even more so in later times when the reasons for his replacement were known. He had shown that the Japanese could be beaten. However, Vasey, who took command of 7 Division, was also well known and respected.

On 29 October, New Guinea Force HQ informed all units that

air-dropped mortar fuses were not to be used, and the weapons were not to be used until fuses could be delivered by landed aircraft. In the 7 Division formations, 25 Brigade was to secure Kokoda; 3rd Battalion was allocated to 16 Brigade, for use at Alola to recover air drops, while 2/31st Battalion returned to 25 Brigade from its actions at Kagi. After 16 Brigade turned right for Oivi, 25 Brigade was to go on, with 2/33rd and 2/25th, around to the left of Eora, with 2/25th to take Isurava and 2/33rd Alola.

2/33rd spent three days in the jungle making its way from Templeton's Crossing to Alola, a journey that normally took six hours along the track. The expedition into the wet greenery was remembered by the battalion as an exhausting and futile march; no Japanese, tracks, villages or other sign of humans was seen. The radios were useless, and once swallowed by the jungle, 2/33rd was alone.

At Eora, 2/1st began to move out to follow the Japanese, with two companies to move parallel to the axis of the track and the other two following on the high ground. There was time for a basic hot breakfast to be provided. A young cook told to take two dixies up the slope to B Company was hesitant, so 'Sandy' Rayward took them and set off. With the heavy dixies in each hand, he climbed the slope head down, and as he reached the crest looked up and saw he was in the Japanese positions. All around were log and dirt bunkers – luckily empty of Japanese. B Company was surprised when he delivered breakfast from the enemy positions.

For many, there was a great psychological relief. The enemy, dominating them from impregnable positions above, was gone; no more casualties would be inflicted for a time; the day was fine. Then as they marched towards Alola, by the track was the body of a battalion member, with most of a buttock and thigh removed. Feeling against the enemy was described as 'explosive'. Accounts of such Japanese behaviour circulated among all the units, and later similar tales would be told by the units from Milne Bay, with, later still, accounts of the murders of the missionaries and civilians at Buna. Almost daily, the image of the Japanese was being reduced to that of an evil beast, an enemy of humanity.

Later that day, Japanese were seen ahead at Alola, and the 2/2nd

Battalion Vickers machinegun was sent for, but just as it was ready to flail the distant enemy, mist obscured them, and darkness halted further advances.

Japanese Codes Officer Morimoto noted the fine weather, and his arrival at the ration distribution point near Kokoda, where his radio unit was issued rations. They saw some Japanese aircraft fly over, and the improvement in morale was immediate. Morimoto was told that the planes dropped rations at Kokoda. Port Moresby was attacked by Japanese bombers, who managed to destroy two aircraft and kill three men on the ground. At Buna, work continued on various construction projects, including air-raid shelters. At dusk, 'Wada' saw three friendly fighters, an event so rare that he noted it in his diary.

On 29 October, at 9.35 am, three A20s with a fighter escort attacked enemy positions forward of Alola with 20-pound bombs from 50 feet. There was no activity to report, and ceiling and visibility in the target area was unlimited. Nearly six hours later, at 3 pm, another three A20s with eight P39s as escort attacked Popondetta and enemy at Alola and Deniki with 20-pound bombs. It was raining at Yodda but fair visibility at Deniki. The afternoon reconnaissance of Buna–Lae–Finschafen–Gasmata was flown by seven B25s, who found a single twin-engined enemy bomber 10 miles east of Finschafen. The B25s swarmed to attack, but the Japanese Betty had a 20-mm tail gun that was used to good effect, damaging one B25. About 2100 rounds of .50-calibre machinegun were fired by the B25 gunners, and many hits on the enemy were seen, but it was not shot down or even claimed as a probable. Ten B17s set off at 8.30 pm to attack Buin, but on arrival found visibility was very poor. One B17 hit an 8000-ton ship, next day found to be beached, and another ship also was beached, but no one claimed hitting it.

Early on 30 October, in response to Admiral Ghormley's request, two squadrons totalling 14 B17s went to Buin–Faisi. The first five dropped 25 bombs from 4500 to 10,000 feet, claiming one hit and six near misses on a battleship, a cruiser and a carrier. Then came nine B17s with 46 bombs, and crews claimed one direct and two possible hits on ships, but there was nothing else to report. Ken

McCullar went in at 1800 feet, to get under the cloud cover, and found five ships in a line. He attacked through fierce AA and with at least five searchlights on him, but his bombs would not release. He pulled up into the cloud, came back and salvoed onto a 15,000-ton ship, with no results seen. Weather was good on the way to Rabaul, but the harbour was covered by cloud from 2800 to 5000 feet. The speed with which the weather could change was experienced later in the area by 30 Squadron RAAF. Six Beaufighters set off before dawn to attack Kahili, on Bougainville, but were forced back by the weather. A front extended to 16,000 feet, and strato-cumulus with showers went from 500 to 7500 feet.

16 Brigade began moving forward again, passing the litter of retreat. Japanese pack saddles, horseshoes and dead horses were scattered around, then as they neared Isurava the skeletal remains of Japanese and Australian dead, from the fighting of two months before, were found. At Isurava rest house was the remains of an Australian Bren gunner, in correct firing position behind the gun. D Company 2/1st halted where 53rd Battalion had stopped on 29 August, and the platoons found a large quantity of usable ammunition and some cooking utensils, all of which were welcome. A Japanese fire was so recent that the ashes were hot. 2/1st camped for the night. Behind the battalions, headquarters also were advancing, with 25 Brigade HQ arriving at a location just north of Eora Creek, and 7 Division Advanced HQ at Templeton's Crossing.

The Japanese again broke contact and rapidly moved back, destroying bridges and roadworks behind them, leaving the Australian scouts to probe carefully forward into the unknown. The Japanese HQ, I and II/144 began marching to Oivi, with 1100 yards between units. Officially, 144 Regiment ceased to be 'the Stanley Detachment', the title being assumed by Yazawa's force. I/144 was attached to Yazawa. Work continued on Buna airfield by 14 and 15 Pioneer Units. Other units and detachments were employed on road improvements and construction tasks, another sign that the Japanese did not intend abandoning the New Guinea operation, but were preparing to hold on until the Guadalcanal matter was settled, then renew the drive to take Port Moresby.

In the early hours of 31 October, eight RAAF Catalinas attacked Buin–Faisi and another went to Lae–Salamaua. Eighteen B17s attacked Buin–Faisi and Rabaul with a total of 136 bombs, and despite heavy, intense and accurate AA, haze and clouds building up, claimed four hits and four near misses after attacks from 200 to 13,500 feet.

The immense effort by the heavy bombers in support of the Solomons theatre was not reflected in postwar investigation by the Joint Army Navy Assessment Committee, as there was little evidence in Japanese records to verify claims of hits and sinkings for October. All Japanese losses were attributed to Solomons-based Allied units. In daylight over New Guinea, at 9.20 am, Nauro was bombed by three A20s, which reported all 20-pound bombs in the target area, and thin overcast at 1100 feet. It was the only recorded attack mission in support of the Kokoda campaign for the day.

2/1st Battalion received an air drop at Alola, on the usual small kunai clearing on a razor-back ridge. Only two planes dropped, and most of the supplies disappeared for ever down the jungle slopes, but enough for a small ration for one day was recovered. At 10.30 am, 2/31st Battalion under Lieutenant Colonel Dunbar took over the lead, and 2/1st was happy to relinquish the honour. Relief was short-lived, and at 1.30 pm the battalion was ordered to go east to Abuari. Off in the distance Kokoda could be seen; 2/1st was fated not to go there. By late afternoon, the advanced HQs of both brigades and 7 Division were at Alola.

For October, the Allied air supply organisation had dropped five times the quantity of rations it had in September: 1,511,731. This consisted of rations for the Europeans and natives, emergency and chocolate emergency rations, and in addition there were drops of ammunition, medical, engineer, signals and ordnance supplies. The arrival of the US 6th Troop Carrier Squadron at Port Moresby on 13 October had a marked effect. Ironically, transport pilots and crews were not acknowledged as flying 'combat hours', which were credited only to bomber, fighter and reconnaissance crews, yet the air supply flights had at least an equal effect on the outcome. The fixation with results of attack missions on groups of men and a dispersed supply system hidden under jungle treetops continued to the end of the Vietnam War, and US air units dumped immense tonnages of high explosive into the absorbent jungle wilderness.[37]

On this day ANGAU reported that there was a total of 7914 carriers, labourers and boat crews from the local population, supervised by 136 Europeans. However, because of the requirements of other parts of New Guinea, only 1650 of these carriers were employed on the Kokoda Lines of Communication.

On the coast at Buna, 582 patients at Japanese 67 L of C Hospital were prepared for evacuation to Rabaul next day. During the month, a total of 1458 men from all units in the force had been admitted, with 870 coming from 41 Regiment, 144 Regiment and 15 Engineer Regiment. Only 23 officers from those units were included, and a total of only 29 officers were patients. In all, 30 units were represented in the patients' list. The large numbers of patients reflected the situation in the combat units. On this day, I/144 at Ilimo evacuated 48 men, leaving 182 in position. III/144 numbered 123 forward, with 56 on rear duties. However, these men were well-armed, with large supplies of ammunition, in good defensive fighting positions.[38]

Terrain, climate and conditions were equally as harsh on Japanese units as on Australian units. 2/25th Battalion, as an example, had been struggling across country since 27 October. The battalion had suffered two cases of scrub typhus, both fatal, during the month. The men were generally weary, continually wet, were cold at night, unable to light fires at night because of the enemy or because everything was wet, there were no hot foods and no sources of energy in the tins of bully beef and packets of biscuits; sugar was badly needed. The battalion diary stated that it was 'pitiable to see them struggle on, willpower fighting against bodily exhaustion'.

Chapter 6
REAPING THE WEST WHIRLWIND
November 1942

The usual very early morning attacks on Solomons targets were made on 1 November by nine RAAF Catalinas from Cairns, which attacked Buin–Faisi at 2.20 am, followed from Port Moresby by 12 B17s, which dropped 60 bombs, and claimed one hit on a transport, a probable hit on a destroyer and a near miss on another destroyer, but a B17 was missing. On New Guinea itself, at 5 am, Lae airfield was attacked by seven B25s, which dropped 40 bombs through light but inaccurate AA. The Japanese fighters reacted strongly, and 14 A20s, with 16 P40Es as escort, engaged 15 or 20 Zeros 70 miles (112 km) south of Lae, with a Zero claimed probably destroyed, and an A20 crash-landed at Moresby. The fighter escort claimed two Japanese hit and seen to go down, but one P40 was last seen with two Zeros on its tail, in a dive and smoking. In the attacks, no aircraft were seen on Lae airfield, and cloudbase was solid at 4000 feet from Lae to Salamaua. Zeros also intercepted the early morning reconnaissance by three B25s, and seven Japanese fighters fought the bombers from north-west of Buna to south of 'Kokoda Gap'; one badly shot-up B25 crash landed, wrecking the aircraft. Japanese ace Toshio Keneko, of 251 Kokkutai, was lost in the combats. Four P400s escorted transport planes to Pongani, but on the return trip two of the fighters disappeared. Transport planes were dropping supplies at Alola.

Under the aircraft, but blind in the smothering greenness and damp, were 2/33rd Battalion. Lieutenant Colonel Buttrose deduced that the noise meant aircraft dropping supplies, so sent a platoon ahead. The soldiers came out of the jungle uphill from the drop zone, and by midday the battalion was camped on the slopes. Brigadier Eather told Buttrose that 16 Brigade was pushing ahead and that 2/31st Battalion was in Kokoda with no Japanese around the place. 2/33rd was to go on to Kokoda next day.

2/31st was at Deniki, with no sign of Japanese resistance. The battalion had spent several days at Eora Creek, and on 31 October begun advancing to Isurava. A Company was leading, and arrived at Deniki, followed by the rest of the battalion. Four platoon patrols sent out did not make contact with the enemy, but the bridge near the waterfall between Isurava and Deniki was destroyed. Kokoda was in sight from Deniki, and there was no sign of activity. The battalion settled in for the night.

7 Division ordered 16 Brigade to push on, regardless of the situation at Deniki. By 1.30 pm, brigade HQ was moving. The war diarist noted that as a small ration of tobacco had been issued, 'faces were happy'. A hot meal had been eaten the night before, the track was relatively easy, the sun was shining, 'so we were happy'. Such were the simple things that improved the outlook of the soldier in New Guinea, October 1942.

Though the fighting was over for the moment, the casualties were not able to be evacuated beyond Myola. By midday on 1 November, 438 sick or wounded men were collected there.

Lieutenant Colonel F. N. Chenhall, commander of 2/6th Field Ambulance, sent critical signals to Port Moresby, pointing out the great shortage of medical supplies of all kinds, the failure to supply what he did request, the lack of an alternative to air evacuation and the lack of staff planning for the medical situation. 2/4th and 2/6th Field Ambulances had been caring for casualties during the advance in stations along the trail and at Myola. Their experiences, dedication and spirit are worthy of a separate book, and space does not permit more than a brief reference here. As with all other units, everything had to be man-packed, with the additional problems of performing medical and surgical treatments in the prevailing conditions, with hygiene and sterility always a major factor. Operations were generally done at night, by hurricane lantern, with that part of the patient's body not requiring attention protruding from the tent shelter. In one 10-day period, 2/4th Field Ambulance treated 240 battle casualties.

Two Japanese transports came in to Buna, bringing, among their cargoes, canteen goods. Twenty technicians and sick returned to Rabaul. The ships had arrived safely enough, but the return voyage was to be very different.[1]

The Japanese 144 Regiment assembled at Ilimo, and were informed officially by Horii that Colonel Yamamoto was appointed to command the regiment, and now would be known as 'Yamamoto Butai'. The 'Kusunose' title would not be used. This practice of titling each unit and sub-unit after its commander caused a great amount of confusion to Allied Intelligence and Operations staffs, who were continually presented with information indicating 'new' Japanese units. It is, however, another indication of the mediaeval aspects of the Japanese Army, and must have caused confusion in their own system.

Horii told the regiment: 'Some time ago, the force was ordered to cross the Stanley mountains. With bravery and determination, you men advanced as far as Ioribaiwa in the face of stubborn enemy resistance. We had Port Moresby under our mercy and created terror in the hearts of the enemy.

'However, the general situation of the Army forced us into an unwilling withdrawal. For this reason, the Stanley formation had to employ defensive tactics at Iora and the Gap. Fearing the decreasing fighting strength of the troops due to the deficiency of supply, a temporary evacuation of the force from those positions was decided upon, though much against our will. Considering the general situation and the objectives of the force, we will withdraw to the Kumusi River area, where problems of supply are comparatively easy, and prepare for a future offensive.

'To repeat, our withdrawal will not be the result of the superiority of the enemy. It was aimed to recover the health and strength of the troops. To compare this with defeat shows a gross misunderstanding.

'Exert yourselves towards making a healthy recuperation. Be useful to the force, and prepare for brave and active counterattacks. To build up our morale and inflexible fighting spirit is the most important thing at present.

'It is believed that the enemy, as is characteristic of him, will take this advantage of making further persistent attacks on our front lines. They may also penetrate our flanks and rear. If such an occasion arises, the force will make determined counter-attacks and destroy the enemy.

'For the sake of honour, all units, regardless of whether they are combatants, non-combatants or Army employees, are expected to recover...fighting strength spiritually as well as physically, thereby demonstrating the strength of the high-spirited brilliant force.'[2]

Lieutenant Morimoto's unit was camped on the right bank of the Ilimo River. He received a complaint from some of his soldiers concerning the small ration of rice issued – one pint (600 ml). Even after withdrawing from the front line, food was not available to the combat units in adequate quantities, but there was little Morimoto could do. This was his last diary entry, and his book was captured 10 days later, south of Gorari. At Giruwa, 'Wada' received his second lot of mail since arriving at Buna in August. He had noted the air-raids, but did not record any damage.[3]

At dawn on 2 November, 11 B17s attacked the convoy that had left Buna, claiming two hits on one transport and four near misses on another. Watching other squadrons attack, crews reported there was no further damage to the ships. An RAAF strike force of Beauforts, Beaufighters and P40s was to rendezvous, then go on to the ships, but rendezvous was not made and the squadrons returned to base. The Zeros again made an appearance. In an attack at 8 am, six B17s were airborne, but then were warned nine Zeros from Lae were headed east, to the ships. The B17s spread into a search formation, found the ships in clear weather, and the squadron closed in for an attack. The Zeros arrived, split into pairs and circled the ships. The six bombers attacked in pairs, despite intense AA fire, dropped 49 bombs, and claimed a hit on one ship, which stopped dead in the water. Zeros attacked, and the bomber crews claimed three destroyed – one seen to hit the water, one diving losing pieces, one disintegrating, and one more smoking badly in a dive. The stricken ship was *Yasukawa Maru*, 6710 tons, a veteran of many supply voyages for the Imperial Japanese Navy.[4]

There was a break of seven hours before the next air attack was made on the ships. The weather remained clear, helping the attacking squadrons, and at 4 pm, 10 B25s attacked, but 12 bombs were salvoed by mechanical failure, though from the other 33 bombs, four near misses were claimed on a transport. The ships put up heavy AA fire, and Zeros made frontal attacks on two B25s, but none were lost. In a further series of attacks from 4.30 to 7 pm, eight B17s harassed the ships, dropped 46 bombs, and claimed nine near misses, but three Zeros attacked and damaged four B17s, though one Zero was shot down in flames. A flight of three B17s went in to bomb at 5.15 pm, but all 24 bombs hit short and to the right of the ships.

Meanwhile, the origin of the resurgence of Japanese fighter activity was identified when a P38 flew to Lae, and returned with photos showing 24 fighters and four bombers around the airfield, but only four fighters were assessed as serviceable.

As the early morning attacks were being made on the ships, at Deniki, 2/31st Battalion looked out on a fine morning, with mist blanketing the Mambare Valley. The battalion resumed its march to Kokoda, passing abandoned Japanese bicycles in the mud on the trail. Lieutenant Hurrell and HQ Company, with a radio, moved straight to the airfield, but Lieutenant Black's patrol was first into Kokoda, followed by HQ Company, then C Company.

They found some Rabaul natives who had been worked by the Japanese until they could do no more, then were left without food. The tales they told of treatment by the Japanese, of cold-blooded beatings, of killings, of being forced onward by bayonet jabs, had an immediate effect on the carriers who had arrived with the Australians. These men were disgruntled with their lot, but soon came to realise just how well they were treated by comparison. In a very short time, as the news of the Japanese brutalities spread along the carrier lines, their attitude changed markedly to one of distinct approval and support for the Australian forces.

All the rifle companies of 2/31st went on past Kokoda airfield and established themselves in a cultivated area south of Amada. The area was considered so secure that fires were allowed at night, and tea was made for the first time since taking over the brigade lead.

2/1st Battalion was marching east. The remaining rations from the air drop on 31 October were issued: one quarter-pound of chocolate (113 gm), four and a half packets of chewing gum, half a packet of biscuits and a small amount of tobacco. The battalion Medical Officer, Captain O'Connell, estimated that 20 per cent of the battalion was suffering from pronounced dietary deficiency. To add to the problems, as the force went into the lower country, mosquitoes appeared. Some fresh native fruits and vegetables were sampled as the column passed through gardens. Obviously, the Japanese had not been there. At midday, the battalion reached the dropping ground at Kobara, where it was resupplied after 2/2nd, 2/3rd and 3rd Battalions. 2/33rd Battalion marched from Alola down into the Yodda valley, camping at 5 pm, alongside a patch of bananas, paw-paws and coconuts.

7 Division had signalled its brigades, informing 16 Brigade that it was to be prepared to move towards Wairopi from midday on 4 November, when 25 Brigade was then to be responsible for the protection of Kokoda west to Oivi, as well as patrol to Wairopi. Major General Vasey sent a personal message to Brigadier Lloyd: 'I wish to see you move towards Oivi in full strength at earliest. I feel your HQ and 2/1st too far back in view no contact today. Time will be saved if you can keep the same battalion leading.' There was a reference to supply drops intended on 3 November, then finally, 'I want you to capture the enemy guns used in this area'.

To the uninformed, it may have seemed that General Blamey was responsible for the Australian offensive from Imita, as he arrived after the planning and preliminary movements had been done by Lieutenant General Rowell, who soon was removed from the scene. Now Major General Vasey arrived in time to appear to put 7 Division on the advance, when in fact it was the benefits of Major General Allen's work. Similarly, on a larger scale, in North Africa General Montgomery took command of 8th Army after Auchinleck had stopped Rommel at El Alamein.

Meanwhile, from 3rd Battalion, Sergeant Bede Tongs had been

sent by Lieutenant Colonel Cameron on another long patrol, out to the Mt Thumb area, then to approach Kokoda from the north. They had set off from Alola, still in shirt and shorts, aware that they would have to cross mountains at about 8600 feet (2620 metres), with only half a blanket per man. The patrol pushed on through the moss forests, the eerie dimness, among the hanging moss streamers trailing from the trees, forced to step from one buttress root to the next – a missed step resulted in the man going waist deep into centuries of leaf mould. There were occasional signs that someone had passed that way, but no recent marks or indicators of Japanese presence. They became increasingly short of breath, and put this down to lack of sustaining food, not realising it was the effect of climbing into the mountain heights.

The Japanese 144 Regiment strength this day was a total of 891, from an original number of 2932. More than 500 were known to have been killed, the rest were lost to wounds and illness. Horibe's 6 Company was down to 14 men, from an original strength of 162; Sakamoto's MG company had 46 on duty from 137; III/144 was reduced to 176 from a landed strength of 744. Known killed in the battalions were, I Battalion – 167; II – 171; III – 152. The diet of 2 MG Company was supplemented with horse meat, and the company commander noted that 'it tasted surprisingly good'.[5]

2nd Lieutenant Ebuchi, who had arrived at Basabua on 18 August and been employed on various tasks in 144 Regiment, had been making patrols from the unit locations, but without contact with the Australians, and reported in person to Lieutenant Colonel Tsukamoto at regimental HQ.[6]

Early on 3 November, six Catalinas from Cairns attacked Buin–Faisi, but owing to bad weather, there were no further successful attacks on the ships, and anyway General Kenney had only three serviceable B17s. At 9.25 am, two B17s attacked a burning 8000-tonner (*Yasukawa Maru*) 56 miles (90 km) south-west of Gasmata. Three bombs missed, but 30 minutes later the ship was reported to be a solid mass of flames, with smoke to 4000 feet. There were no other recorded attacks relevant to the Kokoda campaign during the day.

Horii's staff issued Operation Order Ko-136 at 6 am at Papaki. The order referred to a 41 Regiment report of 2 November, that enemy had reached the Kokoda–Isurava track, that 41 Regiment had been attacked but held the enemy. 144 Regiment was to send III/144 to Baibari, three and a half miles (six km) south of Ilimo, to cover the left rear of the South Seas formation; Horii would remain at Papaki. Runners were to take the orders to HQ 144 Regiment, and those concerned would take notes from verbal instructions. At 8 am, the staff issued another order, Ko-135, to be passed verbally to those concerned. After considering the various reports, it seemed that 'a superior enemy force' was advancing on the Papaki–Isurava track, but details were not known; the formation would conduct reconnaissance of the main track and its vicinity, with patrols departing over the next few days.[7]

At 8.30 am, 7 Division staff, including Captain Bert Kienzle, arrived at Kokoda. The native carriers were adorned with flowers, and there were smiles all around; they had done well and received praise. Many local people knew Kienzle, and came to tell of hardships under the Japanese. Chiefs volunteered to provide carriers, morale was high; the Australians were winning. To mark the event of the Australian capture of Kokoda, a flag-raising ceremony was held later, with representative parties of soldiers from the available battalions, and medals presented to five worthy natives. In addition, gifts of tobacco, knives and other items of value to them had been made to the carriers. Enough supplies had been brought up for those away on tasks, so no one was missed out, and all received this acknowledgement.

The carriers, displeased with their treatment and the working conditions, had become markedly more amenable since seeing for themselves what Japanese occupation and military discipline meant. The wretched condition of the Rabaul natives who had been found, and the tales told by the people in areas the carriers walked through, were more than enough to convince them. Eyewitness accounts of beatings, bayoneting and shooting were told by all the survivors, and had a great impression. Dr Vernon was persuaded to mount a bicycle by some of his men, and despite it having no tyres, they pushed him along into Kokoda, a laughing party, and at last he felt he was home again.

2/25th Battalion, very tired after seven days on the march, had arrived at Kokoda and in the afternoon was put to work clearing the airfield. This work, then expanded by necessity to provide men for unloading the planes, went on for three days.

Away from the Kokoda celebrations, Brigadier Lloyd, Colonel C. C. F. Spry and other members of Lloyd's HQ staff were having a little excitement of their own. 2/2nd Battalion had departed the Kobara drop zone, but only had three days' bully beef and biscuits, and three miles (4.8 km) of telephone cable. While waiting at the end of this length for more, a company was sent on forward to clear for 1000 yards and patrol out from there along the Oivi track. However, Brigadier Lloyd, conscious of the need for speed after receiving Vasey's personal message the night before, and that there had been no contact, ordered 2/2nd HQ to go on, and with his party strode along the track, passing the infantry perimeter. The waiting Japanese hosed the group with light machinegun fire, not inflicting casualties, but quickening the heartbeats of many. 2/2nd Battalion war diary made sarcastic remarks about the rearward pace of the brigade HQ party. Brigadier Lloyd then set up his headquarters by a creek. Rifle platoons sent out cleared each side of the track, but the Japanese had gone, presumably never knowing how close they had come to dealing a solid blow to 16 Brigade. The brigade reached the Kokoda–Buna track, and found that though it had been reported by aircrews as trafficable to motor transport, even the new wonder vehicle, the jeep, would have had difficulty using the mudbath that existed.

Further on, Sergeant Blackwell and his patrol were fired on by three light and one heavy machineguns and a mountain gun, but despite this they closed in, remaining with the Japanese until 7 pm. Day ended too quickly for Lieutenant Colonel Edgar to attack, but he intended to do so next morning. He would employ B, C and D Companies. D, under Captain Blamey, was to go well to the left, cross the river and attack up onto the high ground; C, under Captain Swinton, was to cross with support from A Company, then attack towards the track from the right. The vegetation in the area was thicker than in the mountains, a tangled, dense mass, and movement off the tracks was very difficult, but water was plentiful. By the end of the day, 16 Brigade had 2/2nd Battalion forward against enemy positions, 2/3rd in rear of 2/2nd, and 2/1st at the drop zone.

The Japanese opposing 2/2nd Battalion was a composite battalion from Yazawa's 41 Regiment, well armed with machineguns and artillery, and with as much ammunition and food as could be carried to the Oivi positions. III/144, with Engineers, was at Gorari, and the other two battalions were with support troops at Ilimo.

After dawn on 4 November, nine B25s and seven B26s searched unsuccessfully for ships off Salamaua, and three A20s with escort attacked Oivi with 20-pound bombs from 2000 feet. Three B17s, in 'unusually clear' weather, set off on the daily reconnaissance of the Buna–Lae–Vitiaz Strait–Gasmata area, dropped eight bombs on a 12,000-ton ship off Salamaua; all missed. By this time, General Ennis Whitehead at HQ US 5th Air Force was becoming enraged at the continual bombing of ships 'off Salamaua', which proved to be the wreck off Gona. A poem was composed threatening dire things to the next person who wasted good bombs on the wreck. Salamaua was attacked by two waves of aircraft in the afternoon. At 2.10 pm, eight B25s dropped 30 bombs, but 16 of them hit in the water, though 14 others exploded across the target area. Twenty minutes later, six Beaufighters came in at treetop height looking for barges and personnel, did not find any, so strafed trucks, buildings and AA positions.

Japanese veterinary officer Yano reported on the condition of the horses of 2 MG Company: 10 dead and 14 alive, prompting the company commander to write that they would be able to eat meat with their rice again that night, adding, 'extremely grateful'. He had included a poem in his diary:

> *When we ran short of rations,*
> *We devoured our own kind to stave off starvation.*[8]

2/2nd Battalion put in its attack on the Japanese positions, but it was found that again they had gone. The nervous strain on the advancing Diggers was considerable. It was known that the Japanese could fight with great determination, that he was well-armed and quickly able to construct formidable defences; he could be waiting anywhere along the track. The cumulative effect of advancing into the unknown, prepared to fight at any time, plus the letdown when a planned attack on a position was found to be unnecessary, was very wearing.

Only 1000 yards from this empty position, the Japanese were waiting again, and fired on 7 Platoon, then withdrew. When 7 took up the advance, an hour and a half later they came under light and heavy machinegun and mountain gun fire. Captain Fairbrother had 7 Platoon pinned down across the track, so sent 9 Platoon to the right and 8 to the left. Japanese fire was intense, with many rounds of shell fire. One Australian was killed and three wounded, then at 5 pm the Japanese again withdrew. The wheel tracks showed that they were pulling a 75-mm mountain gun. Night fell before contact was made again.

Major General Vasey arrived at 16 Brigade HQ to discuss operations and the problems of movement. It was decided to send 2/1st Battalion well to the right. Fires were allowed and tea made, plus an issue of small amounts of chocolate, cigarettes and writing paper combined to raise morale higher. At Kokoda, native carriers were allocated to the brigades, with 230 to 16 Brigade and 323 to 25 Brigade.

2/1st Battalion had stopped to receive an air drop, and recovering the bundles in the kunai was very hot and difficult work. Lieutenant Colonel Cullen used the time to study the situation. He suggested to Brigadier Lloyd that the battalion move east to Gorari or Ilimo to outflank the positions at Oivi. This was accepted, and the battalion was warned to be on the lookout for US troops advancing from the other direction. An additional 70 natives were allocated to the battalion for carrying. Available maps were inaccurate, but had few details anyway. This lack of knowledge of the tracks caused great loss of time and much roaming the country for all units.

The battalion set off along the track, crossed two streams and passed a native village, then after two hours walking halted for the night. The ANGAU staff sergeant in charge of the carriers then pointed out that the nearby village was where they'd spent last night, and was only 300 yards from the drop zone where the supplies had come in. The track had gone in a half-circle. The Aussie sense of humour came to the rescue. Pressing on, the night halt was made on a razorback ridge, with rain pelting down, and many of the men ill with dysentery. The diet was the usual cold bully beef and dry biscuits.

At Kokoda, the first Douglas C47 transport aircraft had been able to land, and all indications were that the supply situation now would become easier, with no wastage from air drops. Also, casualties could be flown back to Port Moresby. All this meant that the unfortunates at Myola were even further down the priority list, and eventually some of the patients there recovered enough to walk back to Moresby, arriving there at the end of December.

2/4th Field Ambulance moved to Kokoda and established a Main Dressing Station, but everything was in such short supply that for a time sick men who arrived had to build their own shelters. Alan Watson was a dentist, but during the advance along the trail had been working as an anaesthetist. At Kokoda, and later, at Popondetta, he also performed the duty of Plane Loading Officer. He found that US transport pilots, having delivered their cargo, were quite prepared to take off empty, and ignore wounded Australians. 'Regrettably, I fell back on "bribery and corruption": one Jap helmet, five sitting cases; one Jap rifle, 10 Australian sick or wounded; so many rounds of ammo per extra body taken back; stretcher cases "cost" more.' RAAF pilots posed no such problem.

The sound of the transport aircraft in the Kokoda area had been heard by Bede Tongs's patrol, passing around to the north, and was a source of some comfort to them. They had come across a deserted village, and found there two Japanese graves, identified by the well-carved wood markers planted on them. Not knowing what the situation was, the patrol was alert. The village warriors appeared in the kunai patch, small, light-brown men armed with bows and arrows, and a tense situation was defused when Bede's men were seen to be friendly. The women and children appeared, and finally Bede gave the headman a quantity of salt, which he carried on advice from ANGAU. He never did find out how the Japanese graves came to be there, but pushed on with the last part of the patrol – still alert for Japanese.

Bede's parent 3rd Battalion, after moving to Myola and coming under command 25 Brigade, had then gone to Kokoda, but now was placed under command of 16 Brigade, and moved to the Kobara drop zone. 3rd Battalion had for some time been short of clothing, equipment, tobacco and mosquito nets, but was not to receive all these things at Kobara. The rumour that on arrival at Kokoda the battalion would be flown back to Moresby, rested, and sent on leave to Australia was fondly nurtured by some of the battalion. It was a pleasant sunny day, the track had dried, the travelling was easy, and as the battalion neared Kokoda, it entered the rubber plantation. Such basic matters as the good weather and walking conditions made spirits rise, and the plantation was thought of as a nice place to camp before flying to Moresby. In the evening, officers and NCOs were called to conferences, runners were hurrying past, and none of this seemed related to flying back to Moresby. The rumours were reconsidered, and Moresby, rest camps and leave to Australia were discarded. Reality was to be bitter fighting in the Buna–Gona campaign.

Meanwhile, 2/2nd and 2/3rd Battalions had been fighting their running battle until at Oivi the Japanese turned and let loose a hail of fire from light and heavy machineguns and mountain guns. The Australians began to attack the high ground. The Fulton and Lysaght companies of 2/3rd combined, but were held by the stiff resistance. The mortars, supplied from Kokoda, were fired, but the Japanese replied with maximum fire from all types of weapons, and this heavy shooting went on all day from both sides.

On 5 November, five Catalinas attacked Tonolei, and on the usual reconnaissance around the northern circle, three B25s attacked a small schooner at Arawe, on the south coast of New Britain. A B17 on reconnaissance to Rabaul was attacked by six Zeros over St George's Channel, claimed one destroyed, but was hit in return. Other B17, B25 and B26 missions were flown in the Lae–

Salamaua area, with no results. Three A20s attacked Oivi, but saw nothing to report. For the second day, the Japanese 144 Regiment logged the flight past of aircraft, but no damage was suffered. The low level of aerial activity continued next day, with no attack missions and only the usual morning and afternoon reconnaissance flights over the northern arc from New Guinea.

On 5 November, Lieutenant Colonel Edgar's 2/2nd had decided on a battle drill: on contact B Company would try the local flanks, while C went deeper to the right, and the companies closed up and linked. This had been done at company level, with platoons, but not with the full battalion. The two Oivi features were obvious places for the Japanese to defend, at least for some time. At 8.10 am, contact was made, with the now-usual heavy volume of Japanese fire, including mortars. Ferguson's B Company was held by the defenders, and two companies of 2/3rd (Gall's and Walker's) who were attached were sent to the left to assist B Company. Meanwhile, D Company attacked on the right, was held, and dug in. By 11.35 am, C Company came back to the main track, having been unable to penetrate the Japanese positions, and was sent to the right of Blamey's D Company. All the battalion was now committed, and the Japanese showed no sign of leaving.

Lloyd's 16 Brigade was not at full strength, and what was available was somewhat fragmented. 2/1st Battalion was with 25 Brigade; two rifle companies of 2/3rd were moving up from Kobara drop zone and two were with 2/2nd Battalion in action at Oivi. Lysaght's and Fulton's companies of 2/3rd, when they arrived at the battle, went around to the right, but were held by machinegun and mortar fire. The Japanese had prepared themselves well. The spurs they held were covered with fire from light and heavy machineguns firing on fixed lines, as well as fire from snipers, mortars and mountain guns. The Australians were dug in only 60 yards away; there was little sleep that night.

2/1st Battalion, pushing east, moved south of Oivi through a succession of deserted villages. At Sengai village, they found the bodies of five members of 2/14th, left by Buckler's party, which escaped that way after Isurava, and arrived at Sengai on 21 Sep-

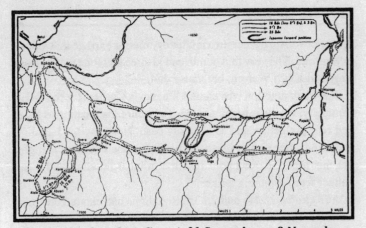

The approach to Oivi–Gorari, 31 September to 8 November.

tember. The Japanese arrived on 4 October. At least, the Japanese were blamed for the murders.

Postwar investigations were made after several Rabaul half-castes and natives gave accounts of the wartime activities of a half-caste Chinese from Rabaul. He had been in trouble prewar for stealing, and when the Japanese arrived had at once become an enthusiastic supporter and gone with them to New Guinea. There he dressed in Japanese uniform, carried pistols of Japanese and US make, a rifle, and in appearance was indistinguishable from the Japanese. He boasted of how he had been allowed to fire the machinegun at Australians, of how he had beaten and killed Rabaul and New Guinea natives, and had killed white Australian troops. One of his boasts concerned shooting a number of Australian wounded found in a hut during the Kokoda campaign. This person returned to Rabaul and remained in Japanese service until the end of the war, as a member of the Kempeitai (military security police). He then took off his uniform and tried to resume civilian life. Apparently, not enough evidence could be gathered to bring the fellow to trial.[9]

2/1st Battalion found signs of Japanese patrols not far ahead of it, then came to the Gorari track junction and paused overnight. Lieutenant Blakiston and 8 Platoon patrolled north along the Gorari track, and surprised three Japanese cleaning weapons and cooking. In the flurry of firing, two Japanese were wounded, but so were two Australians in a retaliatory mortar barrage that quickly was fired. The very first bomb landed three feet (one metre) from Corporal Keith Warren, but was a dud.

The track junction was named 'Leaney's Corner' for the OC A Company, who was to remain there to secure the location as flank and rear protection and as a supply base. Next day the battalion was to advance east to Ilimo. As usual, it rained during the night, but this time the downpour resulted in local flooding and some danger from lightning strikes.

At Kokoda, 2/25th and 2/33rd Battalions had cleared the grass from the strip, then assisted with unloading transport planes. The first US jeeps were delivered, and were cause for much enquiry and interest as they zipped around the area. The Willys jeep may have been the single most coveted item of equipment in the Second World War, after cigarettes, alcohol and nylons. Fresh food, bread and chocolate was flown in, and the battalions revelled in the evening meal, it being two months since the last cooked food was eaten. Just as welcome were complete issues of new clothing. However, the fresh food reacted strongly on the stomachs of many men, causing upset bowels.

Lieutenant Colonel Buttrose, 2/33rd, was able to inform the five men he had nominated that they were now commissioned officers, and allocated them to their platoons. At this time, 2/33rd had A and C Companies commanded by lieutenants, and B, D and HQ Companies by captains. It numbered 16 officers and 271 other ranks; some platoon strengths had been brought up to equal that of others by transfers within the unit. 2/31st Battalion had been patrolling without contact, but the unit diary noted that on this day, for the first time, native women were seen in the area. The locals had accepted that the Japanese were not going to return.

Few of the Australians, or the Japanese for that matter, had the war inflict damage on their homes, unlike many of the native people over whose land the campaign was fought. One man who had a home in the area was Captain Bert Kienzle. He asked permission to leave Kokoda itself and went to his plantation at nearby Yodda. The buildings had been damaged by air strikes and the rubber plantation itself needed care; he returned to his ANGAU duties.

On 6 November, Sergeant Bede Tongs's 3rd Battalion patrol arrived at Kokoda, and were pleasantly surprised at the scale of activity as they emerged from the bush and began crossing the airfield. Suddenly, on the tip of the plateau ahead, they saw the Australian flag flying, and a spontaneous cheer went up. The work parties around looked at the bedraggled party crossing the strip, but Bede presumed the workers had done their own cheering a few days earlier. The appearance of the flag 'is still one of the greatest sights I can picture in my mind'. He asked where 3rd Battalion was, and went on to Oivi. There, Lieutenant Colonel Cameron told him that things had changed so much that the patrol was immaterial, but had been of value, as the Japanese graves in the village showed the enemy knew of the place and had been in the area. The patrol went back to B Company.

Horii's staff issued Order A-137 at 9 am, informing readers that yesterday the Yazawa Unit (41 Regiment) had been attacked by an Australian battalion, but had repulsed them. This referred to Oivi. The Kuwata battalion also had been attacked and also had held. The force would consolidate on key points south of Ilimo.[10]

One of the Japanese HQ 144 Regiment clerks maintained a type of unit diary. For this day, he wrote of 'heavy gunfire in the early morning', and the later meeting of commanders to discuss the move to Baribe, which was reached at 6 pm. Some mortar fire was heard, in the distance. He also wrote, 'experienced difficulty in cooking on damp ground'. 2nd Lieutenant Ebuchi went out on a patrol with three men, but apparently did not make contact with any enemy.[11] The 144 Regiment strength reported at the headquarters location on this day was: HQ 48, II/144 123, Signals 16, Artillery 30, Engineers 15, Military Police 2. At 1 pm, the main strength of 144 Regiment began marching to the battle area at Oivi and Gorari, following III/144.[12]

At the Oivi position, the day began warily: the Japanese were only a short distance away. A patrol from Lysaght's company lost seven men close to the position, but Fulton's men were more successful. Fulton and Lysaght attacked at 2 pm, the firing was continuous and heavy, pinning Lysaght's men, but Fulton's fought through to the highest feature. Japanese fire was so intense that the Aussies were forced off the crest. Major Hutchison, commanding 2/3rd, used the Anti-aircraft Platoon, commanded by Lieutenant F. J. Hoddinott, DCM, to reinforce and hold the ground. Then it seemed the Japanese were about to attack strongly between Lysaght and 2/2nd Battalion. Major Hutchison asked for one extra company, but as that was not enough, requested a second. He was sent the companies of Captains Atkinson and Jeffrey, 3rd Battalion. They took position on the right, and helped repulse a Japanese dusk counter-attack, but soon after Japanese mortars killed one and wounded three Diggers. On the left, Walker and Gall had not been able to locate the Japanese flank. Gall's men, trying to work around the enemy, could hear Japanese chattering and chopping as they improved their defences.

By the end of the day, Australian casualties were 14 killed and 36 wounded. An unarmed stretcher party from brigade HQ was attacked by a patrol of Japanese, and the Australians' only recourse was speed through the bush; all returned safely next day. Brigadier Lloyd informed 7 Division that the Japanese position was three miles in length (4.8 km), that 2/2nd and 2/3rd plus two companies of 3rd Battalion were committed and he had only two companies of 3rd Battalion as a reserve, while he thought that the Japanese had two and possibly three battalions in their positions.

For the Australians, benefits began to flow from the landings by C47s at Kokoda. New rations, although in small quantities, arrived at the battalions: dried potatoes, tinned fruit, sausages, vegetables, jam and butter, meat and vegetables, baked beans, as well as dried fruits and tea. It was difficult to break up the bulk for issue necessary in the forward positions, and there was not much of the new rations, but it was preferable to bully beef and biscuits.

General Kenney flew to Port Moresby with General MacArthur, and this time both were to stay until the 'Buna show' was an Allied success. An advanced echelon of GHQ had been established a few days earlier. The media, controlled by MacArthur's staff, had consistently given a false impression, that MacArthur was often or continuously present at the battle front, when in reality he was in Brisbane, and only made fleeting visits to New Guinea.

2/1st Battalion, trying to find the Ilimo track, was not making much progress, and eventually realised the maps were useless. Next day it was decided to turn back to Leaney's Corner, then go north to Gorari. During the day a runner from Leaney arrived, but disappeared on the return journey. A second runner came in with word that he had seen Japanese near the creek at Wallopa, so he was escorted back.

On 7 November, the usual reconnaissance missions were flown, with nothing to report. The only mission in support of the Kokoda campaign was flown at 10.35 am, in good visibility, when three A20s attacked Kakandetta and Soputa, and reported AA heavy and accurate, but off in bearing. Half Buna airfield was reported to be under water, and the rest very muddy.

144 Regiment logged an attack on its position by Allied aircraft, but no damage was recorded. Regimental HQ issued an order to all units, stating that one-third of unit strength was to be on guard at night in all front line positions; all personnel, in front and rear positions, were to wear ammunition pouches and bayonet at all times; voices were to be kept low, silence was to be observed by day and night, and wood chopping was to be done quietly. Rather than a formation alleged by Horii in his earlier declarations to be not worried about the enemy, and moving back only because of supply and health problems, this order reveals the real situation: the Japanese had lost the initiative, and all ranks now had to be ready to fight at any time.[13]

The diarist at HQ 144 Regiment noted a bombardment by three Australian mortars on 41 Regiment (Oivi), and the estimated loss of 100 men by the Australians in attacking III/144, on the left flank. The regiment was digging trenches, preparing for more attacks. The writer wondered how the Solomons fighting was going. 2nd Lieutenant Shigeru Ebuchi, patrol officer for III/144, reported to his CO at 6 am, and was told that he would be relieving No. 7 Company. This was his last entry, and the diary was captured on 16 November on the Kokoda–Oivi track.[14]

The attack referred to by the regimental diarist was made at 8.15 am by B Company 3rd Battalion and 2/3rd Battalion, but was halted by well-sited Japanese machineguns firing accurately on fixed lines. Fulton's and Atkinson's companies fired from the right, across the front of the attacking men from the companies of Lysaght and Jeffrey, with Edgar's 2/2nd firing similarly from the left, but the Japanese fire killed and wounded another 13 men, and no advance was possible. Later, the battalion mortars silenced some of those machineguns.

Major General Vasey was not going to continue frontal attacks on prepared positions, and began a southward flanking movement with his other battalions. The initiative was firmly in the hands of the Australians. 7 Division had ordered its brigades according to Major General Vasey's view of the developing battle. 25 Brigade was to advance east and secure a bridgehead over Kumusi River, while 16 Brigade was to hold and harass the enemy at Oivi, and hold the high ground there when taken. Casualties in 16 Brigade, for the campaign so far, to the end of this day were 107 killed, 278 wounded and one missing.

25 Brigade departed Kokoda, to capture Gorari. The rest had done much good for the Diggers, though the two days' fresh food had resulted in some diarrhoea. As usual, the weather was stormy, with rain carried along by the wind making life uncomfortable. The battalions marched to Kobara, and 2/25th Battalion diary noted that it was an 11-hour effort, with troops along the trail retching, weak with fatigue and severe diarrhoea, said to be caused by the new food, the heat and excessive exercise. 2/31st Battalion was moving in a right flanking sweep, now commanded by Lieutenant Colonel Miller, formerly second-in-command of 2/1st Battalion. Like the other battalions, 2/31st also enjoyed a couple of days on the new rations, washed, rested, and had been issued new clothes. As they pushed ahead, in the distance the men could hear the sound of the mortars at Oivi. 2/1st Battalion moved north to attack Gorari, under command of 25 Brigade. General Vasey was about to snap shut his pincers on the Japanese.

On 8 November, the daily reconnaissance flights found nothing to report, nor did the first attack mission of the day at 8.50 am, flown in good visibility by three A20s to Oivi. However, the Japanese mountain artillery position was strafed, as noted by 2nd Lieutenant Ino, 41 Infantry.[15] Three B25s checking Buna–Lae–Gasmata reported Buna airfield covered with water, nothing to report at Wairopi, and a heavy front with rain from Gasmata to the east. At 1.10 pm, the weather around Buna was still clear when three Beaufighters at treetop level, with four P40s escorting at 12,000 feet, swept the Wairopi–Buna–Popondetta area, confirmed Buna airfield was flooded, and there was no Japanese activity seen, but AA was accurately placed around the higher-flying P40s. No further attack missions were flown over the Kokoda battle area, but at 11 pm, three Catalinas harassed Kavieng airfield.

However, at Oivi, the land action continued. At dawn on 8 November, when the Diggers in 3rd Battalion began to move around after the night, Japanese snipers who had crept close inflicted some casualties before they were chased off or left of their own accord. During the day, beginning at 6.45 am, the battalion mortars fired more than 130 rounds into the Japanese positions on the right. However, their enthusiasm was reined in somewhat when the battalion was informed that supplies of mortar bombs were not enough for such a bombardment, and the rate of fire was to be reduced to harassment rather than the heavy rate preferred. Japanese could be heard squealing as the bombardment went on. Not to be outdone, the Japanese fired their own weapons in reply. An issue of comforts was made to the attacking battalions: a small amount of tobacco, half a cake of soap, one handkerchief, half a packet of chewing gum per man; 18 pounds (8.1 kg) of cake delivered to 2/2nd Battalion was sent to the forward troops.

To the south, at Gorari, 2/31st Battalion met 2/1st Battalion, then pushed on. There was light contact with the Japanese, and Lieutenant Colonel Miller made a reconnaissance, then decided to put in a right flanking attack assisted by a diversion from A Company. All was ready at 11.15 am; fire was opened at 11.50, but the enemy replied to the mortar bombardment with their own, wounding Lieutenant Mules and a Digger. At 12.30 pm, the 2/31st companies advanced, and hit the Japanese, later reporting them on a front of 300 yards of which the flanks could not be located. The Australians suffered 16 casualties. Several chances to fire at Japanese had been lost, as there was some uncertainty as to the location of two Australian platoons. The day cost the battalion three killed and 25 wounded, for a known Japanese loss of three dead. The night was quiet. The Japanese were Kuwata's III/144, responsible for the mass murders of 2/22nd Battalion on New Britain in February. The AIF battalions, of course, did not know this at the time.

2/1st Battalion, under command of 25 Brigade at Gorari, was to be used to exploit any successes. Eather sent 2/25th around past 2/31st, to get behind the Japanese, and then sent 2/33rd wider still, to cut the track to Buna, and 2/1st went even further to the right. A Company 2/25th got astride the Kobara–Ilimo track, behind the enemy, and held the position for three days while the rest of the battalion cut the track between the enemy and Gorari, despite torrential rain that caused flooding in some areas. There developed a triangular battlefield, with 3rd, 2/2nd and 2/3rd Battalions fighting in the west at Oivi, 2/25th and 2/31st fighting at the southern angle of the triangle, and 2/33rd and 2/1st in action at the third, eastern corner of the triangle. For both sides, ammunition supply was not a great problem. Aircraft were flying it in to Kokoda for the Australians, and the Japanese were close to their dumps. The noise of battle, especially mortars and artillery, was almost ceaseless.

2/33rd was ordered to send a patrol to the east, to check on enemy strength at Ilimo and to act as a flank protection force for the remainder of the division. B Company was so reduced in numbers that after 30 fit men were selected, only 22 were left. These men were not able to go on the patrol, but could not be spared from the intense action all knew was imminent. Five days' rations were taken, and Lieutenant Phil Curry, with the Intelligence Officer Lieutenant Bob Howland, took the patrol off to the east.

The results of the fighting around the Japanese 144 Regiment were logged as: 'Enemy attacked II Battalion's line. Our casualties, five dead.' The regimental diarist wrote that 'the enemy penetrated our positions after lunch, attacking furiously with automatic rifles. We challenged them, and the fire became intense. Yoshimoto died in action, and Private Moriona was also killed. Several others were killed or wounded. We fought in the rain until midnight'.[16]

At 8.40 am on 9 November, six A20s strafed and bombed Oivi, reporting visibility over the target unlimited, but Kokoda and Myola overcast. Fifteen minutes later, nine Beaufighters strafed targets at Popondetta, Giropa and Sanananda, but had nothing to report except a barge burning and two aircraft hit by AA from Giropa Point. Behind them came eight B26s showering 100-pound bombs on supply dumps in the Sanananda–Buna area. Photos showed the airfield contained 13 destroyed or damaged aircraft, but none serviceable. A carrying party of Takasago volunteers on the Popondetta road had to run into the trees several times when attacked during this strike, but there were no casualties. The gunnery log for the Sasebo AA unit recorded the attacks as 'Today's raid was the most severe since landing here. One enemy fighter was shot down by Army guns at Buna.' Another AA unit member noted that at 8.30 am, 'shot down one of three enemy twin-engined planes'. No Allied loss was recorded. One B17 on reconnaissance was attacked over Mono Island by two Zeros, who put seven machinegun holes in the bomber.[17]

The Japanese 144 Regiment strength had shrunk to: HQ 46, II/144 118, III/144 126, Signals 24, Mountain Artillery 42, Engineers 15, Medical 5.[18]

Lieutenant Colonel Edgar was evacuated sick from 2/2nd Battalion, on the opinions of the brigade commander and medical officer. He went back to Kokoda, and Major Buckley administered command; Edgar returned when he had improved. 3rd Battalion kept up the pressure on the Japanese with a bombardment of 30 rounds of two-inch mortar bombs. 2/1st Battalion, for its part, had noticed the difference in 25 Brigade troops brought about by the two days' rest at Kokoda, and the more important two nights of good sleep. The troops looked fresh and healthy, though they said they did not feel rested enough. 2/1st were exhausted and plagued with diarrhoea. 2/33rd Battalion passed through 2/1st, to get behind the Japanese and try to reach the Kokoda–Ilimo track. While waiting to move off, 2/1st was issued with enough supplies to allow each man a small piece of fruit and two sweet biscuits. This was such a memorable event that years after the war it was recalled and was worthy of a place in the unit history. Such was the supply situation in the forward units in November 1942.

South of Gorari, 2/25th Battalion attacked, but failed against the good positions prepared by the Japanese, who had cleared fields of fire, erected barricades, and placed medium machineguns to cover them. In addition, the Japanese counter-attacked twice. Machinegun fire made it impossible to hold the ground that had been gained, and the Aussies had to withdraw to their original positions. The assaults cost four officers and 10 soldiers killed, with two officers and 21 men wounded.

Meanwhile, 14 Platoon C Company 2/31st had enjoyed some success: Japanese withdrawing north-east along the Gorari track were fired on, losing eight killed, and two light machineguns were captured. Two Australians were killed, one was wounded. Later, Lieutenant Colonel Miller told all companies to apply pressure on the Japanese, and informed them of 2/25th Battalion's activities. 2/31st advanced until the leading platoon of A Company was pinned down by automatic weapons fire. A wide field of fire had been cleared, and vine fences erected across it; all was covered with fire and it was impossible to cross the cleared areas. A and C Companies dug in and kept up a volume of fire across the clearing, while D Company went to the flank, where 2/25th was met. 2/31st was to act as 'an offensive block' while 2/25th pushed south. 2/31st was astride the track, with Captain A. L. Hurrell's company on the right, Thorn's in the centre and Beazley's on the left, with Upcher's and Major E. Thorne's Headquarters Company in reserve. 2/31st had lost nine killed and nine wounded, but 12 Japanese were found dead.

2/33rd Battalion, passing to the east beyond 2/25th and 2/31st, pushed on to the north, and was 500 yards from Gorari village when the scouts were fired on. D Company was leading, and Captain Clowes began to manoeuvre his platoons. By 3 pm, the huts of Gorari were visible through the trees. To the left of 2/33rd, the

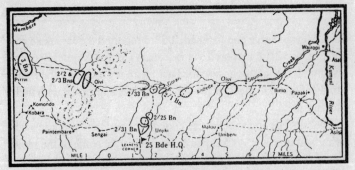

Oivi–Gorari, nightfall on 9 November.

battle for Oivi was in full swing; behind, 2/25th and 2/31st were
in action; Lieutenant Colonel Buttrose ordered C Company, under
Lieutenant Cullen, to go to the right of D Company and clear up
to the village, as well as link with 2/1st if possible. Radio communications in the valley were good, and Buttrose was able to speak
to Brigadier Eather, back beyond the 2/25th combat. Meanwhile,
C Company 2/33rd prepared to get up into the middle of the battle
area. The Japanese were in position on the far bank of a small
creek, and used this to good advantage, with the creek bed covered
by fire. Lieutenant Frank McTaggart's 15 Platoon was caught in
a killing zone, losing one man killed and four wounded. Lieutenant Cullen sent Sergeant Storey's 14 Platoon to assist, at which
time the Japanese put in a left-flanking attack. Cullen realised he
was about to be surrounded, and gave the order to withdraw. This
was easier said than done, and a platoon from A Company had to
assist, but by 5.30 pm the company was back at its starting point.
The dead man had to be left in the creek bed. D Company 2/33rd
had held its position astride the southern track, but no link-up with
2/1st had been made; their battle could be heard going on. A Company moved up to the left of D, C moved to its rear and the small
B Company came in between A and C, with HQ in the centre. To
the rear, 1000 yards away, the sound of 2/25th could be heard.
Night came.

At 5 pm, 2/1st came up to 2/33rd rear positions, turned east, and
500 yards away came to a roaring torrent some 50 feet (15 metres)
wide, which forced the battalion to follow it north. Then firing was
heard and it was presumed 2/33rd was in action. 2/1st tapped into

the telephone cable and listened. 2/33rd reported the Japanese going east, and 2/1st prepared a response. A Company quickly organised with two platoons up, one back, with the creek on the right, and went into the attack as the Japanese were engrossed with their evening meal.

The surprise and shock were enough to send the Japanese scattering and running. A Company swept through, some of the more thoughtful 9 Platoon Diggers grabbing containers of cooking rice from the fires as they passed. A Company then came to a Japanese defensive position, and some 2/33rd wounded from the previous clash. The enemy had been bounced from the high ground where he had already dug in. A little further on, A Company captured a bridge over the torrent, realised the Japanese would be bound to attack to recapture it, and reported the find to 25 Brigade HQ. Also found was enough quinine to issue two tablets per man per day for the rest of the campaign. In fact, this quinine had been originally intended for 2/1st, but was air-dropped to the Japanese by mistake. 2/1st settled in for the night, eastern flank along the creek, northern along the track, determined to prevent enemy movement past and across the bridge.

However, neither side could use the bridge. Just on the far side was a cluster of rocks some 10 feet (three metres) high, which provided a commanding position. Accurate Japanese snipers held out there for two days. 2/1st would have to cross the river upstream, then attack along the east bank and force the Japanese away from positions from which they commanded the eastern end of the bridge. Seizure of the bridge would be crucial to the development of the fighting in the next few days; the Japanese were beginning to realise they were in a desperate situation.

'Enveloping attack by about 150 enemy. Lieutenant Sueki Kawamura died in action,' was the log entry of 144 Regiment for the day's fighting. This was the final entry, and the log itself was captured on 11 November south of Gorari. The regimental HQ diarist: 'Early in the morning the enemy again attacked. Sergeant Major Sakai was killed and there were three or four other casualties. The enemy surrounded us and commenced firing from all sides, the firing continued in the jungle through the night.' This was the last entry, and the pages also were captured south of Gorari on 11 November.[19]

Horii's staff issued Operation Order Ko-140 at 6 pm, at Ilimo:
'1. The enemy's attack against 41 Regiment has subsided since morning. It seems the enemy is increasing his strength against 144 Regiment, and approximately a hundred men with trench mortars is attacking; prisoner admits it is 33rd Battalion. After withdrawal to Oivi area, formation supplies have been replenished slightly, but fatigue of transport personnel and horses has increased and their strength is obviously weakening each day. The hardships have increased due to roads and bridges being destroyed by storms which lasted several days. The Guadalcanal area is attacked now by superior forces but as yet does not appear to be in danger.

'2. According to Army Orders, the formation will withdraw to the east bank of the Kumusi River to occupy the area.

'3. A part of 15 Independent Engineer Regiment will assist the formation in crossing the river. The crossing will be completed quickly from the night of the 10th to the night of the 16th. Crossing will commence at dusk to avoid air attack.

'4. 1 Company 55 Division Engineer Regiment will immediately repair bridges west of Papaki to facilitate formation movements. Together with other units, a strong part of it will remain on each bridge for necessary repairs, then destroy it after all units have crossed.

'5. Each unit between Ilimo and Papaki will go into operations from tomorrow, 10 November. Based on dispositions under Lieutenant Tada, the river will be crossed in approximately the following order: Wireless platoon, Ilimo and Papaki Convalescent Hospitals, Mountain Artillery elements, Service Corps, labourers and Takasago volunteers, after evacuating all patients and moving across all stores, ammunition, etc.

'6. At dusk on 10 November, 41 Regiment will hold the area east of Ilimo and the bridge four km [2.4 miles] west of Papaki, and delay the enemy advance as much as possible, at least until evening 16 November.

'7. At dusk on 10 November, 144 Regiment will cross immediately after 41 Regiment, and will concentrate in the vicinity of the east side of crossing point. The regiment is to occupy the streams between Ilimo and Papaki, and check the enemy advance at least until the evening of 14 November.

'8. 3 MG Company 144 Regiment will secure the three-road junction near Ilimo and cover passage of the other units. Withdrawal has been arranged for morning of 11 November. [Item 9 dealt with wireless communications arrangements for the move back; not relevant to this account.]

'10. If bridges are destroyed, each unit will assist the Engineers with repairs. Take care not to give away the plan to the air, particularly when using the bridge. In the event of air attack, units will take cover to avoid destruction of the bridge [sic]. [Item 11 dealt with distribution of supplies at Ilimo, while item 12 dealt with sectors assigned to transport units.]

'13. On the morning of 10 November, I will move from my present location, and after making arrangements for changing the direction of the various units at the bridge east of Ilimo, will leave on the morning of 11 November for Papaki. After the river crossing, I will be at the east bank at that point. The river crossing is scheduled for 6 pm 12 November. Runners will accompany me. – Tomitaro Horii, Formation commander.'[20]

For the Australians closely engaging the Japanese at Oivi, there was no hint of this intended withdrawal. Yazawa and his force began a professionally executed disengagement from an enemy in close contact. The firing, the resistance was just as strong. News arrived of the successes against the Germans and Italians in North Africa, and 16 Brigade diarist recorded that it 'sent spirits soaring'. Less welcome was the information that the amounts of comfort supplies, such as tobacco and soap, as given by 7 Division were higher than actually received by the brigade, but it was agreed that the lower figures acknowledged by the brigade as received would be accepted.

In the afternoon, three B25s flew the usual northern reconnaissance route and claimed one direct hit on a 5000-ton ship in St

George's Channel. Salamaua AA was heavy, intense and accurate, though some was off in direction. During the night, three Catalinas attacked Kavieng, one Catalina attacked a destroyer with four 250-pound bombs, but missed.

Around Gorari, no rain fell. This simple fact was of importance to the tired and dirty infantry in position there. It meant they would have the pleasure of beginning the next day dry. That was about all the local good news. Japanese were active all around the positions, and could be seen moving on all sides of 2/33rd. Even within the battalion position, one man was lost. Private George Gates was sent from C Company to HQ, and disappeared. He was found dead after the action, bayoneted. His brother was in 18 Platoon.

At dawn on 10 November, the security patrol from A Company 2/33rd clashed with about 30 Japanese only 30 yards from the company perimeter. Two Australians were killed and three wounded, and an unknown number of Japanese fell. The rest of the Japanese then charged forward, yelling and leaping, past A Company and into B Company, inflicting three more casualties. Captain Brinkley, the OC, was badly hit in the stomach and died later. Then a runner from HQ to C Company was shot dead after taking only 20 paces. The worst aspect of the developing action was that the Japanese dragged up a mountain gun and began to fire high-explosive and air-burst shrapnel into D Company 2/33rd at point blank range – 400 yards. This stream of shells went on for three hours, while D Company held on with no means of hitting back. The unit historian described the D Company situation as desperate. As well as the shelling, small arms fire came from Japanese infiltrating or trying to escape. Five men were killed and two wounded. With nothing to dig with except a bayonet, and the ready idea that to remain was to be blown to pieces for no benefit, some men made their own decision and went back. Corporal MacKay was sent to bring them back, and Captain Clowes threatened to shoot anyone else who left the position. D Company, after steady losses at Imita and on the Templeton's Crossing track, had reached a crucial point. It held despite all, grimly enduring. C Company 2/33rd sent out patrols to keep the flanks clear, and more men were wounded and killed in

A Company. By the end of the day, there were 30 dead, dying and wounded around the aid post, which was only a short distance from battalion HQ. All around was the sound of battle, from the other battalions and from the rifle companies themselves. 2/33rd held on through a trying day.

To the south of 2/33rd, D Company 2/25th attacked the enemy there, reached the Japanese positions, but was forced to withdraw by intense fire placed across the open ground; the company lost two killed and eight wounded. 2/25th and 2/31st maintained contact with patrols, and prepared to attack together onto Kuwata's III/144. But the Japanese charged first, at 3.10 pm. D Company 2/31st repulsed them, then at once got up and assaulted, with emphasis on the Tommy gun and bayonet, sweeping forward 75 yards, inflicting heavy casualties, but losing 15 of their own. Thirty-eight dead Japanese were counted, and it was known others had been killed and wounded. Battalion HQ moved up to the old D Company position. By 5 pm, 2/31st dispositions were: D Company forward on the left, B forward on the right, A and C Companies in support, with HQ Company in the rear, astride the track. Lieutenant Colonel Miller told D Company that no assistance was available, asked if they could hold, and back came the confident reply that they would hold for a week if necessary. Battalion casualties since 8 November were 18 dead, five thought to be killed, and 44 wounded. At the end of the day, battalion strength was 16 officers and 332 other ranks; total casualties had been four officers and 26 men killed, 10 officers and 78 men wounded; eight officers and 179 men were in hospital.

This day, 10 November, was the final test of strength between the combatants on the Kokoda Trail. If the Japanese, by whatever means, could have dislodged any of the attacking Australian battalions, particularly the eastern units, they could have exploited the advantage and escaped. It was a test of doggedness, and the AIF battalions hung on.

Early morning sweeps by P40s and P400s did not find any Japanese fighters and there was nothing to report. Six RAAF Beaufighters were ordered to attack targets from Kokoda to Buna, and the first flight of three strafed barges, truck dispersal areas and dumps in the Sanananda–Soputa–Amboga area, in conditions of unlimited visibility, but the second flight failed to get through intervening bad weather. At 9.20 am, a coordinated attack by eight B26s and three A20s attacked targets in the Soputa–Sanananda area. From 1400 feet, the B26s dropped 100-pound bombs, reporting two secondary explosions and a hit on AA positions, while at 75 feet, the A20s showered 23-pound parafrag bombs on the AA position. Crews saw one AA gun blown out of its pit by a B26 bomb. They went back to strafe despite the ground fire, and one A20 was hit in an engine nacelle, but another had a much more exciting pass over the area.

As Lieutenant Ed Larner was coming in to attack, an AA shell exploded behind his A20, pushing the tail up, and the nose down. Before Larner could correct, he found himself flying through the treetops, and the Douglas A20 carved a path through the foliage for at least 30 yards, before he managed to haul it up out of the greenery. The plane was heavily damaged around the nose, cowlings and propeller blade leading edges. A tribute to its designers and builders, the A20 flew back to base. Ed Larner was the sort of man Kenney needed in the 5th Air Force, and following his policy of rewarding actions as soon as possible, Larner was promoted to captain and awarded the Silver Star. By March, Larner commanded the 90th Squadron in the Battle of the Bismarck Sea. In April, he killed himself, his passengers and crew, when trying to do a spectacular low pass, break and landing on arrival at the new base at Dobodura. Elsewhere on 10 November, a B17 checking Buka and Faisi was at 28,000 feet when attacked by seven Zeros, the crew claimed one destroyed; the bomber was slightly damaged.

An unidentified Japanese diarist described the attack on the AA positions, adding, 'Dropped many parachutes. Paratroops did not come down with parachutes, but bombs were attached to them, and became buried in the ground. Most did not go off. There was danger of unexpected explosions, and signs were erected.' At Giruwa, the Japanese diarist 'Wada' noted, 'Fifty bombs dropped at Giruwa. Saw a formation of friendly planes flying towards Port

Moresby'.[21] 2nd Lieutenant Ino, 41 Regiment, was so weak he was posted to the reserve unit. Ino was well aware of the situation, but remembered the earlier instructions on the ultimate aim of the Horii formation, and thought that the formation would need assistance to complete the attack on Port Moresby intended later in the month.[22]

D Company 2/1st Battalion attacked the Japanese at Gorari from the east, and soon there was heavy fire going in both directions. The company objective was higher ground held by the Japanese, who engaged the platoons as soon as they crossed the track. Lieutenant Hollingworth was leading, and ahead saw troops moving towards his platoon as he was briefing his section commanders. After some delay when runners were pinned down by fire, a message from Captain Simpson to the effect that it was not thought friendly patrols were in front was received. In Hollingworth's platoon, Private Fowler took aim and shot the leading man approaching, but as he fell, Hollingworth saw a helmet, rolled gas cape and haversack like those worn by the Australians, so called to cease fire. But the men were Japanese, return fire killed Fowler and the platoon soon was in a serious situation. More men were killed and wounded, and acts of bravery went unrewarded. However, the Japanese also were suffering considerable casualties and began to work backwards, allowing D Company to move back to the area of the bridge and track, but then fire from the Japanese in rocks on the far side also inflicted casualties. Lance Corporal C. W. Ward, the company clerk and runner, five times crossed the dangerous, bullet-swept clearing to assist wounded. This encounter had forced the Japanese to redeploy forces concentrating against 2/33rd, and possibly D Company 2/1st had countered a move against 2/33rd's flanks.

A Company 2/1st also was engaged in a fire fight at the bridge, with Japanese whose fire was quite accurate. During the day their shooting killed three A Company men. B Company, under Lieutenant Powell, was ordered to prepare to be the counter-attack force if the Japanese attacked A or D Companies. Meanwhile, the C Company 2/1st had managed to cross the river, a dangerous,

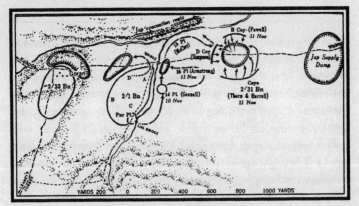

Gorari, 10 to 11 November.

turbulent 50 feet (15 metres). The only assistance was by way of
a log that spanned part of the way, from rocks to the east side.
Placing this had taken many tries and most of the night. Strangely,
the Japanese had not detected the work; they had not sent any sort
of patrol. In some respects, the Japanese were extremely proficient
and dangerous, but in others were unbelievably amateurish. The
river crossing had taken all morning. C Company moved to the
enemy, Lieutenant Gosnell's 14 Platoon meeting three and killing
all. C Company set up a perimeter on the eastern side of the river,
and endured a night of small arms, grenade and bayonet attacks.

During the day, at Oivi, patrols to the left and right harassed the
Japanese, attacking their posts. It was not realised that the Japanese were withdrawing. The advantage was inexorably going to
the Australians. The Japanese now were confronted by confident
and able forces to the south and west, while fast-flowing rivers
were to the north-east. General Horii, at Oivi, was cut off from his
headquarters.

Sergeant Bede Tongs took 10 Platoon, 3rd Battalion, along to
the right of the Oivi position, tasked to get around to the rear of the
Japanese position. At first he tried to navigate by watching the
direction of flow of the creeks, but soon gave this up, and after two
and a half hours turned left to the Japanese and began climbing. A
great stench informed them that they were close to the enemy, as
the Japanese persisted in very basic open latrines, often nothing
more than a log on which to sit, at the top of a steep slope. This was

what they found, and Bede saw a man in the act of tucking his shirt
into his trousers, aimed at him, and tried to see if he really was
Japanese, who usually wore a jacket outside their trousers. But
then firing began and he shot the fellow as the platoon attacked up
the slope. A light machinegun was destroyed, Japanese resistance
was increasing, and it was time to go. Bede took the platoon, with
its one wounded man, back some 130 yards and fired the 10 grenades he'd brought along from the rifle. All landed in the Japanese
position, resulting in a volley of high-explosive in return, but it all
missed. The platoon moved away, and later walked into Brigadier
Lloyd's 16 Brigade Headquarters. Lloyd greeted them, and said
they were not supposed to go to him, to which Bede replied that he
had not known Lloyd was there, but simply had come on the headquarters. Lloyd quickly summoned a staff officer and told him to
get some troops up onto the path followed by the platoon – there
was no one between them and the Japanese. Later, Bede joined
Lloyd and Lieutenant Colonel Cameron in a dixie of rice while
they discussed the patrol.

Early on 11 November, the B17s again went to Buin–Faisi in the
Solomons, and at 4.15 am, five bombers dropped 20 bombs from
5000 to 8000 feet in clear weather, claiming one possible hit. Over
New Guinea, in clear weather, at 8 am, at heights of 20-50 feet,
three Beaufighters attacked targets in the Oivi–Buna area, then
strafed barges near Gona–Sanananda, despite heavy and light intense accurate AA, and crews counted six guns firing at Soputa,
plus five machineguns. At 11.15 am, three A20s found nothing to
report at Wairopi, but made 15 strafing passes under the 3000-foot
cloudbase. Three Beaufighters returned to Oivi and Buna at 3.50
pm, and strafed huts and cars seen on the roads. A Japanese describing the event wrote: 'Since morning, enemy bombers and fighters have attacked our position, but I have not been injured. A number of bombs were dropped up to 16.30 [4.30 pm]. At about 15.30
[3.30 pm], an order came for us to fall out, and we immediately
carried two shells per person to the AA position, as it seems they
had run out of shells and for a time firing had ceased. During this
time, enemy planes came over and bombed us.' Reconnaissance

flights covered the usual areas, with little to report. There was nothing new at Buna airfield, and weather prevented flights to Lae and Salamaua. At 10.45 pm, five Catalinas began to harass Kahili, on southern Bougainville.[23]

On 11 November, the enemy had gone from Oivi. Australian patrols cautiously probed and verified the fact. Yazawa and 900 men had slipped away. The usual strong positions were investigated, and the aids to quiet evacuation were noted: vines along the paths, with shielded candles providing illumination. No equipment, arms, dead or wounded Japanese were found after the skilfully executed military operation. Pushing east, 2/2nd Battalion met 25 Brigade troops at Gorari; the Kokoda campaign was almost over, with final spasms to be endured on both banks of the river.

Meanwhile, at dawn, a Japanese officer appeared in the position of D Company 2/25th, and attacked the Company HQ Corporal, but was killed, then small groups of enemy tried to break through C and D companies, but were killed, for a total of eight dead Japanese and two wounded Australians. At 6.30 am, with 2/31st Battalion, an attack went in on the Japanese. Then the Japanese counterattacked against 2/25th HQ, killing one Australian and wounding the RSM and Medical Officer, but 11 Japanese were killed. Fifty-four dead Japanese littered the battalion's path, and captured material included a mortar, two medium machineguns, seven light machineguns, ammunition and a large amount of food. The battalion reorganised, left two platoons to bury the dead and salvage useful materials, and set off north for Gorari at 11 am.

In its part of the assault, 2/31st troops were ordered to fire single shots only and to use grenades and the bayonet to avoid causing casualties to friendly troops. D Company pushed on through Japanese automatic weapons fire, shoving the enemy onto B Company, resulting in 40 Japanese being killed in an area of less than half an acre (.2 hectare). Later, 2/31st Intelligence Section counted 89 dead Japanese in and around a clearing, plus a mountain gun, two medium machineguns, a rangefinder, ammo and documents. Battalion losses had been three killed and eight wounded.

Nine months after killing the surrendered members of 2/22nd in the area of the Tol Plantation, on New Britain, the Japanese III/144 had been destroyed. Kuwata survived, but committed suicide after the war, before interrogation for the crime could result in legal proceedings. His medical officer, also under investigation for his part in the New Britain killings, managed to suicide. No war crimes trials for the Tol Plantation massacres were held.[24]

The Japanese regarded the war crimes trials as simply the result of anti-Japanese feeling. After the surrender, when the war crimes investigations were in progress, the Japanese commander in the Solomons, General Imamura, clandestinely circulated a letter indicative of Japanese military outlook to his subordinates. Imamura stated that in past wars plundering, rape and other crimes had not been punished, so the current investigations were only a further expression of anti-Japanese feeling. While he did not know exactly what everyone had done during the war, he was sure all had done their best, and urged non-cooperation with the Allied investigators, care with statements about fellow soldiers, but if convicted, the sentence should be regarded as an honourable service. But this was three years after the annihilation of Japanese 144 Regiment.

After destruction of Kuwata's battalion, the Australian companies withdrew to their original positions, and reorganised to face out, against any Japanese in the area, rather than inwards against the trapped force as before. Patrols went out, but had no contact. After reorganising, 2/31st quickly moved off to the north for the final actions, and at 3.15 pm passed through 2/33rd, over the bridge, to join 2/1st in an attack on the village area.

Earlier on 11 November, at 11.15 am, C Company 2/1st Battalion assaulted the Japanese at the eastern end of the bridge. Sergeant Bob Armstrong's 15 Platoon began the attack on the rocky position. By 11.30, 19 Japanese were killed, a prisoner was captured, the position was taken, and troops could cross the bridge.

At 1.30 pm, Lieutenant McCloy's 13 Platoon 2/1st Battalion was moving east on the northern side of the track, found a Japanese position and attacked. They'd put their heads into a lions' den. The camp was later calculated to have held 300 Japanese. All three rifle sections in 13 Platoon were heavily involved as the Japanese reacted strongly. Corporal Shearwin's section had three killed and five wounded; every man was hit. Corporal Schreiber's section killed all Japanese in sight. Corporal Stoddart's section attacked the Japanese right flank, killed 18 enemy, but were forced back by a counter-attack, and Stoddart himself had three wounds, holding the enemy until he was last of his section to withdraw.

However, 2/31st arrived, joined 2/1st, and preparations were made for a two-battalion attack before the day ended. At 5.30 pm, the battalions attacked, and, incredibly, the Japanese were preparing to eat and were put to flight. It was hard for the Australians to understand that the determined enemy could be caught so stupidly, weapons aside while gathering for a meal, after so much close fighting, but it was all too true. 2/31st bounced the Japanese out of their positions, the attack turned into a slaughter of Japanese, and 30 minutes after the assault began they were fleeing down the track to the west, but more determined elements soon began counter-attacks. By 6.15 pm, all companies of 2/1st were in action, except those holding the bridge. At 6.40, the battle was still going on, and the volume of fire, the sheer noise, was thunderous. In an attack on B and D Companies 2/1st Battalion, 40 Japanese had been killed. 2/1st casualties had been six killed and 12 wounded. By 6.55, all was quiet. It was dark, and the action was over.

Cooperation between the two battalions had been excellent. At one stage, Lieutenant Colonel Miller and his party from 2/31st were pinned down by automatic weapons fire and grenades, but Major Robson swung B Company to the right, through 2/1st, and completed the encirclement. Many Japanese were killed as they fled along the track. Australian casualties from 2/31st included Major Thorne, Lieutenant Birnie and five men killed, plus seven wounded. Seventy-four dead Japanese were counted in the battalion area. II/144 had been destroyed. It had been one of the battalions in the assault on Rabaul, and also had been among the original invasion force for Japanese landings on New Guinea in March.

2/33rd had been holding its positions through another night of no sleep and plenty of rain, but lost another 10 wounded when desperate Japanese coming up from the south bounced off 2/1st and ran into 2/33rd's perimeter. Gradually the shelling from the north ceased, but tensions had been high in the battalion over the past two days. Patrols from 2/1st and 2/25th came in to the battalion, gradually the fighting eased, and men began to stand up, then to move around, and later go into Gorari itself. By mid-afternoon, the rear was safe enough for carrying parties of natives to begin taking back the wounded after delivering supplies. Lieutenant Colonel Buttrose, 2/33rd, had been worried as casualties mounted, but was told by Brigadier Eather that, 'You can't expect to run into a hornet's nest without being stung'.

Large numbers of mules and horses with pack saddles were found throughout the area; it was obvious a large force of Japanese had been defeated and dispersed. The fast-flowing Kumusi River took many, including General Horii. There are several accounts of his death, but all describe it as happening in the river trying to escape. A total of 580 dead Japanese were counted after the Gorari actions. The Australian battalions at Oivi began advancing to the Gorari area and the Kumusi River.

The Takasago Volunteer who had arrived at Buna on 13 August and chronicled the fortunes of his unit, the hard carrying duties, the malaria, the air attacks, made his last entry. 'The enemy, who has been resisting [sic!] since day before yesterday about one kilometre [1100 yards] in front, is fighting actively. There are serious losses on both sides. Because battle conditions changed for the worse, the members were assembled and sent to the adjacent 120th Land Service to guard.' The diary was captured next day.[25]

A trickle of prisoners began to come into Australian hands, and their information provided confirmation of the annihilation of the South Seas Detachment. Takiwo Igaue was a member of 2 Platoon 1 Company in Tsukamoto's I/144 and had landed with the leading elements on 21 July; the 170-strong company now numbered 20; Lieutenant Ogawa was killed before Kokoda, Lieutenant Inoue at Kokoda, Lieutenant Hatakenaka at Isurava, followed by Lieutenant Hirano and then Lieutenant Kaji. Hikoichi Tamura, in Takamori's Engineers, was in a party of 50 who found themselves surrounded; an officer called to charge, no one obeyed; 46 were killed. Yoshihiro Yoshimoto was with Yokoyama's Engineers and also landed on 21 July, but was so debilitated with malaria and hunger that he walked to an Australian tent and surrendered. Yuki Kunisawa, of 1 Platoon 8 Company in III/144, had seen three company commanders and two platoon commanders killed, and in his section of 11, three had been killed, four were evacuated ill and only four remained.

Setting off early on 12 November, six B17s attacked Tonolei in the Solomons at 5.15 am. Going in at 4500 feet, with visibility good and through moderate but inaccurate AA fire, the bombers dropped 29 bombs on ships, and crews claimed two hits, a very close miss and near misses. At 6.50 am, three RAAF Beaufighters swept the Buna–Kakandetta area, flying through light rain and mist, with visibility two miles (3.2 km), cloudbase at 4000 feet, strafing barges and huts. The Gona road was assessed as fit for light vehicles only. The usual reconnaissance flights were curtailed by weather, and there was nothing reported.

At 8 am, 2/25th Battalion advanced along the Ilimo track, and made contact at the river and creek junction west of Ilimo. A and B Companies forded the river and attacked from the rear, advancing some 300 yards, but by the end of the day had to halt because of darkness, with the enemy almost surrounded. 2/31st killed three Japanese at first light on 12 November as they tried to escape from the encirclement, then the battalion moved east, after 2/25th. The night before, the troops had eaten a meal of captured rice and Australian chocolate. At the Gorari battlefield, the enemy defeated by 2/1st and 2/31st was identified as Horie's II/144, opponents of 2/1st at Templeton's Crossing and Eora Creek. Among the Japanese dead was found Captain Sanderson's German Schmeisser machine pistol (MP38) and his paybook was found on a body. 2/1st had lost 18 killed and 45 wounded, with two missing, and all ranks strength was 360; rifle companies were down to 50 men. 2/33rd began clearing a dropping zone and a supply dump area, as well as looking for dead and missing. About 200 yards west of the village, some disturbed earth was investigated, and was found to be the burial place of the mountain gun that had made life so dangerous for D Company. 2/2nd Battalion was issued new clothes and boots, enjoyed hot meals, and caught some wandering Japanese horses and mules for use as pack animals.

Australian troops and a company of the US 126 Regiment met at Wairopi. The Kokoda campaign was almost completed and the attack on the Japanese Buna–Gona position was about to begin. The confident but inexperienced US troops and officers were to have a devastating introduction to battle.

On 13 November, seven B17s attacked ships at Buin–Faisi at 4.20 am, and crews claimed two hits and three near misses on a cruiser and destroyers, plus a near miss on a transport, from 28 bombs dropped. Over New Guinea, at 10 am, in clear weather, three Beaufighters swept the Buna area, strafing barges, huts and collapsible boats. Aircraft flying to more distant places on the usual reconnaissance missions had little to report due to weather, but a B17 was attacked by four fighters north-west of Kahili, and escaped with minor damage. Another reconnaissance B17 made three strafing passes on a schooner in Lorengau Harbour. Elsewhere, the developing potential of air transport was shown, when more troops of the US 126 Regiment were flown in, and the regiment was complete at Pongani. General Kenney's enthusiasm for all aspects of air power were of the greatest benefit to the Allied forces in the SWPA.

At dawn, 2/25th Battalion found the partially encircled enemy of the previous afternoon and evening had gone, leaving behind two light machineguns and eight buried Japanese. The battalion pushed on to Wairopi. 2/31st Battalion had gone to the right, but found the enemy gone. Later, it took over the lead, going on to Ilimo, passing Japanese positions that were less than 24 hours old. At 12.30 pm, they reached Wairopi, and deduced that the Japanese were not long gone as horses and mules were found still tethered to corrals. Large stores of rice were found. Patrols went left and right along the riverbank, and one returned to tell of watching six Japanese try to swim the river, but three drowned. Bede Tongs's 10 Platoon 3rd Battalion found many Japanese who had hanged themselves from trees overhanging the river, having apparently crawled out onto a branch, fixed the noose from their neck to the branch, then dropped off into the fast-flowing water, the strength of which hauled on their bodies and hastened the hanging. By this time, the platoon was becoming disgruntled at always leading the company and being sent on all the patrols, and put it down to the fact that they were led by a sergeant rather than an officer. Also found by the advancing battalions were more than 200 carriers who had been used by the Japanese. The battalion diary states that the carriers 'were overjoyed' to be in Australian hands again.

A Takasago officer went to Sambo, 'but the troops at the front line were surrounded by the enemy and we lost track of them. The second line troops crossed the river and are coming down the mountain. 89 men of the volunteers are missing. Company Commander Nao arrived and reported that the force commander and his staff have gone down along the Papaki River and may have been annihilated'.[26]

At 3 pm, 2/25th reached Wairopi. Scattered around were large amounts of medical supplies, pack transport equipment, rubber boats and some horses. The Japanese had bayoneted some of the animals, and those alive were in poor condition, suffering from ill-treatment. Later, an air drop was received in the open area. 2/33rd also arrived at Wairopi; 2/31st was checking the left and 2/25th the right. The river was flowing at 10 knots and was 25 yards wide. Lieutenant Frank McTaggart's 15 Platoon, on patrol, brought in two Japanese found sitting under a tree; they offered no resistance. Late in the afternoon, forward elements of 16 Brigade arrived, and there developed something of a spirit of light-heartedness on the riverbank. There were many suggestions as to how the fast-flowing river could be bridged, but darkness fell before anything was done. A strong swimmer went across and reported good swimmers would be able to make it. 2/33rd was ordered to do so next day.

Faisi was attacked at 7.40 am on 14 November by two B17s, but no hits were made on a 10,000-ton transport there. Three Beaufighters swept the Buna area at 9 am, and attacked canoes and huts along the Kumusi River. Visibility was five to 10 miles (eight to 16 km), cloudbase 5000 feet. Three hours later, another flight of four Beaufighters swept the same area, through inaccurate AA from Buna, and reported 8/10th cumulus, with base at 300 feet. Later, a B25 searched the tracks north of Soputa, found no sign of enemy activity, and reported Buna weather clear, but with clouds inland from 1000 to 15,000 feet and violent thunderstorms. The other usual reconnaissance flights found nothing to report. Five Catalinas began attacking Kahili at 11.10 pm, and reported starting nine or 10 fires, eight aircraft destroyed, an ammunition dump hit, and machinegun passes made on 20 aircraft lined up along the western edge of the airfield, resulting in fires visible 60 miles (100 km) away.

A member of Lieutenant Masaoka's 3MG Company wrote that they had started moving at 4 am, 'but enemy planes were over us at break of day, and we could not move ahead. Report that No. 2 Company, acting as rear guard, is in action. At once prepared to go to their aid, but this was stopped'. 2/25th Battalion had patrols out, and one contacted about 200 Japanese, who were trying to withdraw under protection of large volumes of automatic weapons fire. One Australian died of wounds and the patrol returned to base.[27]

2/1st Battalion moved to Wairopi, to arrange crossing the Kumusi River. At Wairopi, a bosun's chair had been constructed and gradually the force began to cross. By night, C Company, part of B and part of HQ 2/33rd were across. A suspension bridge was planned for next day. Captain Bert Kienzle arrived at the bridge, to take charge of 300 Rabaul natives who had gathered on an island in the river. They were emaciated and sick, and told the usual stories of Japanese ill-treatment. They said the Japanese had built the bridge four times. Kienzle counted 500 dead horses in the area, and estimated there were about 1500 more loose.

Individuals and small parties of Japanese had been seen in the area as stragglers tried to make their way back to the main Japanese force, but none tried to interfere with the crossing operation. At 4 pm, the weary 2/33rd patrol led by Lieutenant Phil Curry came in from their journey to Ilimo. One man had been lost, presumed drowned, but the only Japanese seen by the main body of the patrol had been a prisoner. Their main problems had been those of the terrain and climate. The missing man apparently was captured by the Japanese, and is referred to as having identified '33rd battalion' in their report. As no trace of him was found, he must have been murdered like all the others.

Air activity on 15 November began with the usual heavy bomber operations. Twelve B17s attacked Rabaul harbour from 4 am, in excellent visibility, claiming one direct and one possible hits on ships, and four fires started, which were visible 75 miles (120 km) away. Eight B24s of the newly-operational US 90th Bomb Group attacked shipping at Buin–Faisi. One was attacked by float-planes on the way back, and gunners claimed one as a probable, but another B24 force-landed at sea, and two of the crew were lost. At 8.50 am, six Beaufighters and five B26s attacked AA positions at Buna and Soputa, and fire slackened after the B26 strike on the positions. Some mysterious cloths reported on trees in the Sangara area were positively identified as parachutes, indicating Japanese parachute resupply missions. At 12.35 pm, three Douglas A20 Bostons from RAAF 22 Squadron swept the coast from Sanananda–Giruwa to the mouth of the Kumusi River, and strafed, though there were no signs of enemy activity. As an indicator of things to come, a B17 landed at Moresby's 7-Mile airfield carrying a 105 mm howitzer, an eight-man gun crew, 50 rounds of ammunition, the necessary tractor, tools and a camouflage net. Next day it flew the load to Dobodura.

During the period covered by this account of the Kokoda campaign, 21 July to 15 November 1942, at least 1400 bombs of 250 pounds or heavier were dropped by B17s and B26s in attacks on shipping around New Guinea, New Britain, New Ireland and Bougainville. Hundreds of flying hours and thousands of maintenance hours were consumed in the heavy bomber effort, for little benefit. Crews were sincere in claims of hits and sinkings, but these could not be verified. The greater part of the Allied air effort was allocated to bomber attacks on shipping, for little result. It was not until March 1943, with the destruction of the Lae convoy, that effective tactics were combined with aircraft and weapons to achieve positive results, and those were gained by fast low-level attacks.

16 Brigade HQ arrived at Wairopi, and the diarist wrote of the holiday atmosphere along the banks as the victorious Australian battalions gathered. The HQ had to wait until next day to cross and resume the advance. 2/1st Battalion was given a rest day. 2/33rd was across the Kumusi River by 11 am and set off along the Gona track. The going was flat, weather good, although hot. The companies passed many Japanese huts with rice, biscuits and other supplies in them, which had not been delivered to the suffering Japanese front-line soldiers. Ammunition had taken priority. The battalion halted for the night at Ongahambo, and next day met forward elements of US infantry units, who immediately asked where were the fresh food dumps and canteens. 2/33rd would dearly have wished to know the answer to that one, too. 2/25th was across the river by 1.30 pm, and set off along the track to Buna, marching in rain until 4.30, when a halt was called. 2/31st also crossed, as did 2/2nd. Ahead, for all the battalions, was the bloodletting of the Buna–Gona campaign. The Kokoda campaign was over.

After 14 weeks in the theatre, and having commanded the Allied Air Forces since 4 August, on 15 November General Kenney was at last mentioned in a press release from MacArthur's headquarters as having taken personal command of air units and operations in Papua. MacArthur used as a reward his control of press releases that might include mention of an individual, and later there was his more well-known briefing of General Bob Eichelberger, on the way to New Guinea at the time US Army units were failing miserably in battle. Telling him to take Buna or not return, MacArthur said that if he succeeded, his name would be given to the Press, and he would be recommended for a high British decoration.

MacArthur would go on, driven by his immense ego, to take the surrender of Japan in Tokyo Bay in September 1945. Eventually, he would be removed ignominiously from his position as Supreme Commander in the Far East by President Harry S. Truman, whose highest military rank had been captain in the artillery. MacArthur had tried to ignore the fact that he was subordinate to his nation's elected leader.

While the Australians and Americans were increasing their strength, expanding their mastery of tactics, and developing their logistic capability, the Japanese were sliding deeper into a worsening situation. They had been at their peak in late August, but had failed. A member of the Japanese 3 MG Company 41 Regiment recorded that 'although strict watch was maintained through the rain and cold last night, we found at dawn that the enemy had a strong force on hand to surround our position. I and II Battalions under Lieutenant Koiwai [sic – he was mostly referred to as Major or Lieutenant Colonel Koiwai] decided to give up the position. Company strength is 16 men. Had to bury two MGs and 50 ammunition strips, as it would not be possible to carry them away. Withdrew quickly to the Kumusi [River], lightly equipped, under command of the battalion commander'. The Japanese diarist 'Wada' was 'informed by an NCO that our situation is dangerous'. He continued to make diary entries for another 13 days, the last being on 28 November. He chronicled the worsening situation of the Japanese at Buna, and his final entry was, 'Raided by enemy planes. No friendly planes seen. Our end is near. Emperor heard of the crisis at Buna, and sent a message to fight to the last man'.

Fukuichi Watanabe had commanded the Machinegun Company in Koiwai's II/41 and was captured when wounded. He said that the four-platoon company had been reduced to one platoon, and on one occasion 20 men had been killed in an attack when many bombs exploded all around them, a reference to low-level A20s. He also said that Colonel Yazawa was despised by the troops, as he hid in a hole in the ground after giving the order to attack; the soldiers called him '2nd Class Private Yazawa'.[28]

On 15 November, as the Kokoda campaign closed with the destruction of the Japanese force sent to capture Port Moresby, 67 L of C Hospital had 1851 patients and 233 surgical cases; 180 cases had arrived on 14 November. Staff were to prepare as many as possible for evacuation on the ships expected to arrive. Within the hospital, the staff were reporting serious matters, and officially it was recognised that disaster was near. Patients were stealing food, and there were few bearers to get patients to the hospital. Fifty-four patients had died in the first half of November. In a move that indicated the implacable mindset of Japanese officers and the savagery of the coming Buna–Gona fighting, patients were organised to fight.[29]

Horii's formation was destroyed. Those men who evaded the Australians at Oivi–Gorari and made their way to the Buna–Gona area were a liability to the force there, as they had few weapons, little food or equipment and were exhausted and demoralised. Of the senior officers, only Major Mitsuo Koiwai, II/41, is known to have experienced the entire Kokoda campaign from 18 August, and survived. He was evacuated on 28 January 1943 for medical reasons, and escaped the second annihilation at Buna–Gona. In quick succession, but at great cost to the Allies, the Japanese in the New Guinea–Solomons region were to be defeated at Milne Bay, Kokoda, Buna–Gona and Guadalcanal. Then, in March 1943, a convoy of eight ships bringing the 51st Division to Lae was sunk by RAAF and US aircraft, with four destroyers also sunk and two more damaged. The balance of power in the South West Pacific Area had changed; the Japanese were soon to reap the whirlwind.

It is perhaps fitting that the final Japanese quotation comes from a soldier in a unit sent to New Guinea by commanders in Rabaul, who were incapable of accepting the real situation confronting them. Hiroshi Sakai kept a diary, and was one of the reinforcements sent to Buna in late November. The Kokoda campaign was just ended, he saw what remained of Horii's formation, and wrote: 'The condition of the South Sea Detachment is beyond description. It is worse than you think. In Giruwa there are Engineers and Line of Communications hospital, but no fighting power. Patients in the hospital have no food to eat. The condition is so bad that I have no words to describe it.'[30]

The Australian Army Militia and AIF units had won a vital campaign fought in conditions that had not been imagined only six months before. The Australians had done so without assistance from powerful Allies, except that provided by an unreliable air support system and a generally ineffective bombing campaign, against an enemy who had enjoyed superiority at sea, in the air and on land when on the offensive. That the Japanese were incapable of exploiting their air superiority or developing a suitable logistics system for the campaign led to their defeat. That defeat was inflicted by Australian infantry fighting in conditions they had never envisaged.

The Japanese, despite extensive planning to land and support a force to advance over the Owen Stanleys to capture Port Moresby, did so with little information. The Australians had not really considered fighting in the mountains, and were preoccupied with the defence of Port Moresby against attacks from the sea. Neither side knew what the campaign would entail; there had not been a previous operation from which to draw lessons. Just as Air Chief Marshal Sir Hugh Dowding and his group and squadron commanders fought the Battle of Britain with little useful information or procedures from previous campaigns of air attack, learning and adapting defensive aerial warfare tactics between July and November 1940, so did the Australian commanders in New Guinea fight and learn the lessons of jungle warfare as the campaign went on from July to November 1942. It is easy for those who do so to criticise such matters as tactical handling after the event, when comfortably in possession of all the information, without the pressure and stress of personal responsibility.

Just as no serious thought had been given to fighting in the Owen Stanley Ranges, so no conception was reached of the enormous stresses to be endured by the young Australians committed to fight – the great physical hardships to be endured in the cruel terrain and climate, with inadequate clothing, equipment and food supplies; the relentless mental strain of close combat in jungle; the knowledge that a wound meant days of painful travel before proper treatment could be received; the diseases that would have a lifelong legacy of distress for those afflicted; a merciless and barbaric enemy who had stepped from the Dark Ages, and who had to be exterminated rather than simply defeated.

Yet Militia and AIF alike persevered, won at great cost, and set a standard for military achievement that is the equal of any other in Australian history...

KOKODA

Appendix A

Many of those who fought across the mountains died in the continuing actions on the northern coast or soon after. The year is 1942 unless stated otherwise. A partial list of those mentioned in the preceding pages is:

Major Bill Benn	18 January 1943	
Captain J. M. Blamey	26 November	
Captain A. K. Bosgard	27 November	
Captain Peter Brewer	20 Oct 1944	*aircraft accident*
Captain P. L. Brinkley	10 November	
Corporal G. K. Clark	2 July 1945	
Captain T. M. Clowes	22 November	
Private G. E. Dwight	29 November	
Lieutenant A. C. Haddy	7 December	
Lieutenant G. T. Hicks	5 December	
Lieutenant L. G. Inkpen	8 December	
Lieutenant G. L. Leaney	20 November	
Lieutenant J. McClure	20 November	
Major Ken McCullar	12 April 1943	
Captain A. S. McGavin	28 November	
Lieutenant Colonel Miller	14 December	*scrub typhus*
Lieutenant B. W. Moloney	20 May 1945	
Warrant Officer G. Mowat	30 December	
Lieutenant F. Owen	20 November	
Lieutenant G. E. Pearce	6 December	
Lieutenant R. S. Phelps	22 November	
Lieutenant A. L. Sargent	7 July 1945	*killed when Japanese POW*
Captain A. M. Simpson	20 November	
Lieutenant R. H. Sword	9 December	
Captain C. R. Thorn	19 November	
Captain J. W. Thorn	7 December	
Captain G. H. Vernon	16 May 1946	*died at Samarai Hospital*
Major I. F. Vickery	27 November	
Lieutenant C. M. White	6 December	
Lieutenant H. C. Wiseman	20 November	

Appendix B

B17 OPERATIONS IN SUPPORT OF THE KOKODA, MILNE BAY AND SOLOMONS CAMPAIGNS 21 JULY TO 15 NOVEMBER 1942. It has been evident from the foregoing pages just how large was the flying effort made by the relatively few B17 Flying Fortresses from the beginning of the Kokoda campaign.

Following the principles of strategic air power, General Kenney was right in sending what heavy bomber force he had to targets at Rabaul and other Solomons locations, and of course he was ordered to do so to support US Navy actions there.

Also, he realised that bombing stretches of jungle in hopes of hitting an important Japanese position along the Kokoda Trail was unlikely to provide benefits equal to those possible from attacking Rabaul and the distant convoys, before the ships unloaded at Buna. However, when transport aircraft were in such short supply, and it was plain that supply missions to the Australian forces on the trail were of paramount importance, it does seem that a few B17s would have made a valuable contribution to the campaign by being used temporarily as supply-dropping aircraft.

Kenney sent as many B17s as possible to Rabaul and the Solomons, and seemed to have accepted claims by crews for sinkings and damage, which claims, as he must have known from confirmatory Intelligence sources, were quite far from reality.

Some 383 sorties were flown by the bombing squadrons of the 19th and 43rd Bomb Groups between 21 July and 15 November, by far the greater proportion against distant Solomons targets or against convoys. The single, long ranging and dangerous reconnaissance flights that went out each day, to the same vital areas, have not been given due credit. Many found nothing to report, but others resulted in quite intense engagements with defending fighters.

Always there was the weather: impartial, partly understood, and capable of destroying a four-engined bomber by sheer force. The reconnaissance effort by the 435th Squadron was substantial, largely unsung, and gradually undertaken by the main bomber groups, who used these flights as a means of giving new crews some experience.

Crews arriving from the USA, in four-engined bombers at this time, were flown by pilots in command who had about 300 hours of flying time. They had not been trained for the weather conditions in the South West Pacific. It should be remembered that both the B17 and B24 were relatively new aircraft, barely out of the experimental stage, and that only a few years previously the pilots who crossed the world's oceans were hailed as international heroes. Now such flights were merely a first step into combat zones by inexperienced pilots, navigators and engineers.

Vivid memories of the theatre remain with surviving crews, and many of those memories are of the dangerous flying conditions. More crews were lost to weather than to the enemy. Aircraft simply disappeared. Pilots who did return from bad weather encounters told of suddenly finding the big bomber rising at rates of up to 3000 feet a minute, despite all engines throttled back and both pilots holding the control column fully forward. Then the ascent would suddenly cease, with frightening creaks, cracks and groans from tortured and flexing airframe and wings. There might be an equally violent descent, this time with engines at full throttle having little effect to counter the plunge. It was quite probable that missing aircraft simply had been suddenly over-stressed. The B17s, identified from records, that flew most of those reconnaissance missions were:

#12666 22 missions
#12645 21 missions
#19194 21 missions
#19193 20 missions
#12648 18 missions
#12639 18 missions
#12627 18 missions *Miss Carriage*
#19208 15 missions (take-off crash 12 October 1942)
#12609 15 missions
#19207 10 missions
#14355 10 missions *Diana Might*

Six other B17s flew between five and 10 reconnaissance missions, there are 27 sorties for which the aircraft identity cannot be determined, and B24/LB30s flew an additional 20 sorties.

Acknowledgements and sources

Assistance given by the following individuals is gratefully acknowledged: Ian Affleck, Margaret Barter, L. A. 'Teddy' Bear, Jan Beck, Steve Birdsall, Stan Bisset, John Brogan, Lindsay Burge, Mick Fielding, Bill Fogarty, Kevin Ginnane, Charles W. King, David Marsh, Elva Mowat, Jim McAllester, Robert K. Piper, Phil Rhoden, Ray Royal, Cy Stafford, Frank Sublet, R. Swanborough, Bede Tongs, Syd Trigellis Smith, Dick Vudra, Alan O. Watson, Roy Watson, R. F. 'George' Woodward.

Bede Tongs thoughtfully made available contributions from ex-members of 3rd Battalion from his own collection for the unit history: Noel Geraghty; Jimmy Holmes; Tom Hone; Brian McIntosh; Ron Seaman; Bob Tolly; a separate thanks, Bede.

As ever, the staff of the Australian War Memorial Research Centre were unfailingly courteous, helpful and even cheerful, despite my many requests for heavy, bound volumes, and lots of them, over the years. My thanks to Joyce Bradley, Andrew Jack, Tony Rudnicki, Ian Smith and George Imashev. Information on Allied Air Forces operations was extracted from the relevant squadron operations record books, the Allied Combined Headquarters logbooks, and Attack and Reconnaissance Reports, held at the Australian War Memorial or RAAF Historical Section, Department of Defence.

Information about the infantry battalions, brigades, division and New Guinea Force Headquarters came from Australian War Memorial Collection 52 (AWM 52) of such records. AWM 52 contains division, brigade and battalion war diaries, and those consulted for this book were:

ANGAU (AWM 52) 1/10/1
NGF 1/5/51
7 Division 1/5/14
16 Brigade 8/2/16
21 Brigade 8/2/21
25 Brigade 8/2/25

The infantry battalions are in the AWM 52 8/3/- series, so that 2/1st Battalion is 8/3/1, and the others numbered accordingly. Information about the people or units mentioned many times is provided here once, rather than in numerous footnotes, the bane of modern writers.

AWM 55 is the collection of translations of captured Japanese documents by the Allied Translator and Interpreter Section (ATIS), GHQ, and is composed of Spot Translations; Enemy Publications (EP); Current Translations (CT); Bulletins (Bull). Some documents from the Combined Intelligence Centre South Pacific Force (CICSPF), the Solomons theatre, from AWM collection 58, are also included. The AWM 54 collection is printed material dealing with Australian and Allied forces in the Second World War.

I/47 AA Battalion AWM 55; ATIS 162
15 Pioneers AWM 55; ATIS 177
Lieutenant Ebuchi AWM 55; ATIS 157
Lieutenant Horibe AWM 55; ATIS 193
Bert Kienzle AWM 54; 577/6/8
Charles King diary and mission reports
Lieutenant Morimoto AWM 55; ATIS 165
George Mowat diary, by permission of Elva Mowat
Lieutenant Noda AWM 54; 577/7/26
Saburo Sakai via Henry Sakaida
WO Sadahiro AWM 55; ATIS 116
Sakigawa Tai AWM 55; EP 27
Sasebo 5SLP AWM 55; ATIS 105
Toshio Sato AWM 55; ATIS 112
Harry Staley diary, via Steve Birdsall
Takasago Volunteers AWM 55; ATIS 104
Akiro Teruoka AWM 55; ATIS 80
Dr Geoffrey Vernon AWM 54; 253/5/8

The prisoner of war interrogations from which detail was taken are in the AWM 55 Collection, ATIS PW Interrogations, numbers 1-49. The clandestine letter from General Imamura to his subordinates – telling them that the war crimes were only an anti-Japanese action, not to cooperate, and to regard a sentence as something to be borne with honour – is in AWM 54, file 423/4/58.

Footnotes

For those who feel that copious footnotes create a form of respectability, individual footnote references to some source materials are:

Chapter 1
1. AWM 55 ATIS Spot #7 (hereafter, 'AWM 55' has been omitted for brevity)
2. ATIS Bull 132
3. ATIS Bull 60
4. ATIS Bull 132
5. CICSPF Item #595

Chapter 2
1. AWM 54 577/6/8
2. AWM 54 577/6/8
3. CICSPF Item #1167
4. ATIS EP 27
5. ATIS EP 27
6. AWM 52 1/10/1
7. AWM 54 577/7/32
8. ATIS EP 27
9. ATIS Bull 16; 20
10. ATIS Bull 105; Spot #1
11. AWM 52 1/18/1
12. ATIS Bull 210
13. AWM 52 1/10/1
14. ATIS Spot #2; Report #29
15. AWM 52 1/10/1
16. ATIS Bull 139
17. ATIS Bull 105
18. AWM 52 1/10/1

Chapter 3
1. ATIS Bull 104; 177
2. ATIS Bull 105
3. ATIS Bull 80
4. ATIS Bull 105
5. ATIS EP 28
6. ATIS Spot #15; Bull 112; 177
7. ATIS Spot #24; 15; Bull 112

8. AWM 52 1/10/1
9. AWM Murdoch sound archives
10. ATIS Bull 68; 69; 112
11. AWM 64 11 Sqn ORB
12. ATIS Bull 15
13. AWM Murdoch sound archives
14. ATIS 105; 100
15. ATIS Bull 11; CT 104; Bull 177; 40; 24; 104
16. AWM 54 577/7/32
17. ATIS CT 6 p. 23-24
18. ATIS Bull 111; 8
19. ATIS Bull 111
20. ATIS EP 28
21. ATIS Bull 73; 15; 66
22. AWM 54 577/7/26; ATIS Bull 16; 193; 78; 20; 157
23. ATIS EP 28
24. ATIS Bull 23; 27
25. ATIS Bull 66
26. ATIS Bull 29
27. ATIS Bull 66
28. ATIS Bull 149; 189
29. ATIS Bull 40; 66; 248; CICSPF Item #0345; Bull 146
30. ATIS Spot #1; Bull 73
31. AWM 52 8/2/21
32. ATIS Bull 40; 66
33. ATIS Bull 189
34. ATIS Bull 12
35. ATIS Bull 40
36. ATIS Bull 36
37. AWM 54 577/7/32
38. ATIS Bull 36; 191; 40
39. ATIS EP 32
40. AWM 54 577/6/8

41. ATIS Bull 157
42. ATIS Bull 12
43. ATIS Bull 40; 146; CICSPF #0345; CT 28; Spot #15
44. ATIS Bull 20
45. ATIS EP 32
46. ATIS EP 32
47. ATIS Bull 40; Spot #15; Bull 66
48. ATIS Bull 40
49. ATIS Bull 146
50. ATIS Bull 10; 20
51. ATIS Bull 73; 157; 88; 184
52. CICSPF Item #0345

Chapter 4
1. ATIS Bull 146
2. ATIS Bull 41; 162
3. ATIS EP 32
4. ATIS EP 28
5. ATIS Bull 102
6. ATIS EP 28
7. ATIS EP 32
8. ATIS Bull 104
9. ATIS Bull 40; EP 28
10. ATIS Bull 104
11. ATIS EP 32
12. ATIS Bull 685
13. AWM 54 577/7/32
14. ATIS Bull 193; 106
15. ATIS Bull 93
16. AWM 54 577/7/32
17. ATIS Bull 125
18. ATIS Bull 40; 105; 177; 102
19. ATIS Bull 165
20. ATIS EP 32
21. ATIS Bull 102
22. ATIS EP 32
23. ATIS Bull 149; 125
24. ATIS Bull 10; 73
25. ATIS EP 32
26. ATIS Spot #15; Bull 177

27. ATIS EP 32
28. ATIS Bull 193
29. ATIS EP 32
30. ATIS EP 32
31. AWM 52 1/5/14
32. ATIS Bull 104
33. ATIS EP 32
34. ATIS Spot #20
35. ATIS Spot #15; Bull 66; 106
36. ATIS Bull 162
37. ATIS Bull 162; 13
38. ATIS EP 24; Bull 157
39. ATIS Bull 162
40. ATIS Bull 162
41. ATIS Bull 40; 104
42. ATIS Bull 162
43. ATIS Bull 163; 162; EP 24
44. ATIS EP 28
45. ATIS Spot #1
46. ATIS Bull 162
47. ATIS EP 28
48. ATIS Bull 73
49. ATIS Spot #20
50. ATIS Bull 125
51. ATIS Bull 193; EP 27
52. ATIS Bull 162; 163; 103
53. ATIS Bull 155
54. ATIS Bull 125
55. ATIS Bull 112
56. ATIS Bull 162; 177
57. ATIS Bull 64
58. ATIS Bull 163
59. ATIS EP 24

Chapter 5
1. ATIS Bull 171
2. ATIS Bull 10
3. ATIS EP 39
4. ATIS Bull 189
5. ATIS Bull 167
6. ATIS Bull 125
7. ATIS Bull 40; 101; 104; 105

8. ATIS EP 39
9. ATIS Spot #1; Bull 132
10. ATIS Bull 125; 74
11. ATIS Bull 125; 171
12. ATIS Spot #1
13. ATIS Bull 8
14. ATIS Bull 131
15. ATIS EP 24
16. ATIS Bull 125; 8
17. ATIS Bull 153
18. ATIS Bull 163; 177
19. ATIS Bull.125
20. ATIS Bull 66; 177
21. ATIS Bull 125
22. ATIS Bull 168
23. ATIS Bull 125
24. ATIS Spot #37
25. ATIS Bull 125; 165
26. ATIS Bull 66; 177
27. ATIS Bull 125; 163; 74
28. ATIS Spot #15
29. ATIS Bull 125
30. ATIS Spot #8
31. ATIS Bull 125; 165
32. ATIS Bull 11; 66; 177
33. ATIS Bull 125; EP 24
34. ATIS Bull 177
35. ATIS Bull 125
36. ATIS Bull 66; 104
37. ATIS EP 24; Spot #15; CT 5; Spot #8
38. AWM 54 577/7/29 (9); 85/4/ 10 II

Chapter 6
1. ATIS Spot #15
2. ATIS Bull 192
3. ATIS Bull 163
4. JANAC – AWM Dewey catalogue 940.545952 U74j
5. ATIS Spot #8; Bull 37
6. ATIS Bull 157
7. ATIS EP 39
8. ATIS Spot #37
9. AWM 54 1010/9/105
10. ATIS Spot #8
11. ATIS Spot #8; Bull 137
12. ATIS CT 5
13. ATIS Bull 125; Spot #8
14. ATIS Bull 157
15. ATIS Bull 155
16. ATIS Bull 125; Spot #8
17. ATIS Bull 104; 78
18. ATIS CT 5
19. ATIS Bull 125; Spot #8
20. ATIS EP 39
21. ATIS Bull 153; 163
22. ATIS Bull 155
23. ATIS Bull 171
24. AWM 54 577/7/32
25. ATIS Bull 104
26. ATIS Bull 168
27. ATIS Bull 162
28. ATIS Bull 162; 163
29. ATIS EP 29
30. ATIS Bull 40

Permission to quote from the following unit histories is gratefully acknowledged, as is the interest shown by members of the unit associations, and the time given in commenting on relevant portions of the draft:

2/1st Australian Infantry Battalion: The First At War, Editor: E. C. Givney, Macarthur Press Pty Ltd, Parramatta NSW 1987; *2/3rd Australian Infantry Battalion: War Dance*; Ken Clift, Streamlined Press, Brookvale, NSW 1980; *2/14th Australian Infantry Battalion: The Second Fourteenth Battalion*; W. B. Russell, Angus & Robertson, Sydney 1948; *Men of the 2/14 Battalion*, J. C. McAllester, Griffin Press, South Australia 1990; *2/33rd Australian Infantry Battalion: The Footsoldiers*, W. M. Crooks, Printcraft Press, Sydney 1971; *39th Australian Militia Battalion: To Kokoda and Beyond*, Editor: Victor Austin, Melbourne University Press 1988.

MAPS
Permission to reproduce the maps from the official history volume – *South West Pacific Area, First Year, Kokoda to Wau*, Dudley McCarthy, Australian War Memorial, Canberra 1959 – is gratefully acknowledged.

I have used information from the above people and written sources to assist me in this portrayal of the Kokoda campaign, July to November 1942. If any errors or misconceptions remain in the book, they are mine.

Bibliography

American Caesar, William Manchester, Hutchinson 1979

A Thousand Men At War, Malcolm Uren, Heinemann, Melbourne 1959

Big Distance, D. Hough & E. Arnold, Duell, Sloan & Pearce 1945

Douglas MacArthur The Far Eastern General, Michael Schaller, Oxford University Press 1989

Flying Buccaneers, Steve Birdsall, Doubleday 1977

Full Circle, S. F. Rowell, Melbourne University Press 1974

General Kenney Reports, George C. Kenney, Duell, Sloan & Pearce 1949

Moresby's Few, Leslie Jillett, The North Western Courier, Narrabri 1945

Peter Three Eight, John Stanaway, Pictorial Histories 1986

Retreat From Kokoda, Raymond Paull, Heinemann, Melbourne 1958

That Mob, F. M. Budden (author/publisher)

The Brown And Blue Diamond At War, John Burns, Griffin Press, Adelaide 1960

The First At War, The Association of First Infantry Battalions, Sydney 1987

The Footsoldiers, W. M. Crooks, Printcraft Press, Sydney 1971

The Second Fourteenth Battalion, W. B. Russell, Angus & Robertson, Sydney 1948

These Eagles, RAAF Directorate of Public Relations, Australian War Memorial, Canberra 1942

The Other Ultra, Ronald Lewin, Hutchinson UK 1982

To Kokoda and Beyond, Victor Austin, Melbourne University Press 1988

Victory List No. 3, Frank J. Olynyk 1985

War Dance, Ken Clift, 1980

Winged Samurai, Henry Sakaida, Champlin USA 1986

Index

Note: In the interests of space and resultant size of the book, it was decided to reduce the index to a minimum. All units that were engaged in action in the campaign, and senior officers, are included, as are place names for the significant actions. Other units, particularly those in the Port Moresby and Milne Bay areas, were omitted. Kokoda, Port Moresby, and other local places that appear in the text so many times have been omitted. Apologies in advance for the names of individuals that may have been left out.

The index is divided into five sections, and entries are alphabetised within each section:

1. Allied forces – air and land.
2. Japanese forces – air, land and sea.
3. People – Allied and Japanese
4. Place names – significant actions.
5. General.

1. ALLIED FORCES
AIR
Royal Australian Air Force

Beaufighter 238-39, 243, 246, 249, 260-62, 268-69, 271-72, 278, 286, 296, 305, 357, 364, 370, 376, 387, 396, 400, 405-09

Beauforts 283, 370

Boston 409

Catalina 6, 7, 44, 47, 51, 54, 59, 60, 65, 70, 73, 78, 81, 86, 152, 165, 172, 243, 245, 253, 260, 264, 269, 271-72, 275, 278, 280, 284, 294-95, 297, 305, 319, 328, 331, 350, 357, 365, 367, 373, 379, 387, 395, 401, 408

Hudson 6, 34-7, 39, 41, 44, 47, 59, 331, 335

Kittyhawk 38, 136, 253, 370

United States Air Force

A20 118, 163, 170, 173, 180, 182, 186-87, 197-98, 209, 214, 221, 224, 232, 245, 249, 253, 257, 265, 269, 271, 274-75, 280, 283, 287, 191, 294, 297, 299, 302, 311, 314, 341, 351, 357, 363, 365, 367, 376, 380, 385, 389, 397, 409

A24 36, 41-2, 52, 56, 59, 63, 124

B17 12, 25, 31-8, 43-5, 51-2, 54, 58-9, 61, 63-5, 69-71, 78, 80-1, 92, 95-6, 99-100, 103, 111, 114, 117, 119-22, 124, 127, 131, 136, 152, 159,

163, 165, 172, 174-75, 180-
82, 189, 213, 221, 229, 232,
238, 243, 245, 259, 263, 265,
267, 269, 271-78, 280, 283,
285-87, 295-97, 305, 311,
314-15, 319, 324-25, 331-32,
335, 340, 348, 350-51, 357-
58, 363, 365, 367, 370-71,
373, 376, 379, 389, 397, 400,
405-09
B24   25, 31, 51, 61, 69, 348,
409
B25   24, 35, 38, 43-4, 47-8,
54, 63, 69-71, 77, 173, 175,
181, 196, 219, 229, 243, 260,
283, 286, 291, 294, 296-97,
302, 309, 311, 314, 320, 325,
331, 334-35, 349, 354, 358,
363, 367, 371, 376, 379, 387,
394, 408
B26   7, 33, 36, 38-40, 42-3,
47, 50, 55, 54, 63, 65, 69-71,
77, 81, 95-6, 108, 131, 136,
152, 163, 172, 208, 214, 218,
232, 245, 376, 379, 389, 397,
409
C47/DC3   12, 48, 53, 77, 81,
124, 175, 196, 290, 318, 334,
349, 365, 367, 377-78, 384,
388, 392
P38   54, 58, 196, 204, 209,
243, 255, 274, 358, 371
P39/P400   24, 26, 31-2, 35-6,
38-9, 41-4, 47, 52, 57, 65,
67, 69, 75, 83, 108, 126-28,
131, 152, 163, 165, 167, 170,
172-73, 180, 182, 186-87,
189, 214, 232, 249, 257, 260,
272, 275, 278, 280, 299, 302,
305, 363, 367, 396
P40   41, 238, 249, 257, 260·
61, 265, 268, 272, 283-84,
311, 357, 367, 387, 396

LAND
**Australian Infantry Forces
(AIF) Brigades**
16 Brigade   256, 283, 298,
300, 309, 311, 314, 323,
326-27, 335, 347, 349, 352,
354, 362, 364, 367-68, 372,
375-77, 379-80, 386, 394,
410
21 Brigade   76, 96, 104, 107-
09, 116, 118, 120, 123, 130,
134-35, 139, 145, 150, 152-
53, 159, 179, 181, 183, 185,
190-93, 195, 198-202, 205,
208-10, 236, 244, 247, 252,
293-94, 337
25 Brigade   194, 201-04,
208-09, 230, 236, 239, 241,
244, 258, 262, 268, 272-73,
289, 294, 298, 300, 308, 313,
318, 320, 326, 328, 347, 349,
362, 364, 372, 377, 379-80,
386, 388, 392, 401

AIF Infantry
2/1st Battalion   197, 288,
297-98, 300, 329-65, 372,
376-77, 380-81, 385-92,
398-99, 402-10
2/2nd Battalion   157, 197,
298, 326-27, 329-33, 352,
356-57, 362, 372, 375-76,
379-80, 384, 386-89, 401,
410

2/3rd Battalion   197-98, 298, 328, 332-38, 344, 346, 349, 352-53, 356, 360-61, 372, 376, 379-80, 384, 386, 388

2/14th Battalion   76, 91, 106-08, 113, 116-17, 123, 129, 131-61, 165, 171-72, 175-78, 183-88, 192-200, 205-06, 209-13, 218, 222, 225, 231, 234-36, 247-48, 281, 284, 293, 380

2/16th Battalion   76, 91, 100, 111, 113, 116, 123, 134, 136, 140-44, 150-58, 162, 165, 166, 168, 170-79, 183-86, 190-93, 200, 204-05, 209-10, 213-18, 222, 225-27, 231, 234-36, 244, 247-48, 284, 313, 400

2/25th Battalion   181, 204, 226, 228, 232-37, 244-46, 250, 265-68, 270, 274, 277, 281-82, 284, 287-88, 293-95, 298-99, 306, 311, 313, 316, 318, 323, 326, 328, 331, 334, 349, 352, 357, 361-62, 366, 375, 382, 386, 388-91, 396, 401, 404-10

2/27th Battalion   129-30, 167-68, 175-85, 188-94, 198-205, 209, 218, 230, 244-48, 253, 255, 258, 274, 282, 290, 294

2/31st Battalion   8, 204, 218, 222, 224, 231-33, 236-37, 245-46, 259, 273, 282, 290, 298, 318, 323, 334, 352, 362, 365, 368, 371, 382, 386-88, 390-91, 396, 401-07, 410

2/33rd Battalion   181, 201, 203, 207-08, 211, 213, 215, 218, 220, 222, 228, 230, 232, 234-39, 241, 245-46, 266-67, 270, 273-74, 282, 284, 287, 290, 293, 298-99, 301-20, 325-27, 349, 354-55, 360, 362, 367-68, 372, 382, 388-92, 395-96, 398, 402-10

Australian Army

ANGAU   6, 10, 11, 23-4, 32, 39, 42-6, 54, 66, 70, 74, 88, 92, 107, 121, 192, 198, 228, 282, 285, 290, 297, 361, 366, 378-79, 383

Papuan Infantry Battalion   15, 32, 38, 40, 42, 44, 51, 60, 70, 73, 75, 90-2, 105, 116, 131, 158, 215, 361

Militia Brigade

30 Brigade   4, 5, 88, 105

Militia Infantry

3rd Battalion   24, 189, 203, 208-15, 222, 226-32, 236, 252, 262, 273, 281-82, 285, 293-95, 298, 300, 309-22, 326, 328-29, 331, 362, 372, 379, 383-84, 386-89, 399, 406

39th Battalion   4, 5, 7-9, 15, 23-32, 38-40, 43-52, 54, 56, 58, 60-4, 68, 70-95, 97, 101, 103-04, 106, 109-26, 129-35, 139, 145, 148, 150-52, 155, 158, 160, 166, 171, 173, 176, 178-79, 182, 211, 216, 248, 301

49th Battalion   4, 5, 88, 110

53rd Battalion   4, 5, 105, 113, 116, 122, 125-26, 129-33, 139, 144-48, 153, 155, 158, 160, 176, 178-79, 181, 184, 210-11, 364

Note: Other Militia and AIF Brigades in the Moresby and Milne Bay area not included

Other

7th Australian Division

AIF   59, 88, 120, 123, 126, 129, 148, 169, 178, 199, 219, 228, 230, 244, 258, 287, 290, 300, 307, 323, 347, 355, 361-62, 364-65, 368, 372, 374, 384, 386, 394

General Headquarters South West Pacific Area   12, 14, 21, 27-8, 32, 66, 81, 88, 92, 96, 113, 124, 127, 168, 185, 241, 253, 256, 279-80, 288, 291, 327, 336, 384

New Guinea Force Headquarters 9, 46, 97, 103, 121, 124, 219, 253, 290, 323, 361

2. JAPANESE FORCES

AIR

Mitsubishi A6M 'Zero'   1, 25-6, 37, 41, 44-5, 47-8, 53-4, 57, 65, 71, 81, 92, 95, 99, 112, 116, 121, 126-28, 131, 152, 172, 229, 260, 286, 296, 319, 324, 358, 367, 370-71, 379, 389, 397, 405

LAND

17th Army Headquarters   28, 30, 141, 163, 216, 251, 254, 259

Nankai Butai/South Seas Detachment   17, 30, 110, 150, 244, 267, 276, 281, 289, 293, 295, 374, 404, 412

Sakigawa Transport Unit   31-6, 38-9, 41, 43-5, 50, 53, 56, 60, 63, 68-70

Sasebo 5 Special Landing Party (5SLP])   17, 33, 35, 51, 59, 67, 70, 78, 95, 98, 112, 117, 196, 207, 286, 354, 357, 389

Takasago (Formosan) Naval Volunteers   18, 33, 64, 81, 87, 96, 114, 147, 161, 163, 167, 173, 181, 207, 216, 225, 242, 244, 246, 249, 254, 257, 267, 281, 286, 302, 357, 389, 404, 407

14 & 15 Naval Pioneers   17, 64, 69, 73, 96, 121, 127, 131, 136, 159, 160, 171, 174, 180, 201, 208, 229, 269, 285-86, 314, 318, 329, 332, 347-48, 352, 354, 357, 364

15 Independent Engineer Regiment   17, 18, 121, 263, 366, 376, 389, 393, 394, 405

47 Field Anti-Aircraft Battalion   30, 112, 229, 238, 243, 246, 257, 260-61, 267, 269, 271, 274-76

55 Mountain Artillery Battalion   17, 112, 122, 133, 138, 263, 284, 339, 387, 389

41 Infantry Regiment/Yazawa

Force   30, 53, 67, 73, 109,
112, 17, 138, 151, 154-56,
161, 163, 170-74, 205-06,
212, 216-18, 220, 223, 251,
254, 267, 269, 279, 287, 289,
311, 328, 334, 339, 354, 366,
374, 376, 383, 385, 387,
393-94, 398, 401, 411
I/41   117, 168, 173, 212, 217,
223
II/41   117, 166, 168, 177, 179,
188, 223-24, 263, 265, 354,
411-12
III/41   117, 123, 141, 177,
212, 223, 285
144 Infantry Regiment/
Kusunose & Yamamoto
Force   5, 6, 17, 106, 111-
12, 124, 129, 131, 139, 151,
154, 161-62, 170, 173, 177,
188, 207, 212, 216, 223-24,
251, 254-55, 263, 268, 271,
273, 275-76, 287, 289, 293,
309, 312, 315, 320, 325-26,
331, 334, 354, 357, 361, 364,
366, 369, 373-74, 380, 383,
385, 388-89, 392-94, 402
I/144   17, 18, 34, 39, 42, 64,
72, 76, 80, 93, 109, 119,
120-22, 212, 234, 254, 276,
289, 293, 312, 325-26, 329,
331, 352, 361, 364, 366, 373,
404
II/144   6, 106, 109, 111, 114,
116, 118-19, 121-24, 126,
129, 132, 137, 143, 153-55,
161, 167, 177, 179-80, 186,
190, 201, 212, 220, 222-23,
239, 243, 246, 250-51, 254,

258, 262-63, 265, 267, 272-
73, 275-76, 279, 282, 287,
293, 296, 327, 331, 364, 373,
388, 403, 405
III/144   135, 139, 141-42, 155,
162, 167, 170, 177, 179, 187,
195, 223, 246, 263, 267, 276,
293, 312, 366, 373-74, 376,
383, 385, 387, 396, 402, 405

SEA
Japanese Naval Air Unit
Tainan Kokkutai 37, 47-8, 65,
108, 118, 152
Japanese ships
Ayatosan Maru   18, 31, 33,
35-6, 38, 59, 96, 112
Kazuura Maru   168, 172,
249
Kenyo Maru   69, 70, 96
Kinai Maru   69, 70, 81
Kinryu Maru   34, 255
Kotoku Maru   56-7, 59, 63
Matsue Maru   174
Myoko Maru   117
Nankai Maru   64, 69, 70, 95-
6, 112
Ryoyo Maru   35-6, 56, 106-
07, 112, 279
Yasukawa Maru   172, 370,
373
Yokohama Maru   59

3. PEOPLE
(Japanese personnel in italics)
Allen, Major General Arthur
130, 227-28, 234, 242, 287,
290, 292, 300-01, 309, 311,
314, 323-24, 331, 339-40,

347, 351, 355, 361, 372
Bear, Corporal L. A.   146, 176
Benn, Major W. 'Bill'   34, 47,
    99-100, 124, 252, 265, 335
Blamey, General Sir
    Thomas   14-6, 88-9, 124,
    230, 238, 242-43, 253, 256,
    259, 263, 270-73, 275, 288,
    300-01, 309, 323-24, 340,
    355, 372
Cameron, Lieutenant Colonel
    Alan   68, 70-1, 74-5, 90,
    92, 97-8, 100, 111, 120, 179,
    189, 211, 252, 281, 300, 318,
    320, 373, 383, 400
Cowey, Staff Sergeant Jim   76,
    85-6, 89, 90, 94-5
Curtin, Prime Minister John   13,
    14, 16, 242, 273
Eather, Brigadier Ken   208,
    220, 227-28, 231, 234, 236,
    244, 258, 272, 298, 300, 309,
    312, 320, 367, 404
Hirano, Lieutenant   82, 84, 101,
    103, 142, 238, 264, 331
Honner, Lieut. Colonel
    Ralph   104-05, 111, 131-
    34, 139, 151-52, 155, 160,
    167, 178
Horibe, Lieutenant   107, 109,
    111, 114, 116, 118, 121-22,
    143, 167, 170, 177, 179,
    186-87, 223-24, 227, 233-34,
    239, 243, 246, 250, 254, 258,
    262, 265, 267, 270, 272-73,
    278, 284-85, 287, 289, 296,
    299, 302, 305
Horii, Major General
    Tomitaro   17, 30, 53, 62,

73, 104, 106, 112, 114, 119,
    122-23, 129, 131, 135, 137,
    150-51, 168-9, 173-74, 182,
    188, 190, 194, 199, 206, 211,
    215-17, 220, 224-25, 233-34,
    239, 247-51, 259, 263, 264,
    271, 277, 280, 302, 305, 309,
    339, 345, 354, 361, 369, 374,
    383, 385, 393-94, 398-99,
    404, 411
Hyakutake, Lieutenant General
    Harukichi   17, 43, 53, 62,
    212
Katue, Sergeant (PIB)   51, 60
Kenney, Lieutenant General
    George C.   34, 47, 53, 59,
    60-3, 66, 68-71, 81, 83, 86,
    99, 100, 108, 118, 120, 124,
    174, 196-97, 217-18, 221,
    230, 241, 247, 252-53, 255,
    259, 277, 282, 285-86, 290,
    295, 311, 319, 335, 348-50,
    358, 373, 384, 406, 410
Key, Lieutenant Colonel A.
    S.   138-39, 148, 152, 155-
    56, 161, 171, 212, 281, 331
Kienzle, Captain Bert   6, 10,
    23-5, 28, 43, 46-7, 62, 65-9,
    77, 80, 92, 99, 113, 195, 279,
    287, 297, 305, 315, 374, 382,
    408
Kingsbury, Private Bruce   146-47
Kusunose, Colonel   17, 106,
    122, 154, 173, 182, 289, 309
Lloyd, Brigadier J. E.   283, 331,
    335, 337, 372, 375, 377, 380,
    384, 400
MacArthur, General Douglas   11-
    16, 21, 23, 27, 34, 53, 59-60,

63, 66, 71, 83, 88-9, 92, 96,
108, 113, 118, 124, 127, 168,
174, 185, 196-97, 201, 221,
241-43, 247, 255-56, 259, 273,
275, 277, 279, 283, 288, 309,
319, 323-24, 335, 340, 358,
384, 410

McCallum, Corporal
Charles 148, 193

McCullar, Captain Ken 174,
218, 252, 296-97, 311, 319,
324, 341 350, 364

Morimoto, Lieutenant 177,
205, 246, 257, 331, 344, 349,
363, 370

Morris, Major General Basil 5,
6, 15, 43, 64, 69, 7, 87

Mowat, Warrant Officer
George 28-30, 32, 39, 44,
46, 49, 52-3, 58, 60-1, 64,
76, 80, 90, 95, 103, 106, 115,
118-19, 152, 158, 166, 301

Noda, Lieutenant 107, 109,
112, 114, 119, 121, 123-25,
129, 131, 135, 139, 142, 161,
170, 1777, 182, 188, 195,
242

Onogawa, Lieutenant 64, 69-
71, 76, 80, 84, 90, 93, 98,
100, 103, 111, 119, 120, 174,
182, 195, 237, 269, 275, 278,
288, 291, 298, 312, 349

Owen, Lieutenant Colonel W.
T. 28, 38, 40, 44, 46, 48-9,
51-2, 54-5, 68, 72, 79, 105,
110

Porter, Brigadier S. H. W. C. 8,
9, 105, 115, 208, 222

Potts, Brigadier Arnold 76, 96,
100, 107, 109, 116, 118, 120,
123, 129-30, 133-34, 139-40,
144-47, 149-50, 152, 158,
166, 169, 178-79, 184, 190-
92, 195, 198-99, 205, 208,
244, 248, 347

Rogers, Major Floyd 'Buck' 41,
56, 57, 63

Rowell, Lieutenant General Sydney 86-8, 91, 96, 108, 113,
116, 127, 168, 185, 217, 228,
230, 234, 242, 252-53, 255-
56, 259, 263, 270-71, 273,
275, 372

Royal, Driver Ray 26, 27, 108,
292

Sadahiro, Warrant Officer 106-
7, 109, 111-12, 114, 116, 119,
121-22, 124, 132, 143, 162

Sakamoto, Lieutenant 123,
132, 167, 180, 184-85, 188,
194-95, 233-34, 238, 327-28

Sanopa, Lance Corporal
(PIB) 50, 73, 84, 111, 115,
158

Sato, Toshio 69, 81, 114, 152,
159, 196, 219, 229, 274, 299

Shin, Seaman 1st Class 33, 51,
59, 95, 96, 99

Staley, Captain Harry see
McCullar, Ken

Templeton, Captain Sam 9, 30,
40, 42, 44, 49, 58, 67, 72, 83,
110

Teruoka, Private 64-5, 68, 78,
83, 90-3, 98, 104, 108, 114,
119-20, 162, 167, 182, 187,
197-98, 204, 215, 221, 224,
237, 239, 243, 246, 250, 254,

258, 266, 270

Tongs, Sergeant Bede 210, 222, 252, 262-63, 281, 285, 287, 293-95, 300, 314-15, 320-22, 328, 372, 378-79, 383, 399-400, 406

Tsukamoto, Lieutenant Colonel 17, 34, 58, 72, 264, 271, 287, 289, 299, 325-26, 352, 373

Tsukioka, Commander see Sasebo 5SLP under 'Japanese land forces'

Vasey, Major General George 31, 127, 168, 185, 355, 361, 372, 375, 377, 386

Vernon, Doctor Geoff 47, 49, 51-2, 55-6, 81, 374

Watson, Major W. T. 32-3, 38, 40, 42, 50-1, 55-6, 58, 72, 192

Yazawa, Colonel see 41 Regiment under 'Japanese land forces'

Yokoyama, Colonel 17, 18, 36, 43, 58, 110, 121, 250, 293

4. PLACE NAMES

Efogi 176, 178-79, 181, 184-89, 194, 196, 198, 206-07, 209, 217, 220, 224, 232, 247, 250, 253, 269, 273, 280, 283-85, 290, 293, 298-300, 305, 309, 314, 318

Eora Creek 263, 267, 275-76, 278, 284-85, 287, 289, 293, 299, 300, 302, 309, 312-13, 316, 320, 325, 331, 335-36, 341, 347-49, 351-52, 354-55, 357-58, 362, 364, 368-69, 405

Gorari 370, 376-77, 381, 383, 385-88, 390, 392-95, 401, 404-05, 411

Imita Ridge 213, 218, 222, 227, 233-34, 236-37, 239, 241, 244-46, 258, 265, 287, 395

Ioribaiwa 109, 189, 206, 208, 210, 213, 215-16, 218, 220-28, 230, 232-34, 238, 243-45, 249-50, 262, 265-66, 269-74, 276, 277, 282, 284, 299, 300

Isurava 94-5, 97, 101, 106, 111, 115, 123, 132, 139-41, 147, 149-52, 154-5, 161, 163, 167-70, 175-6, 181, 205-7, 216, 239, 247-8, 250, 253-4, 269, 278, 280, 285, 299, 302, 315, 357, 361-2, 364, 368, 374, 380

Kokoda 52-56, 73-91, 371-375

Kokoda 'Gap' 20, 66, 88, 100, 126, 182, 250, 315-16, 334, 339, 354, 367, 369

Oivi 289, 347, 357, 361-62, 364, 372, 376-77, 379-80, 383, 385-89, 393-94, 399-404, 411

Templeton's Crossing 299, 301, 303-13, 316, 320, 325, 334, 347, 349, 352, 362, 364, 395, 405

5. GENERAL

cannibalism 314, 325, 327, 344, 352, 362, 376

prisoners, Japanese treatment
    of   19, 32, 49, 51, 67, 95,
    98-100, 110, 131, 136, 160,
196, 205-06, 212-13, 216,
281, 285 287, 302, 335, 371,
374, 380-81, 387, 408-09